Visual Methods in Psychology

This comprehensive volume provides an unprecedented illustration of the potential for visual methods in psychology. Each chapter explores the set of theoretical, methodological, ethical and analytical issues that shape the ways in which visual qualitative research is conducted in psychology. Using a variety of forms of visual data, including photography, film-making, drawing, internet media, model making and collages, each author endeavours to broaden the scope for understanding experience and subjectivity, using visual qualitative methods.

The contributors to this volume work within a variety of traditions, including narrative psychology, personal construct theory, discursive psychology and conversation analysis, phenomenology and psychoanalysis. Each addresses how a particular visual approach has contributed to existing social and psychological theory in their topic area, and clearly outline how they carried out their specific research project. The contributors draw on qualitative sources of verbal data, such as spoken interview, diaries and naturalistic conversation alongside their use of visual material.

This book provides a unique insight into the potential for combining methods in order to create new multi-modal methodologies. The range of topics covered includes sexuality, identity, group processes, child development, forensic psychology, race, and gender, making this volume a vital contribution to psychology, sociology and gender studies.

Paula Reavey is a senior reader in psychology at London South Bank University. She has published widely on topics relating to child sexual abuse, social remembering, mental health, space and embodiment, using memory work, discursive approaches and visual methods.

Visual Methods in Psychology

Using and interpreting images in qualitative research

Edited by
Paula Reavey

Psychology Press
Taylor & Francis Group

HOVE AND NEW YORK

First published 2011
by Psychology Press
27 Church Road, Hove, East Sussex, BN3 2FA

Simultaneously published in the USA and Canada
by Routledge
711 Third Avenue, New York, NY 10017

Routledge is an imprint of the Taylor & Francis Group, an Informa business

British Library Cataloguing in Publication Data
A catalogue record for this book is available from the British Library

Library of Congress Cataloguing in Publication Data
Visual methods in psychology : using and interpreting images in qualitative
research / edited by Paula Reavey.
    p. cm.
  Includes bibliographical references and index.
    ISBN 978-0-415-48348-3 (hbk : alk. paper)
  1. Visual perception--Psychological aspects. 2. Psychology–Qualitative
    research. 3. Visual perception--Social aspects. I. Reavey, Paula.
  BF241.V5673 2011
  150.72'1–dc22   2010036804

ISBN: 978-0-415-48348-3 (hbk)

Typeset in Times New Roman by RefineCatch Limited, Bungay, Suffolk
Printed and bound in Great Britain by TJ International Ltd, Padstow,
Cornwall
Cover design by Andrew Ward

For Boris Reavey, my beloved and desperately missed nephew.

Contents

Tables

Figures

Contributors

Meg Barker is a psychology lecturer at the Open University and an existential therapist specialising in sex and relationship counselling. She has co-edited two books on sexuality (*Safe, Sane and Consensual*, 2007, with Palgrave Macmillan and *Understanding Non-monogamies*, 2010, with Routledge) and one on psychotherapy (*Understanding Counselling and Psychotherapy*, 2010, with Sage). Meg is co-editor of the journal, *Psychology & Sexuality*, with *Taylor & Francis*. Her research on sexualities and relationships has also been published in several journals and books.

Helen Bowes-Catton is a postgraduate student at the Open University. Her doctoral research project, described in this chapter, uses visual and creative methods such as photography and modelling to explore the ways in which bisexual identities are experienced and produced, through the body, in 'spectacular' and mundane spaces. Her research on bisexuality has been published in the *Journal of Bisexuality* and *Lesbian and Gay Psychology Review*.

Alexander John Bridger is a Senior Lecturer in Psychology at the University of Huddersfield. He recently completed his PhD which developed how the situationist practice of psychogeography could be used as a new qualitative method in critical psychology. Recent publications include a literature review of academic, artistic and activist work on psychogeography in the *Journal of Social and Personality Psychology Compass*. Current research is focused on psychogeography, sexuality and space as well as yoga practice and theory. Alexander is also involved in various psychogeography walks, talks, groups and events such as the Bored in the City Collective, The Loiterers Resistance Movement and the Leeds Psychogeography Group. He is a member of the Centre for Applied Psychology Research at the University of Huddersfield and the Discourse Unit at Manchester Metropolitan University.

David P. Brown is administrator for the Research Institute for Health and Social Change, Manchester Metropolitan University, Manchester, UK.

Richard Brown is an award-winning artist (Royal Glasgow Institute of Fine Arts) with a degree in Fine Art and Sculpture (Bath Spa University) and a background in graphic design and stone carving. He is a multi-disciplinary artist whose work includes solo shows, artist residences, commercial and public art commissions. He has taught art in schools, youth clubs and to adults and he has curated many exhibitions, including Tribal Gatherings.

Steven Brown is Professor of Social and Organizational Psychology at the University of Leicester. His research interests are around the mediation of social remembering across diverse settings. These include: commemoration of the 2005 London Bombings; personal, family and institutional recollections of childhood traumas and challenges; and self-archiving in virtual social networking. He is author of *Psychology without Foundations: History, Philosophy and Psychosocial Theory* (with Paul Stenner, 2009, Sage) and *The Social Psychology of Experience: Studies in Remembering and Forgetting* (with David Middleton, 2005, Sage).

Angela Cassidy is a Senior Research Associate at the School of Environmental Sciences, University of East Anglia. Her research interests are in science, risk and health communication; public engagement/participation; and science and technology studies. Much of her work has addressed the relationship between scientific knowledge/expertise and everyday life experience, and she has used visual methods to investigate the popular communication of scientific ideas, as well as to explore participants' knowledge of complex risk issues. She is currently researching public controversy in the UK over bovine TB and the role of badgers in transmission of the disease.

Kerry Chamberlain is Professor of Health Psychology at Massey University, Auckland, New Zealand. He is a critical health psychologist with interests in health in everyday life, and specific research interests in the social practices, uses and meanings of medications, media and health, food and health, everyday illness, and social disadvantage.

Lilliana Del Busso is an associate professor in psychology at Ostfold University College, Norway. She recently completed a PhD entitled, 'Being-in-Motion: Femininity, Movement and Space in Young Women's Narratives of Their Embodied Experiences in Everyday Life'. This work enjoins poststructuralist and phenomenological principles and uses memory work, diaries and visual research methods. Current research projects include working with colleagues at King's College London on a qualitative study of doctors who are experiencing complex health needs and obstacles to returning to work, Her research interests are in the fields of critical psychology and feminist studies, and include embodiment, gender, space, emotion and qualitative research methodologies.

Karen Duggan is a Project Manager at Manchester Metropolitan University, Manchester, UK. She works on participative community projects in partnership with educational institutions and community organisations. She is particularly interested in addressing social inequalities and facilitating social and transformational change through collective action. Her special interest and research focus is in exploring innovative and creative ways to widen participation in and through the Higher Education system by using Community Psychology approaches to explore diversity and achievement as well as the power of collaborative partnerships. She has recently been working as the Urban Regeneration: Making a Difference Project Development Manager for MMU which is a collaborative project between four universities in the North of England. The focus is to address key urban regeneration challenges through inter-disciplinary collaboration to develop a distinctive form of knowledge transfer around themes of Community Cohesion, Crime, Health and Wellbeing and Enterprise. Karen is part of an impact analysis working group made up of practitioners from across the North of England group who are exploring and testing metrics for community engagement. She is currently also the Project Manager for The Academy of Health and Well-being at MMU.

Mark Finn is a Senior Lecturer in Psychology at the University of East London having held two research posts at Cardiff University, most recently at the School of Social Sciences with Karen Henwood. With a predominant research interest in the psychosocial productions and regulations of non/normative relationships, Mark has also conducted published research into transgenderism, fatherhood and masculinity, and health-related quality of life. His current research is a psychosocial exploration of 'affirmative' therapeutic engagement with practices of open non-monogamy.

Michael Forrester is a Senior Lecturer in Psychology at the School of Psychology, University of Kent. His interests are in conversation analysis, psychoanalytic studies, and qualitative methods. Recent publications include *Doing Qualitative Research in Psychology*, 2010 (editor, Sage) and co-editor (with Hilary Gardner) of *Analysing Interactions in Childhood: Insights from Conversation Analysis*, 2010 (Wiley-Blackwell).

Hannah Frith is a Senior Lecturer in Psychology at the University of Brighton. She has published widely on topics relating to appearance and identity, qualitative methodology, sex and sexuality, embodiment and body image using visual and discursive methodologies. She co-edited (with Sarah Riley, Sally Wiggins, Pirkko Markula and Maree Burns, 2007, Palgrave) *Critical Bodies: Representations, Identities and Practices of Weight and Body Management*.

Rosalind Gill is Professor of Social and Cultural Analysis, at the Centre for Culture, Media and Creative Industries, Kings College London. She is author of *The Gender-Technology Relation* (Taylor & Francis, 1995, with Keith Grint), *Gender and the Media* (Polity Press, 2007), *Secrecy and Silence in the Research Process: Feminist Reflections* (Routledge, 2010, with Roisin Ryan Flood) and *New Femininities* (Palgrave, in press). Her work is located in two main spheres: first, the intersections between gender, culture, media and subjectivity – in which she is well known for having elaborated a shift from objectification to (sexual) subjectification, as well as for setting out a distinctive understanding of postfeminism as a sensibility; and second the changing nature of work in the cultural and creative industries, with a particular focus on new media. She is currently writing a book about 'mediated intimacy' and collaborating on Marsden-funded research about 'tweens' negotiations with 'sexualised culture'.

Kate Gleeson is the Research Director for the Bristol Doctorate in Clinical Psychology based at the University of Bristol, UK. Her research interests are focused on personhood and visual identity. She is currently working on developing visual research methods and the teaching of research methods. Most recently she has published on topics including qualitative research methods, body image, the appearance of men, and the visual identities of young women and people with learning disabilities. Kate is preparing a book about her process approach to research supervision.

Lewis Goodings is a Lecturer in Social Psychology at Roehampton University. Lewis's research is dedicated to the area of computer-mediated communication and a qualitative form of social psychology. He uses a constructionist approach to study new forms of online communication and focuses on classic notions of identity, community and the self. He is always looking to explore the broader social dynamics of technology, discourse and organisation.

Christine Griffin is Professor of Social Psychology at the University of Bath. Much of her recent work explores the relationship between identities and consumption for young people, with a long-standing interest in representations of youth, femininity and young women's lives. Recent projects include a study of young people's negotiation of branded leisure spaces at music festivals and free parties with Andrew Bengry-Howell; a project on clubbing and dance cultures as forms of social and political participation with Sarah Riley; and a major study on the role of branding and marketing of drinks in relation to young adults' everyday drinking practices. She has published widely in journals including *Feminism and Psychology*, *Discourse Studies*, the *British Journal of Social Psychology*, *Sociology* and the *Journal of Youth Studies*. Monographs include *Standpoints and Differences: Essays in Practice of Feminist Psychology* (with Karen Henwood and Ann Phoenix, Sage, 1998); and *Representations of Youth* (Polity Press, 1993).

John Griffiths is a Lecturer in Psychology at Manchester Metropolitan University, Manchester, UK. His research interests are in the area of men and masculinities, community social capital, and issues of individual, social and community health.

Shiloh Groot is a social psychologist with research interests in indigenous worldviews and communities, resilience, poverty and illness. Shiloh is currently working towards completing her Doctoral research into street homelessness at the University of Waikato, New Zealand.

Janice Haaken is Professor of Psychology at Portland State University, USA, a clinical and community psychologist, a documentary filmmaker, and media activist. An interdisciplinary scholar, Haaken has published extensively in the areas of psychoanalytic feminism, gender and psychiatric diagnosis, memory, violence, trauma, and the psychology of storytelling. Haaken is author of *Pillar of Salt: Gender, Memory and the Perils of Looking Back*, co-author of *Speaking Out: Women, War, and the Global Economy*, and co-editor of *Memory Matters: Understanding Recollections of Sexual Abuse*. She is author of the forthcoming *Hard Knocks: Domestic Violence and the Psychology of Storytelling*. Her documentary films include *Diamonds, Guns and Rice* (co-producer), *Queens of Heart: Community Therapists in Drag* (writer/director), and *Moving to the Beat* (producer). She is currently working on a film on patients who enter the Oregon State Hospital through the insanity defense.

Jennifer Hawkins is an Associate Lecturer in Education on Inclusion and Disability Studies courses at Liverpool Hope University, Liverpool, UK. She teaches Curriculum Issues and Practitioner Research modules to final year degree students. Over the past 10 years, since her former career as a secondary Special Needs teacher in English and Art, she has been conducting independent research working on a new theory about the function of feelings in learning. During that time Jennifer has worked as a home tutor to school refusers, a mentor to action researching teachers and artists and as an educational evaluator of arts-based projects in schools. Jennifer's PhD includes her own and her participants' art and reflexive writing as a means of accessing and researching subconscious thought processes. Her participants' role, as fellow researchers and collaborators, is central to her research approach. She is interested in ways in which creativity can facilitate learning and demonstrate feelings as subconsciously reasoned thoughts within the deductive networking processes involved in cognition. Jennifer is now working on a book proposal outlining her theory and its practical implications for learners and teachers, while continuing to be involved in developing her ideas through lecturing and researching with her students.

John Haworth has a PhD in psychology and a Masters degree in fine art. He is currently a Visiting Research Fellow in the Research Institute for Health and Social Change at Manchester Metropolitan University, Manchester, UK. Formerly at Manchester Metropolitan University and The Victoria University of Manchester, he has been Visiting Professor at the University of Technology, Sydney, Australia; and Visiting Research Scientist at the Center for Consciousness Studies, University of Arizona, Tucson, USA. He is the spokesperson for the British Psychological Society on the topics of Creativity and Embodied Mind, and Work, Leisure and Wellbeing. His two overlapping areas of research together constitute a focus on 'Consciousness, Creativity and Well-being'. He has published and exhibited widely, and given presentations at international conferences world wide. He has established a website on well-being, www.wellbeing-esrc.com, as part of a seminar series funded by the Economic and Social Research Council, and in July 2007 Palgrave MacMillan published *Well-Being: Individual, Community and Social Perspectives* edited by J. Haworth and G. Hart. His practice-led research on creativity and the embodied mind has been funded by the Arts and Humanities Research Council. It can be seen on the website www.creativity-embodiedmind.com and in Haworth, J. T. (2009) Explorations in Creativity, Technology and Embodied Mind. In T. Freire (ed.) *Understanding Positive Life: Research and Practice on Positive Psychology*. Lisboa: Climepsie Editores.

Karen Henwood is a Professor in the School of Social Sciences, Cardiff University. Her substantive research interests are in the forging of identities and subjectivities in personal lives and socio-cultural context; troubled and troubling identities; lived experiences and social constructions of gender, risk, embodiment, and well-being. Her methodological work spans interpretive thematic approaches (such as grounded theory), discursive and narrative methods, qualitative longitudinal methodology, and visual methods. Her work is mainly published in high-quality academic journals (e.g. *British Journal of Social Psychology, Social Science and Medicine, Discourse Studies, Transactions*) and edited books (e.g. *Handbook of Qualitative Methods in Psychology*, edited by Carla Willig and Wendy Stainton Rogers). She is currently a co-Principal Investigator (2007–2012) of the ESRC Timescapes network, leading the Men-as-Fathers project.

Darrin Hodgetts is a Reader in Social Psychology at the University of Waikato, New Zealand. Prior to this appointment Darrin held posts in Community Health at Memorial University in Canada and Psychology and Media and Communications at the London School of Economics and Political Sciences. Darrin has over 10 years experience working in a range of diverse community settings. His research spans the media, health, homelessness, social inequalities, place and civic engagement.

Caroline Howarth is Lecturer in Social Psychology at the London School of Economics. Her research and teaching seek to push social psychology in general and social representations theory in particular in a more critical direction by addressing questions of racism, power, identity, exclusion and resistance. This has demanded the conceptualisation of the role of re-presentation in identity formation, in the marginalization and racialisation of specific communities and in the possibilities of belonging, resistance and transformation. She has published across these areas in a wide range of journals such as the *British Journal of Social Psychology, Journal for the Theory of Social Behaviour*, and *Culture and Psychology*. She is also editor of *Papers on Social Representations* and on the editorial board of the *Journal of Community and Applied Social Psychology*.

Alex Iantaffi is currently working as a fellow at the University of Minnesota, USA, Program in Human Sexuality, as a researcher and clinician. She received a PhD from the University of Reading (UK) and an MSc in Systemic Psychotherapy from the University of Bedfordshire (UK). Alex's research interests and publications have focused on gender, sexuality, disability, polyamory, and BDSM and she is also the editor-in-chief for the *Journal of Sexual and Relationship Therapy.*

Katherine Johnson is a Principal Lecturer in the School of Applied Social Science at the University of Brighton. Her research interests are in the fields of sexuality, transgender and queer studies, critical and community psychology, psychosocial studies, mental health and suicide, and qualitative research methods. She is currently completing a book *Sexualities: A Transdisciplinary Approach* (Polity – due 2011) and co-editing *Community Psychology and Economies of Distress: Global Perspectives* (with Carl Walker and Liz Cunningham, Palgrave – due 2011).

Carolyn Kagan is Professor of Community Social Psychology and Director of the Research Institute for Health and Social Change at Manchester Metropolitan University, UK, where the first action learning UK Masters programme in community psychology is based. Much of her work concerns the wellbeing of those marginalised by the social system, and the ways this can be enhanced or obstructed through creative engagement. She has published extensively on collaborative and action research processes and her work has contributed to UK and international service and policy. Her most recent research projects include those on arts for health, urban regeneration, forced labour and university–community engagement. See www.compsy.org.

Anne Kellock is a Senior Lecturer at Sheffield Hallam University, Sheffield, UK. She teaches Early Childhood Studies and Childhood Studies on under and post graduate degrees. She has nearly completed her PhD which was fully funded by the Manchester Institute for Research and Innovation in Art and Design (MIRIAD) at Manchester Metropolitan University. Her PhD focuses on using creative and participative methodologies with primary school children to understand wellbeing from their own perspective in England and New Zealand. She has a background in primary school teaching in both countries over several years. Her visual research techniques have also been used with young adults around problem-solving and wellbeing in the workplace as part of her MSc. She has been a curator and exhibitor for an exhibition: 'Tapping into Visual Worlds' which featured visual research projects at Manchester Metropolitan University in 2008. Her publications range from research methods with children and adults, the use of visual and creative methods with participants as well as Sen's Capability Approach and working in marginalised communities. Anne's current research interests include the Experiential Sampling Method and creative methodologies with young people, and specifically children's disability in Malaysia.

Rebecca Lawthom is a Reader in Community Practice in the Psychology Department at Manchester Metropolitan University, UK. She is a feminist and community psychologist and has published widely in areas such as life history methods, disability and psychology, community psychology and feminism. She is currently involved in three research projects: Disability and Cultural

Sensitivity, Refugee and Asylum Seeker Health, and Forced Labour of Chinese Migrants. Recent works include *Researching Life Stories: Method, Theory and Analysis in a Biographical Age* (with Goodley, Clough and Moore, Routledge, 2004), and an edited collection *Disability and Psychology: Critical Introductions and Reflections* (with Goodley, Palgrave, 2006). A text in preparation is *Community Psychology: Critical Action and Social Change* (with Kagan, Burton, Siddiquee and Duckett – due 2011, Blackwell).

Helen Lomax is Senior Lecturer in Health Policy. Her research interests include the role of policy, popular culture and professional expertise in shaping parenting experiences and practices. Methodological interests encompass the development of video-based and photographic techniques for understanding social identity and as a method by which people can make visible their own lives and inform local and national policy agendas. She is the principal investigator of the ESRC seminar series *Visual Dialogues: New Agendas in Inequalities Research* (www.visualdialogues.co.uk). This two-year project brings together academics, practitioners and policy makers from across the arts and social and health sciences in order to explore the potential of the visual for understanding the forms and experiences of inequality that shape societies, communities and individual lives.

Anamika Majumdar has recently completed her doctoral research titled 'South Asian women's narratives of intimacy and marriage in the UK: making sense of experience through cultural scripts, space and objects' at London South Bank University. Her research interests lie in intimacy, personal relationships and culture(s). She has previously worked as a research assistant on an NHS study exploring understandings of sexual health and service provision with the Bangladeshi community of Tower Hamlets, and an ESRC-funded research project exploring South Asian women's experiences of sexual violence in the UK.

John Maule is Professor of Human Decision Making and Director of the Centre for Decision Research at Leeds University Business School, UK, and has until recently been President of the European Association of Decision Making. He has spent many years undertaking research on how individuals, groups and organisations take decisions and how we can use this knowledge to help them improve the effectiveness of these activities. He has published many journal articles, books and book chapters on the psychology of risk and decision making and is currently involved in research projects concerned with communicating risk to the public and the effects of emotion on risk taking. He has a very strong commitment to applying academic theory and research on human decision making to professional and work contexts.

Yvette Morey is a Research Fellow at the Bristol Social Marketing Centre (University of the West of England). Her primary research interests are youth, identity and practices of consumption, including the use of drugs and alcohol in young people's leisure activities. She has conducted research on a range of youth(ful) cultures, including recent research into the underground free party scene in the South West, and music festival culture in the UK. Her research has contributed to current understandings about the recreational use of the drug ketamine in the free party scene and more broadly. She is particularly interested in the use of social media and Web 2.0 platforms in digital ethnography and online research. She has published in *Sociology*; *Young*; and *Addiction, Research & Theory*.

Johanna F. Motzkau is Lecturer in Psychology at the Faculty of Social Sciences, The Open University, UK. She has a background in philosophy, German Kritische Psychologie, theoretical psychology, developmental psychology and forensic psychology. She is interested in research methodology, memory and suggestibility, as well as issues surrounding children's rights, sexual violence, and the way in which psychological knowledge is used by the law. Recent research has looked at the history and theory of suggestibility research and compared child witness practice in England and Germany (*Cross-examining Suggestibility: Memory, Childhood, Expertise*). Her research is inspired by the work of Bergson, Deleuze and Stengers.

Ilana Mountian is an honorary research fellow at Manchester Metropolitan University, Manchester, UK. She lectures and researches in psychology and critical psychology. Currently she is a Visiting Professor on Political Psychology at the Psychology Department of the Universidade Federal de Minas Gerais, Brazil. Mountian is a member of the Discourse Unit. Her research interests are on research methods, ethics, immigration, gender and drug use. Her inter-disciplinary approach draws on psychoanalysis, philosophy, social theories, feminist research and post-colonial studies. Ilana has previously worked as a clinical psychologist with drug users, mental health patients, street kids and elderly people. Ilana has published a number of articles and papers on these themes. Some of her most recent publications include titles such as: 'On utilising a visual methodology: shared reflections and tensions'; 'Social imaginary for critical research'; 'Race, class and affirmative action in Brazil: reflections from a feminist perspective' and; 'Culture in psychology'.

Christina Purcell is a doctoral student at Manchester Metropolitan University Business School, Division of Human Resource Management and Organisational Behaviour, UK. Her research interests are labour process analysis, labour market segmentation, low-skilled contingent workers, and cross-national comparative research. She has worked as a research assistant on a European Commission funded project on gender, parenthood and the changing European workplace.

Alan Radley is Emeritus Professor of Social Psychology in the Department of Social Sciences at Loughborough University, UK. He is founding editor of the journal *Health: An Interdisciplinary Journal for the Social Study of Health, Illness and Medicine*. He has used visual methods to study social experience in material contexts, including hospital wards and urban spaces used by homeless people. He has recently published a book on artworks in relation to life-threatening disease, *Works of Illness: Narrative, Picturing and the Social Response to Serious Disease* (InkerMen Press, 2009).

Paula Reavey is a Senior Reader in Psychology at London South Bank University. She has published widely on child sexual abuse, social remembering, mental health, space and embodiment, using memory work, discursive approaches and visual methods. Recent works include two co-edited volumes (with Sam Warner, Routledge, 2003), *New Feminist Stories of Child Sexual Abuse: Sexual Scripts and Dangerous Dialogues* and *Memory Matters: Contexts for Understanding Sexual Abuse Recollections* (with Janice Haaken, Psychology Press, 2009). She is currently working on a book on *Mental Health and Distress* (co-authored with Richard Bentall, John Cromby and Dave Harper, Palgrave – due 2011) and preparing a book on *Memory and Affect* with Steven D. Brown.

Christina Richards is the Senior Specialist Psychology Associate at the Charing Cross National Gender Identity Clinic, UK, and is a member of the World Professional Association for Transgender Health. She is currently undertaking her Doctorate in Counseling Psychology specialising in gender and sexualities. She also publishes and lectures on critical mental health, gender and sexualities.

Sarah Riley is a Senior Lecturer in the Department of Psychology at the Aberystwyth University, UK. Her research takes a psycho-social approach to explore issues of identity in relation to gender, embodiment and youth culture. Her work employs discourse analysis, co-operative inquiry and visual methods. Recent projects include a study of young people's negotiation of branded leisure spaces at music festivals and free parties with Andrew Bengry-Howell and colleagues; a project on clubbing and dance cultures as forms of social and political participation with Chris Griffin and Yvette Morey; and a cooperative inquiry study on 'dilemmas of femininity'. She has published widely and is an editor for *Critical Bodies: Representations, Identities and Practices of Weight and Body Management* (Palgrave MacMillan, 2008).

Fiona Shirani is a research associate for the Timescapes Men-as-Fathers project, based at Cardiff University. Her research interests include: life course and transitions; fatherhood and families; with a particular focus on time and temporality. She is currently working on her PhD about the right time for fatherhood.

Asiya Siddiquee is a Lecturer in the Department of Psychology at Manchester Metropolitan University, UK. Her research interests revolve around community psychology, marginalisation, wellbeing, and online technologies. She is currently one of the editors for the journal *Community, Work & Family.*

Judith Sixsmith holds the positions of Professor of Adult Social Care at Manchester Metropolitan University in the UK and Professor of Public Policy at Simon Fraser University, Vancouver, Canada. Aiming to bridge divides between theory, policy and practice, Judith's work often takes 'bottom up', experiential perspectives through which issues of policy and practice are explored. Here, the role of evaluation of health and social care service delivery has been particularly important, not just in terms of facilitating shared understandings between professionals, service providers and community residents, but also in trying to 'make a difference' to everyday quality of life and well-being. Consequently, her research interests lie in the areas of health and social care, exploring the experiences of people living in deprived communities and locating these within cultural and gendered processes of marginalisation. Often working within collaborative, participatory and multi-disciplinary approaches, Judith has directed several local, national and international research projects on issues of healthy ageing, social capital, advocacy, urban regeneration, prevention and social inclusion. She has published widely in the fields of health, ageing and community/environmental psychology.

Valerie Walkerdine is Research Professor in the School of Social Sciences, Cardiff University. Trained as a psychologist, artist and filmmaker, she has used visual methods in a number of research projects, including using photographs, video, video games, film and installation. The work discussed in this book comes from a study on transition to womanhood, funded by the ESRC and Channel 4 television.

Claire Worley is a Senior Lecturer in Social Policy at Manchester Metropolitan University, UK. She has a particular interest in issues of race, ethnicity and gender and her current work relates to community cohesion policies in the UK. She has published a range of work on community cohesion, urban regeneration, user involvement, housing, homelessness and substance misuse.

Acknowledgements

Writing for, and editing a book is never an isolated venture. That is why there are quite a few people I wish to thank (although I will resist the urge to onerously list all and sundry). My first dalliance with visual methods emerged from the collective work of an embodiment group, made up of Val Gillies, Angela Harden, Katherine Johnson, Vicky Strange and Carla Willig. The research we carried out as part of that group continues to be an inspiration to me and my constant search for more nuanced approaches to the psychological study of experience. I would also like to thank my postgraduate students, Ava Kanyeredzi, Laura McGrath and Joanna Silver for their invaluable feedback on the book at all stages. Following this, my hat remains firmly off to my cherished and much-loved friend and colleague, Steve Brown, who has at all times made writing totally unconventional and ridiculous fun. Thank you so much for everything Steve...

My brother, Jonathan Reavey, has also been a tremendous inspiration to me this last year, when so much was taken from him. His continued struggle and bravery has encouraged me to finish this book and to try to remain focussed when everything around us was in chaos.

And finally, my family, Alex, Oskar and tiny Viktor who continue to make life so much better than ordinary. I wish to thank them all for their humour and unfailing silliness – with the deepest appreciation and love.

Foreword

Carla Willig

This book is a timely and very welcome response to a noticeable lack of accommodation of 'the visual' in contemporary qualitative psychology. Paula Reavey is one of a small number of qualitative psychologists who have been drawing attention to the importance of incorporating non-linguistic data into the qualitative research endeavour for some time. I have very fond memories of working with Paula within the context of our Embodiment Research Group (together with Val Gillies, Angela Harden, Katherine Johnson and Vicky Strange) when we were trying to find ways of transcending discourse-based analyses of accounts of embodied experience. In our six years of working together, we grappled with many of the questions which Paula went on to tackle in her later work and which are addressed in this volume. How we would have appreciated a book like this one at the time … *Visual Methods in Psychology* brings together a wide range of examples of how visual data can be gathered and analysed in order to enrich our understanding of meaning-making and experience. It demonstrates how psychological concerns such as emotions, identity, memory, embodied states and practices, can be explored through visual data and how these can add to our understanding of human experience. Whilst the book promotes and celebrates visual approaches, the contributors do not shy away from engaging with the ethical, conceptual, theoretical and methodological challenges of such work. They raise fascinating questions about the status and ownership of images, and the process of their production and interpretation. What I like very much about this book is the way in which its 23 chapters provide a wide range of different perspectives from which to approach visual methodologies. Each chapter offers a different 'way in' to using images as data. The chapters communicate a sense of shared purpose as well as an acknowledgement of the very significant differences between approaches. This book does what it sets out to do – it demonstrates the creative potential of visual approaches and it helps to remove the study of everyday experience from what Reavey so appropriately describes as 'the grip of language-based methodologies' (Chapter 1, p. 3). It also inspires the reader and creates a sense of excitement which comes from opening up a whole new set of possibilities for qualitative research.

Introduction

Paula Reavey

Images are powerful forms of communication, forming a vital part of our everyday worlds. They communicate how we ought to look and feel and what we ought to consider normal or desirable. And social life bustles along using images in complex ways. Educators, health advisors, drug companies and the fitness industry all use images to sell their ideas and promote their services. In very recent times, we have also witnessed the emergence of new technologies that have opened up new forms of social interactions. Social networking sites, for example, have given rise to alternative forms of communication and mediation, where thoughts, feelings and identities are expressed and performed in online verbal-visual synthesis. In disciplines other than psychology, these emerging forms of communication have long been recognised as important nodes in the formation and performance of identity, embodiment and subjectivity. In psychology, the recognition has been more recent and somewhat limited (Frith *et al.*, 2005; Reavey and Johnson, 2008).

In the social sciences, visual research has grown significantly over the past 30 years, in part due to a growing emphasis on the importance of culture and cultural practices in making sense of human experience (Evans and Hall, 1999; Pink, 2007; Prosser, 2006). It is now acknowledged by a range of sociologists and anthropologists that the visual is an integral part of the way in which culture operates (as a result of mass media especially). One of the major concerns for those working within psychology is how such cultural practices, including visual practices, impact on how people *experience* the world they live in. A growing emphasis on experience-based qualitative methods (our actual encounter with or exposure to something – how it is felt, is seen, the space in which it occurs as opposed to how it is described) as opposed to *discourse* (written or spoken informal interactions or a formal kind of debate) has led some researchers to search for alternative forms of data and analytical procedures (Brown *et al.*, 2008). Until recently, investigations into experience have mostly concentrated on experience expressed through verbal communication (Henriques *et al.*, 1998). However, the authors of this volume have expanded the range of modes through which experience can be studied, to incorporate visual as well as verbal/written modalities.

We encounter images constantly in the ongoing flow of experience, for they constitute a vital part of the existing cultural resources we have to make sense of our lives. Visual anthropologists have recognised this for quite some time, and have made a clear distinction between thinking and speaking about different cultural systems to an emphasis on the rich texture of our experience of those systems (Banks, 2006). We are so much more than we say we are, as we inhabit a world saturated with images, sounds and smells that enter our conscious and unconscious experience in a variety of ways. When listening to the news, when reading magazines, and communicating via the web through social networking sites such as MySpace or Facebook, images mediate our experience of the information being presented and the persons we are exchanging/interacting with. Psychology has been somewhat slow to move with these ideas and has often studied individuals and groups as if communication came only through the modes of language or cognition. And, traditionally, within psychology, images have been confined to use with children or those deemed less 'able' to communicate thoughts and feelings, rather than those who use supposedly more sophisticated modes of language, such as written language and narrative. In this sense, the 'visual' has traditionally been given the status of a naïve or more simplistic form of communication, despite there being no simple or uniform way of reading children's visual communication, through drawing etc. (Wakefield and Underwager, 2006). Yet, in contradiction to this, it is somehow assumed that the visual will communicate clearly what children (and other 'vulnerable' individuals) cannot, or experiences they struggle to articulate. As the works in this volume demonstrate, the way in which we use the visual, however, is far from naïve, simple or uniform. And it certainly cannot be deployed in any definitive diagnostic or projective sense to indicate personality, trauma or mental distress (see Chapter 1).

Multi-modal accounts

Qualitative researchers in psychology have written volumes on how to collect and analyse 'textual data' (the spoken word usually), without sufficient attention to the wider variety of modalities that surround us (visual, verbal, bodily, audio, spatial). An attention to multi-modal communication thus embraces descriptions of a number of different types of psychological activities, environmental spaces and cultural artifacts – including the spaces that either encourage our agency or restrict us, the objects we touch and reminisce with and through, and the sounds we hear that create emotional resonances, for example. Multi-modality is a complex interplay between a number of meaning-making resources that are part of our experience and can be part of the way we communicate those experiences to others. This may include the use of photographic material in remembering people or events, in the use of visual markers when describing how we experience our bodies, and to locate our experience by showing the spaces in which they emerge. When we take seriously how people's experiences are made and the contexts in which they emerge, it becomes difficult to ignore the rich complex of visual media through which experiences come into being.

Of course, images are never used by individuals in any straightforward or 'correct' way. We are constantly interpreting and re-interpreting images and ascertaining meaning, to and from them. Stuart Hall, an eminent visual sociologist who has explored visual methods (1997), has argued, images do not contain a true or singular meaning and are constantly subject to interpretation and re-interpretation, depending on certain personal, social and cultural conditions. In this particular volume, the authors are concerned with how our participants (which may include ourselves) interpret and create images to say and represent something about their lives. This process is inherently interpretive and we as researchers are thoroughly immersed in the manner through which participants engage in this interpretive process.

This volume seeks to provide further discussion and debate about the use and interpretation of visual media in psychology, including the use and interpretation of paintings, photographs, graphic design, models and film in a variety of community, academic and therapeutic settings. More specifically, many of the authors attempt to address theoretical issues through the use of visual methods, such as the role of embodiment and emotions in experience, or the variety of spaces within which our experiences emerge from.

Of course the images already produced in wider culture or the images that participants produce themselves are never 'innocent' or 'a-cultural' (Rose, 2007). They are always already situated in various cultural practices, knowledges, technologies and power regimes. Just as language systems produce subject positions and hierarchies, so do images. As Haraway (1991) has argued, *who* is seen, *how* they are seen and *who* is viewing, are all part of social power relations, producing specific versions/visions of social hierarchies. All of the contributors to this volume thus share a 'critical visuality', where the meanings of images are not taken for granted or seen as either neutral, or reflections of the 'real'. What makes the focus of this volume ever more psychological, however, is the emphasis given to the participants' constructions of meaning from the images given or produced. Thus, emotions, personal narrative, embodied states and practices and identity formation are central to the way in which the combination of verbal and visual data are read by the contributors here. And a variety of psychology-related topics, such as memory, child development, appearance, intimacy, powerlessness, gender and sexuality, embodiment and social identity form the basis for these discussions relating to theory and method.

Aims of the volume

This volume aims to make visible the set of theoretical, methodological, as well as ethical and analytical issues that shape the ways in which visual qualitative research is conducted in psychology. However, the aim of the book is not to expose other qualitative methods that rely on verbal language, as inadequate or outdated. All of the authors writing in this volume combine both verbal and visual data in their work in an integrative way, emphasising the multi-modal nature of experience, which researchers and participants alike are called on to access during the course of research. The authors of the volume have used a variety of forms of visual data, including photography, documentary film-making, drawing, internet media, model making, walking and map drawing, video recording and collages.

As well as describing the research process itself (including the methodological and analytical aspects of the research), each of the chapters illustrates the attempt by psychologists to engage participants in more participatory forms of research. Authors writing in the section on community visions, for example, discuss in detail how participants with a range of social, health and mental health needs are provided with the opportunity to adopt a more creative and agentic role in the research process. Furthermore, all authors in the volume acknowledge the set of theoretical, methodological or ethical difficulties encountered during the course of their work. This volume is not a naïve attempt to herald the virtues of visual approaches in psychology, but aims to explore, in a heuristic fashion, the potential use of these approaches for psychologists and qualitative researchers. Thus, the emerging issues that each of the authors encounters in using visual approaches will be summarised and discussed throughout the volume.

Organisation of the volume

The contributors to this volume work within a variety of traditions, including narrative psychology, personal construct theory, discursive psychology and conversation analysis, phenomenology and psychoanalysis to inform the kinds of research questions they ask and the subsequent interpretations they form of their data. Each addresses how and why they chose a particular visual approach and how it has contributed to existing social/psychological theory on their topic area, as well as clearly outlining how they carried out their specific research project. The sources of verbal data that combine with the visual approach are qualitative rather than quantitative. Thus, the contributors have combined spoken interview data, ethnographic notes, diaries, autobiographical material, focus group discussions and naturalistic conversation alongside their use of visual material.

While the combined authors offer a diversity of perspectives, they nevertheless share a focus on how best to combine visual and verbal data to address the psychological issues under study. Furthermore, they each discuss how to use the visual in a way that does not assume images can stand alone, as purveyors of truth, but are used to add to multiply layered representations of experience. All the contributors engage in critical reflection when discussing their work, in order to illustrate the complexities of working with visual materials to address psychological questions.

Visual Methods in Psychology is organised into four parts. The first part 'Static media: the use of photography in qualitative research' includes chapters by authors who have used static images, such as photography in order to discuss (a) how such images may be interpreted and used within qualitative research or (b) how the different uses of photography can enhance research projects concerned with embodiment and the environmental/spatial setting. The various uses of photographs can lead to different sets of questions and possible interpretations, which the authors discuss in detail.

The second part, 'Moveable features: using Facebook and video in qualitative research', presents empirical research using video-based data and data from existing social networking sites. The focus of this part is to examine how the moving visual mediates both self-presentation and interaction in real-time, for the participant and for the intended (and unintended) audience. The third part of the volume 'Shared visions: opening up researcher participant dialogues in the community and beyond' has a distinctly community and action-oriented flavour. The authors of this section have used a variety of visual methods, including art exhibitions, film-making, photography, tapestry and drawing to address how to increase dialogue between not only the researcher and participant but also the 'audience' of the research. Although the authors of this section have used different types of visual images to achieve their goal, what they share is a commitment to participant-led involvement in the research process within a broad range of action-oriented projects, which they hope to see used to reduce stigma, change social attitudes and increase social justice.

In the final part, 'Ethical and methodological reflections on visual research', authors focus on issues of ethics, methodology and reflexivity for researchers using visual approaches. Here they consider some of the difficulties encountered in using and interpreting images, be it existing images or images produced by their research participants, or they provide reflexive commentary on the process of carrying out the research. A further question is the place of the participants' 'voice' in the research process and how visual researchers can work towards a model of participant involvement that is more inclusive or more mindful of the social hierarchies within the research process.

The chapters

Before the first part of the volume begins, I introduce in Chapter 1 a number of key concepts in visual approaches that are relevant to psychology in particular. The aim of the chapter is to set a scene; a scene that includes some of the history behind the emergence of visual methods in psychology, as well as their exclusion. This chapter contains an overview of how psychology's engagement with the visual has changed over time: from the beginning of psychological methodologies, through to more contemporary issues relating to the qualitative study of experience. Amongst other issues relating to the possibilities for furthering participant agency in the research process, I concentrate on the role of the visual in opening up a channel for examining the material settings of experience (space) as well as examining people's accounts of experience through time (narrative).

Static media: the use of photography in qualitative research

In Part 1, 'Static media: the use of photography in qualitative research', the contributors discuss a variety of qualitative research projects involving the use of photography to explore issues relating to memory, illness, embodiment, appearance and intimacy, using theoretical approaches drawn from social and health psychology, feminism, phenomenology, and post-structuralist theory.

Alan Radley begins this Part in Chapter 2 by examining the importance of looking 'behind' as well as looking 'at' images in photographs in his discussion of two separate visual research projects (one using photo-elicitation, the other using photo-production). He describes how important it is to make a distinction between the content of an image (*image*) and a person's emotional and overall response in relation to that image (*depiction*). For example, he illustrates how photographs made by the participant provide an opportunity to go far beyond the actual content of the photograph (which may or may not be immediately meaningful) and into a realm where moments in life can be once again envisioned (through taking a photograph of an experience), encouraging the participant to articulate an image of an emotion (even though it may be different) after the event has passed. More than simply 'reading' the image, the participant is able, through the photograph, to conjure or imagine the experience of a particular moment and realise once more the context within which particular experiences took hold. This is more than looking 'at' the image; it is looking 'behind' the image also.

In Chapter 3, Ros Gill takes on the challenge of reading visual culture, as it relates to issues of body image for both men and women. Much of the writing exploring this feature of visual culture over the past decades has pointed to the enduring differences in the ways in which men's and women's bodies are put on display. Attention has been drawn to differences of pose, stature and gaze, with many authors asserting that, despite what might look like parity in the objectification of the body, men are still largely depicted in ways that allow them to hold on to power, and are not rendered entirely passive to an undifferentiated gaze. A large body of work has explored how these representations both work with and disavow homoeroticism, without challenging patriarchal power. All this looks set to change after a radical shift in the regime of representing the male body in advertising in 2007/8, with a variety of male 'crotch shots' appearing, posed by men in traditionally 'feminine' pose. In this chapter, Gill examines a range of images taken from recent high-profile advertising campaigns to address the issue of whether both men and women have become 'equally objectified' by this shift in visual representations. Within this visual analysis, Gill's chapter also raises a number of difficult questions about what it means for psychologists or other social scientists to 'read' such visual representations; she asks whether we can 'read off' other changes such as shifts in men's and women's subjectivities from the more general shifts in visual culture. Gill finishes with addressing the question of how we might begin to theorise the relationship between representations and identity, between (visual) culture and subjectivity.

In Chapter 4, Lilliana Del Busso explores two empirical studies that use photographs in different ways to explore young women's embodied experiences in everyday life. This takes the question beyond young women talking about their bodies to address how young women *feel and move* in their bodies. In the first study, photographs from different time periods in women's lives were used alongside life-history interviewing in order to bring the body *into* the interview conversation. Furthermore, the photographs were used as visual aids as well as tools to aid women in remembering key experiences and bodily sensations of importance. In a second study a photo-production and diary method were used by the young women to explore how objects, spaces, places, and other people helped shape their experience of being embodied in everyday life, and specifically in relation to their embodied experiences of pleasure. Del Busso argues that the approach she has used has the capacity to produce more detailed and meaningful research data as well as furthering theoretical development through exploring 'the body' beyond discourse. In particular, the use of photographs can encourage the production of phenomenological detail in relation to women's embodied experiences in their material and spatial contexts, avoiding the reproduction of the female body (object) solely as surface for the inscription of power dynamics.

In Chapter 5, Hannah Frith explores issues of appearance, embodiment and identity for women undergoing chemotherapy for breast cancer, by using a photo-production technique from the beginning to the end of treatment. Here, Frith argues that taking photographs of illness experiences engages participants in the task of producing significant memories (rather than using the photographs as mere reflections of a past event). Thus the act of remembering here is seen as part of a social and communicative practice (of which the visual is an integral part), as opposed to a realist notion of there being static fixed memories revealed directly by the photograph. In re-viewing these photographs during the interview, women are more directly involved in remembering past events, and are confronted by images of past selves which serve to anchor their present narratives in complex ways. And yet, women's refusal to capture a particular experience via photography, according to Frith, is equally significant. In the context of women taking and not taking certain photographs, she explores the role of missing photographs, or photographs never taken, in creating boundaries around what selves and lives are available to be remembered, and how choosing not to create some visual images is part of the process of active forgetting and distancing oneself from illness experiences.

In the final chapter of this part, Anamika Majumdar considers how the processes of photo-elicitation and photo-production are used to capture, albeit in different ways, the material settings through which experiences of intimacy and closeness in South Asian marriages are brought into being within the research context. In the first study, participants' existing family photographs were used in life-history interviews and only participants' discourse about their close relationships over time and space was analysed. In the second study, participants were asked to take photographs of objects, places and spaces significant to their married lives. The photographs were then used as the basis for in-depth interviews. However, the content of the photographs was analysed jointly between researcher and participant, the participant being given the opportunity to organise and select particular photographs for discussion. Majumdar argues that the photo-production technique provided a more successful engagement with the material settings of intimacy and closeness as it encouraged participants to break free from normative narration, which was still evident in the first study. The photo-production technique also encouraged greater participant agency in actively showing how intimacy was practically accomplished and visibly mediated through objects and spaces. The 'showing', therefore, actively shaped participants' engagement with the 'telling' in a way that disrupted narrative rehearsal.

Moveable features: using Facebook and video in qualitative research

Lewis Goodings and Steve Brown in the first chapter of this part deal with the role of the visual across online mediated communities. The arrival of new online social network sites (SNSs) offers the opportunity to rethink the application of the visual in new areas of social psychological research. New SNSs contain a strong sense of the visual through the increased capability to post photographs and other graphical images to a profile page. Recent work in psychology has emphasised that the increased ability to 'see' someone in these new spaces is evidence of narcissistic behaviour. However, in this chapter the authors explore the complex way that the visual is managed in the actual use of online communication, one which attempts to fully comprehend communication in one of the most popular forms of SNS (MySpace.com). The research is driven to look at the actual use of the visual and the textual in the MySpace community as opposed to the individualistic attempts to study this new phenomenon that begin at a particular version of the self. Alternatively, the aim is to explore the multiplicity of the visual and the textual in the *mediated* form of communication that occurs in MySpace. Goodings and Brown explore this phenomenon by drawing on examples of empirical data from MySpace. Their analysis is then directed by three distinct themes. First, the existence of *urcommunication* in the MySpace profiles. The use of urcommunication is to describe the inherent potential to communicate that is managed by the visual and the textual. Second, the ability to communicate across MySpace profiles in a way that changes the urcommunicative function. And third, the way that the visual and the discursive are able to lend their form across a range of different profiling practices. Goodings and Brown argue that MySpace users are able to mediate their everyday life through the use of a range of urcommunicative practices that keep the possibility of conversation open. This involves a performance of both the visual and the textual in the mediation of the profile pages. Final sections of this chapter are intended to propose a relationship between psychology and the virtual that does not intend to underestimate the complex multiplicity of the visual and textual in the ability to convey meaning in new forms of communication.

In Chapter 8, Johanna Motzkau explores the role of the visual in legal practice and psychological research through a reflexive exploration of forensic video data. Drawing on experiences and findings from a research project that compared child witness practices in England, Wales and Germany, the chapter illustrates how the visual asserts itself *throughout* the research process, emerging as an important and often equivocal arbiter within practices negotiating children's memory and credibility in the context of child sexual abuse investigations. The chapter focuses on the role of video technology introduced to provide better access to justice for children and vulnerable witnesses. Drawing on courtroom observations and data from interviews with legal professionals, it illustrates how in practice the video asserts itself as a participant, an autonomous proxy witness with a gaze and an ambiguous voice of its own. Examining closely how video operates in legal practice can make clear the need for researchers and practitioners to reflect critically on the direction and efficacy of the video's gaze.

In Chapter 9, Michael Forrester outlines a participant-observer approach to the 'naturalistic' study of language development in a pre-school child. To illustrate this, he draws on hours of video data taken of his own daughter between 12 and 41 months. The methodological approach he describes is informed by the principles of ethnomethodology and conversation analysis, in order to study in fine detail the sequence of the child's language as it emerges in everyday interaction. In studying the child's emerging language skills over time, Forrester was also able to observe the mediating role of the video in changing the child and parent interactions. Using data to illustrate, he reveals how the camera re-organises the child's engagement with certain tasks, conversations and experiences. Forrester is able to demonstrate how the child, even at a very young age, is able to acknowledge that the camera is 'watching' them, and that through this gaze they are able to perform social acts that serve to alter the course of their interactions. The child discovers, for example, that the camera is an object to interact with (pointed at, gestured toward), or a kind of mirror through which to perform or rehearse different behaviours and modes of expression, and within this a variety of self positionings and emotions.

In Chapter 10, Maria Pini and Valerie Walkerdine continue with a reflexive stance towards video data through their exploration of video-based, empirical research material. Drawing upon a project with a range of young female video-diarists, discussion initially centres on issues of 'authenticity' that are commonly associated with the video-diary. Questions of access, empowerment and surveillance (all of which were central to the project's formation) are addressed in detailing the study's development and its place within the social scientific research field. In exploring the different diaries produced by (working and middle class, black and white) young women, the analysis moves beyond the diary's seductive claims to 'authenticity' and recasts it as a form of informal 'auto-ethnography'. This chapter is, then, both theoretical and empirical, tackling pressing questions about the use of the visual within social-psychological research and demonstrating the different ways in which young women draw upon the resources to hand (including material, linguistic, imaginary and social resources) to fabricate varied and multiple visual fictions of self and subjectivity. In addition to the video affording greater room for these young women to explore different aspects of their subjectivity and presentations of self, the video was a constant reminder to them that they were being watched, and were thus subject to scrutiny by an audience. Subject, in other words, to a normative psychological gaze that restricts as much as it enables communication.

In the final chapter of this part, Helen Lomax examines how video-based methodology can be used to enhance the study of identity formation. Her discussion centres on a piece of empirical work focussing on the interactional exchanges of mothers and midwives in relation to mothers' birth experiences. Drawing on the theoretical and analytical framework of conversation analysis, Lomax examines how certain social orders (the prioritising of clinical discourse on the birth story and midwife–mother distancing) and identities are accomplished through locally and sequentially co-ordinated gaze, body movement and speech. The visual disengagement performed by midwifes (not looking at the mother and attending to paperwork), for example, significantly disrupts the usual order of conversational turn taking and requires the mother to respond in a compliant and passive way, as she readjusts her posture and gaze and realigns them with the midwife's more disengaged body movements. Lomax argues that this visual realignment provides the situational conditions for a more 'clinical' discourse on the mother's experience of childbirth to emerge. In addition to a discussion of the empirical work, Lomax reflects on her position as a researcher recording visual data, as well as her participants' engagement with this visualising process. Rather than 'spoiling' the data, she argues that the mothers' recognition and interaction with the recording equipment provides valuable insight into their engagement with the research process. In addition, this recognition and interaction helps to expand the researcher's knowledge of why participants might recruit them into the interaction and the effects of this recruitment on the flow and content of the conversational exchange.

Shared visions: opening up researcher-participant dialogues in the community and beyond

In this part, the contributors discuss a variety of qualitative research projects involving the use of visual methods, such as photography, collage, film and drawing. These visual approaches enable the exploration of issues relating to mental health, race, identity and emotion, using theoretical approaches drawn from social and community psychology, feminism, psychoanalysis and post-structuralist theory. To varying degrees, the chapters describe visual research that encourages greater participant involvement and ownership over the research process.

In Chapter 12, Katherine Johnson discusses visual methods in relation to experiences of mental distress for lesbian, gay, bisexual and/or transgendered (LGBT) people. The research presented in this chapter is driven by a commitment to the principles of community psychology (empowerment, participation) and knowledge-exchange and emerges out of an existing research partnership with Mind, the UK voluntary-based organisation dedicated to improving social attitudes and services for individuals who are mentally distressed. The project uses participatory-action research methods for creating a space where participants can exercise greater control and ownership over the research process, including the research aims, objectives and analysis. In addition to the use of a photovoice project, where participants were asked to take photos relating to their feelings and experiences of both sexuality and mental distress, the researchers also developed a visual exhibition of these experiences, creating a space for audience dialogue with the participants and their photographs. In describing the main analytical themes to arise from the project data, Johnson also discusses the audience response to the exhibition and asks how we might make sense of them in relation to challenging stigma and changing attitudes towards LGBT mental health.

In Chapter 13, Sarah Riley, Richard Brown, Christine Griffin and Yvette Morey follow on from Johnson in describing how they used a community-based art exhibition as a more creative and immediate form of research dissemination to increase audience engagement. The project behind the exhibition was designed to address how neo-tribalism (how people move between small and temporary groups and how these groups reflect shared values) is reflected in people's engagement, in relation to politics and identity, with electronic dance music culture (EDMC). The exhibition 'Reverberating Rhythms' was based on a series of interviews, focus groups and participant observations (where audio recording as well as photographs were taken) with individuals who participate in the EDMC scene. A reading group based on a theoretical work about tribalism, formed by the psychology academics of the project, was also used as a source of data for the exhibition, alongside participant data. The chapter builds on collaborative work between academics and artists in developing and disseminating psychological research. The collaborative process described here involved learning how to summarise and simplify without losing depth; how to communicate and interact with the artist in order to produce a joint vision; the construction of the materials themselves; and other practical activities (e.g. identifying a suitable venue, publicity, press, feedback questionnaires). Examples of the exhibits shown are provided throughout the chapter, describing the processes involved in their production, which often orient around a shift from the verbal (academic) to the visual (artistic). Ultimately the different media forms of graphic design, photography and fine art were argued to create a more vibrant and accessible form of engagement with a range of complex psychological ideas. Furthermore, the images allowed for a more subversive, contradictory, and disruptive form of audience engagement with these ideas.

In Chapter 14, Angela Cassidy and John Maule discuss the possibilities of using a visual approach to explore food risk knowledge amongst a variety of stake holders, including scientists, risk policy managers, farmers, food industry workers, and the public. One of the aims was to assess the similarities and differences in the way each of these groups represented food risk. A further aim was to devise a strategy for minimising any differences between the groups, through the adoption of more effective and ubiquitous forms of risk communication. Their initial qualitative data, using interviews and focus groups, were unsuccessful in eliciting the kind of responses they needed, especially with the public whose knowledge of food risk was limited. In response, Cassidy and Maule developed a visual approach employing 'fuzzy felt' to elicit mental models and social representations of food risk and to increase participant engagement with the issue, both at a community and industry level. In this, participants were asked to visually represent the food chain and any attendant risk by assembling the ready-made images made of the fuzzy felt provided. They were then asked to write down more information on the possible risk posed by various foods and what they would do to minimise or mitigate such risks. In addition to the visual techniques, Cassidy and Maule carried out a series of individual interviews to elicit more in-depth information relating to risk management and responsibility, amongst other issues.

In Chapter 15, Janice Haaken focuses on video ethnography, psychoanalytic social theory, and social action research, making use of a community documentary film project produced by the author, *Moving to the Beat*, as a case study. Here she not only outlines the theoretical underpinnings of the project but also identifies key areas for critical reflection. *Moving to the Beat* focuses on how African and African American youth are actively making use of hip-hop to communicate with one another and as a force for social change. The themes and storyline of the documentary were derived from key motifs identified by youth portrayed in the film, many of whom also participated as production assistants. Themes include differing understandings of hip-hop as a language for social change, including conceptions of both male and female artists and activists, differing fantasies black youth hold of America and Africa, and differing identifications with authority and rebellion. *Moving to the Beat* is a collaborative project, with crew in Freetown, Sierra Leone and Portland, Oregon, that grew out of an earlier field project on women and the Sierra Leonean civil war. The chapter addresses key questions that emerged out of the two years of producing *Moving to the Beat*, in particular it focused on the process of representing aspects of the black diaspora and/or black culture that have been devalued or degraded in mainstream popular culture, and by what criteria the activist documentary filmmakers evaluate the 'progressiveness' of visual media.

Caroline Howarth, in Chapter 16, examines representations of identity, power, self-reflection and stereotypes via a participant observation of, and collaboration with, a community-led arts-based project with young people of mixed heritage. Here she argues how images are a powerful way through which racism is reinforced through the *seeing of* minority individuals as different. This form of visibility, she argues, can lead to feelings of entrapment and potentially the desire to change physical attributes to reduce such visibility (hair straightening, nose reduction etc.). This London-based arts project (MOSAIC) was designed to facilitate shared discussion and to provide a space for these young people to challenge representations of 'race' and develop positive images of difference. Visual data (including photography and fabric weaving) drawn from extensive participant observation of the project reveal two things. First, how creative photography can capture the gaze of the other and the symbolic violence of racism as well as the possibilities for recasting the self in the eyes of others. Second, how weaving together different threads and fabrics that resonate with cultural associations and social memories can produce shared images and narratives of connection and disconnection, belonging and exclusion. These visual data were analysed alongside textual data (consisting of free-flowing discussions that occurred within the workshops and more structured interviews) within a social representations framework. In this, Howarth assesses the extent to which images draw on or contest dominant representations of 'race' are current in British society.

Helen Bowes-Catton, Meg Barker and Christina Richards, like Howarth, examine the complexities of sexual identity through their work within existing community-based groups. In their project, they explored bisexual identity at the annual UK BiCon (2008) event, which frequently involves participants in creative and arts based workshops. Here, the authors describe a visual project which aims to move beyond 'talk about bisexual identity' to an approach that encourages a more experiential and embodied account of bisexual identity. The empirical work they describe is based on a number of studies, including two photo-production studies of embodied experiences at (a) the actual BiCon event and (b) a photo-diary of a week in their everyday life. Three further group workshops at the BiCon event were held, which invited BiCon members to participate in model-making activities, involving Lego™, plasticine, and other craft materials. Through preliminary reflections on these data, the authors discuss how creative visual techniques open up a significant space for participants to describe and more thoroughly explore embodied feelings, which move beyond traditional and dominant categories of gender and sexuality. Furthermore, they argue that many of the participants are better able to integrate the importance and impact of setting (space) into their accounts of embodied subjectivity.

In Chapter 18, Alex Iantaffi moves into the realms of education and therapy to explore how a drawing technique, 'the river of experience', can be used to enable participants to explore life narratives collaboratively with the researcher. Iantaffi develops her argument by drawing on examples in research with disabled women in higher education and in therapeutic settings, to illustrate the use of this tool. The individual drawings of the participants' rivers can, in fact, support the researcher in exploring the participants' worlds during the qualitative interview by highlighting moments that may have otherwise been lost in a purely verbal dialogue driven by the researcher.

In the final chapter of this part, Alexander John Bridger introduces an analysis of maps and cities to explore the role of place in relation to emotions and reflective thoughts, drawing on ideas from psychogeography, critical psychology and urban studies. Within this, he provides a reflection on the use of walking, narrative and creative maps, in exploring the interrelationship between subjective experience and material environments. To illustrate this, Bridger focuses on empirical work from a project based at Ground Zero, New York and draws on two central situationist concepts – the détournement (a deliberate changing of words, images and sounds) and the dérive (a playful but mindful drift through one's material environment) to theorise the impact of space on subjective experience. That Ground Zero of course has come to crystallise mass-media representations of September 11th (for 'Western' societies at least) allows Bridger to adopt a range of creative visual techniques, including photography, auto-ethnography and the creation of an alternative and disorienting map of Ground Zero (using the principles of the détournement and the dérive) to explore themes such as injury, power and memory.

Ethical and methodological reflections on visual research

In this final part, the authors reflect upon the use of visual research in psychology by discussing certain elements of the modes of data collection, analysis and the conceptual underpinnings of visual approaches. In this, they draw on theoretical and conceptual issues in community psychology, feminist theory and social constructionism.

In Chapter 20, Darrin Hodgetts, Kerry Chamberlain and Shiloh Groot provide a reflexive account of the use of photovoice and photo-production techniques in community-based participatory research (in particular, their research with homeless people). Photovoice techniques have commonly been used for showing deprivation to those in power and lobbying for change, with the participant positioned as 'expert' in the research process. The authors argue that while this approach to research is useful in bringing the perspectives and voices of marginalised groups to the fore, it may also invoke relatively naïve assumptions about the concept of voice. Images, like other modes of discourse are subject to social conventions around what is acceptable to show and are continually subject to comparison with already existing (media) images. The photography participants are also subject to constant re-negotiation and re-construction within the resultant dialogue emerging from the research process. As participants reflect upon the images they have taken, for example, their accounts can lead to very different places from the ones represented in the images, including futures imagined but not yet realised (such as leaving the streets). Hodgetts, Chamberlain and Groot thus argue that the reading of images must take place through a longitudinal engagement with participants' changing circumstances, with their emerging dialogue and the different relationships they have with their own space/setting.

In Chapter 21, Kate Gleeson examines how to make explicit the analytical procedures we might use to examine visual data. She argues how visual methodology within psychology (and other social sciences) rarely makes explicit its mode of analysis, and certainly not at a level to encourage replication. The analyses that do exist (in semiological studies, for example) tend to focus on the close reading of individual examples of images, where the selection of material for analysis is idiosyncratic or not commented upon. Such approaches, she argues, do not sit well with psychologists who, even when qualitative researchers, are still steeped in the notions of systematic analytic procedures with clear sampling strategies that allow comparison across data sets. Gleeson's chapter sets out a systematic account of her analysis of photographic portraits and accompanying text (contained in a calendar) of individuals with learning disabilities. She refers to this form of analysis as Polytextual Thematic Analysis. Polytextual because it assumes the visual, the verbal and the written must be read in conjunction with one another. Gleeson provides a detailed description of the steps in the analysis, and an exposition of the texts used to interpret the images are provided as a means to expose the analytic process involved.

In Chapter 22, Karen Henwood, Fiona Shirani and Mark Finn provide a reflexive account of their use of three different visual techniques in working with men on a qualitative, longitudinal project about fatherhood. One of the major methodological and analytical tasks for the 'men as fathers' project was to highlight the diverse ways in which men position themselves psycho-discursively (including in terms of their 'imaginary positions') in their private and public relationships, and within the changing times and settings in which they live their lives. Although Henwood, Shirani and Finn clearly see a positive role for the visual in working with ideas of space and time, they also encountered a number of difficulties. In the chapter they compare three types of visual methods including collage (made up of existing media images), visual sequence (showing images of fatherhood sequentially, from different time periods) and personal photographs, which they combine with rich interview material. They describe, as an example, how a collage of images used at an early phase of the research to stimulate accounts of fatherhood and masculinities, at times set up a judgmental good father/bad father frame, and compromised the elicitation of more experiential data. Subsequently, they took to using visual images (e.g. in the form of family photographs) that were chosen by the men themselves to offset the problem of culturally primed images and to return men to more concrete and personal accounts of experience and the fractured underlying identities that intersect them. Each visual technique has value, they argue, in producing research-relevant data but each must be closely scrutinised in terms of its ability to address specific research questions.

In the final chapter, Ilana Mountian and colleagues provide a reflexive account of the use of photographs as part of an experience sampling method (ESM) in the study of wellbeing in higher education. The ESM is used to study pre-programmed segments of time. In this study, diaries and snapshot photography were used to capture experiences of enjoyment at pre-programmed moments throughout the day. As the participants were also the researchers, they were then able, in the context of group discussions, to reflect upon the process of producing visual accounts of experience. The authors discuss a number of ethical dilemmas arising from the use of the visual, especially with regard to power and reflexivity. More specifically, they examine the power dynamics associated with the intended audience (work colleagues) of the visual data, the impact of the intended audience on the production of the photographs, and how to balance self-reflection against confidentiality in the context of ongoing work relationships. The work described in this chapter once again emphasises the need to take into account the contexts surrounding the production of visual materials, and the power dynamics that inform them.

Summary

What I hope the reader will gain from this volume is a sense of the creative potential for visual approaches, in developing, expanding and enhancing qualitative methods in psychology. Our experiences of the world are so undeniably rich, layered and complex that they require a set of multi-layered or multi-modal theoretical and empirical tools to better grasp this plentiful landscape. The approaches outlined in Visual Methods in Psychology offer some insightful ways in which to work with such complexities in the spirit of contribution (rather than solution) to the ongoing debate about the processes through which *experience* and *subjectivity* can be known and understood.

References

Banks, M. (2006) Visual anthropology: image, object and interpretation. In J. Prosser (ed.) *Image-based research: a sourcebook for qualitative researchers*. London: Brunner Routledge.

Brown, S. D., Reavey, P., Cromby, J., Harper, D. and Johnson, K. (2009) Psychology and embodiment: Some methodological experiments. In J. Latimer and M. Schillmeier (eds) *Un/knowing bodies*. Sociological Review Monograph Series. Oxford: Blackwell, pp. 199–215.

Deleuze, G. (1986/1992) *Foucault*. Minneapolis: University of Minnesota Press.

Evans, J. and Hall, S. (1999) *Visual culture: the reader*. Buckingham: Open University Press.

Frith, H., Riley, S., Archer, L. and Gleeson, K. (2005) Imag(in)ing visual methodologies. *Qualitative Research in Psychology*, 2(3), 187–198.

Hall, S. (1997) *Representation: cultural representations and signifying practices*. Buckingham: Open University Press.

Haraway, D. J. (1991) *Simians, cyborgs, and women: the reinvention of nature*. London: Routledge.

Henriques, J., Hollway, W., Urwin, C., Venn, C. and Walkerdine, V. (1998) *Changing the subject: psychology, social regulation and subjectivity*. London: Routledge.

Pink, S. (2007) *Doing visual ethnography: images, media and representation in research*. Revised and expanded 2nd edition. London: Sage.

Prosser, J. (ed.) (2006) *Image-based research: a sourcebook for qualitative researchers*. London: Brunner Routledge.

Reavey, P. and Johnson, K. (2008) Visual approaches: using and interpreting images. In C. Willig and W. Stainton Rogers (eds) *The Sage handbook of qualitative research*. London: Sage.

Rose, G. (2007) *Visual methodologies: an introduction to the interpretation of visual materials*. London: Sage.

Wakefield, H. and Underwager, R. (2006) The application of images in child abuse investigations. In J. Prosser (ed.) *Image-based research: a sourcebook for qualitative researchers*. London: Brunner Routledge.

1 The return to experience
Psychology and the visual

Paula Reavey

The visual has always been there: an (in)visible history of continuity in psychology?

Psychology has a long-standing concern with the visual and with technologies of visualisation. This goes way beyond the specialised subdiscipline of the psychology of perception; it is instead part of the conceptual roots of the discipline as a whole. The emerging visual technology of photography was after all a central part of how the nascent discipline of psychology established its scientific credibility in the late nineteenth century – through the visual recording of scientific observation. For example, in *The Expression of the Emotions in Man and Animals*, Charles Darwin made comparisons across photographs and illustrations of children and animals as the evidential base for his theory of universal emotional expressions. This approach greatly influenced the growth of *Comparative Psychology* in the late nineteenth century (Richards, 2002). Moreover, photographs and minute observations of his son William Erasmus Darwin, which Darwin and his wife collected as a 'developmental diary' from his birth, are arguably the template from which *Developmental Psychology* established itself (Fitzpatrick and Bringmann, 1997).

The use of visual records to differentiate species and meticulously categorise plants and animals into various types and subtypes became the hallmark of nineteenth-century natural science. It marked the systematisation of observation, indicating accuracy, evidential recording, and careful attention to detail. What is measurable, therefore, is assumed to be what is observable. In the case of psychology, the fledgling discipline sought to separate itself from philosophy, and the myriad metaphysical difficulties which appeared to prohibit a 'science of mind', by emulating the natural sciences such as functional physiology as far as possible (Richards, 2002). Recent successes at that time in physiology had arisen from mapping functional connections between anatomy and behaviour. This same logic was applied to what Gustav Fechner (1860) called 'an exact theory of the functional relationships between body and soul and between the bodily, mental, somatic and physiological world' (cited in Meischner-Metge and Meischner, 1997: 102).

Two technologies of visualisation made this *Functional Psychology* possible. The first of these was the development of time-measuring devices such as the kymograph and chronoscope. This made it possible to record the time taken for the perception of stimuli and the execution of a response. Careful manipulation of stimuli under controlled laboratory conditions along with precise recording of the timing of responses became the basis of psychological experimentation (see Danziger, 1990). The second, and no less important, was the use of 'graphic notation' and 'chronophotography' by Etienne-Jules Marey and Eadweard Muybridge to study the behaviour of animals and subsequently humans (see Rabinbach, 1992). Chronophotography is a process of taking rapid exposures (around a dozen per second) on either a single photographic plate or on a series of cameras. The aesthetically striking images which result – such as Muybridge's famous photographs of galloping horses – provide a detailed visual description of the body's movement in space over time. This impressive oeuvre clearly anticipated moving film and the culture of viewing more generally. And yet, Muybridge's descriptions proved invaluable also for *Industrial Psychology* (e.g. the time and motion studies conducted by Frank and Lillian Gilbreth) which aimed to restructure and retrain the bodily movements of workers in order to maximise efficiency.

Photography also greatly influenced the development of *Psychopathology* and *Clinical Psychology*. Visual categorisation of different personality types and the categorisation of the 'mad', 'subnormal' or 'criminal' was performed by assembling photographic arrays in which purported mental differences could be made legible to the 'trained eye' (Jackson, 1995). Photographs were also commonly used to lend visual credibility to diagnostic categories of mental defects or 'feeblemindedness'. Through careful visual recording, the spaces between a person's eyes, the size of a forehead or the body posture of an asylum inmate could provide direct evidence for an observable and thus categorical difference in the person under study from a 'typical' person. The multiple exposure technique used by Marey – where a series of images are exposed on the same photographic plate – was also used by Francis Galton (see Draaisma, 2000). Galton argued that his 'compound photographs' of criminals and of 'consumptives' taken one-by-one onto the same photographic plate showed their common features, since individual or non-common features would be effectively washed out during the process. The technique was, Galton claimed, a sort of 'pictorial statistics' where norms of human development and diversity could be visually represented. This idea fed into popular notions of normality and abnormality around mental health which gained currency in the late nineteenth and early twentieth century (Porter, 2003). Visual techniques such as the Rorschach ink blot tests – surely one of the most recognisable representations of psychology – and the Thematic Apperception Test (see Cramer, 1996) were and still are used to provide insight into a person's personality type, his/her unconscious motivational state, or used to detect signs of mental illness. Finally, contemporary forms of visualising the differences between 'normal' and 'abnormal' individuals are now reported to be 'captured' in the magnetic resonance techniques commonly used in psychiatry, behavioural genetics and neuro-psychology. However, the dangerous over-interpretation of these visual markers – that they represent enduring and static biological markers of diseases and brain dysfunction – should be approached with extreme caution (Bentall, 2009; Cromby, *et al.*, forthcoming).

Social Psychology has throughout its history used film and photography as a means of documenting research and shoring up the 'face validity' of its claims. The images of participants presented in Stanley Milgram's (2005) infamous studies on obedience in the early 1960s appear to leave little room for doubting the validity of his claims. Close analyses of the statistical evidence (and the ecological validity of the experimental set-up) about the tendency for 'ordinary' people to follow orders that can lead to the harming of others is somewhat overshadowed by these powerful images. Similarly the video recordings taken by Philip Zimbardo and colleagues of the Stanford Prison Experiment (SPE), have been promoted as powerful testimony to the ease with which people take on the aggressive or passive behaviour in their respective roles as prisoner or guard. This material was captured using the sort of 'hidden camera' techniques that have become the mainstay of reality-TV shows such as *Candid Camera*, or more recently, Big Brother. Interestingly Zimbardo himself has claimed that Alan Funt, creator of the first reality-TV show Candid Camera, was 'one of the most creative, intuitive social psychologists on the planet' (Zimbardo *et al.*, 2000: 197). Kurt Lewin also used hidden camera techniques to make a series of films which focused on the spaces of child development, the best known being the 1931 film *The Child and the World*. This film work led to a meeting with the Russian auteur Sergei Eisenstein (director of Russian classics including *Battleship Potemkin* and *October*) and subsequent plans for a psychological laboratory to be established in Moscow in collaboration with the local state film academy (Lück, 1997: 285). To summarise, an historical analysis of the role of the visual within psychology can reveal its instrumental effects in providing the context for 'the psychological' to become observable and, therefore, measurable and more 'scientific'. In using visual images as evidence, and in employing visual technologies to increase the accuracy and thus the status of psychological observations, the discipline of psychology has also made its findings more publicly accessible. And yet, despite these noteworthy uses of visual images throughout psychology, there has been very little in the way of methodologies that have attempted to accommodate the visual. This is especially difficult to understand with regards to qualitative methodologies that claim to capture more readily meaning making in everyday experience. To understand why this is so, it is necessary to review briefly the emergence of qualitative research in psychology to grasp why it is that everyday experience has been in the grip of language-based methodologies for the past three decades.

Qualitative research in psychology and visual myopia

Qualitative research is now well established in certain subdisciplines of psychology (critical, community, social, clinical, educational), even though as a methodology it continues to sit on the margins of psychology's mainstream. Rather than searching for generalisable laws (which is psychology's ultimate aim), qualitative researchers are concerned with uncovering the variety of ways in which people make and interpret meaning, how they tell stories about their lives and communicate with others (Willig, 2001; Parker, 2004; Stainton Rogers and Willig, 2008). Thus, the aim of this type of approach is to explore in depth the rich texture of people's accounts and conversations, for the purpose of research only or to work towards radical social change (see Parker, 2004). The participant, and not the researcher, becomes the focus of meaning generation and active agent. In recent years, numerous publications have emerged that describe in detail how to collect, store and analyse qualitative data in a systematic and logical fashion, depending on the theoretical tradition one is working from.

In the United Kingdom, qualitative psychology has been informed by theoretical traditions such as post-structuralism and postmodernism, and to a lesser extent phenomenology and existentialism. However, it is noteworthy that the take up of post-structuralism has been somewhat esoteric and has tended to promote the linguistic and the discursive above other modalities (e.g. visual, sound, affect). There are a number of reasons underpinning this. First of all, Anglo-North American critical social science has been greatly influenced by ordinary language philosophy (e.g. Wittgenstein, Austin, Ryle) and the development of linguistically oriented 'phenomenological sociology' in the form of ethnomethodology. It is notable, for example that three of the major figures in Anglo critical psychology of the 1970s and 80s were deeply immersed in the work of Wittgenstein (i.e., the works of Ken Gergen, Rom Harre and John Shotter). Second, the reception of the semiotic tradition in the UK has tended to focus on a narrowly linguistic reading of De Saussure rather than the huge variety of other forms of semiotics which deal with other modalities of understanding and expression – such as C. S. Peirce's pragmatist semiotics, A. J. Greimas's comparative/structuralist semiotics, Thomas Sebeok's zoosemiotics/biosemiotics and Felix Guattari's schizoanalytic semiotics. Finally, key post-structuralist authors such as Derrida and Foucault have been read as discourse theorists. Derrida's (1976) phrase 'there is nothing outside the text' (p. 158) has been itself read outside of the text as a claim that there is no intelligibility outside of discourse, when in fact it is a highly nuanced technical point about the hermeneutics (interpretation) of philosophical discourse and the metaphysics of graphism (writing in a very broad sense).

The treatment of Foucault is of particular note, not least because a methodology known as 'Foucauldian Discourse Analysis' is now recognised in UK social psychology. The method draws inspiration from *The Archaeology of Knowledge*, where Foucault makes the claim that 'discourse constructs the objects of which it speaks' (Foucault, 1972/2008: 54). As with Derrida, this very playful claim is made as part of a broader set of arguments, in this case with the history of ideas and Frege's philosophy of language. Moreover, the book, along with the lecture *The Discourse on Language* from the same period, make it abundantly clear that at this time Foucault was concerned explicitly with the relationship between the discursive and the 'extra-discursive'. This concern came to full fruition in Foucault's subsequent investigations of the relationship of knowledge and power, where the visual plays a central role in terms of the organisation of bodies (i.e.

panopticism) and the representation of the population in terms which enable its management as a productive and reproductive force (i.e. biopolitics). To selectively read Foucault as a discourse theorist is then to miss the richness and subtlety of his thinking for psychology (for a 'non-discursive' reading of Foucault and psychology, see Brown and Stenner, 2009).

The majority of qualitative work uses spoken semi-structured and unstructured interview data, natural conversations, focus group discussions, diaries or written reports, which all focus on either the broad sense-making patterns, or the minute detail of the way in which the language is structured and performed in social interactions. What every technique shares in common, however, is a reliance on the spoken or written word as a source of data – a fundamentally *mono-modal approach*.

Elsewhere, Katherine Johnson and I (Reavey and Johnson, 2008) have argued that the reason for the reluctance to engage in multi-modal forms of qualitative analysis is related to visual data being more ambiguous or polysemic (multiple meanings) – as the interpretation of the image cannot always be fixed and does not always relate to any spoken account by the participant (see also Frith and Harcourt, 2007 and Motzkau, this volume). Despite this reluctance among some qualitative researchers, the visual has grown significantly in the social sciences and more recently in psychology. In the section that follows, some of the topics that researchers in psychology have examined using visual approaches will briefly be explored, in order to illustrate how the rich embodied and spatial (amongst others) texture of experience cannot be fully captured by language-based/mono-modal perspectives.

Why qualitative psychology could use visual approaches: the potential for multi-modal approaches

To date, visual approaches in psychology have tackled a range of experiential issues, including embodiment (Del Busso, 2009; Gillies *et al.*, 2005), health and illness (Radley and Taylor, 2003a, 2003b; Radley, 2009), the process of remembering (Middleton and Edwards, 1990; Radley, 1990; Middleton and Brown, 2005; Brookfield, Brown and Reavey, 2008), identity and appearance (Gleeson and Frith, 2006) and mental health difficulties (Silver and Reavey, 2010, in press). This multi-modal work has combined visual and verbal data to create a richer picture of the topic under study and has used a variety of visual techniques, from the use of already existing images (e.g. in the form of family photographs, here referred to as *photo-elicitation*) to the use of images generated within the context of the research, here referred to as *photo-production*[1] (participant-generated photos, photo-diaries, paintings and drawings). What these authors share is the acknowledgement that (a) individuals *experience* the world not only through narrative, but through setting (space) and embodiment and (b) that individuals are *already* using multi-modal forms of expression and communication when (re)presenting their experiences in everyday life. As people become more proficient in using new communication technologies to convey ideas and feelings and engage in new forms of social interaction, relationality and subjectivity, it is ever more vital that researchers in psychology engage with these everyday forms of communication and representation.

How we use and interpret the visual in research, of course, is in turn informed by the kinds of questions we wish to ask and the theoretical frameworks that inform those questions. A number of researchers in this volume have used visual techniques in a variety of ways to address complex issues relating to the study of experience. By outlining how visual methods are used to address particular experiential issues throughout the volume, we can begin to see their utility in taking the study of experience beyond textual representations and into the realm of multi-modality. We will also see how researchers have begun to open up a space to examine 'hard to reach' issues, such as the environmental spaces that individuals experientially inhabit and the emotional and embodied elements of experience that are always present but rarely directly acknowledged in qualitative research (Brown *et al.*, 2008). In visual research (using painting, drawing, photography and film) I have carried out with colleagues, on topics ranging from mental health, space, embodiment, memory and ageing, we have also found that the visual can successfully act to disrupt well-rehearsed present narratives on a topic (Gillies *et al.*, 2005; Brookfield *et al.*, 2008; Reavey, 2008; Silver and Reavey, 2010). Participants, when faced with a photograph from their past, for example, can suddenly be confronted with, and are able to *imagine* the emotions or their embodied states from that time, such that the past can enter into the present moment and create a new narrative or more complex account (especially if the re-emergence of the past collides with narratives of the present). This is not to say that somehow the visual catches the person out or forces him/her to tell the truth about the past, but nevertheless it can serve to provide a more complex and layered account, and one that is more seeped in emotional resonances and reminders, and one in which the setting (the actual place) of the experience is brought into sharper view. In one research group meeting I was involved in,[2] where we were looking at photographs of ourselves for the purpose of exploring embodiment, it was of interest that one of the group members was genuinely surprised by how the photograph of a particular time in their life completely disrupted their initial narrative memory of that time. Where they were certain before viewing the photo that they had 'messed up' that period of their life, the photo reminded them that this memory was far from straightforward; in the photo they appeared well presented, clean and celebratory in an exciting place. Thus, the account became more complex and more layered as a result of combining the visual with the subsequent verbal discussion. The visual jolted them into an alternative narrative position, which cohered *and* collided with their initial narrative recollection.

Other researchers have also noted that visual data can alter the emotional tone of the interview and engage the senses more powerfully than conversation alone. A photo-elicitation study by Kunimoto (2004), with Japanese-Canadians interned during the Second World War, revealed how different kinds of memories and emotions emerged through the use of domestic photographs from that time period. Though the conversational exchange began in a fairly formal manner, the photographs evoked memories that were more emotional, rich and enlivened through the course of the interview. Joanna Silver and I have also found photographs to be a valuable source for addressing issues of self-hood for individuals diagnosed with Body Dysmorphic Disorder (BDD – a condition marked by a distressing preoccupation with an imaginary or minor defect in a facial feature or a localised part of the body). By inviting participants to bring to interview photographs from different periods in their lives, we found that they moved away from diagnostic discourses on BDD and presented an intensely emotional account of their idealisation of their childhood self, on which present judgements about facial disfigurement were grounded. The photographs were particularly powerful in the way they provoked an emotionally led discussion about the discrepancies between their beautiful, innocent and ideal childhood self and their present deteriorating and flawed self (Silver and Reavey, 2010). This emotional connection between past and present in the clinical literature on BDD was absent; photographs were a useful way of accessing and exploring this connection because participants had ready to hand a visible portrait of the self physically (and thus emotionally) changing over time.

Part of the reason for greater opportunities for 'emotionality' is the emphasis visual researchers place upon *participation* and *agency* within the research process. In many visual studies, participants are actively encouraged to make their own choices about the photographs they take or select to discuss in any subsequent interview (Mitchell *et al.*, 2005; Radley and Taylor, 2003b). In other words, they are more involved in *what* is seen, as well as *how* the images are used in the research process. This in itself can allow participants to focus on images that have emotional resonancy. However, the emotional resonancy of some images may also lead to active avoidance by the participant, especially in times of loss or grief, so it is vital that we do not assume images will *necessarily* evoke emotions; and if they do, we cannot assume individuals will want to talk about, or engage with them in a research context.

A further argument to for using visual research within qualitative research is the potential for increased participant *participation* in the generation and organisation of data, thus allowing the participant to shape the context out of which personal stories are told. If participants are given the opportunity to 'show' their experiences and lives, rather than 'narrate' them only, they are able to expand their story to show where and when their experiences occur, with greater freedom. One could say that in some sense this process invites the reader and researcher to begin from the position of bearing witness to the participant's 'world-making' (to borrow a phrase from Radley, 2009), rather than acting from the position of detached observer of a person's verbal narrative only (see Radley, 2009 for an extended discussion of narrative, art and testimony). Many researchers using photographs, for example, involve participants in organising images for further discussion within an interview or focus group. This provides greater space for participants to order the material and speak to issues in a particular sequence that make more sense to them (Radley and Taylor, 2003b). As a result, participants find they have more time to reflect on their experiences when they are given the opportunity to be more in charge of the data collecting and organising process.

For some visual researchers, involving participants in data organisation as well as collection is central to the aim of further democratising the research process. Although this is a far from straightforward process and not always successful (see Henwood *et al.*, and Mountian, this volume), there are examples of greater participant agency, at least in terms of defining the parameters of the research activity, and providing a space to challenge dominant cultural and social labels and representations (see Howarth, this volume).

Viewing experience from the perspective of time and space

Another success relating to the use of visual methods is its potential for widening the focus of participants' accounts by attending to the setting in which their experiences take place. Almost all qualitative methods involve asking participants to recall and reflect on past experiences and, when using purely verbal methods, this has been observed to lead to such narratives being overwhelmingly organised in terms of time. Studies incorporating visual methods have on the other hand been shown to succeed in disrupting such narratives and encourage participants to also reflect on the social and material contexts of their experiences. Not just *when* but *where* experiences emerge.

Whenever qualitative researchers talk to people about their experiences, they are asking people to speak about events that have occurred in the recent or even distant past. Biographical or narrative research in psychology has stressed how important it is to gain a more intimate knowledge of people's experiences as they occur across time, in order to establish patterns of continuity as well as change (Wengraf *et al.*, 2000). Unless we are studying real-time interaction (as many conversation analysts and discursive psychologists argue we should), qualitative research is dealing with *recollections* of events and versions of self, or discourses relating to personal narratives/stories, that are both past *and* present. Time and memory thus looms large in the experiences that individuals recall in the context of qualitative research. But time and memory do not stand alone, and are interlaced with space – in other words, the settings/places where experiences occur. Whilst many narrative researchers have long argued for a greater sensitivity to the specifics of personal narratives over time (Wengraf *et al.*, 2000), there has been less attention to the setting out of which such narratives emerge. A number of authors in this volume, however, point to the importance of viewing experience and subjectivity as *situated* in specific locations (see Pini and Walkerdine, Majumdar, Hodgetts *et al.*, this volume). The process by which we story ourselves into being is thus spatially framed, not just time-framed. We can accept this if we embrace the self as a process and form that shifts according to context. As Foucault wrote (2000: 290–291):

It [the self] is not a substance. It is a form, and this form is not primarily or always identical to itself. You do not have the same sort of relationship to yourself when you constitute yourself as a political subject who goes to vote or speaks at a meeting and when you are seeking to fulfil your desires in a sexual relationship. Undoubtedly there are relationships and interferences between these different forms of subject; but we are not dealing with the same type of subject. In each case, one plays, one establishes a different type of relationship to oneself. And it is precisely the historical constitution of these various forms of the subject in relation to games of truth which interests me.

Following Foucault (2000), the argument here is that recollections of experience should not be read as a product of a coherent self, or a self made up of a stable substance (which we then believe makes our biographies coherent). By treating the self as a substance, the implication is that whilst there is a change and development over time, which can lead to reframing and interpreting the past in line with our current state of self-hood, it nevertheless implies a certain kind of narrowing of interpretive flexibility.

Thus, self should be treated as continually varied, depending on the setting in which it emerges. As Brown and Stenner (2009: 168) note,

If it is possible to speak of a subject at all then it must be done with reference to the 'various forms' subjectivity takes and the multiplicity of relationships and connections that pertain between these forms.

Furthermore, the spaces wherein the self unfolds literally leave their mark on any subsequent recollection of this self. By 'leaving their mark' what I mean is the space is an integral part of the sets of relations that contribute to the patterns of self-hood over time (Reavey, 2010).

Different kinds of spaces also make possible different versions of agency; our capacities for acting and self-making are affected by the meanings associated with certain spaces. In a photo-production diary study by Del Busso (2009) on young women's experiences of embodiment, participants were asked to take pictures of objects or spaces that reflected experiences of embodied pleasure (eating, having sex, exercise etc.). In the subsequent interviews with women, who brought along their photos and diaries, it became clear that the manner in which participants experienced embodied pleasure was intimately tied to the setting in which those experiences occurred. For example, some women felt greater embodied agency in outside natural spaces where they were able to move *freely* without being restricted by expectations of what they should look like and without fearing for their safety. In other public spaces, such as built-up spaces or heterosexualised spaces (clubs and pubs) their agency was felt to be restricted and feelings of powerlessness increased. The visual display of spaces and settings thus afforded greater room for women to be able to explore the different possibilities for self-hood and agency that were available to them. Space is therefore an integral influence on the selves that we can be. Attention to space thus affords a greater awareness of experience as *embodied* in a variety of intersecting locations in which different various aspects of self-making are practiced (McDowell, 1996).

Bringing concepts of space into qualitative research is by no means straightforward. However, visual approaches can be useful in bringing to the fore the spatial locations (and the objects that inhabit them) in which experiences occur by at least putting them on the discursive agenda in the research context (Brookfield *et al.*, 2008). If we can take a visual record at the time at which we experience something or can gather together existing visual images of an event (e.g. our existing personal photographs), we can bring the space and setting of the experience to the foreground and make it explicit in the context of discussion. Radley and Taylor (2003a) in a photo-production study of recovery experiences, for example, asked patients to take photographs of the salient spaces and objects of the hospital ward they were in, in order to examine the impact of the physical setting of the ward on the process of recovery. Participants were subsequently interviewed, using the hospital images as major leverage for discussing their memories of recovery. Radley and Taylor found the images of the material objects and spaces of the hospital prompted painful memories of their hospital stay whilst also allowing them to actively distance themselves from the hospital, because the images were 'from the past' *and* from 'another place'.

In sum, visual research in psychology can bring to the fore the spaces and objects through which people experience themselves so that the various forms of self-hood reported (verbally) and shown (visually) are contextualised. The gap between the material and the discursive thus becomes significantly reduced and seen in connection with one another – 'as one in a web', as Brown and Pujol pronounce (Brown and Pujol, 1998; Brown, 2001).

Summary

Psychology has a long history of engaging with the visual. And yet the visual has not been a prominent feature of methodological procedure in psychology, including social constructionist or more broadly qualitative approaches. I have proposed a number of reasons for this, including the uptake of language-based philosophies in social constructionist traditions, and the over-emphasis of language/discourse in readings of Foucault's work, among others. Following this, I have pointed to the process through which visual approaches can open up possibilities for understanding people's experiences – as the multi-layered and multi-modal phenomena they inevitably are. This, I contend, is why we may be better able to engage individuals in the process of exploring the link between past and present in a way where the past can be more present – in terms of its setting (space), emotion and embodiment – through the use of ready to hand visual (re) presentations of it. I have of course cautioned against reading this process as one that assumes 'a/the truth' lurks behind those images, or that images serve to catch people out or force them to confront a 'true self' or what is 'really there'. We have already seen how the visual is just as much subject to interpretation as any other modality, replete with plurality and ambiguities. With this cautionary note in mind, the visual nonetheless can be seen to bring to mind emotions, embodied states and spaces that enable us to ground or contextualise our experiences more readily. It can also provide the opportunity for participants to begin the research process by *showing* us how they have made their worlds, rather than answering our questions or beginning with an explanation. In doing so, the multi-layered aspects of those experiences – that include both space and time – can be explored by the participant and researcher as a joint negotiation.

Acknowledgments

I am indebted to Steve Brown for his invaluable insight and help with the writing of this chapter. I would also like to thank Alex John, Laura Mcgrath, Joanna Silver and Ava Kanyeredzi for reading and commenting on the chapter in its earlier stages.

Note

1 Sometimes authors refer to *photo-elicitation* to describe both approaches. However, for the sake of clarity, I have decided to separate the two terms to distinguish between these two very different approaches. The authors of this volume, in the main, also make this distinction for continuity and clarity.
2 This research group was made up of six researchers dedicated to the empirical study of embodiment. In the group, we experimented with a variety of methodologies to examine the question of how one might access embodiment, which we took to mean how one feels, senses and expresses bodily sensation and action.

References

Brookfield, H., Brown, S. D. and Reavey, P. (2008) Vicarious and post-memory practices in adopting families: the re-production of the past through photography and narrative. *Journal of Community and Applied Social Psychology*, 18: 474–491.
Bentall, R. P. (2009) *Doctoring the mind.* London: Allen Lane.
Brown, S. D., Cromby, J., Harper, D., Johnson, K. and Reavey, P. (2011, in press) Embodiment, methodology, process: a preliminary report. *Theory & Psychology.*
Brown, S. D., Reavey, P., Cromby, J., Harper, D. and Johnson, K. (2008) The psychological legacy and the limits of embodiment. In J. Latimer and M. Schillmeier (eds) *Knowing/ unknowing bodies.* Sociological Review Monograph Series. Oxford: Blackwell.
Brown, S. D. (2001) Psychology and the art of living. *Theory and Psychology*, 7: 171–192.
Brown, S. D. and Pujol, J. (1998) As one in a web: discourse, materiality and the place of ethics. In I. Parker (ed.) *Social constructionism, discourse and realism.* London: Sage.
Brown, S. D. and Stenner, P. (2009) *Psychology without foundations: history, philosophy and psychosocial theory.* London: Sage.
Cramer, P. (1996) *Storytelling, narrative and the Thematic Apperception Test.* London: Guilford Press.
Cromby, J., Harper, D. J. and Reavey, P. (forthcoming) *Understanding mental health and distress: from disorder to experience.* Basingstoke: Palgrave.
Danziger, K. (1990) *Constructing the subject: historical origins of psychological research.* Cambridge: Cambridge University Press.

Darwin, C. (1872/1999) *The expression of the emotions in man and animals: definitive edition*. Fontana: Fontana Press.

Del Busso, L. (2009) *'Being in motion': femininity, movement and space in young women's narratives of their embodied experiences in everyday life*. Unpublished PhD manuscript, London South Bank University.

Derrida, J. (1976) *Of grammatology*. Baltimore, MD: Johns Hopkins University Press.

Draaisma, D. (2000) *Metaphors of memory: a history of ideas about the mind*. Cambridge: Cambridge University Press.

Fechner, G. T. (1860/1966) *Elements of psychophysics*. Orlando: Holt, Rinehart & Winston.

Fitzpatrick, J. F. and Bringmann, W. G. (1997) Charles Darwin and psychology. In W. G. Bringmann, H. E. Lück, R. Miller and C. E. Early (eds) *A pictorial history of psychology*. Chicago, IL: Quintessence Books.

Foucault, M. (1972) *The archaeology of knowledge* (Trans. A. Sheridan). London: Routledge.

Foucault, M. (2000) *Power: the essential works of Michel Foucault 1954–1984*. Volume two. James Faubion (ed.), Robert Hurley (Trans.) London: Allen Lane.

Frith, H. and Harcourt, D. (2007) Using photographs to capture women's experiences of chemotherapy: reflecting on the method. *Qualitative Health Research*, 17: 1340–1350.

Gillies, V., Harden, A., Johnson, K., Reavey, P., Strange, V. and Willig, C. (2005) Painting pictures of embodied experience: the use of nonverbal data production for the study of embodiment. *Qualitative Research in Psychology*, 2: 199–212.

Gleeson, K. and Frith, H. (2006) Deconstructing body image. *Journal of Health Psychology*, 1(11): 79–90.

Jackson, M. (1995) Images of deviance: visual representations of mental defectives in early twentieth-century medical texts. *The British Journal for the History of Science*, 28: 319–337.

Kunimoto, N. (2004) Intimate archives: Japanese-Canadian family photography, 1939–1949. *Art History*, 27: 129–155.

Lück, H. E. (1997) Kurt Lewin – filmmaker. In W. G. Bringmann, H. E. Lück, R. Miller and C. E. Early (eds) *A pictorial history of psychology*. Chicago, IL: Quintessence Books.

Meischner-Metge, A. and Meischner, W. (1997) Fechner and Lotze. In W. G. Bringmann, H. E. Lück, R. Miller and C. E. Early (eds) *A pictorial history of psychology*. Chicago, IL: Quintessence Books.

McDowell, L. (1996) Spatialising feminism: Geographic perspectives. In N. Duncan (ed.) *Body space: geographies of gender and sexuality*. London: Routledge.

Middleton, D. and Brown, S. D. (2005) *The social psychology of experience: studies in remembering and forgetting*. London: Sage.

Middleton, D. and Edwards, D. (eds) (1990) *Collective remembering*. London: Sage.

Mitchell, C., DeLange, N. Moletsane, R., Thabisile, J. S. and Buthelez, T. (2005) Giving a face to HIV and AIDS: on the uses of photo-voice by teachers and community health care workers working with youth in rural South Africa. *Qualitative Research in Psychology*, 3: 257–270.

Milgram, S. (2005) *Obedience to authority: an experimental view* (new edition). New York: Pinter and Martin.

Parker, I. (2004) *Qualitative psychology: introducing radical research*. Buckingham: Open University Press.

Porter, R. (2003) *Madness: a brief history*. Oxford: Oxford University Press.

Rabinbach, A. (1992) *The human motor: energy, fatigue and the origins of modernity*. Berkeley, CA: University of California Press.

Radley, A. (2009) *Works of illness: narrative, picturing and the social response to serious disease*. Ashby-de-la-Zouch: InkerMen Press.

Radley, A. and Taylor, D. (2003a) Images of recovery: a photo-elicitation study on the hospital ward. *Qualitative Health Research*, 13: 77–99.

Radley, A. and Taylor, D. (2003b) Remembering one's stay in hospital: a study in photography, recovery and forgetting. *Health: An Interdisciplinary Journal for the Study of Health, Illness and Medicine*, 7: 129–159.

Reavey, P. (2008) Back to experience: material subjectivities and the visual. Key note address at *Visual Psychologies*. 4 June, University of Leicester, UK.

Reavey, P. (2010) Spatial markings: memory, narrative and survival, *Memory Studies*, 3: 314–329.

Reavey, P. and Johnson, K. (2008) Visual approaches: using and interpreting images. In W. Stainton Rogers, and C. Willig (eds) *The Sage handbook of qualitative research*. London: Sage.

Richards, G. (2002) *Putting psychology in its place: a critical historical overview* (2nd edition). London: Routledge.

Silver, J. and Reavey, P. (2010) Body Dysmorphic Disorder and the life narrative. *Social Science and Medicine*, 70: 1641–1647.

Stainton Rogers, W. and Willig, C. (2008) (eds) *The Sage handbook of qualitative methods in psychology*. London: Sage.

Wengraf, T., Chamberlayne, P. and Bornat, J. (eds) (2000) *The turn to biographical methods in social science*. London: Routledge.

Zimbardo, P., Maslach, C. and Haney, C. (2000) Reflections on the Stanford Prison Experiment: genesis, transformations, consequences. In T. Blass (ed.) *Obedience to authority: current perspectives on the Milgram paradigm*. London: Lawrence Erlbaum Associates.

Part I

Static media

The use of photography in qualitative research

2 Image and imagination

Alan Radley

Any visual psychology should include within its concerns 'the act of picturing'. This is something more than using pictures to access other topics of interest, which makes visual material merely illustrative of what is signified. While there is a place for research that uses pictures as a record, or even as a prompt to better interview material, this falls short of a critical approach to visual studies. A methodology that limits itself to analysing visual records as content – or worse still, to analysing verbal accounts about visual data – fails to address how people make sense *with* pictures as well as making sense of them.

I will pursue this line of argument by making a distinction between the terms *image* on the one hand, and *depiction* or *picture* on the other. The word image is often used interchangeably with other terms to mean 'what the picture shows', which is consistent with a copy theory of perception.[1] The use of the term to cover two separate entities – what is 'in the photo' and what is 'inside the viewer's head' – can only lead to confusion when trying to understand what picturing involves (Mitchell, 1984). If one speaks to people about photographs that they have made, or even about ones they would like to have made, it soon becomes clear that the print is often an approximation to what they wanted to show but could not (Hodgetts *et al.*, 2007). Or else the photograph can be said to capture the person exactly, so that the (mental) image one has of them somehow coheres with the (physical) depiction on the print. These two possibilities, along with others, are defined within a potential space of viewing that enables a consideration of making, showing and explaining using visual methods.

This possibility is soon revealed to anyone using visual methods as part of psychological research. Rather than being a problem to be avoided, the question of how people make pictures – as well as explain with them – provides a useful way of investigating some of the indeterminables in everyday life. For my part, as a social psychologist acknowledging the primacy of embodiment (e.g. in illness, in homelessness), approaching problems via photography is a way of foregrounding the material settings in which people live their lives. This is not a reduction to the physicality of existence, but rather an attempt to hold still (for a moment) the fragments in which everyday experience attains psychological and social significance. It is not that the detail of physical settings is especially significant: rather, making and talking about a photograph can help explain or express (these are not the same thing) something that would otherwise be difficult to show about how we live in the world. It is in the context of this interest that the matter of pictures and images becomes salient, especially in relation to the use of visual methods in psychology more generally.

In order to further the distinction between images and depictions, I will discuss two examples of research using visual material, one involving photographs provided by an overseas aid agency, the other using photographs made by respondents themselves while in hospital. In the first study, people ranked, ordered and discussed a series of photographs used by UNICEF for fund raising, explaining which of the pictures would be more likely to spur them to give money for this cause (Radley and Kennedy, 1997). In the second study, patients who were on a surgical ward took photographs in hospital and then used these to talk about their experience, both at that time and later on when they were recuperating at home (Radley and Taylor, 2003a, 2003b).

Using pictures as an aid to interviewing is a well-established technique in social science, while getting people to take photographs of their situation and discuss these is an increasingly popular method (Collier, 2001; Pink, 2006). The first case – photo-elicitation – draws attention to the scenes or images pictured in the photographs, so that it is the content that appears for examination. The second – photo-production – treats the prints as evidence of the act of photography, so that how the pictures are produced and in what context are matters of central concern. These two options give rise to different but overlapping strategies for research. Rather than being static frames that enclose pictures of things, photographs made by respondents can be interrogated and justified from when they are taken (and even before that) through to the end of any subsequent interviews. This makes it possible to include the context of production as data, and hence reflect something of the action-frame of the researcher as well as the intentions of the respondents concerned.

This perspective is usefully related to Wright's (1999) distinction between readings that 'look at' and those that 'look behind' photographs, which in turn can be linked with accounts given by respondents and interpretations made by investigators. Both sets of people have the scope to look at and to look behind photographs, though from different positions. The analytic framework shown below allows us to unfold the ways in which respondents use visual imagery to mediate their understanding of their world. It can be summarised as shown in (Table 2.1).

Importantly, just as interviews can be made *in the anticipation of* photographs to be taken, and then *on the basis of* prints being looked at, any analysis involving more than one investigator also has a conversational form. The accounts given and the interpretations made are then a result of a dialogic relationship between different positions, not an outcome of prescribed movements from one person to the other. As interpretive practice, this comes near to Mitchell's description of representation as something assembled over time out of fragments, where these fragments might be considered as moments that are articulated into significance through the joint analytic process. The aim is to 'make materially visible the

Table 2.1 Approaches to using visual methods in social science research

	'Looking at'	*'Looking behind'*
Primarily told by respondent	Focus of the photo (intended content)	When taking the photograph
Primarily told by investigator	What the photos show – denote/express	The research aim – assumptions

structure of representation as a trace of temporality and exchange, the fragments as mementos, as "presents" re-presented in the ongoing process of assemblage, of stitching in and tearing out' (1994: 419). This means that the aim of research becomes not so much an understanding *of* the pictures, as an understanding *with* the photographs about the lives of the respondents concerned. A key part of this is that the act of research photography is itself an experiential fragment, providing a biopsy of the respondent's world.

Good images and bad pictures

Investigating the way that people think about overseas aid, we showed a set of photographs (supplied by UNICEF) to a range of people from different backgrounds. There were three groups chosen – manual workers, business people and professionals. These included both men and women, with the majority being in the range 40–60 years of age (Radley and Kennedy, 1997). The aim of the study was to explore responses to photographs that show different degrees of need and dependency among people in developing countries.

What became apparent was that respondents reacted according to whether they judged the photographs to depict what (they believed) the agency was trying to show, or ought to show. The legibility of the pictures rested upon the degree to which the signifier (what was shown in the print) and the signified (in this case, needy individuals) phenomenally cohered. A picture of emaciated babies was judged as a 'good charity picture', this photo's *functional aesthetic* enabling the observer to endorse the camera's objective intention to offer an ethical judgement. By *functional aesthetic* Bourdieu (1990) referred to judgements made about a photograph on the basis of how 'well' it depicts its subject matter according to cultural convention. 'Good' photographs are those that are clear, well composed, include what is relevant and exclude what is irrelevant, and enable an appropriate response from the viewer in that context. A 'bad' photograph is either technically lacking or depicts its subject inappropriately – where that appropriateness extends to the scope and direction of response invited from the viewer. Photographs that disturb, are unclear or are not understandable breach the conventions of the functional aesthetic. This shows that inspection of any photograph draws upon conventional ways of looking and of making pictures, a practice with which everyone in developed societies is familiar.

In this study respondents drew upon 'rules of appropriateness' for showing; how subjects should be pictured, in what contexts, with what decorum, as well as how they should be displayed and for what purposes. Using these criteria, some respondents picked out photographs from amongst the UNICEF set that they saw as being inappropriate. One photograph showed a group of smiling children playing near some oil drums, which one respondent thought looked rather like the kind of birthday card one could buy in a local shop. While she could see that the photograph showed clearly the children living in poor conditions, it yet failed to establish itself for her as an exemplar of a proper charity picture.

Another failure of a similar kind was attributed to one picture that was judged incompatible with the aim claimed by its inclusion in the UNICEF set. The photograph showed a teenage boy dressed as a soldier, carrying a gun and smoking a cigarette. As one respondent said, 'if I had the authority I would tear that photograph up and throw it away'. In this case the inappropriateness of the picture touched upon contradictory signifiers concerning race and childhood, as well as perceived need. For that reason, some respondents cared more that the boy in the picture held a cigarette than that he carried a gun.

While this discussion of 'kinds of' pictures implies that different genres are mutually exclusive, we found that an image purportedly belonging to one sphere was sometimes intensified in its meaning by comparison with images from another. The following quotation illustrates this point, being part of an answer to a question about which photographs might prompt this particular woman respondent to give. (She had said earlier on in the interview that she always turned the page at pictures of starving children.)

> Well, the one that I was thinking about this morning, because I was thinking about you [the interviewer] coming ... And the photograph that sums it up – the problem for me is not – it wasn't a photograph for charity, it was the Vietnamese picture of the girl covered in napalm. But I think that is what a lot of the – the aid people took – the idea of that photograph. And used it in other – and used it in other ways. But that is the photograph that – that says it all. But it's also the one that makes me think, 'No, I can't bear it'. I don't want to believe that the world is like that. But that's the photograph that sums it up, although I know that [it] was taken as a news photograph.
>
> (Female, bookseller)

People are aware of how pictures are used, of the various genres of representation employed, and of the expected cultural reactions to pictures of various kinds. In the charitable giving study, what they made of these photographs – what they said about them – was framed in terms of these considerations, along with feelings about the pictures that they could not easily articulate. Features that were picked out in the photographs were used as part of a justification of culturally held views about need, desert, the developing world and ethnic differences. These features were also used as referents in the respondents' accounts of their own views, intentions and experiences.

Figure 2.1 Girls at pump (copyright: UNICEF, with permission).

Compare these two excerpts relating to a photograph showing two girls, smiling, drawing water from a mechanical pump (see Figure 2.1). The first quote is from a woman who was suspicious of requests for support overseas, and the second from a man who had experience of visiting Africa and said he understood the need for help.

Erm – well, the children seem happy. They've got a smile on their face. Because usually, when you see them on telly, they haven't. And they've got water and that.... usually, when it's shown on telly, they've got no water, they're in these sorts of puddles, trying to get water out, what's covered in – God knows what.

... the water, I would see this as very positive. Again, because it involves ... the involvement of children who are obviously poor. Having seen people pushing barrows of water around Kenya, miles and miles, to provide water for villages, it has a personal attachment. And the faces are familiar, in that I can imagine the sort of faces that people – would find it, not having to push their barrow five miles, or whatever – they have access to a pump, and clean water ...

The difference between the two excerpts concerns not just the background experience that the respondents bring to the viewing, but also the way that they articulate their views by reference to different parts of the photograph. In the case of the woman, she notes the girls' 'smile on their face', which suggests to her their relative advantage compared with other pictures she has seen of distressed children. Again, the possibility of distress depicted in the photograph is consistent with the idea of charity photographs having a functional aesthetic that legitimates feelings of pity on the part of the viewer. In contrast to this, the man notes the girls' poverty, so that their smiles (though he does not mention them) are consistent with need that has been relieved in some way. What we concluded from this was that,

> their accounts were ways of 'making the world sensible', using the visual material to define their own location with respect to a world that is 'as it should be'. The analysis showed how some people emphatically rejected particular photographs on the grounds that they portrayed all too vividly a state of social affairs that the observer did not wish to entertain. By the same token, other accounts showed that liked pictures were those that enabled a preferred sense of the world to be put forward, including an identity for the speaker that warranted a place in such a positive 'order of things'. From this perspective, the image is not so much read out of the photograph as it is fashioned in the course of 'world-making by sense-making'.
>
> (Radley and Kennedy, 1997: 453)

The 'image' referred to in this quotation is not the 'image on the print', but rather the affective attitude or overall response that people made to a picture; how they handled it, their expressions of liking and disliking, distaste etc. The responses that respondents conveyed about the photographs were sometimes closer (in the sense of liking), sometimes further away from the depictions shown, depending upon how comfortable they were with the photograph. What was mentioned, highlighted or downplayed in terms of the print content depended upon the *imaginary* relationship between the viewer and the subject that respondents articulated. This relationship was imaginary in the sense that respondents had to *envision* the world in which they and the people in the photographs were contained, to anticipate their actions in relation to them and to justify the position they had taken on such matters in the past. That is what is meant in saying that 'the image is ... fashioned in the course of world-making by sense-making', where what is seen in the photograph is made meaningful in the course of justifying the viewer's relationship to the people depicted. In the course of this justification the 'image' is explicated by reference to the print, so that what the picture is said to show justifies the affective relationship that the viewer has to the material being offered.

On the basis of this analysis, the image that is formed of any single photograph – or photographs as a set – is not to be confused with the depictions in the pictures. Nor is the image to be reduced to the words that respondents use to articulate and to justify their positions about need and its monetary relief. In this study these photographs, like others, occupied a double role in the demands they placed upon respondents. First, they brought before viewers events 'that had happened'; this sometimes led to feelings (some contradictory) that respondents could not predict they would experience. Second, they provided definite resources on which viewers could draw in order to articulate into significance their relationship to the subject. The organisation of what was depicted in the photographs, and the viewer's relationship to the subjects portrayed therein, were constituted together in the justification of the act of viewing. Experientially, the bringing together of past experiences, together with the need to justify one's reaction in the present *is the image* that the respondent holds.

Why should it matter whether we separate out image from depiction in this way? It matters because it moves the argument away from a concern with interpretation of what is 'there in the picture', to one of explaining how we communicate, using pictures, about the images we have of the world. Or to put it another way, it highlights how we 'make visible or keep hidden through representation' those things that enable a relationship to others, or a world-view to be brought into being. Pictures of needy people do a certain kind of work because they make particular cultural demands upon the viewer; these demands are met by envisioning the kind of world in which such pictures arise, are sustained or might be discredited. The resultant 'image' is what the viewer is left with *after the photograph has been removed.*

Respondents become photographers

Asking people to take and then talk about their photographs is a link forged between the world of the investigator and the world of the respondent (see Table 2.1). This is because the aims of the research are conveyed in the instructions to people about how to take pictures, and may become realised in the conversations that investigator and respondent have about the photographs under consideration. By taking the camera the respondent first becomes an extension of the investigation, an interpreter of the requirements of how the study is to be conducted. By returning with the photographs she/he satisfies what has been asked of him or her, and yet supplies pictures that 'go beyond' what the investigator has asked for.

To talk about photographs one has taken is to make claims for them – to explain, interpret and ultimately take responsibility for them. This is a matter of accounting for acts of production where the camera catches more than anticipated and omitted what might have been intended. As Mitchell (1994: 421) has pointed out, a break or gap between representation and responsibility is not only possible but also a structural necessity, in that the photograph cannot explain itself. Into this gap falls every possibility about telling about pictures, being subject to the constraints and opportunities offered by the context in which viewing takes place. We might think of this gap as a discursive space that is opened by the act of photography, a potential for naming not just what is there to be seen, but also what is barely shown, unclear or even beyond the edge of the picture (Hodgetts *et al.*, 2007).

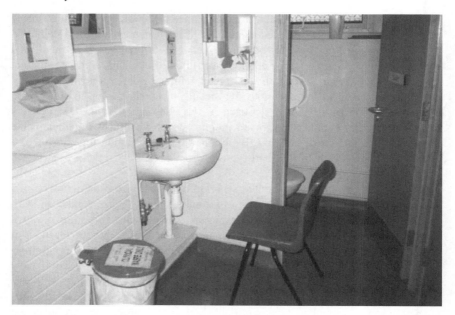

Figure 2.2 Bathroom (copyright: Alan Radley).

It is important to note that the ways in which people talk about photographs they have taken themselves is not simply a description of what is given on the print. It is a justification of the act of picturing, in which what is claimed is sustained or supported by reference to features pictured. These justifications will often relate to the reasons and ways of producing the photograph. This includes not only the rationale of the investigation but also cultural knowledge about photography, about 'research' and the interests of needy people, as discussed above, or of hospital patients as will be discussed below. In studies using photo-production the 'responsibilities of telling' are actualised in the transaction of request/compliance that the research involves. The agreement to be a participant in research – and to act accordingly – is not outside of the participants' understanding of being, for example, a hospital patient or a potential donor to charity. This is a further reason to comprehend how the production of photographs is integral to the descriptions made of them that are offered by respondents in any research investigation.

To illustrate this, consider a photograph shown here (see Figure 2.2), the first of two taken in hospital by a woman some seven days after she had undergone abdominal surgery (Radley and Taylor, 2003a). This is what she said about the picture during an interview conducted two days later in her home:

> This one isn't a very nice picture for me. It has bad memories. I took this picture because I was in a bit of trouble one night – I think it was the second night after my operation. And (pause) I was struggling a little bit. Well, I wasn't too happy because I had already asked for assistance two or three times, and sort of been brushed aside,

saying 'we'll come in a minute'. What it was was that I was bleeding from one of my wounds, so to speak, and by the time they got round to seeing me I was in a bit of a state. In the end I tried to walk to the toilet myself – to the bathroom – and with all my pipes and my – what do you call it? – [Int: drips] – drips, and of course I was trying to sort of change myself with all the pipes mixed up and I was getting into a bit of a state. So one of the patients came in and saw me and said: 'Oh dear, you are in a bit of a state aren't you?' So she went to fetch one of the nurses and then she came to help me out. Now that was the really only bad feeling I had while I was in there, and I was really upset because I felt really alone then, you know, because there was nobody there to help me and a feeling of uselessness.

Here is the story behind the picture, if you like. The account describes the series of events that made up the situation prompting the photograph, and the parts played by the patient and others in what occurred. It has narrative form in providing a plot, the different roles played by the actors involved, the narrator's evaluation of people's actions and a description of the temporal and spatial setting in which this all took place. She says that 'it isn't a very nice picture' for her, and that it has 'bad memories'. This keys the story as a remembered event whose significance is locatable in the pictures that had been brought to her home.

This is not a neutral image onto which a painful story was eventually grafted. The qualities of the experience are apparently there in the picture when she looked at it. In saying this, I am not trying to elevate the picture above the story she tells, but to indicate that, for her, the story is somehow anchored to the photograph. In spite of that, what she sees in that picture – on the photographic print – is hardly mentioned. There is mention of the toilet and the bathroom – the place depicted – but she gives no description of the photograph at all. Instead, the account is redolent of what we would expect from narrative, in that she tells of having asked for assistance from a nurse, of it not being forthcoming, of going to the bathroom where another patient recognises her need and calls for a nurse who does eventually come to help her. The words take over. Listening to the story, we do not actually need to see the bathroom to understand what is being told, and I am not really sure that our perception of the photographs is much changed once we have heard it. Here was where this happened, but we see no patients or nurses in the picture, no dressings or wounds, no drips or pipes. For us as third parties, the image has a forensic quality to it, rather like a picture of the scene of a crime (Benjamin, 1970).

However, something else is going on in this narrative as well as emplotment, temporal sequencing and the presentation of an, albeit small, moral universe. There are several descriptions of her condition (struggling, bleeding, bit of a state, of feeling alone and upset). These feelings are related in her story to the actions (or non-actions) of others but are not totally consequent upon them. Her condition, her suffering at that moment, *is* the condition for the story, and is given to us in the descriptive passage that says: 'with all my pipes and what do you call it, drips'. 'What it was was that I was bleeding from one of my wounds.' She goes on to describe walking to the bathroom and changing herself with all these pipes getting mixed up. To use a leading expression, she paints a picture of her situation that depicts what getting into a bit of a state means in that bathroom, with all those pipes attached to her.

When first looking at the photograph she said, it 'isn't a very nice picture for me. It has bad memories'. What the picture depicts for her are spaces and objects that she experienced in the course of struggling with her pipes and drips. These depictions are not neutral, because they have acquired the power to stare back at her, even if they do not have this power over us, the viewers. In this they are more than depictions of the site of her misfortune, because they are integral with her image of her time in hospital, an image grounded in her struggles when she was frightened. None of this is 'in' the picture to be read out by anybody else, nor is it even guaranteed by listening to her story.

The woman makes use of the picture of the bathroom to tell in another way, by means of the photograph. In this way she articulates into significance the bare spaces and objects depicted. What is being told is actually not about the picture and its content per se but the experience of that room *made possible by her having photographed it*. I am suggesting that the room (which for her is an experienced setting, not a neutral, physical space) was *re-figured* in the act of taking a photograph of it. Let us not forget that taking photographs of one's hospital ward is quite unusual. It is no less than turning upon the technologies and apparatuses of the hospital system. It is this, the act of making the photographs, of turning upon the ward environment to mark her time in the hospital that she takes into account (takes into *the* account). It is not just the happening of events in the bathroom that is being discussed here: it is 'the bathroom pictured' that needs to be justified in her story. In fact, she took a second picture of the doorway – not shown here – from the inside out, to show (and to recapture?) the leaving of this space and its episode of distress.

We might say that the moment of photography is a kind of resistance to the flow of hospital experience. This resistance is evidentially there when she looks at the print – the print is proof of the moment that the picture was taken. But it is more than this. The act of photography also re-makes another moment, a momentous one. It is a constructive act through which she imagines – conjures – her previous experience in that room. It is this act of *imagining* that produces the photograph as its trace. The trace of the physical setting alone is all that is there to be seen by us, the viewers, but the 'image of her suffering' is what makes the photograph meaningful to her. This image is not there to be seen, but is what she told us about by reference to the photograph. Her story is a transform, if you like, of ways of symbolising this experience that have been made possible by the act of picturing this setting.

Whether this woman could have or would have told this story without the aid of the photographs we cannot be sure. I feel certain that she would have told *some* story about this event, because it stood out in her experience of her hospital stay. However, whether she would have told us some of the other stories elicited with the aid of the photographs that she took is far less certain. The act of photography makes a difference because the story then told is built upon this other (visual) way of representing the world. This world is always represented, but is one not always represented in *just this way*. Essential meaning is not located in her story any more than it is located in the photographs. Meaning and significance are distributed across these media, so that pictures and words together provide opportunities for both presentational knowing and discursive explanation.

I said earlier that when looking at 'pictures of need' respondents communicated how comfortable they were with the (imaginary) world that these photographs invoked for each of them. Describing what the pictures showed was part of making closer or more distant their relationship to the people depicted, and to the values they engaged. In the case of the photographs made by this woman patient, she was concerned to explain (while still keeping distant) a painful moment during her time in hospital. How does this relate to images and their place in the use of visual methodologies? We might concur with Bartlett that her image of the moment described a stage in the act of remembering, 'characterised by doubt, hesitation, surprise, astonishment, confidence, dislike, repulsion and so on' (1932: 207). These terms are worth repeating in full in order to show their implications for what can be described in a photograph: what can be 'remembered about', and what can be 'remembered for'. In Bartlett's terms the 'memory image' that arises is an extensive scheme, referring to an affective relationship in a setting, often elusive to explication.

Seen in this way, the woman treated her photographs as visual cues to the setting (i.e. bathroom) from which they were *deliberately* sampled. This setting was more than the physical context of the bathroom, more than a place and time, even. It refers to 'an affective relationship', the image that she wanted to convey, and which the act of photography engaged through enabling her to re-imagine it. Her photograph served, therefore, as a transform, a mediating device for communicating about a distressing moment. An important part of its value was to provide a way of envisaging that moment once again, but *in a different way*. This different way was not for her 'to suffer again' but to be able to articulate the image of distress that remained with her after discharge. Rather, like other patients, she made use of her photographs as bridges to and from an imagined projection of recovery from illness (Radley and Taylor, 2003b). In that sense, it is insufficient to speak of her 'reading' her photographs, or even 'placing an interpretation' upon them.

Conclusion

Making a distinction between image and photograph, and removing the idea of image from picture content, hopefully encourages us to 'look behind' as well as to 'look at' photographs. It alerts us to the need to investigate not just what pictures show, but the *act of picturing*, its potential and its limitations. It moves us away from the view that photographs show what is there (a realist view), or that the content of pictures is sufficient as data. It also questions the idea that photographs are simply talked into being, so that an analysis of talk about pictures provides, on its own, an adequate investigation of their potential. If psychologists are to look behind pictures, it is to the practices of showing that they should attend, so that how people make sense with pictures becomes important.

Earlier I used the term 'action frame of research' when discussing what respondents believe is expected of them. The idea of justifying why a person took particular pictures, why that content, in this way rather than that, or failed to show what they really wanted to show, is part of the present demands that any study of sense-making must meet. This means that understanding how people use photographs should include some consideration of the requirements placed on respondents by the researcher, and (equally important), some statement by the researcher of the status in which the pictures are held (Wagner, 2006). From what I have said above, it follows that there is no such thing as a photograph – existing neutrally – outside of action frames in which they are made and viewed. There are, instead, pictures being made, shown, explained and even hidden. What makes visual media psychologically significant is that they are, along with text, another means of communicating what cannot be shown directly about our dealings with the world and with each other; in a sense, they help to provide a vision of what cannot be visualised.

Acknowledgement

I am grateful to UNICEF for allowing me to reproduce a photograph from their library.

Note

1   I have to say that I have not always maintained this distinction in my previous writing.

References

Bartlett, F. C. (1932) *Remembering: a study in experimental and social psychology.* Cambridge: Cambridge University Press.

Benjamin, W. (1970) The work of art in the age of mechanical reproduction. In W. Benjamin, *Illuminations.* London: Jonathan Cape.

Bourdieu, P. (1990) *Photography: a middle-brow art.* Cambridge: Polity Press.

Collier, M. (2001) Approaches to analysis in visual anthropology. In T. van Leeuwen and C. Jewitt (eds) *Handbook of visual analysis.* London: Sage, pp. 35–59.

Hodgetts, D., Chamberlain, K. and Radley, A. (2007) Considering photographs never taken during photo-production projects. *Qualitative Research in Psychology*, 4, 1–18.

Mitchell, W. J. T. (1984) What is an image? *New Literary History*, 15, 503–537.

Mitchell, W. J. T. (1994) *Picture theory.* Chicago, IL: University of Chicago Press.

Pink, S. (2006) *Doing visual ethnography: images, media and representation in research* (2nd edition). London: Sage.

Radley, A. and Kennedy, M. (1997) Picturing need: images of overseas aid and interpretations of cultural difference. *Culture & Psychology*, 3, 435–460.

Radley, A. and Taylor, D. (2003a) Images of recovery: a photo-elicitation study on the hospital ward. *Qualitative Health Research*, 13, 77–99.

Radley, A. and Taylor, D. (2003b) Remembering one's stay in hospital: a study in photography, recovery and forgetting. *Health: An Interdisciplinary Journal for the Social Study of Health, Illness and Medicine*, 7, 129–159.

Wagner, J. (2006) Visible materials, visualised theory and images of social research. *Visual Studies*, 21, 55–69.

Wright, T. (1999) *The photographer's handbook* (2nd edition). London: Routledge.

3 Bend it like Beckham?

The challenges of reading gender and visual culture

Rosalind Gill

Introduction

It is now nearly 25 years since – on TV screens across the UK – Nick Kamen was seen strolling into a retro-looking launderette and slowly and suggestively removing his clothes, to the soulful soundtrack of Marvin Gaye singing 'I heard it through the grapevine'. This advert for Levis 501s was so successful that – according to legend – the factories producing the jeans struggled to keep up with the resulting 700 per cent increase in demand. For cultural analysts, however, it was the impact of this advert on representations of men that made it so significant. It inaugurated – or at least became the iconic example of – an ongoing transformation in depictions of the male body, a shift that seemed to overturn the unwritten rule of visual culture in which, as John Berger famously put it, 'men look and women appear'. Since that moment back in 1985, men's bodies have been 'on display' in the mediascape as never before: oiled 'sixpacks' stare back at us from magazine covers, superwaifs mince along the fashion catwalk, and beautiful young male bodies are offered up for our consumption in any number of advertising campaigns on billboards, television or the cinema screen. Rather than men being simply 'bearers of the look' (Mulvey 1975) as an earlier generation of feminist film scholars argued (Kaplan 1987; Doane 1992), men's bodies are now regularly and routinely portrayed as objects of the gaze, visually depicted for their 'to-be-looked-at-ness' (in a manner previously reserved for women).

In this chapter I want to look back at this shift in the depiction of male bodies, and also at the critical writing that discussed it. For some analysts the representation of men as sexual objects in sites across mainstream popular culture represented nothing short of the fracturing of patriarchy, indeed of heteronormativity, and the binary of sexual difference itself (Simpson 1994; Mort 1996). Others, however, were more sceptical, and sought to show how, despite an *apparent* equalisation in sexual objectification, idealised-eroticised representations of men were constructed in such a way as to allow men symbolically to hold on to power (Dyer 1982; Neale 1993). Here I want to re-engage with these important but somewhat neglected debates to do three things. First, to ask how we might read visual culture, and specifically, what theoretical, methodological, cultural and political vocabularies might enable us to critically engage with representations of the male body/male bodies? Second, and following from this, I want to ask whether, after more than two decades in which sexualised representations of the male body have been a feature of mainstream popular culture, we are now seeing significant shifts in the way the male body is depicted? To that end, I will discuss recent advertising campaigns, which seem – potentially – to encode different meanings about masculinity from the earlier representations of muscular manhood. In particular I will look at images from Armani's (2007/8) campaign featuring David Beckham, and Dolce & Gabbana's (2007) Light Blue advertising campaign starring model David Gandy. Do these campaigns constitute a break or shift in depictions of the male body? And if so, in what ways? Finally I want to raise the question of whether, in the wake of the ongoing sexualised presentation of the male body in popular culture – and particularly the more recent examples – 'we are all equally objectified now'? I have not seen any critical writing about this, but it's frequently voiced in the media with assertions that 'men are the new women' that men are now vilified and attacked in advertising in ways that would not be permitted if it were women, and even calls for a Minister for Men to look after their (allegedly neglected) rights. It is something my students – who have largely grown up in visual landscapes in which the sexualised display of men's bodies is taken for granted – say to me often: any claim I might make about the objectification of women will be met with the response 'but men are equally objectified'.

I have long been interested in the way in which this claim functions rhetorically to silence concerns about the representation of women, but I believe also that it does need to be taken seriously in its own terms. *Do* 'we' want to argue that representations of women constitute more of a cause for concern or anger than those of men? And if so – if feminists (including me) want to continue to argue that the objectification of women is different (read 'worse') than that of men – then we need to be able to say *what it is that makes the difference*, rather than simply assert it is so. How might we do so in a way that is principled and has integrity? Are the differences that exist ones that can be identified through *formal visual analysis of the images* themselves (looking for example at mise en scène, posture, gaze, degree of flesh exposed, etc), or is it a question of the *volume of the representations* ? Or, more broadly, do we also have – simultaneously – to read *culture, subjectivity and history* in order to advance such arguments? In reading visual culture, then, how might we think about the relationship between the texts themselves and the context in which they appear?

'In a world ordered by sexual difference …' (Mulvey 1975)

This question has been central to many debates about visual culture since Laura Mulvey's groundbreaking article 'Visual pleasure and narrative cinema', published in 1975. Drawing on Lacanian psychoanalysis, Mulvey's aim was to investigate the ways in which the cinematic apparatus operates psychically to produce meanings and modes of spectatorial subjectivity organised around sexual difference. Mulvey was writing about Classical Hollywood Cinema – a set of institutional practices and textual forms which were at their height in the period between the 1930s and 1950s. Textually, the films were usually built around two intertwined narratives: the generic story (solving a crime, rescuing someone, putting on a show, etc) and a heterosexual love story. In a detailed psychoanalytic exposition, Mulvey argued that visual pleasure in Classical Hollywood Cinema was built around two contradictory processes: scopophilia, or pleasure in looking, and narcissism. One involved a separation and distancing from the figures on the screen, the other demanded identification. Mulvey argued that these pleasures became structured by a heterosexual division of labour: the woman is passive, there as a display, to be looked at; the man is a protagonist, driving forward the narrative. As she famously put it:

> In a world ordered by sexual imbalance, pleasure in looking has been split between the active male and passive female. The determining male gaze projects its fantasy onto the female figure, which is styled accordingly. In their traditional exhibitionist role women are simultaneously looked at and displayed, with their appearance coded for strong visual and erotic impact so that they can be said to connote to-be-looked-at-ness. Woman displayed as sexual object is the leitmotif of erotic spectacle: from pin-ups to striptease ... she holds the look, plays to and signifies male desire.
>
> (1975: 11)

However, Mulvey's point was not simply that the woman displayed is there as an erotic object for the male protagonist of the film, but also that she becomes as such for the audience. Three masculine gazes – the gaze of the camera, the gaze of the male protagonist within the film and the gaze of the cinema spectators – map onto each other leading inevitably to the objectification of women.

Mulvey's work generated a huge amount of debate that has both critiqued and developed her ideas. Critical engagement is focused on the lack of an address to an active female gaze or spectating position, and on dissatisfaction with the notion that the only options for women were to identify with a masculine position (in a sort of psychic transgendering) or to take up a feminine – necessarily masochistic – position. Critics also pointed to the problematic elision of masculine spectating positions with actual male subjects, as well as to its privileging of gender – or sexual difference – above all other axes of identity (such as age, sexual orientation, race or class). Mulvey's work has also been criticised for its rather universalising and deterministic assumptions about the functioning of filmic texts. Against this, much contemporary work on media and visual culture stresses the polysemic nature of texts and the possibility of multiple, contradictory and shifting readings and identifications. As John Ellis (1992) argued, identification is never simply a matter of men identifying with male figures on screen and women identifying with females. Cinema involves many forms of fluid desire that may transgress identities, positions and roles.

In relation to display of the male body, Mulvey's work is notable for its argument that men are bearers not object of the gaze, and for the suggestion – much developed in later work – that women are narratively punished for actively desiring men in the film. Only musicals escaped this because, she argued, in musicals *spectacle* took precedence over *narrative* [see also Gaylyn Studlar (1992) on Rudolf Valentino and Steve Cohan (1992) on Fred Astaire].

If active (heterosexual) female desire was disavowed, so too was homoerotic male desire – which might after all be produced in men by the invitation to identify with powerful and glamorous male protagonists. A number of strategies have been identified in films that might be said to lessen the anxieties associated with this: e.g. the 'reassuring' depiction of a woman, the use of humour (especially in locker room scenes), through explicit disavowals, as well as through the presence of excessive violence or mutilation (Neale 1993). If women are *punished* narratively for desiring, men are *tested*, and this testing sometimes enables the production of a set of eroticised images of the male body to be depicted. As Yvonne Tasker (1993) succinctly puts it: 'torture operates in the narrative as a test for the hero to survive, but also as a set of aestheticised images to be lovingly dwelt on'.

Tasker was writing about the proliferation of action movies and spectacular male heroes which came out of Hollywood in the late 1980s and 1990s, rather than the 'Classical' earlier period. It was already clear that depictions of the male body were changing radically in film – but also in advertising, fashion, magazines and other parts of visual culture. What changed in the mid-1980s was not simply the *volume* of representations of the male body but, more importantly, the representational strategies used to depict it. Whilst there had long been depictions of attractive men in popular culture – from screen matinee idols to the rugged 'Marlboro man' – what marked the shift was the new (re)-presentation of men as *objects of the gaze* rather than simply bearers of the look. Nick Kamen's striptease in the launderette, the rise of dance/stripping troops such as the Chippendales, the emergence into the mainstream of publications such as 'For Women', the sudden explosion of fashion imagery from men … all these were indications of a profound shift in visual culture in which men's bodies – like women's – could be offered up to us 'to be looked at'.

Reading the shift

Over the last two decades a considerable body of writing has explored this shift, from several different angles. One tradition of research has examined the *catalysts* for this transformation in depictions of the male body. At a general level the representations were understood as part of the shift away from the 'male as norm' in which masculinity lost its unmarked status and became visible as gendered. Sally Robinson (2000) argues that white masculinity was rendered visible through pressure from black and women's liberation movements which were highly critical of its hegemony. A variety of new social movements galvanised the creation of the 'new man', the reinvention of masculinity along more gentle, emotional and communicative lines. More specifically, the growing confidence of gay liberation movement in Western countries, and the increasing significance of the 'pink economy' helped to produce a greater range of representations of the male body in gay magazines and popular culture (Chapman 1988; Mort 1996; Nixon 1996). Part of the shift can be understood in terms of these images 'going mainstream' and, as they did so, opening up space for an active gaze among heterosexual women (Moore 1988). The shift also had significant economic determinants: retailers, marketers and magazine publishers were keen to develop new markets and had affluent men in their sights as the biggest untapped source of high-spending consumers (Edwards 1997). Style magazines like *The Face* helped this enterprise by producing a new visual vocabulary for the representation of men's bodies, and this too opened up space for eroticised practices of representation (Mort 1996; Nixon 1996). As Rowena Chapman (1988) argued, 'new man' was a contradictory formation, representing both a response to critique from progressive social movements, and a gleam in the eyes of advertisers, marketers and companies aspiring to target young and affluent men. Perhaps the figure of the metrosexual that has come to prominence more recently symbolises the extent to which marketing-driven constructions won out over more explicitly political re-articulations of masculinity.[1]

A second trajectory of research has been concerned with the *implications* of the changing depictions of the male body. From within psychology, there has been interest in what impact the proliferation of idealised-eroticised images might have on young men's body image and self-esteem, with questions raised about the growing equalisation of 'pressures' – often refracted through a set of concerns about masculinity 'in crisis' (see Gill 2008). More sociological research has located the shift in relation to questions about body culture and identity, also raising questions about the relationship between representational practices and gender relations (Gill *et al.* 2000; Gill 2003)

But it is a third tradition of scholarship that I am most interested in here: a body of writing influenced by psychoanalytically informed feminist film criticism and art practice, queer theory and critical race studies, which looks critically at the *nature* of contemporary representations of the male body and the ways in which they may be organised to deal with the anxieties and threats produced by such a significant shift in visual culture. This work reads contemporary representations of men in intersectional terms as simultaneously gendered, racialised, classed, aged and intimately related to sexuality. It suggests that far from there being a diverse range of representations of the male body in mainstream visual culture, most can be shown to conform to a very specific 'type'. The models are generally white, they are young, they are muscular and slim, they are usually clean-shaven (with perhaps the exception of a little 'designer stubble'), and they have particular facial features which connote a combination of softness and strength – strong jaw, large lips and eyes, and soft looking, clear skin (Edwards 1997). As Tim Edwards (1997) has argued, this combination of muscularity/hardness and softness in the particular 'look' of the models allows them to manage contradictory expectations of men and masculinity as strong and powerful but also gentle and tender – they embody, in a sense, a cultural contradiction about what a man is 'meant to be'. The famous poster 'L'enfant' showing a muscular, bare-chested man cradling a baby perfectly exemplifies this, and was Athena's (the poster company) best-selling item for many years (Chapman and Rutherford 1988).

Older bodies are strikingly absent and there are strong and persistent patterns of racialisation to be found in the corpus of images of the male body in advertising. White bodies are over-represented, but they are frequently not Anglo-American or northern European bodies, but bodies that are coded as 'Latin', with dark hair and olive skin, referencing long histories of sexual Othering and exoticism (Nixon 1996) (though this may be changing, particularly in the USA, where, in 2004, Abercrombie and Fitch settled a class action for racism out of court after accusations that its 'all American' image was all white, blonde and blue-eyed). Black African American and African Caribbean bodies are also regularly represented in an eroticised manner, but these bodies are usually still reserved for products associated with sport, drawing on long held racist cultural myths about black male sexuality and physical prowess. It is also worth noting that adverts depicting black men frequently use black male *celebrities* (e.g. Tiger Woods, Thierry Henry), in contrast to the unknown models who are used when the 'sexy' body is white. As Peter Jackson (1994: 88) has argued, this does nothing to challenge the underlying racialised logic of representation, but in fact reinforces it by presenting the 'acceptable' face of black masculinity 'shorn of the more threatening associations of a stereotypically anonymous' black manhood. In contrast, male Asian bodies are rarely presented in advertising as sexually desirable – again indexing different racist ideologies, this time of 'a-sexuality'. As I have argued elsewhere, class is also central to the construction and reading of such representations. The use of 'arthouse' techniques such as black and white photography or 'sculpted' models that make reference to classical iconography connotes affluence and sophistication, as well as offering a kind of distance to the consumption of such images.

Writing is polarised on the issue of how significant this shift in the portrayal of male bodies is. Some see in it a fundamental challenge to patriarchy and heteronormativity. Frank Mort (1996) argued that the objectification of men's bodies and the use of 'cropping' to focus upon selected, eroticised areas (eg upper arms, chest, 'sixpack') represents nothing less than the symbolic fracturing or fragmentation of male power. In turn, Mark Simpson predicted that male dominance and heterosexuality would not survive this transformation in visual culture:

> Men's bodies are on display everywhere; but the grounds of men's anxiety is not just that they are being exposed and commodified but that their bodies are placed in such a way as to passively invite a gaze that is undifferentiated: it might be female or male, hetero or homo. Traditional male heterosexuality, which insists that it is always active, sadistic and desiring, is now inundated with images of men's bodies as passive, masochistic and desired. Narcissism, the desire to be desired, once regarded as a feminine quality par excellence, is, it seems, in popular culture at least, now more often associated with men than with women. Sexual difference no longer calls the shots, active no longer maps onto masculine, nor passive onto feminine. Traditional heterosexuality cannot survive this reversal: it brings masculinity into perilously close contact with that which must always be disavowed: homosexuality.
>
> (Simpson 1994: 15)

Against this, however, a considerable body of work has examined the strategies used to *undercut or offset* the potential threat produced by depicting (white) male bodies in a manner more familiarly used for women. The early writing of Richard Dyer and Stephen Neale is particularly important, but has also been taken up by more recent work by Fowler (1996), Kress and van Leeuwen (2006), and Schroeder (2007). What, then, are the strategies that appear to operate to offset the transgressiveness threatened?

On the one hand, many adverts use models with an almost 'phallic muscularity' – the size and hardness of the muscles 'standing in for' male power. Indeed, writing about an earlier generation of male pin-ups, Richard Dyer (1982) talked about representations of the male body having a 'hysterical' feel. Likewise, Susan Bordo (1997) argued that many male striptease routines tend to eroticise the teasing display of *male power* rather than the sexiness of the bodies themselves [but see her later argument in *The Male Body* (1999) and see also (Smith 2007)].

The posture and facial expressions of eroticised-idealised males in adverts also diminish the potential threats discussed by Simpson. Men tend not to smile or pout, nor to deploy any of the bodily gestures or postures discussed by Goffman (1979) as indices of the 'ritualised subordination' of women in advertising (canting, knee bends, being shown smaller or lying down, etc), and nor are they depicted in mirror shots – so long a favoured mode for conveying women's narcissism. In contrast, in what I have elsewhere called 'sixpack advertising' (Gill 2009a) men are generally portrayed standing or involved in some physical activity. Moreover, they are mostly pictured alone in ways that reference the significance of independence as a value marking hegemonic masculinity (Connell 1995), or they are pictured with a beautiful woman – to 'reassure' viewers of their heterosexuality.

However it is not *simply* the case that these representations must disavow homoerotic desire. On the contrary, gay men are a key target audience for such advertising representations, being acknowledged as fashion leaders in clothing, 'grooming' and the purchase of fragrances. Indeed, through the figure of the 'metrosexual', marketing professionals sought to re-articulate these interests in 'looking good' to a heterosexual agenda. The representations advertisers construct have to appeal simultaneously to (at least) three different constituencies: gay men, heterosexual women and heterosexual men – in such a way as not to antagonise, alienate or frighten straight men. Discussing the way advertisers manage this, Tim Edwards (1997) highlights the paradoxical nature of men's magazines as a site for such images, pointing to the 'fundamentalist' assertion of heterosexuality in written texts juxtaposed with page after page of homoerotic images of the male body as one example of how this contradiction was managed, through a splitting that operated between the visual and written texts.

Attention to the organisation of gazes also points to differences with depictions of idealised-eroticised females in advertising – though this may be changing. Writing about this in a now-classic article in *Screen*, 30 years ago, Dyer argued that male pin-ups tend to look back at the viewer in ways reminiscent of 'street' gazes to assert dominance, or they look up or off, indicating that their interests are elsewhere. Kress and van Leeuwen (2001) distinguish between an *offer* and a *demand* in relation to gazes in visual images. When the model looks away from the camera this is an indirect gaze that makes an offer to the spectator to become the subject of the gaze (that is, it offers him or her the possibility to render the model an object). In contrast, when the model looks directly at the camera it constitutes a direct address that is a demand, they argue. However, as I argue elsewhere (Gill 2010), this split between subject and object is problematic, particularly when it is mapped onto gender in a seemingly straightforward manner. I have discussed this in relation to representations of women, arguing that one key feature of what I have called the shift from objectification to sexual subjectification is this change in gazes: compared to 20 years ago women in adverts are much more likely to look directly – to address or tease the viewer – a shift that is underwritten by textual cues that stress women's assertiveness, independence and playfulness. Yet, as I have argued, the written or spoken texts operate as an alibi for 'sexualised' representations which, without them, would be much more likely to garner attacks for sexism (Gill 2009a).

In addition to the threats posed by homoeroticism, there are also anxieties related specifically to gender hierarchy – namely to the presentation of male bodies as objects of a heterosexual female gaze. The anxieties threatened here are often dealt with through humour. This can be seen in the well-known advert for Diet Coke on British television (and elsewhere) in which the camped up, exaggerated desire of the women (depicted in over-the-top state of sexual anticipation, with much heavy breathing, biting of lips and re-arranging of hair), and the comic nature of the '11 o'clock appointment' serve to place the scene in humourous, ironic quotation marks – plus the 'comedic' reversal of use of a labourer, the embodiment of a white working-class version of sexism [see also Buchbinder's (1998) discussion of similar ads].

Interestingly, advertisers have also started to deploy strategies designed to appease men's anger at being addressed by idealised images (in a way that parallels what happened in relation to women – i.e. L'Oreal's 'Don't Hate Me because I'm Beautiful' campaign): a Nivea skin balm advert shows a blue-eyed blonde man with the slogan 'his good looks may be irritating, but his skin isn't'. Does this suggest an increasing similarity in modes of address and visual depiction of men and women? I will return to this in the final part of the paper, but first want to turn to ways in which representations of men's bodies in adverts are changing.

Beyond 'sixpack advertising'? When Armani met Beckham

Twenty years after Nick Kamen's invitation to watch as he undressed, it seems to me that idealised-eroticised images of men in visual culture (especially advertising) are changing. In 2003 an advert for Yves St Laurent broke taboos by using a naked man to promote a fragrance. Almost as significant was another advert showing a model with abundant body and facial hair – marking a departure from earlier, more typical representations that are 'manscaped', to use the current parlance. Thinner, more vulnerable looking models have also become more popular – in contrast to the muscular 'sixpacks' I have discussed elsewhere (Gill 2009a).

A campaign for Dolce & Gabbana also broke the mould in 2006 with a series of strikingly homoerotic locker-room adverts, in which, rather than being pictured alone, a group of men (members of the Italian football team) are shown posing together in tight fitting underpants, their sexy bodies oiled, in one case even touching.

In 2007/8 two campaigns were launched which seemed to underscore the shift in representational practice and raise questions about ongoing transformations of visual culture. In an advert for the Dolce & Gabbana fragrance Light Blue, model David Gandy is shown reclining in the sun, his crotch occupying centre shot (see Figure 3.1). While some features of the representation remain similar to the 'sixpack' – particularly the accentuated muscularity of the arms, the oiled hardness of the body, and the nature of the model's gaze – the advert is notable for the relatively 'passive' depiction, the centring and prominence of the genitals (so often previously hysterically 'evoked' rather than shown – (see Dyer) and the

Figure 3.1 A 'feminised' pose?
Source: Image reproduced courtesy of the Advertising Archives

conventionally 'feminine' pose adopted (in fact an almost identical pose is adopted by a female model in the 'sister' advert for the women's version of this fragrance).

The same year, the first in a series of adverts for Armani underwear featuring David Beckham was launched to an avalanche of press coverage (see Figure 3.2). This is how the British paper *The Guardian* covered it:

> Last week we got a sneak peek of one of the most iconic advertising images of 2008. Of course I'm talking about that piece of art-cum-porn for Emporio Armani's underwear featuring David Beckham – his chiseled face and perfect pecs and oiled abs and lean thighs, but mainly, and most prominently, his Armani underpanted groin.
>
> (Ramchandani 2007)

Media coverage focused on the traffic-stopping qualities of this image (Sibbles 2009), the breathless reactions of the many thousands of fans who came to see the giant versions of the adverts unveiled in locations such as New York's Times Square or London's Oxford Street, the explicit sexiness of the advert and its possible impact on men, with the potential to 'make an entire gender feel inadequate' (MacInnes 2010) – a theme that was heightened when Cristiano Ronaldo was hired as the new face/body of Armani in 2010.

The centring of the groin in all of these campaigns is significant. Ten years earlier, in the UK an underwear campaign for Brass Monkeys was removed by the Committee of Advertising Practice for being 'unsuitable for public consumption'

Figure 3.2 Breaking the mould for representing men.
Source: Image reproduced courtesy of the Advertising Archives

because it focused explicitly on the model's groin and turned him into a 'sex object' (Jobling 2003). That this is no longer the case is an indication that something has changed, and helps to account for the reactions of those who claim men and women are 'equally objectified' now, and indeed that 'being reduced to a quivering jelly of insecurity is no longer just for women', as one journalist put it (MacInnes 2010).

According to some readings, the 'exposure' of the penis (or at least its outline, tightly clad) should translate into an exposure and demystification of male power – along the lines of the feminist postcard of the 1970s in which line drawings of a girl and boy shown peering into their underpants is given the caption 'so is that all that explains the difference in our pay?'

Yet an alternative way of reading these images is not as an exposure or deconstruction of male power, but as its teasing, thrusting display. Far from equalising the gender politics of representation, of revealing male power as the masquerade, perhaps these newer groin shots in fact represent a celebration of phallic power? This would be redolent of the scenarios discussed by Rachel O'Neill (2010), witnessing the reactions of male cinema audiences to the film Top Gun, in which the slogan 'worship the cock' was apparently spontaneously chanted. The sheer size of the groin shots on hoardings outside Selfridge's, Macy's and other key locations might be said to underscore such a reading. Victoria Beckham is said to have commented that she was 'proud to see his penis 25 feet tall. It's enormous. Massive' [quoted in (Fisher 2008)].

This points to the complexities of reading the image. On the one hand, heterosexual female sexual agency seems to be given space in a way that marks a significant rupture with previous representations; yet on the other, this is reframed less in terms of *desire* than *admiration*, in a way that seems to reinstate or even heighten unequal gender power relations. 'It's about shock and awe and phallus-worship', as one friend put it, highlighting the way in which the images were apprehended in terms of traditional masculine concerns about size and performance. Moreover, the focus on Victoria Beckham's reaction – that of the *wife* – seems to attempt to position the advert within a heteronormative economy, in which Beckham's groin is acceptable precisely because it is a sportsman's, a father's and above all a *heterosexual groin* (notwithstanding Beckham's status as a gay icon and metrosexual).

It may well be, as Paul Jobling has argued in relation to an earlier generation of underwear advertising, that the meanings are 'not so easily or safely contained' (2003: 148), but nevertheless the homophobia of some of the coverage is striking. Martin Kelner (2009) writing in the British liberal daily *The Guardian*, asserted 'these are confusing times for followers of the national game ... shots of an oiled up David Beckham modeling Armani underpants will have some of us sporting our bobble hats and rattles a little uncomfortably'. Perhaps such a frank acknowledgement of the discomforting experience of being confronted – in public places – with large homoerotic images is itself a marker of change – for in an earlier era even the homoeroticism would have been disavowed entirely – yet at the same time with the acknowledgement comes a further enactment of heterosexuality; the expression of anxiety *itself* perhaps a new way of 'doing heterosexual masculinity', a mode of what I have called 'new homophobia', part of a wider trend in 'confessional' 'lad lit' and 'lad flicks' which plays with anxieties about both homosexuality *and* homophobia (Gill 2009b; Hansen-Miller and Gill 2010). This new 'ironic' homophobia (which, it should be noted,/has not displaced but exists with 'older' forms) is seemingly less an attack on an existent sexual minority than a self-deprecating 'joke' about the homosexual potentials of heterosexual men. What is clear is how complicated the terrain of visual culture has become; how difficult it is to 'read' these representations of masculinity.

Conclusion

In this chapter I have documented a shift in representations of the male body in mainstream visual culture, and have looked back to an earlier generation of writing that tried to make sense of how 'objectifying' images of men were designed – through their composition and mise en scène – to disavow homoeroticism as well as to hold onto patriarchal power. Charting a shift over the last three decades, I have asked whether those same strategies (e.g. particular postures, organisation of gazes, presence of a woman, etc) are still in place, and, in particular, whether two advertising campaigns from recent years represent a rupture with previous modes of representation.

I have suggested that the advertising images of David Beckham and David Gandy (for Armani, and Dolce & Gabbana, respectively) do indeed represent a shift in mainstream depictions of the male body, with their focus on the male groin, offering a clear outline of the penis and balls, at the very centre of the images. Whether this, in turn, constitutes a break in relation to the power of heteronormativity and male power is less clear. It seems to me that the images may simultaneously *do and undo* patriarchal power and the normative force of heterosexuality. The existing terms of reference provided in the groundbreaking work of Dyer and Neale are useful, to be sure, but they can no longer (if they ever could) offer us definitive readings of such representations, for their meaning depends in part upon the volume of such representations, their intertextual relationships with other media (including the ways in which the 'models' are made to signify particular meanings, and the ways in which such advertising campaigns are talked and written about in the media), and, above all, on an understanding of the history of such representations and their cultural significance. Perhaps ironically, then, it seems to me that in order to contest the notion that 'we are all equally objectified now', we need to go beyond the specificities of any particular representation to interrogate the corpus of images that make up visual culture, and the unequal ways in which these continue to play out on men's and women's subjectivities.

Note

1 See my earlier work for a discussion of constructions of the figures of the new man and the new lad, which highlights the extent to which a range of cultural intermediaries are

involved in not simply representing new masculinities through such figures, but quite literally constructing and materialising them.

References

Bordo, S. (1997). Reading the male body. In P. L. Moore (Ed.), *Building bodies*. New Brunswick, NJ: Rutgers University Press.

Bordo, S. (1999). *The male body: a new look at men in public and in private* (1st ed.). New York: Farrar Straus and Giroux.

Buchbinder, D. (1998). *Performance anxieties: re-producing masculinity*. St Leonards, NSW: Allen & Unwin.

Chapman, R. (1988). The great pretender: variations on a new man theme. In R. Chapman and J. Rutherford (Eds), *Male order: unwrapping masculinity*. London: Lawrence & Wishart.

Chapman, R. and Rutherford, J. (1988). *Male order: unwrapping masculinity*. London: Lawrence & Wishart.

Cohan, S. and Hark, I. R. (Eds) (1992). *Screening the male – exploring masculinities in Hollywood cinema*. London and New York: Routledge.

Cohan, S. (1992). 'Feminising' the song-and-dance man: Fred Astaire and the spectacle of masculinity in the Hollywood musical. In S. Cohan and I. R. Hark (Eds), *Screening the male – exploring masculinities in Hollywood cinema*. London and New York: Routledge.

Connell, R. W. (1995). *Masculinities: knowledge, power and social change*. Berkeley, CA: University of California Press.

Doane, M. A. (1992). *Femmes fatales: feminism, film studies and psychoanalysis*. New York: Routledge.

Dyer, R. (1982). Don't look now: the male pin-up. *Screen* 23(3–4): 61–73.

Edwards, T. (1997). *Men in the mirror: men's fashion, masculinity and consumer society*. London: Cassell.

Ellis, J. (1992). *Visible fictions: cinema, television, video*. London: Routledge.

Fisher, A. (2008, 27 May). Beckham factor boosts briefs as men tighten up. *The Guardian*.

Fowler, R. (1996). *Linguistic criticism*. Oxford: Oxford Paperbacks.

Gill, R. (2003). Power and the production of subjects: a genealogy of the new man and the new lad. In B. Benwell (Ed.), *Masculinities and men's lifestyle magazines: the Sociological Review monograph*. Oxford: Blackwell.

Gill, R. (2008). Body talk: negotiating body image and masculinity. In C. Philips, S. Riley, M. Burns and H. Frith (Eds), *Critical bodies: representations, identities and practices of weight and body management*. London: Palgrave.

Gill, R. (2009a). Beyond the 'Sexualization of Culture' thesis: an intersectional analysis of 'sixpacks', 'midriffs' and 'hot lesbians' in advertising. *Sexualities* 12:137– 60.

Gill, R. (2009b). Lad lit as mediated intimacy: a postfeminist tale of female power, male vulnerability and toast. *Working papers on the Web*.

Gill, R. (2010). *"Objectification": what is it good for?* Paper presented at Economic and Social Research Council Seminar Series on Inequalities and Visual Culture, January.

Gill, R., Henwood, K. and McLean, C. (2000). The tyranny of the sixpack: men talk about idealised images of the male body in popular culture. In C. Squire (Ed.), *Culture in Psychology*. London: Routledge.

Goffman, E. (1979). *Gender advertisements*. London: Macmillan.

Hansen-Miller, D. and Gill, R. (2010). "Lad flicks": discursive reconstructions of masculinity in popular film. In H. Radner and P. Stapleton (Eds), *Feminism goes to the multiplex*. New York and London: Routledge.

Jackson, P. (1994). Black male: advertising and the cultural politics of masculinity. *Gender, Place and Culture* 1: 49–60.

Jobling, P. (2003). Underexposed: spectatorship and pleasure in men's underwear advertising in the 20th century. *Paragraph* 1 & 2: 147–162.

Kaplan, E. A. (1987). Feminist criticism and television. In R. Allen (Ed.), *Channels of discourse*. Chapel Hill, NC: University of North Carolina Press.

Kelner, M. (2009, 12 June). A whole new ball game. *The Guardian*.

Kress, G. and van Leeuwen, R. (2001). *Multimodal discourse: the modes and media of contemporary communication*. London: Arnold.

Kress, G. & van Leeuwen, T. (2006). *Reading images: the grammar of visual design*. London: Routledge.

MacInnes, P. (2010, 15 January). Ronaldo and the planet of the abs. *The Guardian*.

Moore, S. (1988). Here's looking at you kid! In L. Gamman and M. Marshment (Eds), *The female gaze: women as viewers of popular culture*. London: The Women's Press.

Mort, F. (1996). *Cultures of consumption: masculinities and social space in late 20th century Britain*. London: Routledge.

Mulvey, L. (1975). Visual pleasure and narrative cinema. *Screen*, 16(3): 6–18.

Neale, S. (1993). Masculinity as spectacle: reflections on men and mainstream cinema. *Screen* 24.

Nixon, S. (1996). *Hard looks: masculinities, spectatorship and contemporary consumption*. London: UCL Press.

O'Neill, R. (2010). *Products of a sexed-up culture: Contextualising 'pickup' and the seduction community*. Paper presented at the ESRC seminar series Complicating the Debates About the Sexualisation of Culture, May.

Ramchandani, N. (2007, 17 December). Golden balls strikes again. *The Guardian*.

Robinson, S. (2000). *Marked men: white masculinity in crisis*. New York: Columbia University Press.

Schroeder, J. (2007). *Visual consumption*. London: Routledge.

Sibbles, E. (2009, 15 May). Crowds gather to hail Emperor Beckham's new pants. *The Guardian*.

Simpson, M. (1994). *Male impersonators: men performing masculinity*. London: Cassell.

Smith, C. (2002). Shiny chests and heaving G-strings: A night out with the Chippendales. *Sexualities*, 5(1): 67–89.

Smith, C. (2007). *One for the girls: the pleasures and practices of reading women's porn*. Bristol: Intellect Books.

Studlar, G. (1992). Valentino, 'Optic intoxication' and dance. In S. Cohan and I. R. Hark (Eds), *Screening the male – exploring masculinities in Hollywood cinema*. London and New York: Routledge.

Tasker, Y. (1993). *Spectacular bodies: gender, genre and the action cinema*. London: Routledge.

4 Using photographs to explore the embodiment of pleasure in everyday life

Lilliana Del Busso

This chapter explores examples from two empirical studies of young women's embodied experiences in everyday life. As opposed to generating talk about embodied experience through a traditional qualitative interview, the studies explored here used photographs as a way to tap into and ground accounts in specific and concrete experiences. As such, participants' explorations of their own pre-existing photographs and photographs produced in relation to the topic of research aided the focus on particular experiences, providing access to rich detail in relation to living through specific embodied events.

Furthermore, the research presented attempted to take account of the multiple modalities through which lived experience is constituted, such as the visual, touch, sound and language. In the current research, embodiment thus was considered beyond 'the body' inscribed by discourse, particularly by highlighting the felt and sensed spatial and temporal aspects of being-in-the-world.

Influenced by Cartesian dualism, privileging mind over body, the discipline of psychology has focused its attention on sites of specific psychological functionality (e.g. cognition); a practice which often abstracts 'the body' from social, relational and embodied psychological experience (Stam 1998; Brown *et al.* 2009). As such, people's embodied existence in the social, relational and material world has rarely been the starting point for investigating psychological phenomena. Hence, although 'the body' has an implied presence in psychology, mainly as a vehicle for the production of thought, 'the body' or embodied experience has rarely been theorised explicitly in relation to specific areas of concern to psychological study. In contrast, explicit and focused theorisation of 'the body' has been far more forthcoming within the disciplines of sociology (Featherstone *et al.* 1991; Weiss and Haber 1999; Fraser and Greco 2005; Howson 2005; Williams and Bendelow 1998; Welton 1998), anthropology (Csordas 1999) and feminist studies (Young 2005; Grosz 1994; Davis 1997; Harraway 1990; Ussher 1997; Price and Shildrick 1999). Nevertheless, albeit representing a greater interest in 'the body' for itself, all these fields can be characterised as having been heavily influenced by and privileging a post-structuralism of 'the body'. For example, it can be argued that both the present/absent 'body' in psychology and the abstracted, inscribed 'body' of post-structuralism suffer from severe reductionism as suggested by Stam (1998: 5):

Whereas psychology splits and compartmentalizes the body into functions that deny the embodied nature of psychological life and experience, so can an individualistic language of 'bodies in discourse' deny the crucial manner in which the body is already and always social in its expressions and impressions.

As suggested by Stam, these conceptualisations and treatments of 'the body' fall short of taking account of the 'embodied nature of psychological life and experience', thus neglecting the sensuous, spatial and relational aspects of being-in-the-world (Merleau-Ponty 1962).

'The body' and embodied experience

The dominance of a post-structuralist focus reluctant to acknowledge materiality and lived experience has often produced an abstracted 'body' far removed from people's everyday lives. In relation to the post-structuralist language of 'the body', which dominates most social science disciplines, Csordas (1999) has suggested that in the literal world of the social sciences 'the body' is often far abstracted from the lived experiences and material realities of people's lives. In line with these ideas, Price and Shildrick argue that lived embodiment has been neglected and what has transpired in the literature is an 'emptied out body-without-organs leaving only an undifferentiated surface of inscription' (1997: 7). Although post-structuralist analyses have been invaluable in terms of understanding power dynamics in relation to social categories such as for example gender, sexuality and ethnicity, it can be argued that such analyses, particularly in relation to embodiment, are limited by an over-reliance on discourse.

In contrast, the approach of phenomenology focuses on the central concept of *lived experience*, emphasising the continuous engagement and reciprocity between person and world. In this context, embodied existence is understood as being-in-the-world (Merleau-Ponty 1962), where world and person ('self') are inseparable and simultaneously produced in continuous process. In line with phenomenological principles, embodiment can be articulated as a process of sensuous and embodied being in and living through a relational, spatial, material and socio-political world. As opposed to the static, discursively inscribed body, embodiment is the person's process of continuous motion oriented through a world of spaces, objects and others (Ahmed 2006). As described by Denzin, embodied experience is a process of living through time and space:

> The lived body is a temporalized spatial structure. That is, the person's spatial move-ments, locations, and relocations can be understood only as movements within time ... The body does not fill up space in the same way that other real, physical things do or a piece of equipment does. The person takes space in and determines her own locations, making room for herself as she moves about and draws things near.
>
> (2007: 58)

Hence, persons, as described by Denzin, are in continuous interaction and negotiation with their spatial limitations and possibilities, not as body-objects but as persons in motion who orient around and engage with multiple spaces and objects. Whereas traditional phenomenological approaches can be critiqued for 'naively' accepting first-person descriptions of lived experience (Brown *et al.* 2009), hermeneutic phenomenological approaches seek to contextualise individual lived experiences in wider social structures and dynamics. In the context of such an analysis, descriptions of lived experience are read in terms of how they have been made sense of by the individual (e.g. embodied) detail, as well as being subjected to an *interpretation* in relation to wider social and political dynamics (e.g. discursive dynamics, power). For example, Iris Marion Young's (1980/2005) groundbreaking work 'Throwing like a girl' draws simultaneously on the phenomenological and post-structuralist works of Merleau-Ponty and Foucault in exploring the terms of feminine embodiment in the world. In doing so, Young uses case examples to illustrate ways in which women carry out physical tasks such as throwing a ball, arguing that women are encouraged to live through their physical existence in particular ways related to heteronormative contexts. For example, Young notes that more often than not women do not engage their full potential for movement, producing instead more passive states of embodiment. As such, she asserts that women often experience restriction in relation to comportment, in terms of generally occupying space but more specifically engaging in motion, experiencing a sense of their bodies as object-like:

> An essential part of the situation of being a woman is that of living the ever-present possibility that one will be gazed upon as a mere body, as shape and flesh that presents itself as the potential object of another subject's intentions and manipula-tions rather than as a living manifestation of action and intention.
>
> (Young 2005: 45)

Hence, through Young's focus on embodied *experience* in the context of everyday settings and practices she is able to identify specific ways in which women's subjectivities are formed in relation to the restriction of embodied agency in heteronormative spaces. In summary, the framework outlined here offers understandings of embodiment which simultaneously take account of the rich detail and structure of experience as 'lived and felt in the flesh' (Young 2005: 7), *and* the socio-political context and power dynamics through which such experience is lived.

Brown, Cromby, Harper, Johnson and Reavey (2009) suggest there has been a 'turn to experience across the social sciences', specifically aiming to address and move beyond the discourse reductionism characterising much of the existing literature (Williams and Bendelow 1998; Langdridge 2003; Bigwood 1998; Marshall 1999). In particular, empirical researchers have attempted to develop methodologies which take into account the multi-modal nature of lived experience (e.g. discourse, vision, touch), and aim to produce accounts of specific and contextualised embodiment which give rich detail in relation to what it's like to live through specific experiences (e.g. bodily and spatial detail of an experience) (Gillies *et al.* 2004, 2005). Building on this work, the following sections suggest ways in which pre-existing photographs and photo-production methods are suited for and can be utilised in the context of the theoretical and methodological framework presented here for exploring embodiment.

Exploring embodied experience through photographic images

> The focus on 'what the eye can see' is partly a movement against what some might see as the extraordinary dominance of talk and text in our research imaginations and methods, extraordinary because of the one dimensional nature of this foray into, or construction of, what most would agree is a multi-dimensional, multi-sensory 'reality'.
>
> (Mason 2002: 104)

As suggested by Mason (2002), a research engagement with 'a multi-dimensional, multi-sensory reality' requires methods which incorporate but also attempt to go beyond discourse or 'text' (e.g. 'the body' as text), and take account of, for instance, the visual modality through which the world is experienced. The traditional semi-structured research interview, utilised mainly in relation to discursive, conversational or thematic analyses, more often than not produces talk *about* a specific topic (object of the text). Introducing the use of photographs, in contrast, offers ways of *tapping into* and *grounding* participants' accounts in remembered experiences, time and space/place. Rose (2007: 238) suggests that using photographs in social science research is of particular use in relation to evoking 'information, affect and reflection'. Hence, visual materials such as photographs can generate rich description in relation to specific or concrete experiences through an image by allowing participants to tap into or access remembered detail of 'what an experience was like' (sensuous, emotional, spatial and relational) (Willig 2008). In the process of exploring their photographs the participants' focus is shifted away from 'what they think about' a particular embodied experience and onto the details of what the experience was like when they were living through it. Hence, a photographic image can prompt detailed description in relation to being-in-the-material-world of places, objects and others, emphasising being as motion-through-space, as opposed to reproducing a static (discursively inscribed) 'body'. Both pre-existing photographs and photographs produced for the research can highlight temporal aspects of lived experience, for example in terms of different life 'stages', or in exploring everyday life (e.g. times of day/embodied practices).

In studies where participants' pre-existing photographs are used, images are often selected in adherence to the researcher's instructions and in relation to the research topic, enabling particular accounts and perhaps silencing others. Participants thus reflect on and make choices in relation to the selection of photographs and the narratives made possible/impossible by their images prior to the interview. It can be argued that this approach, nevertheless, is particularly suited for exploring issues of change, process and life stage. In contrast, photographs produced by participants for the research offer a more *active* approach, in terms of engaging with material and social contexts, reflecting on the selection of images to be taken and the accounts made possible from the photographic production (Radley and Taylor 2003; Frith and Harcourt 2007). The photo-production method thus requires participants to communicate their lived experience through images as well as speech, producing contextualised accounts involving material and relational realms of space/place, objects and others. In the context of both methods, however, the participants are afforded the opportunity to explore and interpret their own images, showing the researcher what their experience 'is like', in the context of a research interview.

The following sections of this chapter explore two examples of using photographs in the context of two empirical studies. The first study used pre-existing photographs in exploring women's embodied experiences at different life stages and over time, whereas the second study used photo-production in exploring women's current experiences of embodying pleasure in everyday life. Hence, in the first study women's own pre-existing photographs from different time periods in their lives were utilised alongside life-history interviewing in order to aid the exploration of particular experiences and events of relevance to everyday embodiment over time. In the second study, of heterosexual women's experiences of embodying pleasure, the women who participated produced a set of photographs representing the material and social contexts of their embodied experiences alongside a daily diary of their experiences. The participating women took a number of photographs of objects, spaces, places and other people they considered as being of importance to their experience of being embodied in everyday life, and specifically in relation to their embodiment of pleasure. In both studies women reflected on and interpreted their own images in the context of an interview.

The use of pre-existing photographs: remembering the embodiment of time and place

The purpose of the study was to allow women to identify and explore a number of specific experiences across life stages which had contributed to their overall sense of being embodied. The research thus asked which everyday experiences were central and significant to women's experience of being embodied over time.

Eight young women took part in a topical life-history interview, in which they were invited to talk about everyday experiences and events that they thought were particularly relevant to the ways in which they have experienced their embodiment (Plummer 2001). One of the aims of conducting life-history interviews was to allow women to identify and talk in detail about specific experiences which they considered to be important to their overall experience of being embodied. Furthermore, women's own pre-existing photographs were used as a visual aid in encouraging the remembering of specific events taking place during the time period depicted in the photograph (e.g. adolescence). Hence, the participating women were asked to bring along pre-existing photographs of themselves to the interview, which they felt were relevant to the research topic. At the start of the interviews they were asked to arrange the photographs on a table in full view of themselves and the researcher, and describe each one to the researcher in terms of the content depicted and its relation to embodied experiences over time (Radley and Taylor 2003). The aim was to ground, and in turn access, *specific* memories of embodied experiences during the time periods represented in the photographs.

For example, Lucy, a 26-year-old heterosexual woman, brought along to the interview a photograph of herself in her early twenties, taken just after she had swum through a rock cave, and in describing the photograph she said:

> it's not a very flattering angle and it's all kind of thighs and chin and nothing par-ticularly attractive but I actually really like it because ( ) there's no make up, there's no hair, there's not a huge amount of clothing um, and although it isn't flattering I really like it, I like it because it's, it's me ( ) what you were saying about how you think about your body, it's like the most perfect example in here of what your body can do, I could climb a cliff, I could dive into the sea, I could swim, I could go through the rocks, I could climb back again and it just felt really, it was freezing so that was part of it ... when you're like that was energising, because it was a very stimulating day and I do realise I like it [the photo] for the memories rather than because I like how I look in it...

Lucy uses her photograph here to describe her experience of being physically capable. She emphasises how she has engaged in active aspects such as climbing, diving and swimming. In the interview, Lucy went on to recount a number of experiences of movement which allowed her to experience herself as 'tomboy' and 'athletic', and contrasted these with a felt social expectation of more passive femininity. For example, in her heterosexual relationships she had often felt that she was expected to dress and show off the part of her body favoured by her partner (e.g. breasts, legs) in order to appear adequately feminine and 'heterosexy'. In contrast to a felt sense of ownership of herself in her sexual relationships, she stated that being able to swim through the rock cave had made her 'feel very powerful' and suggested that physical capability through movement allowed her a felt sense of empowerment which was more important to her than how she looked during the experience. Lucy contrasted her experiences of being physically capable and 'active', with experiences in which she had 'performed' femininity, constructed by Lucy as 'passive', disempowered and something that 'other' women engaged in more frequently than herself. As argued by feminists, the production of women as feminine 'ornamented surface' (Bartky 1993: 455) relies on a performance of a groomed and relatively static body-object (Choi 2006; Young 2005). This production of femininity, however, can be and is disrupted by women's engagement in movement, which often results in a dishevelled and untidy appearance through, for example, sweating and other physiological processes (Choi 2006).

In the interview, the photograph of Lucy on top of the rock enabled her to produce a narrative in which her embodiment was characterised by physical movement and capability. The photograph was particularly meaningful in relation to Lucy's experience of and ambivalence towards social expectations of embodying (static) femininity. Although the image showed Lucy in full figure wearing a bathing suit, her analysis of the photo centred on the remembered experience of swimming through the rock cave. She stated that the importance of the image to her embodied experience over time was not how she *looked* in the photo, but rather what she could *do*: '… I could climb a cliff, I could dive into the sea, I could swim, I could go through the rocks, I could climb back'. In the interview, Lucy utilised the photograph to evidence her *experience* of being in motion, intentionally manoeuvring through a difficult landscape (Chisholm 2008), and importantly, focused away from *looking at* herself (as body-object in the photo).

The photograph enabled Lucy to tap into the remembered experience of being at the rock cave and explore the bodily sensations of importance in experiencing the event. In addition to providing rich detail of this particular experience, in the life-history context the photograph encouraged the remembering of similar, as well as contradictory, experiences (e.g. of being physically capable, in motion) over the life span. As illustrated by Lucy's example in the current study, the utilisation of pre-existing photographs allowed not only descriptions of the 'surface' aspects of the image (e.g. myself as the body in the image), but enabled the exploration of specific experiences in rich detail, emphasising being in motion and engaging in actions in the material and spatial world.

Participant photo-production: experiencing pleasure in space

The purpose of the study presented in this section was to allow heterosexual women to identify and explore in detail everyday experiences of embodying pleasure. The research thus asked which experiences women identify as pleasurable and how these were lived through in women's immediate spatial, material and relational everyday contexts. Women recorded descriptions of their experiences of pleasure in a daily diary, and produced a set of photographs in relation to their everyday social and material contexts.

Hence, the seven heterosexual women who took part each received a pack with a disposable camera and a notebook for diary writing. The women were instructed to write a daily diary of their experiences of embodying pleasure over a period of two weeks, and to produce a set of photographs of spaces, places, objects and people which they thought related to their experiences of everyday embodiment and pleasure. In producing their accounts, the women were encouraged to reflect on specific experiences of embodying pleasure in relation to touch, taste, sight and smell. Having produced their diary accounts and photographs, the women each took part in an interview, allowing them to discuss their experiences of embodying pleasure and to reflect on their experience of producing the diaries and photos. The interviews were an important part of the data collection process and provided the participants with a space for self-reflection and interpretations of their own data. As in the previous study, the photographs were arranged by the participant on a table in front of herself and the researcher. In all the interviews the participants used the photographs continuously in exploring their experiences.

One of the main aspects through which women reported experiencing pleasure in their diaries, photos and interviews was moving through outside spaces. For example Ann, a 29-year-old Irish woman, took a photograph of the woods and used it to describe how only particular, outside spaces allowed her experiences of embodying pleasure in her everyday life (see Figure 4.1):

> It's like I've said in there [diary] a lot of the time when I'm walking around thinking about what I'm going to be teaching or what I am writing or anything like that it feels as if my consciousness is sort of not even in my body but sort of off a little bit to the side or that I'm sort of out of myself, but walking through the woods it's like the awareness sort of sinks down in me rather than all just being focused in my head it sort of moves down through my body and I'm aware of my legs and my feet moving and almost like a point of connection between me and the ground … (the woods) it's almost like a place of worship in a way … connects me with my body.

In the extract, Ann described her experience of embodying pleasure as characterised by her felt movement through the outside space of the woods. In particular, she emphasised a sense of her 'awareness' moving through herself and connecting her feet to the ground she was walking on. This was reminiscent of other experiences of embodying pleasure through movement described by Ann as a felt sense of her awareness becoming embodied: '… a feeling of all the parts of

Figure 4.1 Ann's photograph of the woods.

me kind of being melted together into a whole instead … it's just a sensation that I can move forward because I'm working as one'. These experiences contrasted with a felt sense of herself as fragmented brain/body/parts, described by Ann as a more common way of experiencing her embodiment. In the interview, Ann used the photo of the woods to describe her felt experience of the woods as a unique space in which experiencing herself 'as one' was made possible. Although the daily movement of walking can be characterised as an ordinary routine experience for able-bodied people, many of the women in the current study suggested that their experiences of walking became 'special' in particular outside spaces (Rose 1999).

It can be argued that photo-production methods allow participants an active position within the research process. This is not only achieved through their ability to move around in the immediate surroundings of their everyday lives, capturing aspects of lived materiality in terms of the spatial world, but also through setting the agenda by identifying aspects of particular relevance to their experience of the research topic.

As illustrated by Ann's example, the participant-produced photographs emphasised young women's experiences of being in and moving through particular spaces. Essentially, the photographs enabled rich descriptions of embodied experiences of spatiality, and allowed participants to *show* the researcher what being in space is like.

Reflections on the use of photographs in capturing embodied experience

Contextualised within the post-structuralist phenomenological framework proposed here, it can be argued that the exploration of pre-existing photographs and participant-produced photographs allow accounts which *tap into* and are *grounded in* lived experience (time/space/process). In contrast to asking participants to *talk about* embodiment in the traditional qualitative interview, introducing photographs into embodiment research thus has the capacity to disrupt narrative rehearsal and produce more complex accounts of lived experience (Reavey and Johnson 2008).

In the first study presented here the use of photographs was particularly beneficial in terms of aiding the remembering of a life stage (e.g. childhood), particularly the felt and sensed experience of living through the period of time in question, and the identification of particular experiences of significance in relation to embodiment. Women were thus prompted by the researcher to use the photograph as an aid to tap into the felt experience of being at the specific life stage, and to identify specific experiences of relevance to their embodiment as made sense of over time. One of the challenges of using pre-existing photographs of women themselves in the context of embodiment research, however, is that participants are looking at themselves in the photograph and may focus on their body (as object in the image) as opposed to the felt and sensed experience of being embodied. It was thus important for the researcher to continuously prompt women to identify and describe particular experiences taking place during the time period illustrated in the photograph. In contrast, participants in the second study explored their lived experiences in terms of the spatial, material and relational contexts in which they live through their embodiment, recording spaces/places, objects and others. This approach was particularly successful in terms of highlighting the spatial and temporal aspects of embodiment, encouraging explorations of what it's like to be in the (socio-political) world. As such, in this study women were less concerned with their appearance and their body (object) as 'for-others', and more concerned with how they *experienced* pleasure in their everyday contexts.

Consistent with feminist ethics of sharing power and direction in the research process, it can be argued that the use of photographs in qualitative methods allows participant agency. For example, the use of pre-existing photographs allows participants to select images in relation to the research topic and thus to produce narratives of experience focused on issues central to the participant. Photo-production methods offer participants an active position within the research, as the producer of images for interpretation, and to some extent enables the participant to pursue their own agenda through the selection of images to be taken and issues to be considered in relation to the topic of research (Reavey and Johnson 2008). In addition, in both studies presented here the photographs were analysed in terms of women's own reflections and interpretations of their images and formed part of their overall narratives, as opposed to being subject to an independent analysis by the researcher.

On the other hand, the researcher's use of participants' images in publication may present specific power dynamics and dilemmas in relation to the participants' ownership of the image and the research agenda. For example, embodiment research can be considered a *sensitive* research topic (Renzetti and Lee 1993) and pre-existing photographs in particular may hold sensitive and highly personal significance for the individual participant. In the research presented here participants' pre-existing photographs were considered participants' personal property, and thus unsuitable for publication, whereas photographs produced for the research have been appropriately anonymised and presented publically. In both studies, importance was placed on participants' descriptions, meaning-making and interpretations of what was represented in their own photos, rather than the presentation of photos to the research audience.

Concluding comments

This chapter has explored the use of pre-existing photographs and photo-production in research on young women's embodied experiences in everyday life. As opposed to the traditional interview, which more often than not produces talk *about* 'the body', as abstracted and inscribed surface, the use of photographs offers an *experientially grounded* approach to exploring embodied experience. It can be argued that the use of visual methods is particularly fruitful for analyses which seek to understand lived experience as multi-modal and multi-sensory, and thus located in and lived through space/time. As illustrated by the examples explored here, the use of photographs enabled rich descriptions of women's experience as lived through spatial and material contexts. Some of the ethical dilemmas inherent to this approach, however, emerge in relation to the researcher's use of the photographs, for example in relation to published material, and the treatment of participants' own interpretations of their images and experiences. In the research presented here, photographs produced by participants for the research were considered suitable for publication. Nevertheless, in relation to the utilisation of pre-existing photographs, what participants said about their photographs was privileged over the use of their photographs in published materials, ensuring anonymity and ownership of personal photographs.

References

Ahmed, S. (2006) *Queer phenomenology: orientations, objects, others.* Durham, NC: Duke University Press.

Bartky, S. L. (1993) The feminine body. In A. M. Jaggar and P. S. Rothenberg (eds) *Feminist Frameworks: alternative theoretical accounts of the relations between women and men.* New York: McGraw Hill.

Bigwood, C. (1998) Renaturalizing the body (with the help of Merleau-Ponty). In D. Welton (ed.) *Body and flesh: a philosophical reader.* Maldan, MA: Blackwell Publishers.

Brown, S. D., Reavey, P., Cromby, J., Harper, D. and Johnson, J. E. (2009) Experimenting with embodiment. In J. Latimer (ed.) *Sociology, health and the body.* Sociological Reviews. Oxford: Blackwell.

Chisholm, D. (2008) Climbing like a girl: an exemplary adventure in feminist phenomenology. *Hypatia,* 23(1): 9–40.

Choi, P. (2006) The gendered nature of sport and exercise. *Psychology of Women Section Review,* 8(2): 4–11.

Csordas, T. J. (1999) Embodiment and cultural phenomenology. In G. Weiss and F. Haber (eds) *Perspectives on embodiment: the intersections of nature and culture.* London: Routledge.

Denzin, N. K. (2007) *On understanding emotion.* New Jersey: Transaction Publishers.

Davis, K. (ed.) (1997) *Embodied practices: feminist perspectives on the body.* London: Sage.

Featherstone, M., Hepworth, M. and Turner, B. S. (eds) (1991) *The body: social process and cultural theory.* London: Sage.

Fraser, M. and Greco, M. (2005) *The body: a reader.* Oxon: Routledge.

Frith, H. and Harcourt, D. (2007) Using photographs to capture women's experiences of chemotherapy: reflecting on the method. *Qualitative Health Research,* 17: 1340–1350.

Gillies, V., Harden, A., Johnson, K., Reavey, P., Strange, V. and Willig, C. (2004) Women's collective constructions of embodied practices through memory work. *British Journal of Social Psychology,* 43: 99–112.

Gillies, V., Harden, A., Johnson, K., Reavey, P., Strange, V. and Willig, C. (2005) Painting pictures of embodied experience: the use of non-linguistic data in the study of embodiment. *Qualitative Research in Psychology,* 2: 3–17.

Grosz, E. (1994) *Volatile bodies: toward a corporeal feminism*. Bloomington: Indiana University Press.

Harraway, D. (1990) *Simians, cyborgs and women: the reinvention of nature*. London: Routledge.

Howson, A. (2005) *Embodying gender*. London: Sage.

Langdridge, D. (2003) Hermeneutic phenomenology: arguments for a new social psychology. *History & Philosophy of Psychology*, 5(1): 30–45.

Marshall, H. (1999) 'Our bodies, ourselves: why we should add old fashioned empirical phenomenology to the new theories of the body'. In J. Price and M. Shildrick (eds) *Feminist theory and the body: a reader*. Edinburgh: Edinburgh University Press

Mason, J. (2002) *Qualitative researching*. London: Sage.

Merleau-Ponty, M. (1962) *Phenomenology of perception*. London: Routledge.

Plummer, K. (2001) *Documents of life 2: an invitation to a critical humanism*. London: Sage.

Price, J. and Shildrick, M. (1999) *Feminist theory and the body: a reader*. Edinburgh: Edinburgh University Press.

Radley, A. and Taylor, D. (2003) Images of recovery: a photo-elicitation study on the hospital ward. *Qualitative Health Research*, 13 (1): 77–99.

Reavey, P. and Johnson, K. (2008) Using the visual image in qualitative research. In C. Willig and W. Stainton Rogers (eds) *The Sage handbook of qualitative research in psychology*. London: Sage.

Renzetti, C. M. and Lee, R. M. (eds) (1993) *Researching sensitive topics*. Newbury Park, CA: Sage.

Rose, G. (1999) Women and everyday spaces. In J. Shildrick and M. Price (eds) *Feminist theory and the body: a reader*. Edinburgh: Edinburgh University Press.

Rose, G. (2007) *Visual methodologies: an introduction to the interpretation of visual materials* (2nd edition). London: Sage.

Stam, H. J. (1998) *The body and psychology*. London: Sage.

Ussher, J. M. (1997) *Body talk: the material and discursive regulation of sexuality, madness and reproduction*. London: Routledge.

Weiss, G. and Haber, H. F. (1999) *Perspectives on embodiment: the intersections of nature and culture*. London: Routledge.

Welton, D. (1998) *Body and flesh: a philosophical reader*. Oxford: Blackwell.

Williams, S. J. and Bendelow, G. (1998) *The lived body*. Oxon: Routledge

Willig, C. (2008) *Introducing qualitative research in psychology* (2nd edition). Maidenhead, UK: Open University Press.

Young, I. M. (1980/2005) *On female body experience: 'Throwing like a girl and other essays'*. New York: Oxford University Press.

5   Narrating biographical disruption and repair

Exploring the place of absent images in women's experiences of cancer and chemotherapy

Hannah Frith

Pictures of our first day at school, a special birthday, holidays, weddings, friends, and new additions to the family; photograph albums capture particular moments in a life. In providing opportunities for storytelling, generating laughter over out-dated fashions or changing hair-styles, and allowing the rehearsal and creation of family histories, photographs are also a site for constructing a sense of the past and creating a bridge between the past, present and future. Photograph albums offer a means for narrating the lives of ourselves and of others (Van House *et al.*, 2004; Brookfield *et al.*, 2008) and for charting biographical continuity. In contrast, an illness, such as cancer, can provoke a sense of 'biographical disruption' – a critical break between past (before the illness), present and future lives (Bury, 1982). The diagnosis of an illness, and in particular cancer, forces people to experience many changes in their lives, including the reality of an uncertain future, threats to identity and sense of self, and a re-evaluation of the person's place in the world (Frank, 1995). As such, the stories that cancer patients tell about themselves as they negotiate their way through diagnoses, treatment regimens, changed bodies, and disrupted identities are not just a way of making sense of an illness, but also a life (Mathieson and Stam, 1995). Narratives and storytelling are a medium through which people can make sense of, organise and draw together fragments of their lives into a cohesive whole, and are characterised by a temporal ordering of events (Hydén, 1997). Narratives are considered an invaluable source of experiential knowledge, a resource for developing empathy and patient-centred care, and an important conduit for aiding coping among patients (Charmez, 1999; Frank, 1995; Greenhalgh and Hurwitz, 1999). Drawing on a photographic study of women's experiences of chemotherapy treatment for breast cancer, I consider the ways in which asking women to visually represent their lives engages them in the task of creating memories and doing 'biographical work' to establish the place of their illness within their identities and life worlds. Asking women to mark out particular moments as significant, invites them to enact a bittersweet experience of creating memories that they might rather forget (a cancer diagnosis can be traumatic, and chemotherapy treatment unpleasant), while documenting a move towards recovery and a re-integration of the self into 'normal' activities (Radley and Taylor, 2003a). Re-viewing these images and using them to narrativise their experiences during an interview calls on women to remember past events and to confront images of past selves. Against this backdrop, this chapter explores the work that women do to re-image 'missing' photographs, and explores the role of absent images in creating boundaries around what selves are available to be remembered. In other words, I examine how the materiality of photographs is implicated in the biographical work done by women undergoing chemotherapy treatment for cancer as they narrate their experiences. But first, I will briefly describe the study from which the data are drawn.

The study

Nineteen women (aged 35–68) who underwent adjuvant chemotherapy treatment for breast cancer volunteered to take part in a photographic study exploring their experiences of having an altered appearance. For all but one, this was their first experience of chemotherapy; twelve had undergone a mastectomy, and of the remaining seven several were expecting surgery at a later date. An altered appearance, particularly hair loss, is one of the most feared aspects of chemotherapy (Batchelor, 2001; Frith *et al.*, 2007), and provokes a threat to identity as one is visually identifiable as a person-with-cancer and no longer looks like one's 'usual self' (Harcourt and Frith, 2008). Although using photographs and other visual methods alongside interviews is growing in popularity among researchers of health and illness experiences (see, for example, Guillernin, 2004; Radley and Taylor, 2003a; Rich *et al.*, 2002), it is still relatively unusual. We opted for photographs in this study because we wanted to use a visual method that would be familiar to participants and forms part of people's usual storytelling practice. We also wanted something that would require little skill and expertise, and which would be easy for participants to engage with as and when they felt well enough or inspired to do so. The women were initially interviewed about their expectations and concerns about how the treatment would impact on their appearance (see Frith and Harcourt, 2007 for an overview of the initial interviews). Next, with the aid of a disposable camera, they were asked to represent their experiences, thoughts and feelings about their changed appearance over the course of their treatment. As the temporal aspect of illness narratives is important, and because chemotherapy typically takes place over several months, we felt that photography would be a useful way of capturing the unfolding of their experience over time without constant intrusion from the researchers. The women were invited to take as many or as few photographs as they wanted (the 15 participants who returned their cameras produced an average of 17.6 photographs). Given our focus on appearance it seemed appropriate to use a visual method, but because we anticipated that women might find this problematic we emphasised that they did not have to include photographs of themselves or use the cameras to document actual changes to their appearance, but could instead include pictures that represented their experiences of chemotherapy without actually showing these changes. We wanted women to have control over images of themselves and how they would be represented (see Frith and Harcourt, 2007 for further discussion about the benefits of using photography in this kind of research). The photographs formed the basis for a second interview which took place at the end of their treatment; all interviews were conducted by myself or Diana Harcourt with whom the research was conducted (for further details of the method see Frith and Harcourt, 2007).[1] The women were asked to speak to each of the photographs they had taken in turn, to describe it, talk about why they had taken it, and to explain how it reflected their experience of having an altered appearance. As the photographs were taken in chronological order and because we adopted a relatively unstructured approach, the interviews were designed to evoke a narrative about the chemotherapy experiences as well as specific stories about events within this narrative.[2] As such, the photographs were not analysed in and of themselves, rather they were used in the interviews as a focus for narratives and stories about the chemotherapy experience. In addition, the women were also asked to reflect on the process of creating a photographic record of their experiences, what they planned to do with the photographs, which images they thought were particularly important, and whether there were any images missing from their collection.[3] The interview transcripts were then inductively analysed to identify common themes or elements which run across the stories (Polkinghorne, 1995). As the focus of this chapter is on the ways in which photographs are implicated in the biographical work undertaken by women experiencing chemotherapy treatment, the data presented here are drawn primarily from the second interviews.

Using photographs produced by research participants alongside interviews is typically referred to as *photo-elicitation* (Harper, 2002; Clark-Ibáñez, 2004; Epstein *et al.*, 2006), but this term has been problematised since it suggests that the image already exists and is simply elicited or extracted from the participant. This both obscures the work that goes into choosing what to photograph and into creating the visual image (Radley and Taylor, 2003b), and implies that photographs can draw out pre-stored and otherwise fixed memories (Pink, 2001). Following Hodgetts, Chamberlain and Radley (2007), we prefer the term *photo-production* since this encompasses a focus on the labour of assembling the images and attention to the context and circumstances of their fabrication, as well as on the pictures themselves. Photo-production allows for an exploration of the myriad ways that women approach the task of representing their lives, the practical and emotional difficulties they face in attempting to visualise their experiences, and the embodied experience of using the camera in a particular space and time. This is important as it can illuminate some of the ways in which storytelling can be facilitated or hindered with the use of photography and can reveal more about the context in which narratives have been generated. Moreover, the shift from elicitation to production also reflects a move in understanding the relationship between photographs and memories. Rather than acting as triggers for pre-existing, relatively fixed memories which are internally held, we understand photographs to have an important role in constructing memories and a sense of the past (Edwards, 1999; Radley, 1990; Sontag, 1977). We are not concerned here with the mechanics of memory and whether photographs can facilitate remembering or even create false remembering. Rather, we are interested in the ways in which talk about the photographs are constructed by participants as acts of remembering and forgetting, and we explore how this is implicated in the work of 'biographical repair' following ill-health. Talking about photographs is a form of 'social remembering' (Brookfield *et al.*, 2008). This constructionist approach treats 'remembering' (and forgetting) as a social and communicative practice. Here, recollection is 'not a neutral activity, involving the recall of stored information, but rather a social act in itself through which the past is invoked in relevant, meaningful ways in the course of some activity in the present' (Brookfield *et al.*, 2008: 479). It is these two strands – exploring the processes of photo-production/non-production, and the construction of remembering and forgetting – which we discuss in relation to absent images.

Creating memories

> [I] started to realise that my hair was starting to grow back and that I thought I'll take a photograph of that because it's a really important thing to remember.
>
> (Jane)[4]

> ...certain things were planned – like when I knew they were having their heads shaved – I thought that would be a good thing to take, I'll take my camera.
>
> (Georgia)

As these quotes illustrate, the act of taking a photograph imparts social significance to the moment (Sontag, 1977), and is constructed as a way of 'making memories'. It is precisely this feature of photographs which researchers exploit and which makes participant-led photography a valuable research tool. People take photographs to capture moments in their lives, and to preserve on film significant memories which might otherwise be forgotten (Walker and Moulton, 1989). Many of the images taken by the women in this study were designed to capture a particular event or allow for the telling of a particular story. These stories involved a chronological representation of the chemotherapy journey, and were poignant, vivid, and relayed with tears and laughter. Like many stories, they had distinct beginnings, middles, and ends, and included milestones (e.g., losing hair, wearing a wig, hair re-growth, and last treatment) that took place over several months. These stories charted the journey through biographical disruption and repair as this was written onto the bodies of these women. Several women took photographs of themselves before their treatment in order to capture and retain an image of their 'normal' selves: 'That was just the start, before I'd lost my hair . . . it reminded me of how I should have looked' (Barbara). During their chemotherapy treatment not only did they feel ill and debilitated, they also looked different and not like their normal selves: 'you look like something out of a concentration camp' (Caroline) or 'something out of Star-Trek' (Louise). Towards the end of treatment hair re-growth was seen as marking a shift back to normality, as Anne observed, 'it's only now, now I've got a head of hair, I mean it's very, very short, but now I'm beginning to feel that I'm getting back towards being me again'. For the women themselves, and for those around them, hair re-growth was welcomed as a sign of recovery. For example, Caroline notes how for her young children hair-loss was 'symbolic of my illness and then the hair growing back for them was a sign for them of me getting better'. However, hair re-growth does not necessarily signal a return to the pre-chemotherapy self as hair can grow back a different colour, texture or waviness. Georgia who had had very long hair, couldn't get excited when her hair grew back 'short and spikey' because she kept thinking 'even this time next year when we've got another Christmas, my hair is still not going to be back to how I had it'. In contrast Julia, whose hair had grown back grey and very short at the time of the interview, said 'I quite like the colour' and 'if it stays like this I won't dye it, I'd rather leave it like it'. For some, getting their appearance back to exactly how it was before chemotherapy was seen as the only way to repair the biographical disruption precipitated by the treatment, for others their changed appearance was re-integrated into their sense of self. The photographs were used to explore the continuities and changes between past and present selves, in charting the shifts through biographical disruption and repair. What, then, of photographs which go missing from the collection or which were never taken?

'Missing' photographs can take different pathways from presence to absence – some are carefully planned but never taken, others are taken but then lost, and some are neither planned nor taken yet their non-appearance is still noticeable. Despite their material absence, missing images can evoke discussions as vivid, engaging and detailed as those stirred up by those photographs which can be handled, stored, stroked and examined during the interview (see Lassetter *et al.*, 2007; Hodgetts, *et al.*, 2007). Exploring why these images didn't make it into film is important. While photographs are sometimes 'missing' because practical constraints limit the kinds of images which can be produced, others are purposively absent – both tell us something about the nature of the life tasks (and research tasks) in which participants are engaged. Practically, these women found that they sometimes forgot to take the camera with them when they needed it, or that they simply missed the moment to capture an image (see also Klitzing's, 2004 account of the experiences of homeless women). Lucy described how she missed the opportunity to photograph the 'big boils on my neck' which she developed after taking steroids. By the time she visited the doctor they had 'already started to go down' and she thought, 'oh well next time I'll take a picture when they're nice and big, but they never came again'. Lucy had not spoken about these boils, or about her skin (which she described as being usually a bit spotty but had been exceptionally clear once the boils disappeared), up until the point where we asked about the missing photographs. Nonetheless, this was a worrying and embarrassing side-effect of her treatment which influenced her appearance and which she felt was an important part of her biographical journey through chemotherapy. 'Missing' images are also sometimes carefully planned, imagined and envisioned, and considerable creative thought invested in ways of representing the sensory nature of the illness experience. For example, Louise described how she planned photographs of 'manky old mince meat' that had gone all 'yellow and yukky', or to 'just walk into the supermarket and take pictures of the bleach section' to represent how she felt about the toxicity of the chemotherapy treatment and the way in which she felt it was harming her body at the same time as helping it to fight cancer. These women could provide vivid descriptions – or narrative pictures (cf. Hodgetts *et al.*, 2007) – of the images they would like to have produced. Narrative picturing means that the images can be described and interrogated *as if* they were available. However, although these descriptions can stand in for the missing photographs, they cannot completely replace the images which include many details which would take too long to articulate, and a picture of rotting meat or pustular boils may more readily evoke visceral reactions (e.g. of disgust). But, by including a discussion of 'missing' photographs in the interviews, we were able to access elaborated accounts of experience. Perhaps the disruption of the photographic biography can, to some extent, be repaired by the use of narrative picturing.

Sometimes, however, narrative picturing is not enough. If photographs are seen as conduits or containers of memories, their absence can bring with it a sense of loss. When photographs which women remember taking are 'missing' (perhaps because they had failed to use the flash mechanism or because the images had not been processed), they open up a gap in the story. The material absence of a photograph is treated as if a significant moment has been lost, a memory forgotten, or an opportunity to remember lost. Jane, for example, spoke about her distress at having to have a central line (a tube that is passed through a vein which ends up in the heart) inserted during her treatment. For her, this was extremely significant because it symbolised the seriousness of her illness. Consequently, the removal of the central line some months later was a great relief and represented a significant turning point in her recovery – one she was keen to include in her photographic record. Her disappointment when this photograph failed to materialise reflected the loss of the material image for aiding future re-tellings of her story. Alex described warmly and with much amusement the time when her daughters 'had a bit of fun' shaving off her hair and playing around with different haircuts. She too, was disappointed that the photographs had not come out, and felt a sense of loss that this event was not available for reviewing in the interview (and beyond). Photographs are often treated as concrete records of events and occasions (Cronin, 1998), and are used to provide concrete evidence of the existence of a moment (Walker and Moulton, 1989). Many of these women were keen to have a permanent record of what was often a hugely significant period of their lives:

> we take photographs to remind ourselves of things in our life and this is a hugely significant part of my life ... I think it would be important to remember, to have these because I think I may want to look at them at different times in my life.
>
> (Jane)

Similarly, Anne says that she 'may well keep them in an album' (as you might keep other family snapshots) and will 'never destroy them', so she can 'always just look back sometimes'. As important resources for biographical work, these photographs have a life beyond the project and are incorporated into the ongoing work of narrating their lives. However, it is the assumed permanence of photographs and their ability to bring events, activities and selves into existence which also explains why some images are deliberately never taken (which we return to later).

So, some images are carefully planned but never taken, others are taken but then lost and a sense of loss remains, and yet more are neither planned or taken yet their non-appearance is still noticeable. It is to this last set of absences which we now turn. Some images were missing because at times these women simply felt too unwell to take pictures or were unwilling or unable to engage in the research process. We anticipated that participants would often feel fatigued or ill during their chemotherapy treatment, and that this may impact on their ability to engage in research tasks. Our choice of participant-led photography as a method was based on our desire to be as sensitive and unobtrusive as possible, and we emphasised that women could take as many or as few photographs as they wanted, and that they could decide when and where to take them. We hoped that participating would not be too demanding or burdensome. But, perhaps inevitably, women sometimes felt too ill or too demoralised to take photographs: 'I didn't take photographs of the most painful times, because it was sometimes too all consuming' (Louise), and 'I was sometimes feeling so bad that sometimes I didn't have the energy and inclination to get the camera out' (Caroline). Understanding the constraints which limit photo-production and exploring the contexts and processes around 'missing' images, can do more than simply 'fill in the gaps'. Missing photographs may also tell us something about the nature of the experience we are attempting to capture, and the boundaries which are placed around this experience. By asking about the context of photo-production, we gain an insight into how debilitating women found their treatment:

> I hardly ever took [photographs] when I was feeling rough … I knew I had to do it but I couldn't really be bothered with anything. Not really, apart from the usual routine.
>
> (Linda)

This reminds us that photography is an embodied act (Ziller and Smith, 1977; Thoutenhoofd, 1998), and that the effort involved in creating and making photographs may be considerable (Crang, 1997). The idea that there are experiences which are too painful to represent, and too difficult to capture is itself very telling. For example, the homeless respondents in one study failed to take some photographs because they couldn't access the necessary spaces, didn't have the time or resources to revisit areas, or were concerned about being moved on by the police if they went to take pictures (Hodgetts *et al.*, 2007). Exploring these absent images not only allows for narrative picturing to complete the stories, the telling of the process of photo-production (or in this case, non-production) in itself reveals something about the spatial constraints, monitoring and surveillance, and the social exclusion under which these people live their lives. In this sense, the absences are as revealing as the photographs themselves.

In summary, the aim of remembering in the interviews was the re-presentation of experiences so that we might understand what these women went through and why it was important. Photographs as culturally understood ways of 'capturing memories' allow for the re-telling of a story about biographical disruption and repair (both in the content of the interview, and in the doing of the interview). Adopting a photo-*production* approach enables an exploration of 'missing' photographs which makes possible a process of narrative picturing to 'fill in the gaps' in the biographical story. Moreover, a focus on the context and circumstances of the making, or non-making, of images can inform understanding of the experience itself. However, the materiality of the pictures, being able to handle, store and re-visit them on future occasions in order to reminisce also meant that missing photographs were sometimes greeted with a sense of loss. The following section further explores the role of photographs in remembering and forgetting by exploring how, in creating a bridge between past, present and future, photographs facilitate the work of social remembering and enable the doing of biographical work around the shift from illness to recovery.

Engendering forgetting

Reflecting on their study of remembering one's stay in hospital, Radley and Taylor (2003a) observe how re-viewing photographs during interviews 'disrupts the separation of then and now, of the hospital and home', and sets up a tension for one participant of 'having to remember what she was trying to forget' (p. 144). Recovery from illness and hospitalisation necessitates a distance from the experience, 'forgetting' allows this distance. In re-telling the story of one's stay in hospital, 'forgetting' some of the detail of this stay serves to signal this distance even as, in the re-telling, the experience is brought into the present to be re-lived. It is this slip-sliding back and forth from past to present, and between remembering and forgetting, which creates opportunities and challenges for biographical work during the interviews. For these women undergoing chemotherapy, moving between the past and the present also meant shifting between the ill-self and the healthy-self, and creating a biographical story about the return to the normal self, or the adjustment to a forever changed self. It is in this context that we discuss the role of absent images in managing biographical work and rendering the ill-self unavailable for the future.

If photographs are constructed as a way of 'capturing the past', re-examining and accounting for the photographs in the interview is an invitation for participants to 'relive' their experiences, albeit through the lens of the present. Women noted that the pictures 'brings it more back' (Alex) or 'brought all those things back to me' (Jane). As Anne said, 'it took me back, and made me remember the good and the bad'. The feelings evoked by the photographs don't only reside in the past, they are felt there and then in the interview. Photographs are 'extraordinarily important, emotionally resonant objects' (Rose, 2004: 549), and these emotions are mirrored in the ways the photographs are handled (passed over quickly, pushed away, turned face down) and in the looks of disgust and revulsion that accompany their viewing. As Jane relayed, 'I felt quite emotional when I looked at them, particularly seeing me without any hair' because 'I didn't think I looked that bad …' , or as Julia said, 'I cried [when I looked back through the photos] because you forget don't you […] they're horrendous photographs, I mean I didn't think I was the most attractive woman in the world but good grief'. These women are shocked and distressed as they re-view the images both because their illness is written on their bodies and because they are re-living what it felt like to be ill. The biographical disruption is re-experienced in the interview when women revisit their illness, their changed appearance and the rupture of their sense of self:

> I found that was probably the most harrowing photograph for me, I really, when I looked at that I thought 'oh God' you know. Yeah I think I look really ill in that photograph . . . . I think I look really awful it doesn't look anything like me.
>
> (Jane)

Although some of the photographs depicted positive images and were described with fondness, many served to remind women of their ill-selves – selves which are transformed, different looking, and debilitated. In their study of recovery from a hospital stay, Radley and Taylor (2003a) argue recovery from illness has as its aim the distancing of the hospital experience from the interview experience, and that photographs (and the memories they are constructed to contain) become resources for patients to present themselves as a 'kind of patient' who is now recovered from her hospital stay. In this study, the women drew on the photographs as resources for distancing themselves from the ill-self. In talking about having 'forgotten' the ways in which the chemotherapy altered their appearance, or how ill they felt at the time, women place themselves at a distance from the illness experience and position themselves as speaking from the present in which they are recovered:

> going through them [the photographs] reminded me of feeling all those things, it's amazing how quickly you forget how you feel. Um, looking back on it now, and I think it's not really that long since I finished my chemotherapy and yet I feel amazingly so much better, I know I don't feel as well as I did beforehand, but I feel so much better […] I couldn't bear the thought of going back to feeling like that again.
>
> (Jane)

Garlick (2002) argues that the temporal nature of photographs, where events in the past are brought to bear on the present, is inextricably bound to the construction of self-identity. Photographs function to 'anchor ourselves within the past' (Harrison, 2002: 104), and connections between our present situation and the other spaces, places and times captured in the photographs allow for a construction of change or stability in our biographical narratives. In the example above, the separation of the self depicted in the past of the photographs from the present self speaking in the interview allows for a fracture between the ill-self and the recovered self which presents illness as a thing of the past. So, if photographs can be used to do biographical work in constructing the separation of past from present, and ill-self from recovered self, what is the work done by missing photographs?

If memories are made in the taking of a photograph, and if deciding what is 'photographable' marks it as significant and notable, then choosing not to create some images may serve to ensure forgetting or to deny the importance or existence of some experiences. Missing pictures may be absent *not* because they are considered 'not worth taking' but because they are *so* significant that to capture them on film would somehow make them more concrete and 'real'. For Louise it was difficult to 'admit that this really, really, sucks – you know, because I'm taking a photo of it', and she says that her 'coping mechanism' was 'edging away a little bit' by refusing to commit an image to film. Rather than *capturing* moments and events, Spence and Holland (1991) argue that photographs can be said to *create* moments, events and occasions. Because of their cultural associations with 'capturing reality', photographs are a way of bringing events into being. For Louise, taking a photograph of her worst experiences would make them more real, and would mean admitting the significance and emotional power of the event. For women struggling to come to terms with an altered appearance due to cancer or related treatments, committing these changes to film could be extremely challenging. Some pictures were just too difficult, sensitive or embarrassing to take, and women did not want to make some images of themselves available – either to the researcher or to other women. For example, Linda did not want to include an image of her 'small breast' because she doesn't like 'being photographed like that' and that it might 'bother lots of people'. Georgia commented that 'the only thing missing is me with a bald head, but you're not going to get that, I couldn't have done that'. As Walker and Moulton (1989: 157) note, the 'act of photography anticipates the future by ripping the appearance of a moment out of its time and creating a tangible image for the future of what will be the past'. Just as photographs are seen as a means of capturing the past, they are also seen as resources to be drawn on in the future. Photographs 'express a desire for memory and the act of keeping a photograph is, like other souvenirs, as act of faith in the future' (Edwards, 1999: 222). Choosing not to take particular pictures may be a way of controlling the availability of images for future reminiscence. In contrast to bereaved parents who use photographs to create a bridge between past, present and future in order to retain a sense of themselves as parents (Riches and Dawson, 1998), here women may refuse to create particular images so as to render them unavailable for future remembering. For example, Linda who did not want to include a picture related to nausea and vomiting (one of the major side-effects of chemotherapy which she experienced as especially difficult) reflected on its absence by saying, 'I never actually had my photograph taken when I was being ill, perhaps I was a bit too proud'. She later adds, 'I don't want to remember it, these [the photographs] are memories'. In these extracts, photographs are treated as if they are synonymous with memories – the existence of a photograph ensures the continuance of the memory, while the absence of a photograph allows the memory to fade. Whether or not this really *is* the case, we would argue that women are using the notion of forgetting to manage the place of their illness within their biographical story. Georgia, who heatedly remarked that she 'didn't want any photographs of me at all during the whole thing', explained this in the following way:

> I don't want any reminders, I don't want to look back at pictures of me wearing a wig. That's a reminder. I don't want to be reminded. If there's no photographic evidence your memory fades, but if you've got photographs they don't. They're permanent and I don't want that.

> (Georgia)

People can use objects (such as photographs) to shape how they will be remembered by others in years to come (Radley, 2002). Just as it was important for some women to keep their photographs for future reminiscence, for others it was just as important to excise these images from their lives. Georgia, who threw her photographs away at the end of the interview and had also burnt her wig, remarked 'I want it all gone and out of my life'. She said she would 'probably put them in a drawer and never look at them again [...] the emotions I had when I took them are not the sort of emotions I want to carry on feeling'. There is a paradox for these women, in describing and alluding to photographs that they decided not to take or did not want to take, they bring these images into being. From a social remembering approach, we can see this as communicating the idea that some things should not be captured. By refusing to take some photographs and deciding not to create images of themselves, women are seeking to control the place of illness in their biographical narratives.

Photographs are, then, commonly understood as a means for creating, capturing and making memories. It is this cultural understanding of photographs that researchers exploit when they ask participants to produce photographs for research purposes. Researchers need to take seriously the idea that participants are involved in constructing material objects which may potentially have a life and a place beyond the reach of the research process. Our participants were much more keenly aware of this than we were as researchers, and had thought carefully about what kinds of objects they wanted to manufacture and make available to the world and to themselves. As resources for remembering, photographs are imbued with the power to make experiences 'real' or available and participants may want to share these experiences without allowing them this more solid or enduring existence. Placing this choice within the hands of participants was for us an important decision. Understanding how participants implemented this choice, and how they made sense of and engaged the research tasks that we invite them to undertake, added a richness to our analyses and a depth to our understanding of their biographical journeys. These women were not simply narrating their story, they were actively engaged in deciding what stories could be told and re-told about their lives.

66 *Frith*

Notes

1 Dr Diana Harcourt and I conducted the interviews when we were both based at the University of the West of England, UK. The research was funded by the Centre for Appearance Research based at the university. Further details of the centre can be found at http//science.uwe.ac.uk/research/car.aspx
2 Following Polkinghorne (1988) I use the terms narrative and storytelling somewhat interchangeably as they share a clear emphasis on the temporal ordering of events associated with a change, although others have argued that they can and perhaps should be distinguished (Reissman, 1993; Scholes, 1981).
3 See Harcourt and Frith (2008) or Frith and Harcourt (2007) for further methodological details.
4 Pseudonyms have been used to protect the identity of participants.

References

Batchelor, D. (2001) Hair and cancer chemotherapy: consequences and nursing care – A literature study. *European Journal of Cancer Care*, 10: 147–63.
Brookfield, H., Brown, S. D. and Reavey, P. (2008) Vicarious and post-memory practices in adopting families: the re-production of the past through photography and narrative. *Journal of Community and Applied Social Psychology*, 16: 474–491.
Bury, M. (1982) Chronic illness as biographical disruption. *Sociology of Health & Illness*, 4(2): 167–182.
Charmez, K. (1999) Stories of suffering: subjective tales and research narratives. *Qualitative Health Research*, 9(3): 362–382.
Clark-Ibáñez, M. (2004) Framing the social world with photo-elicitation interviews. *American Behavioral Scientist*, 47(12): 1507–1527.
Crang, M. (1997) Picturing practices: research through the tourist gaze. *Progress in Human Geography*, 21(3): 359–367.
Cronin, O. (1998) Psychology and photographic theory. In J. Prosser (ed.) *Image-based research: a sourcebook for qualitative researchers*. London: Falmer, pp. 69–83.
Edwards, E. (1999) Photographs as objects of memory. In J. Aynsley, C. Breward and M. Kwint (eds) *Material memories*. Oxford: Berg.
Epstein, I., Stevens, B., McKeever, P. and Baruchel, S. (2006) Photo Elicitation Interview (PEI): using photos to elicit children's perspectives. *International Journal of Qualitative Methods*, 5(3): 1–9.
Frank, A. W. (1995) *The wounded storyteller*. Chicago: IL: University of Chicago Press.
Frith, H. and Harcourt, D. (2007) Using photographs to capture women's experiences of chemotherapy: reflecting on the method. *Qualitative Health Research*, 17(10): 1340–1350.
Frith. H., Harcourt, D. and Fussell, A. (2007) Anticipating an altered appearance: women undergoing chemotherapy treatment for breast cancer. *European Journal of Oncology Nursing*, 11: 385–391.
Garlick. S. (2002) Revealing the unseen: tourism, art and photography. *Cultural Studies*, 16(2): 289–305.
Greenhalgh, T. and Hurwitz, B. (1999) Why study narrative? *British Medical Journal*, 318: 48–50.
Guillernin, M. (2004) Understanding illness: using drawings as a research method. *Qualitative Health Research*, 14: 272–289.

Harcourt, D. and Frith, H. (2008) Women's experiences of an altered appearance during chemotherapy: an indication of cancer status. *Journal of Health Psychology*, 13(5): 597–606.

Harper, D. (2002) Talking about pictures: a case for photo elicitation. *Visual Studies*, 17(1): 13–26.

Harrison, B. (2002) Photographic visions and narrative inquiry. *Narrative Inquiry*, 12(1): 87–111.

Hodgetts, D., Chamberlain, K. and Radley, A. (2007) Considering photographs never taken during photo-production projects. *Qualitative Research in Psychology* 4(4): 263–280.

Hydén, L. C. (1997) Illness and narrative. *Sociology of Health & Illness*, 19(1): 48–69.

Klitzing, S. W. (2004) Women living in a homeless shelter: stress, coping and leisure. *Journal of Leisure Research*, 36(4): 483–512.

Lassetter, J. H., Mandleco, B. L., and Roper, S. O. (2007) Family photographs: expressions of parents raising children with disabilities. *Qualitative Health Research*, 17(4): 456–467.

Mathieson, C. M. and Stam, H. J. (1995) Renegotiating identity: cancer narratives. *Sociology of Health & Illness*, 17(3): 283–306.

Pink, S. (2001) *Doing visual ethnography: images, media and representation in research.* London: Sage.

Polkinghorne, D. E. (1988) *Narrative knowing and the human sciences.* Albany: University of New York Press.

Polkinghorne, D. E. (1995) Narrative configuration in qualitative analysis. In J. A. Hatch and R. Wisniewski (eds) *Life history and narrative*. London: The Falmer Press, pp. 5–23.

Radley, A. (1990) Artefacts, memory and a sense of the past. In D. Middleton and D. Edwards (eds), *Collective remembering*. London: Sage.

Radley, A. (2002) Portrayals of suffering: on looking away, looking at, and the comprehension of illness experience. *Body & Society*, 8(3): 1–23.

Radley, A. and Taylor, D. (2003a) Remembering one's stay in hospital: a study in photography, recovery and forgetting. *Health: An Interdisciplinary Journal for the Social Study of Health*, 7(2): 129–159.

Radley, A. and Taylor, D. (2003b) Images of recovery: a photo-elicitation study on the hospital ward. *Qualitative Health Research*, 13(1): 77–99.

Reissman, C. K. (1993) *Narrative analysis.* London: Sage.

Rich, M., Pataschnick, J. and Chalfen, R. (2002) Visual illness narratives of asthma: explanatory models and health related behavior. *American Journal of Health Behavior*, 26: 442–453.

Riches, G. and Dawson, P. (1998) Lost children, living memories: the role of photographs in processes of grief and adjustment among bereaved parent. *Death Studies*, 22(2): 121–140.

Rose, G. (2004) 'Everyone's cuddled up and it looks really nice': an emotional geography of some mums and their family photos. *Social and Cultural Geography*, 5(4): 549–564.

Scholes R. (1981) Afterthoughts on narrative: language, narrative and anti-narrative. In W. J. T. Mitchell *On narrative* (pp. 200–208). Chicago, IL: University of Chicago Press.

Sontag, S. (1977) *On photography*. New York: Farrar, Straus and Giroux.

Spence, J. and Holland, P. (1991) *Family snaps: the meaning of domestic photography.* London: Virago.

Thoutenhoofd, E. (1998) Method in a photographic enquiry of being deaf. *Sociological Research Online*, 3(2). Retrieved from http://www.socresonline.org.uk/3/2/2.htm

Van House, N. A., Davis, M., Takhteyev, Y., Ames, M. and Finn, M. (2004) The social uses of personal photography: methods for projecting future imaging applications. Unpublished paper retrieved from: www.http://people.ischool.berkeley.edu/~vanhouse/photo_project/publications.php

Walker, A. L. and Moulton, R. K. (1989) Photo albums: images of time and reflections on self. *Qualitative Sociology*, 12(2): 155–282.

Ziller, R. C. and Smith, D. E. (1977) A phenomenological utilization of photographs. *Journal of Phenomenological Psychology*, 7: 172–182.

6 Using photographs of places, spaces and objects to explore South Asian women's experience of close relationships and marriage

Anamika Majumdar

This chapter explores the subjective experience of closeness in UK married life using photo-elicitation and photo-production with women of South Asian origin.[1] Personal relationships have become an important object of study within psychology and the social sciences in the last 30 years, reflecting the need to understand more fully experiences which are taken for granted in many people's lives. South Asian women cannot be viewed as a homogenous category, but are differentiated by region, language, religion, wealth, education, caste, as well as the geographical area in which they now reside. Two studies are described where photos were used as a tool to focus participants on their experiences of close relationships in particular material settings, for example the home. This orientation towards the material world was thought by the researcher to trigger memories of specific experiences and feelings associated with close relationships. While the first study involved life-history interviews, where participants reflected on the different experiences of closeness over time with the aid of existing family photos (e.g. *photo-elicitation*), the second study considered how participants made sense of closeness in everyday married life through taking photos of objects and spaces related to married life (e.g. *photo-production*). It is argued here that the use of photos in narrative interviews about close relationships can move participants beyond established cultural narratives or ways of talking about closeness to the complexities of what 'doing closeness' actually entails. In each of the two studies, photographs were used in different ways and each will be examined in order to establish how each approach contributed something different to the study of closeness.

In recent academic and professional literature, there has been a focus on the experience of intimacy, which has mostly been judged as reflecting sexual relationships, romantic involvement or self-disclosure (i.e. the content of what people say to each other) in relationships (Giddens, 1992; Hinde, 1997; Jamieson, 1998). Different conversation styles for men and women in intimate relationships have also been highlighted (e.g. Tannen, 1998), implying that men and women may have different ways of 'doing' intimacy. While intimacy and closeness have been used interchangeably by many authors, this chapter will focus on closeness rather than intimacy as it can be seen to include as wider range of experiences. Both intimacy and closeness can be seen as more than 'speech acts', as people can also communicate or share meaning through non verbal means such as gestures (e.g. touch, facial expressions, moving towards or away from somebody, eye-contact), symbols and silences (Anderson *et al.*, 1999; Weingarten, 1991). The sociologist Jacqui Gabb has argued that all forms of intimacy are 'embodied' whether they involve a sensation of touch or a physical sensation in response to what someone says (Gabb, 2006). Rather than only being accessible through language, intimate or close relationship experiences can therefore be seen as grounded in the body and the physical setting in which people have these experiences. Factors such as housing, the geographical area in which married couples live, whether other family members are living with them and routines of everyday life can resource and also constrain women's experiences of marital closeness (Robinson, *et al.*, 2004).

To understand better everyday practices in family and couple relationships, social scientists have studied people's relationship with the material space of their homes. It has been argued that houses, rooms and objects have the power to evoke memory and emotion (e.g. Hecht, 2001; Middleton and Brown, 2005; Petridou, 2001; Reavey, 2009) and reflect individual self identities in different contexts (e.g. Miller, 2001). In a study of houses as a reflection of the self, Marcus (1995) asked her participants to draw their houses and talk about the pictures in an interview. Similarly, Hunt (1989) asked her participants to take photos of aspects of their home that they particularly valued and interviewed them about the photos in a study of gender and home life. Other research has involved participants being interviewed about their mantelpiece displays during life-history interviews about the places they have lived (Hurdley, 2006, 2007). More recently, Pink (2004) conducted video interviews where she collaboratively explored participants' homes with a video camera to draw attention to sensory experiences of smell, sound and texture of objects in relation to memory, emotion and gendered identity construction.

Visual research methods have been particularly useful in studying people's relationship to their material environment and in capturing experiences which are difficult to put into words (Frith and Harcourt, 2007; Gabb, 2008) or too abstract (Hurworth *et al.*, 2005). The technique of 'emotion maps' (Gabb, 2008) uses coloured stickers to represent emotional interactions with family members, which are placed on floor plans of family homes. The floor plans are then used to facilitate discussions about where intimate encounters occur in families. It has been argued that in conjunction with narrative interviewing and diary-based research methods, emotion maps can provide a holistic picture of family life grounded in materiality by drawing out where, when, how and why intimacy is actually done in practice (Gabb, 2008). Photography is also considered to orient participants to where intimate encounters occur as physical settings are more ready at hand when people come to describe particular experiences (Deacon, 2000). As such, the use of 'family snapshots' in interviews has been thought to enhance memory retrieval and facilitate wider discussion of family relationships (Rose, 2003). Auto-photography, where research participants are given cameras to take photos has also become popular in researching significant life experiences such as hospitalisation (Radley and Taylor, 2003a, 2003b), chemotherapy (Frith and Harcourt, 2007), homelessness (Hodgetts *et al.*, 2007), and inner-city schooling (Clark-Ibáñez, 2004). Auto-driven photo-elicitation interviews have helped to emphasise the link between the psycho-social and the material as participants do not only talk about their photos but also the relationships and issues that they associate with them (Hodgetts *et al.*, 2007). Additionally, auto-photography has been shown to be a useful tool in research with minority ethnic communities and other marginalised groups as it can allow individuals to decide what aspects of their lives to photograph and discuss at interview, rather than answering researcher-defined questions. This can be particularly useful with groups who have traditionally been less visible or heard participants in the social world (Reavey & Johnson, 2008). For example, in research on identity and self esteem, Noland (2006) considered that she was able to see the world through the eyes of her Latina and Indian women participants in the USA, whom she asked to take photos in their environment related to their identity. Other research has highlighted auto-driven photo-elicitation as a tool to increase understanding of relevant cultural and social contextual factors in Hispanic women's experience of physical activity in the USA (Fleury *et al.*, 2009; Keller, *et al.*, 2008).

Theoretical framework

Experience-based narrative research follows the work of Paul Ricoeur (1984, 1991), resting on the phenomenological assumption that the sequential temporal ordering of experience into narrative is part of what makes us human (Squire, 2008). For Ricoeur, narratives are produced through the process of emplotment, where significance is conferred on earlier events and experiences by what comes later in time. While a narrative can be traditionally described as a sequence of events over time, experience-based narrative research attempts to study particular experiences over time, thereby highlighting transformation, continuity and change. When talking about emotional experiences, individuals inevitably produce 'representations' constrained by words, phrases, and concepts that are available to them in a particular cultural context. For example, existing cultural stories of 'marriage', 'relationships' and 'South Asian women' can become resources for individuals to use in narrating their own experiences of marriage (Plummer, 1995). Critics of purely discursive approaches to research have suggested that identification with an image can be a more powerful way of capturing emotions which may be more removed from verbal articulation (Reavey and Johnson, 2008).

Reavey and Johnson (2008) also suggest that visual images can generate further talk around life experiences which do not fit neatly into pre-rehearsed personal or cultural narratives. In the current research, it was hoped that the use of photos would encourage participants to reflect more on the complexities and ambiguities of their relationships than narrative interviewing alone. Within a narrative framework, visual materials are seen as being contained within broader understandings of narrative sequence and meaningfulness (Squire, 2008). The focus is on how disjointed memories, fragments, and thoughts are brought together through emplotment as a way of making sense of experiences of close relationships over time and space. As such, visual research methods do not stand alone but are analysed in conjunction with verbal or written narratives (Pink, 2007; Radley and Taylor, 2003a; Reavey and Johnson, 2008) .

The current research

Participants for both studies were women of South Asian origin who were married and currently living in the UK. Women from different ethnic and religious groups, age groups, class backgrounds and nationalities were interviewed in order to reflect the various identifications and experiences of South Asian women in the UK. A total of 11 women took part in the first study and 8 women in the second study. Participants' ages ranged from 25 to 43 years. All interviews were conducted in English. Pseudonyms have been used to protect anonymity. Due to space constraints, narrative analysis will not be presented here in full, instead it will be illustrated how the visual methods of photo-elicitation and auto-photography were utilised by participants in order to articulate experiences of marital closeness.

Study 1 – Images and life histories: photo-elicitation

A life-history interview was conducted wherein participants were asked to talk through the different places they had lived during their teenage years and up to their present married lives and the close relationships they had in these places. To aid this process, they were asked to bring existing family photos of the homes or places in which they had lived. It was hoped that the use of family photos of homes would encourage wider discussion of experiences and family relationships. In practice, participants often brought photos of themselves or their family members and friends as these were more available to them.

At the start of the interview, the researcher asked participants to lay out their photos on the table, in no particular sequence or order. A semi-structured interview schedule was followed in which questions were asked about who participants were close to in the different places they had lived and in what ways they were close. Sometimes participants gave spontaneous accounts of their pictures, and this was used as a starting point to talk about where they had lived and the relationships they had. Where they did not engage spontaneously with their photos, the researcher attempted to encourage participants to make links to the photos. In some cases, they chose to make minimal references to the pictures, or preferred to speak without them. Overall, participants were not pushed to focus on their photos and where they were not available or not used, they were instead asked to describe their family homes and the relationships between family members and other people in these settings. To protect confidentiality, no copies were taken of participants' family photos and only interview data were transcribed and analysed.

Some participants simply drew on the photos as documentation of events or relationships, for example to point out different family members to the researcher, while others used the photos in a sequence to tell a story about their life, moving from one photo to another. References were often made to the physical intimacy apparent in certain photos, in order to comment on how close relationships had changed over time. For example, one participant compared a photo of her and her father when she was a child to a more recent photo of them. In the first photo, her father was carrying her on his shoulders, while in the later photo, her father was sitting down and she had her hands placed on his shoulders. The participant interpreted these photos as depicting changes in her closeness to her father over time, which reflected socio-cultural norms of reduced physical contact between father and daughter in adulthood. Another participant who spoke at length about being closer to her father than her mother while growing up referred to a photo which showed the 'factuality' of her and her father holding hands on her wedding day, while there were no similar photos of her and her mother. Photos were therefore used in some cases as 'evidence' for documenting closeness in family relationships, as they often depicted the embodied practices of close relationships (e.g. touching, standing close together, hugging or holding hands).

Photos were also used as a platform to connect with and explore particular emotions which were difficult to put into words or explain rationally. In one case, a participant brought out an artist's book of photos during an interview to show a photo which helped to make sense of how she didn't feel comfortable living in a particular area during her teenage years. The photo depicted an Asian woman and her children standing round a street corner staring at a white family who were dressed up and coming out of a house. The participant reflected that this was the opposite of her experience of growing up as the only Asian girl in a white area where she felt that she and her family were hyper-visible.

Analysis

Overall, photos were not used as much as it was hoped in Study 1, as most participants were not interested in engaging with them in detail, preferring to give verbal narrative accounts of their close relationships in different places. It could be that some felt that photos limited or disrupted their flow of thoughts and narratives about the relationships rather than aiding them. For the analysis, a case-study approach was adopted where narratives of closeness/lack of closeness were delineated over the course of each interview. Attention was paid to emplotment and sequencing, focussing on how close relationships (e.g. with family members, romantic partners or husbands) were described as changing or continuing over time and over different spaces and places (e.g. houses, towns, cities and countries). The particular focus was participants' ambivalent and conflicting feelings in close relationships. Each participant's interview was analysed as a case study, and similar storylines of relationships over time were then delineated across participants.

The photos themselves were not analysed in this study, however there are several examples where they trigger particular memories of interactions or episodes in close relationships, thereby inviting participants to reflect on conflicting feelings. In the following extract, Shabana, a 28-year-old British Pakistani Muslim participant who has been married for 12 years to a Pakistani man, uses a sequence of three photos to describe her ambivalent feelings about a particular time in her marriage. The first photo is of her and her husband with his male friends, the second is of her holding a teddy bear and the third is of her and her husband holding hands.

EXTRACT 1: SHABANA

S: these are also pictures of when we went to visit somebody's house but they were away so we (*her husband, his friends and herself*) stayed in their house for like 4 days or something ... like I said everybody was so much older than me, I was just alone and I used to sit around mostly and I just thought ... I'd sit and chat and stuff but everyone just used to think I was a child or you know I'm the child of the group and nobody used to talk to ... erm much, they would just laugh amongst each other and have their own little conversations – which you can see in the next picture, I'm holding a teddy bear, so I'm the child – so (...) – even there you can see – I mean we're holding hands there so ... it was alright-ish till then

R: ok

S: I remember this time as well, we had had an argument there and it was really funny [R: ok] I was feeling really left out – they've taken the picture, you can't see

R: yeah

S: coz obviously everyone's on this side

R: yeah

S: but there was about 6 other guys there at the time and I was just feeling really really left out – you know when you feel kind of inadequate, left out, because obviously they're all men and you're the only woman, and you have to keep your mouth shut and stay to one side and whatever

R: hmm

S: and I just got really annoyed and I felt really bad and I said 'I'm beginning to hate all this' and he was like ... he had this habit of telling me off like you know I'm just a kid or something – so I used to feel like 'oh god maybe I was wrong' – I mean there's a lot of self doubt coz I used to think maybe I am wrong

R: sure

S: but then ... I mean it doesn't matter now, it's done, but at that time I just felt that you know maybe if I had had a chance to sort of say that 'I don't like this, it's not fair, it's not fun' but I always had this ... I was always easily undermined – that 'oh you're wrong' – so I'd be 'ok I'm wrong'

The main narrative developed throughout Shabana's interview is the lack of emotional intimacy between her and her husband and the gradual break down of their marriage. Looking at the first photo, Shabana reflects on habitual memories of going on trips with her husband and his male friends. She describes feeling alone and ignored by the group who see her as a 'child'. At this point, she draws on the second photo as evidence, stating 'which you can see in the next photo, I'm holding the teddy bear so I'm the child'. The 'factuality' of the image suggests that holding a teddy bear, which can be seen as a powerful cultural image of childishness places Shabana in the position of a child in this situation. She quickly moves on to the last photo, of her and her husband holding hands, taken by one of her husband's friends. The physical evidence of them 'holding hands' in the photo appears to invite Shabana to reflect that 'it was alright-ish till then'. She then recalls a detailed memory of the set of events during which this photo was taken, describing an argument with her husband and feelings of being left out as the only woman in the group. She reflects on her complex and troubling feelings of being annoyed at being undermined by her husband and his male friends. She then brings us back to the present time by stating 'it doesn't matter now, it's done' signalling that her life is very different now. She concludes her reflection by employing an imaginary narrative saying 'you know maybe if I had had a chance to sort of say I don't like this …', suggesting that if she had had a chance to express her feelings to her husband without being undermined, things might have been different.

In Shabana's account, the first photo sets the scene for her to describe events and the second photo supports her narrative. The last photo, however, depicts signs of intimacy between her and her husband which cause her to reflect further on her narrative. This reflection possibly opens up a detailed memory and interpretation from Shabana about her agency in being able to communicate effectively in her marital relationship.

Study 2 – Taking photos to depict marriage: photo-production

The majority of participants in Study 1 did not engage with photos of the places where they had lived during the life-history interview, preferring to speak freely without them. Study 2 was therefore designed to make photos of places where close relationships occurred more central to the interview process. It was felt by the researcher that a focus on the objects and spaces which participants relate to in their everyday married life would allow more of an emphasis on the experience of the marital relationship than asking participants to purely speak about their married life. Such a focus was considered to potentially bring into participants' awareness aspects of their married life and relationship that do not fit easily into existing cultural narratives or ways of talking about marriage, while participants' reflections will inevitably be constrained by such narratives (Reavey and Johnson, 2008).

Different participants were recruited to take part in Study 2. They were given written instructions which invited them to take 10–12 photos, using a disposable camera provided, of objects, spaces and places that they felt were important to their experience of marriage in everyday life. Furthermore, participants were asked 'not to think about it too much', but to take photos of 'the first things that came into their heads' and were specifically asked not to take photos of people, as it was thought that most participants would otherwise take photos of their husband and family members instead of engaging with the objects and spaces of their wider material environment. Once the photos had been taken, they were asked to post the camera back to the researcher within three weeks. The instructions also stated the final part of the research would involve an informal conversation style interview with the researcher where they would be asked to briefly tell the story of their marriage and then discuss their photos which would have been developed by the researcher. Similar to Noland's (2006) research, participants often kept the cameras for a longer period of time, sometimes for 2–3 months, explaining that they were finding it difficult to find the time to think of what to photograph. The researcher developed the photos but did not view them until the participants had a chance to organise and arrange them at interview. It was felt that this would give participants a chance to filter out any that they regretted taking or did not wish to discuss at interview (Clark-Ibáñez, 2004). In contrast to the broad life-history approach taken in the previous study, participants were asked to describe how they met their husband and talk about different episodes or stages in their marriage up to the present time. This was asked to provide a background to the photos for the researcher, so that the participants would not have to constantly explain their marital history when talking about their photos.

Most participants chose to describe significant events such as their engagements, weddings, honeymoons, moving house or buying a house, and having children. While some gave a brief description of their marriage, others spoke for more than an hour in this part of the interview. They were not asked to talk specifically about marital closeness and the researcher did not often probe for further information. It was felt by the researcher that asking participants to talk specifically about closeness may allude to a canonical social science or clinical account of a 'good' marriage involving emotionality and communication. It was considered that participants might feel under pressure to present their experience in line with normative social expectations of marriage. Participants were then asked to lay their photos out in a sequence and to describe each photograph in turn, along with their reason for taking it. At the end of the interview they were asked to choose a photo or photos that best depicted their marriage and were asked which other photos they would have liked to take if they were not restricted to objects and spaces.

Some participants described difficulty in deciding what to photograph, as they would have liked to have included family members. Photos were often taken in collaboration with their husband and/or other family members, and some were taken alone. For some participants, their photos therefore reflected a joint presentation of the marriage by husband and wife or brother and sister, while for others the photos reflected a very personal account of their marriage. They were additionally asked about the process of taking photos, namely about their thought processes in deciding what to photograph and how they found the experience overall. Several participants started by thinking about important themes or issues such as emotional closeness, sexual intimacy, shared interests or passions and took photos to reflect these. Some participants attempted to take photos to tell a story of their marriage over time, while others chose to focus their photos on a particular situation in which they currently found themselves, e.g. life after the birth of a child and family members coming to live with them. One participant described walking around her house taking photos of 'whatever jumped out'. All participants described enjoying the act of taking pictures, with some valuing the time to reflect in depth on their relationship. The photos and interview together often provided a time and space to acknowledge the value of their marital relationship. A couple of participants described being a little anxious prior to the interview about what relationship issues might 'come out' of discussing the photos. Digital copies were made of the photos and participants were offered a copy of their photos at the end of the interview but they mostly declined, with only one person deciding to keep only one of her photos. It was agreed in advance that the photos would be used for research purposes only through written consent prior to interview. However participants were asked throughout the interview process to point out any photos that they would not like published in the research.

Several participants chose to tell a chronological narrative of their married life through their sequence of photos, describing different stages of their marriage. Those that did not build a chronological sequence chose particular 'themes' or 'aspects' which they considered important in their marriage overall (e.g. the sharing of culture or religion, household tasks, furnishing a home together, hobbies, and the husband's personality) and placed photos that were on similar topics together and spoke about each topic in turn. It is significant that participants often chose similar objects to photograph (e.g. houses, cars, cookers, beds, computers and televisions). Despite this, these objects symbolised a number of different things for different participants and also within each participant's narrative. Photos taken were often symbols of a marital relationship which indicated shared interests and activities, religious beliefs, values and passions as well as gifts that had been exchanged. Some photos were also used as symbols for particular feelings that were hard to describe in words (see Frith and Harcourt, 2007); for example, one participant took a photo of a flower to symbolise love, intimacy, innocence and companionship in her marriage. Other photos taken were symbols of differences or areas of tension in the marital relationship, such as the negotiation of housework. One participant, who was considering separating from her husband, took a series of photos to depict events and experiences symbolising the gradual breakdown of her marriage, such as arguments or conflict over a house, car and finances, sleeping in different bedrooms, and the husband's relationship with their children.

Analysis

Each interview was analysed by paying attention to the sequencing or thematic arrangement of photos in each interview along with participants' narrative meaning making around them. The researcher considered whether there was a main storyline or plot that each participant was trying to convey, and how the photos aided or constrained this process. Often, particular photos triggered memories for participants, opening up other storylines that they had not previously considered. In some cases, participants used their photos to tell a chronological story over time, while in other cases, the arrangement of photos conveyed a 'snapshot' of their married life at the present time. Since several participants photographed similar objects and spaces, narratives related to different categories of photo (as discussed above) were also analysed across the eight interviews in this study.

Case study: Zahra

In the following interview, Zahra, a 25-year-old British Pakistani Muslim woman who has been married for three years to a British Pakistani man, uses her photos to convey an overall storyline of the couple's closeness and adjustment to each other being recently disrupted by her mother-in-law coming to live with them.

While Zahra's first and last photo indicate a chronological sequence, each remaining photo does not follow a clear sequence or theme, but depicts the disruption of married life for her. Each object or space therefore encompasses her feeling about the past ('how things were') and the present ('how things have changed'). Each object or space is significant in Zahra's daily experience of disruption in her married life. The first photo is the place where her husband proposed to her, while the last photo of an estate agents reflects her hope of

Figure 6.1 The television. 'The photograph was produced by the participant for research purposes to depict a space which she felt was important in her everyday experience of marriage'.

moving away from her mother-in-law by moving house. The sequence of remaining photos includes their car, the cooker, the television, their house, her parents' house, and their bed. Due to space constraints, only one photo will be examined here alongside Zahra's explanation of why she chose it, to illustrate how she uses the image to help her construct and compare narratives of the past and the present.

EXTRACT 2: ZAHRA

Z: that one, erm … that's this room, the telly – that's the way we spend a lot of our time together or we did spend a lot of our time watching TV in the evenings when you come home from work but now not so much … don't really watch TV here coz as I said his mum's watching her programmes here so we don't really watch it anymore. I think that was just something so we could unwind, just relax and you know just lounge about

R: hmm

Z: don't get that relaxing kind of time anymore – there's nothing for you to do (…)

R: so that was a valued part of your relationship that has kind of been lost for the temporary period?

Z: exactly – it was almost like to get dinner ready in time for Eastenders, that was the aim – get through the door, get dinner ready in time for Eastenders, erm you know jump in front of the TV, watch Eastenders and have dinner, that was the time that we had

R: so it's like an unwinding?

Z: yeah – after I drive home from my mum's it's a bit difficult, you prefer to unwind at home but you're having to do it somewhere else, and it's freezing nowadays – (…) I'd prefer it if we could just relax at home and just watch our TV, just put a DVD on or something … It's only because I want that sense of that home, I just want that feeling which is why I think I go there coz I don't think I get that, coz to me it's quite important.

R: sure

Z: so I'm in search of that feeling and once I get it and I feel like I've topped myself up with it, now I'm going to go back home, and that's it. That's what it is.

The photo shows a large television in the corner of a living room with a coffee table, sofa and curtains on either side of it. The floor has a beige carpet, giving the room a feeling of warmth. Zahra appears to have taken it while standing in the corner of the room. This photo comes in the middle of her sequence of objects and spaces. The photo is introduced as 'this room, the telly', as a place where Zahra and her husband spend time together, watching TV to unwind and relax. The present and the past conflict in Zahra's narrative, as she moves backwards and forwards in time, explaining that this way of spending time with her husband is now a thing of the past. This space is now used by her mother-in-law who watches 'her programmes' there. Zahra describes that she and her husband used to have a habitual routine of getting dinner ready in time to watch the soap-opera 'Eastenders'. To relax and unwind, she drives to her mum's house, to get that 'sense of home' and 'top herself up' with that feeling before returning to her own home late at night. The image of the television and living room symbolise for Zahra that sense of 'home', that has been lost even if the space and objects are still there. It also represents a loss of this special time with her husband.

It is significant that Zahra has had time to reflect on the sequence of photos she wishes to present at interview and the story she wishes to show as well as tell to the researcher. As well as evoking memories of the past, arranging the photos and describing her reasons for taking them allows Zahra to reflect more deeply on her feelings of the loss of 'home'. Taken together, her sequence of photos depicts both the cosiness and intimacy of the past and the feeling that it has been lost since her mother-in-law has moved in with her and her husband. Taking the photos in the context of the research interview allowed Zahra to show the researcher the practical issues involved in 'doing intimacy' in marriage, rather than only talking about her married life. The photos themselves therefore have no particular meaning outside of the personal meanings that flow through them, as described in the verbal accounts.

Discussion

The aim of the two studies was to explore the experience of closeness in participants' lives and particularly in marriage. As well as examining how closeness is conceptualised and spoken about using established cultural narratives, it was hoped that the use of visual methods with the focus on spaces, places and objects would emphasise aspects of relationships that are taken for granted such as the everyday 'doing' of close relationships. However, a narrative approach recognises that participants' accounts cannot provide a direct access to their lived experience, but reflect narrative structures and resources available to them as they tell their story. Furthermore, it must be remembered that visual narratives, like oral and written ones, are created for audiences and 'do not generate unmediated, unclassed portraits of an "essential self"' (Riessman, 2008: 177). Empirical research data are not created spontaneously by participants in everyday life but are always created with an audience in mind.

Therefore visual methods may not necessarily generate 'more authentic' representations of experience but may disrupt or rupture cultural or personal narratives by encouraging more reflection and thought in selecting objects and spaces to photograph (Riessman, 2008). While chronological sequencing over time is a defining feature of narrative accounts, the use of photos in both studies appeared to momentarily displace pre-rehearsed narratives of relationships, opening up memories and reflections that were not always readily available to individuals (Reavey and Johnson, 2008). In both of the current research studies, participants were often surprised when photos evoked particular feelings and memories that they had not fully anticipated.

In this brief discussion, I will consider the particular role played by photos in the two studies described. In Study 1, it was hoped that family photos of participants' homes would play a major part in anchoring and structuring participants' life histories through the evoking of particular memories and feelings. However, it was often difficult to find photos of the places they had lived and participants mostly did not wish to engage with their family photos when giving an account of their lives. This may reflect the fact that the majority of participants felt limited and constrained by family photos when presenting a verbal account of their life. For those that did engage with them, the photos were sometimes used to reflect back on particular memories and emotions associated with certain events and experiences in light of the participant's present situation. However, the photos were more often used as documentary evidence of particular events or relationships at particular times. Since the family photos were not taken for research purposes and were mostly not taken by the participants themselves, they may not have held personal meaning for participants in the research context. Additionally, the memories and experiences evoked would be limited by the range of family photos available to participants to bring to the interview. Therefore, it could be that participants felt more freedom to reflect on and construct their life histories without their photos.

In contrast, the photos taken by participants for Study 2 can be seen to reflect their 'way of seeing' their world at the present time (Berger, 1972), for the purposes of the research, rather than a mechanical record. The photos could therefore be used to symbolise feelings and relationships as well as documenting events and activities (Frith and Harcourt, 2007). Auto-driven photo-production has been considered to be useful for allowing research participants to select experiences and aspects of their lives that are meaningful to them and giving them more control over what they discuss at interview (Clark-Ibáñez, 2004; Samuels, 2004). For example, a semi-structured interview schedule was followed in Study 1, where participants were asked who they were close to while living in particular places and how they were close. It is possible that participants felt the need to give normative accounts of their close relationships based on what they felt the researcher wanted to hear and what was socially and culturally acceptable. In Study 2, participants were not asked particular questions about their marital relationship but were able to focus on how the photos they had taken were meaningful to them. This has been described by Samuels (2004), in his auto-driven photo-elicitation study of the lives of young Buddhist monks in Sri Lanka, as, the 'breaking of the frames' of the researcher. He found that participants often highlighted meaningful activities such as sweeping, which he did not initially consider to be important to monastic life.

The data in Study 2 emphasised the private worlds, everyday lives and environments of participants which would not normally be accessible to researchers (Frith and Harcourt, 2007), as well as drawing attention to the more practical side of 'doing closeness' in marriage. Photos of spaces and objects depicted how and where closeness was done and which aspects of everyday life resourced or constrained experiences of closeness in married life (see Ahmed *et al.*, 2008).

Several participants reflected that taking the photos had made them think deeply about the constitutive aspects of their married life. Using visual images to separate married life into different components may therefore provide more depth and may draw out aspects and experiences which may not normally be discussed in verbal interviewing alone. Similarly, Samuels (2004) found that through discussing their photos, his participants gave richer, more concrete descriptions based on their personal experience, emotions and interactions with others than in word-only interviews.

In summary, the use of photos of physical spaces and places where marriage and relationships are played out allowed participants to explore memories and emotions associated with these material settings. It has been argued that photos do not elicit more information, but a different type of information (Harper, 1998). In verbal accounts, participants can be seen as accounting for being in close relationships with particular people (e.g. husbands and family members) as well as for their behaviour in close relationships. In the current research, photos allowed participants access to more specific memories than verbal narrative methods alone and a deeper exploration of subjective, relational and spatially located experiences of close relationships. This was achieved using images, as well as words to represent and articulate a particular experience, memory or feeling to the researcher. A continuous shifting back and forth between verbal and visual meaning making therefore provided the opportunity for new insights and feelings arising from the discussion of photos to be re-integrated back into narrative reflections of marriage and relationships.

Note

1 The term 'South Asian' is usually taken to refer to people who originate from the Indian Subcontinent which may include countries such as India, Bangladesh, Pakistan, Nepal, Sri Lanka, Maldives and Bhutan.

References

Ahmed, B., Reavey, P., and Majumdar, A. (2008). Cultural transformations and gender violence: South Asian Women's experiences of sexual violence and familial dynamics. In K. Throsby and F. Alexander (Eds.), *Gender and interpersonal violence: language, action and representation*. Hampshire: Palgrave Macmillan.

Anderson, H., Carleton, D., and Swim, S. (1999). A postmodern perspective on relational intimacy: collaborative conversation and relationship with a couple. In J. Carlson and L. Sperry (Eds.), *The intimate couple*. Philadelphia, PA: Bruner/ Mazel, pp. 208–226.

Berger, J. (1972). *Ways of seeing*. London: Penguin Books.

Clark-Ibáñez, M. (2004). Framing the social world with photo-elicitation interviews. *American Behavioral Scientist, 47*(12), 1507–1527.

Deacon, S. A. (2000). Creativity within qualitative research on families: new ideas for old methods. *The Qualitative Report, 4*(3 & 4). Available at http://www.nova.edu/ssss/QR/ QR4-3/deacon.html.

Fleury, J., Keller, C., and Perez, A. (2009). Exploring resources for physical activity in Hispanic women, using photo elicitation. *Qualitative Health Research, 19*(5), 677–686.

Frith, H., and Harcourt, D. (2007). Using photographs to capture women's experiences of chemotherapy: reflecting on the method. *Qualitative Health Research*, *17*(10), 1340–1350.

Gabb, J. (2006). *Reviewing intimacy*: Available at www.researchingfamilies.co.uk.

Gabb, J. (2008). *Researching intimacy in families*. London: Palgrave MacMillan.

Giddens, A. (1992). *The transformation of intimacy*. Stanford, CA: Stanford University Press.

Harper, D. (1998). An argument for visual sociology. In J. Prosser (Ed.), *Image-based research: a sourcebook for qualitative researchers*. London: Falmer Press.

Hecht, A. (2001). Home sweet home: tangible memories of an uprooted childhood. In D. Miller (Ed.), *Home possessions*. Oxford: Berg.

Hinde, R. A. (1997). *Relationships: a dialectical perspective*. East Sussex: Psychology Press, pp. 57–61.

Hodgetts, D., Radley, A., Chamberlain, K., and Hodgetts, A. (2007). Health inequalities and homelessness: considering material, spatial and relational dimensions. *Journal of Health Psychology*, *12*(5), 709–725.

Hunt, P. (1989). Gender and the construction of home life. In G. Allen and G. Crow (Eds.), *Home and family: creating the domestic sphere*. Basingstoke: Palgrave, pp. 66–81.

Hurdley, R. (2006). Dismantling mantelpieces: narrating identities and materializing culture in the home. *Sociology*, *40*(4), 717–733.

Hurdley, R. (2007). Focal Points: framing material culture and visual data. *Qualitative Research*, *7*(3), 355–374.

Hurworth, R., Clark, E., Martin, J., and Thomsen, S. (2005). The use of photo-interviewing: three examples from health evaluation and research. *Evaluation Journal of Australasia*, *4*(1/2), 52–62.

Jamieson, L. (1998). *Intimacy*. Oxford: Blackwell.

Keller, C., Fleury, J., Perez, A., Ainsworth, B., and Vaughan, L. (2008). Using visual methods to uncover context. *Qualitative Health Research*, *18*(3), 428–436.

Marcus, C. C. (1995). *House as a mirror of self: exploring the deeper meaning of home*. Berkeley, CA: Conari Press.

Middleton, D. and Brown, S. D. (2005). *The social psychology of experience: studies in remembering and forgetting*. London: Sage, pp. 42–58.

Miller, D. (2001). Behind closed doors. In D. Miller (Ed.), *Home possessions*. Oxford: Berg.

Noland, C. M. (2006). Auto-photography as research practice: identity and self-esteem research. *Journal of Research Practice*, *2*(1).

Petridou, E. (2001). The taste of home. In D. Miller (Ed.), *Home Possessions*. Oxford: Berg.

Pink, S. (2004). *Home truths: gender, domestic objects and everyday life*. Oxford: Berg.

Pink, S. (2007). *Doing visual ethnography*. London: Sage.

Plummer, K. (1995). *Telling sexual stories*. London: Routledge.

Radley, A. and Taylor, D. (2003a). Remembering one's stay in hospital: a study in photography, recovery and forgetting. *Health: An Interdisciplinary Journal for the Social Study of Health*, *7*(2), 129–159.

Radley, A. and Taylor, D. (2003b). Images of recovery: a photo-elicitation study on the hospital word. *Qualitative Health Research*, *13*(1), 77–99.

Reavey, P. (2009). The spaces of memory: rethinking agency through materiality. In J. Haaken and P. Reavey (eds.) *Memory matters: contexts for understanding sexual abuse recollections*. London: Routledge.

Reavey, P. and Johnson, K. (2008). Visual approaches: using and interpreting images in qualitative research. In C. Willig and W. Stainton Rogers (Eds.), *The Sage handbook of qualitative research in psychology*. London: Sage, pp. 296–314.

Ricouer, P. (1984). *Time and narrative*. Chicago, IL: Chicago University Press.

Ricouer, P. (1991). Life in quest of narrative. In D. Wood (Ed.), *On Paul Ricouer: narrative and interpretation*. London: Routledge.

Riessman, C. K. (2008). *Narrative methods for the human sciences*. Thousand Oaks, CA and London: Sage, pp. 141–182.

Robinson, V., Hockey, J., and Meah, A. (2004). 'What I used to do ... on my mother's settee': spatial and emotional aspects of heterosexuality in England. *Gender, Place and Culture*, *11*(3), 417–435.

Rose, G. (2003). Family photographs and domestic spacings: a case study. *Transactions of the Institute of British Geographers*, *28*(1), 5–8.

Samuels, J. (2004). Breaking the ethnographer's frames: reflections on the use of photo-elicitation in understanding Sri Lankan monastic culture. *American Behavioral Scientist*, *47*(12), 1528–1550.

Squire, C. (2008). Experience-centred and culturally-orientated approaches to narrative. In M. Andrews, C. Squire and M. Tamboukou (Eds.), *Doing narrative research*. London: Sage, pp. 41–63.

Tannen, D. (1998). Talk in the intimate relationship: his and hers. In J. Coates (Ed.), *Language and gender: a reader*. Oxford: Blackwell.

Weingarten, K. (1991). The discourses of intimacy: adding a social constructionist and feminist view. *Family Process*, *30*(3), 285–305.

Part II

Moveable features

Using Facebook and video in qualitative research

7 Textuality and visuality in MySpace communication

Lewis Goodings and Steven D. Brown

Ecstasy is all functions abolished into one dimension, the dimension of communication. All events, all spaces, all memories are abolished in the sole dimension of information: this is obscene.

(Baudrillard, 1988: 24)

Introduction

This chapter describes communicative practices amongst users of the social network site (SNS) MySpace. MySpace is one of a growing number of online sites where users are able to connect through a number of activities that have been popular in the wider use of Internet-based communication (e.g. blogging, photo sharing, status updates). In MySpace these activities are co-located in one place – the profile. We are concerned here with the manner in which the visual 'look' and content of individual profiles assists in preparing the way or clearing the ground for communication between users. Drawing on Baudrillard we refer to this preparatory act as 'urcommunication'. This is dominated by the phatic function of signalling one's availability for communication (see Malinowski, 1923). In exploring urcommunicative practices we hope to show how the visual and the textual become intertwined as essential supports for one another.

A common criticism of social networking is that the communication which occurs across these sites (e.g. Facebook, Twitter, MySpace) is essentially empty, lacking in substantive content (Buffardi and Campbell, 2008; Rosen, 2007). 'Posts', 'pokes' and 'tweets' between users are then to be understood as predominantly narcissistic, in effect advertisements or promotions made by individual users rather than genuine attempts to engage in meaningful dialogue. Such a view finds confirmation in both the relative paucity of what is communicated, which tends to be dominated by the visual para-language of emoticons, and the overall design of many profiles, which are often dominated by photographs of users and animated icons.

We regard such criticisms as founded in a mistrust of the role of the visual in communication and a relative prioritisation of the discursive as the primary medium of meaning-making (see Jay, 1994 for historical roots). From a psychological perspective the visual is treated as an adornment or a supplement to the textual. It is not interesting in its own right. By contrast, we view the visual as an essential component of a multi-modal matrix of urcommunicative possibilities. It is through the work of designing and fashioning their profile that individual users are able to position (and re-position) themselves in a social network community. In this chapter we will explore some of the ways in which this happens by focusing on profile changes.

The chapter is organised as follows. First, we provide some context for a social psychological treatment of MySpace profiles. Second, we describe our methodological approach and the theoretical principles out of which it is constituted. Third, we offer an analysis of data from an individual MySpace profile. Finally, we reflect on the status of the visual and its importance for a psychological understanding of mediated communication.

MySpace profiles

MySpace.com is an online social network site (SNS) that allows members to share discussions, photographs, videos and blogs with a global network of members. Since its launch in 2003 the population of MySpace has grown exponentially and it now records around 114 million unique page views per month (ComScore, 2008). Most recently, the number of users seems to have hit a consistent level as sites such as Facebook (www.facebook.com) are now experiencing the high influx of users that MySpace encountered a few years ago. Even though a large proportion of MySpace users reside in the USA, there is also a large fan base of members who live in the UK (Prescott, 2007).

As with most other SNSs the MySpace user is able to communicate with 'friends' (people they have added over the MySpace network) in a number of ways. The most easily recognised area of communication is that which takes place on the 'wall' (a predefined area of the page where other members can leave reverse chronological comments). Comments on the wall are assigned the default photograph of the person who is sending the comment. This photograph will automatically carry a hyperlink that can take the user to the MySpace page of the comment sender. This is one way that communication builds; by the user flipping between their own page and the pages of others. This is an intrinsically public conversation as any other user is privy to both halves of the conversation. This has led to the conclusion for many authors that MySpace is part of a wider identity performance (boyd and Heer, 2006).

MySpace users are connected through the profile pages they create (also called their 'My-Space'). These can vary significantly based on the nature of the SNS, for example, LinkedIN endorses a very professional appearance while Facebook has a more informal feel. However, all profiles are designed in a similar layout that is typically a passport-style photograph at the top of the page and a carefully constructed set of information in self-contained boxes over the rest of the page. boyd and Ellison (2007) argue that organising the layout of a MySpace page is a socialisation process that is at the centre of its popularity.

The profile page is the first place a member checks when they log into MySpace. It is the hub of everything else: the wall, the blogs, shared photographs and all of the personal information. The profile page has been found to be a place of building social capital (Ellison *et al*., 2006) and of facilitating tasks of the group (Preece and Maloney-Krichmar, 2003). The 'friending' application has also been of particular interest as the means through which the profile becomes networked and shared. This has led to the discovery that being in the 'top 8' (a section of the profile that indicates a certain friend is in the select group of the top eight friends) has significance over being on a separate page with the majority of friends (boyd, 2006).

Profile changes can be simply defined as updating or shifting certain aspects of the profile page using the profile editor that is accessible only to the main user. This operates in a separate location away from the profile page itself. In this location users are able to access and update information that is presented on their main profile. The changes could range from a small change (e.g. song choice, display name or mood setting) to a large change (typically an entire background change). Regular visits to the profile page have been found to increase the likelihood of more 'friends' (Thelwall, 2008a). This would appear to be one reason to continually update the profile page.

Psychology, computer mediated communication and the visual

There is a tradition of studying 'computer-mediated communication' from a psychological perspective which predates the emergence of SNSs (see Sproull and Kiesler, 1991; Wallace, 1999; Joinson, 2003; Gackenbach, 2006). Typically such approaches consider the effects of the medium being used on both the form and the content of the messages exchanged between users (i.e. such as in an email, an instant message or a posting). A classic finding in such work is that visual anonymity – the inability to see or be seen by the person with whom you are communicating – has effects on established psychological processes such as self-disclosure, identity management and group polarisation (see Spears *et al*., 1990; Spears and Lea, 1994; Walther, 1996; Joinson, 2001a, 2001b). For example, increased levels of visual anonymity tend to lead to increased levels of self-disclosure (Locke and Gilbert, 1995).

What is striking here is that the visual is narrowly defined as the simple act of looking at the body of another person. Face-to-face verbal interaction is, then, considered the default model of communication. Both communicative partners feel present to and fully aware of the other (see Short *et al*., 1976). The visual provides additional information or cues which enable speakers to overcome potential interactional difficulties such as equivocation and ambiguity and to effectively manage self-presentation. All other forms of communication mediated by technology – from letter writing and telephone calls to emails and instant messaging – are treated as deficient or restricted, as somehow less 'rich' (see Daft and Lengel, 1984) due to the comparative absence of information provided by the visual, resulting in a range of communication problems. For instance, the Reduced Social Cues approach (Kiesler *et al.*, 1984; McGuire *et al.*, 1987; Sproull and Kiesler, 1986; Siegel *et al.*, 1986) shows that a lack of non-verbal cues in online interaction leads to an increase in deregulated, uninhibited behaviour. Such difficulties can be overcome when visual (i.e. non- or para-linguistic) elements are reintroduced into messages, such as 'emoticons' in text messages or icons and small graphics in postings (Wallace, 1999; Krohn, 2004).

The problem with a great deal of work in this tradition is that it remains in thrall to a mechanistic model of communication derived from classical information theory. Communication is understood as the exchange of information via the primary medium or spoken and written language and secondarily through non-verbal/para-linguistic visual cues. The shortcomings of such an approach have been detailed at length in the many trenchant critiques provided by Discursive Psychology (DP) over the past two and a half decades (for example, Potter and Wetherell, 1987; Edwards, 1997; Edwards and Potter, 2005; Potter, 2006). From the perspective of DP, talk-in-interaction is the default model of communication, whereby parties to conversation jointly build meaning and context together in the sequential, rhetorically structured unfolding of naturally occurring talk. Here non-linguistic elements such as pauses, fillers (i.e. 'umm', 'err'), emotional displays (i.e. sobs, sighs) and gestures are all taken to be discursive resources which are woven into the ongoing interaction. Approaches such as Susan Herring's (2004) 'computer-mediated discourse analysis' have applied these principles to look at the interactional design and receipt of text messages, emails and sequential postings (see also Yates, 2001; Lamerichs and te Molder, 2003; Benwell and Stokoe, 2006).

DP-based approaches can deliver detailed micro-analysis of the sorts of interactions which occur on the 'wall' posting area of MySpace profiles. They are more difficult to apply to the entirety of the profile, where it is implausible to treat the combinations of text and images which make up the majority of the profile page as turns in a conversation. We might instead see these juxtaposed elements as invitations or solicitations to communication. Changes to a MySpace profile signal not only that a person is there, but more importantly, that they are ready to communicate. We use the term *urcommunication* to refer to the presentation of material (e.g. text, images) that does not formally constitute a direct opening turn in a communicative act with a given recipient, but is instead positioned to appeal to communication. The act of posting a new piece of information to a MySpace page may *or may not* be the start of a conversation. There are an infinite amount of communication possibilities that could form at any moment. Rather, the profile does a detailed work of establishing communicative possibilities which may (or may not) come to be actualised in subsequent interactions through wall posting.

More specifically, by treating the profile as urcommunication we can see that the visual elements of the profile are not simply in the service of the textual elements in such a way that they may be understood as para-linguistic support for discourse and talk. The combinations of visual and textual elements do not conform to the default communicative model of talk-in-interaction because there is no clearly defined recipient/reader. For example, imagine that one profile prominently displayed an image taken from a category of 'horror films'. If we take a discursive approach to studying this reference then we would assume that the use of the image invoked other members to take this up as a potential first turn – an opening – in an interaction that could unfold by thematising the category of horror films (e.g. 'Great pic! One of my top movies. You know the sequel? That's better IMHO'). What, though, if nobody picks up on the image in this way? Has the potential to communicate been lost? Has it 'failed' or 'mis-fired' in some way? Or is there something more to the visual, something which exceeds the confines of talk-in-interaction? Our argument is that images and text combine in the profile to create a space where communication is possible, but not inevitable. The complex patterns of words, photographs and graphic elements which make up the profile page set up puzzles or problems, which in turn serve as solicitations to discourse rather than explicit 'first turns' for interaction.

Methodological approach

The form of visual analysis which we have developed to study MySpace profiles draws on three principles:

1   *Sequentiality*. Studies in Conversation and Discourse Analysis have demonstrated the sequential organisation of turns in conversation such that each successive turn is 'fitted to' or displays acknowledgement of the preceding turn. Certain kinds of turns, such as questions and invitations, are explicitly designed to facilitate a preferred response (Schegloff and Sacks, 1973; Pomerantz, 1978, 1984; Sacks, 1987). When the next action does not occur as expected this can be overtly noticeable to other members of the conversation (Goodwin and Heritage, 1990). We use the principle of sequentiality to follow the design and receipt of wall postings. We also use this principle to explore the relationship between changes in the visual design of a profile and previous communicative exchanges, whereby a change in the layout may be understood as fitted to or acknowledging a previous exchange.

2   *Relationality*. Semiotics is concerned with the ways that signs carry meaning and significance in everyday life through analysis of the structure of signs in relation to cultural systems, artefacts and rituals (see Eco, 1987; Blonsky, 1985). The concept of 'relationality' is central to semiotic analysis. Any given sign is only explicable through the relations which obtain between it and the other signs which together constitute a system of meaning and comprehension. When applied to visual material, this principle invites analysis of how symbolic and pictorial elements are combined to structure particular kinds of messages. For example, the names given to housing developments coupled with the images displayed on 'for sale' signs act together to connote particular kinds of class and lifestyle aspirations (see Gottdiener, 1987). Here we invoke this principle to question what the purposes may be of the particular juxtapositions of text and image on MySpace profiles.

3   *Signal/noise.* Michel Serres (1980, 1982) draws on information theory to observe that human communication is a mixture of signal and noise. Usually noise is treated as an extraneous element that disrupts communication. Serres argues that noise is instead integral to a message since it is in the process of actively differing from noise that the signal gains its standing. For example, holding the attention of another in casual conversation depends on rendering the rest of the auditory field as uninteresting, as 'noise', against which the present conversation is meaningful and stimulating. But Serres goes on to argue that whilst the sender may seek to perform a particular distribution between signal and noise, there is no guarantee that this will be maintained by the recipient (see Brown, 2002, 2004). For instance, a ringing mobile phone may undo our efforts to sustain a conversation with another, who now consigns our attention as noise to be overcome by a new signal. We follow this principle to explore how combinations of image and text on a MySpace profile serve to define relations of relevancy and irrelevancy which may become reversible across the course of changes to the profile.

Data collection

The nature of this volume calls for a certain depth in describing the use of the visual and textual objects in MySpace profiles. For this reason we have decided to present only one long extract as opposed to a variety of shorter ones. The dataset from which this example is taken was gathered from publicly accessible MySpace pages. In total, 100 profiles were gathered using the 'browse' function from the MySpace site. MySpace browse function uses a complex algorithm to align search criteria based on the MySpace userID. All of the search criteria where aligned to the default settings except 'location' and '[what are you] here for' – they were appropriately set to UK and networking. The profiles selected were monitored for a month, with all activity occurring on the profile, however small, recorded through screenshots from the page. In the example discussed here, all proper names have been replaced with pseudonyms and the unique MySpace userID has been disguised in the presentation of the data. Pictures of users have also been modified to disguise identity.

With regard to research ethics, the data were gathered from publicly accessible MySpace pages and could be researched without the need for formal ethical considerations (in the same way as studying data from newspaper sources). However, several attempts were made to make contact with the author of the data when originally gathered (early 2007) and subsequently. Unfortunately no response was received and the profile was subsequently deleted. MySpace itself deletes those pages that have a high level of inactivity and there is a high likelihood that the profile was deleted by MySpace. There is therefore no possibility that the author of these data could be traced through the site. All other safety precautions have been taken to ensure the protection of the MySpace users that feature in this chapter. Many researchers who have researched MySpace would not protect the authors to the same extent as we have here due to the public nature of the site as a whole (see Moreno *et al.*, 2008; Thelwall, 2008b, 2009 and for discussion of MySpace as a 'technopanic' see Marwick, 2008).

Analysis

The data will be analysed in terms of the three analytic principles described above. We use these principles as guides in our analytic engagement with the profiles. The analysis is organised in terms of three sets of relations.

1: Urcommunicative relations

Jane's profile background is made up of a mixture of black and gold sparks that emanate from an explosive, firework-like blast in the bottom right-hand corner of the screen (see Figure 7.1). This background was most likely downloaded from a large selection of possible backgrounds. The clothes Jane is wearing in the default photo accentuate the colours in the background. It appears that Jane has chosen a photograph that has a close-up style where she is looking directly into the camera. The photograph then builds itself as signal but simultaneously relating to and distinguishing itself from the totality of the MySpace background. The background is elegantly crafted to appear in each of the separate areas of the profile as if it is connected to the overall image as a whole (this is most notably seen in the information box directly beneath the profile picture).

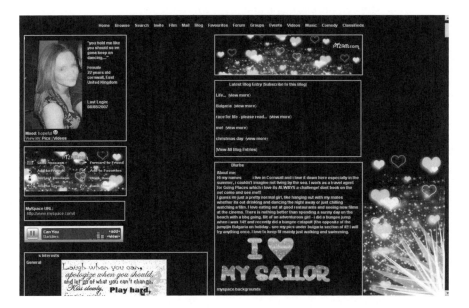

Figure 7.1 Extract 1. Jane's MySpace profile.

How does this visual element afford the possibility of communication? Drawing on the relationality principle, we can see that the image which originates in the bottom right-hand corner draws the eye towards the top of the screen. Once the gaze has been led to the top of the screen it is met by an empty box (which would display '[Jane] is in your network' if the person looking was friends with Jane) that has an identical background image to the interaction box. This similarity then continues to lead the gaze directly to the information box. In this box there are numerous ways to contact Jane. So we see that through relational organisation of the background the page does not reify Jane's existence, it subtly guides the user's attention through the visual towards a possibility of communication.

It is customary for MySpace users to regularly update their 'mood' by changing their status in the profile editor. Unlike other SNSs (e.g. Facebook allows users to type in anything they please as their status), MySpace users have to choose from a list of possible moods, each of which is allocated a representation of the chosen mood as an emoticon [when shown] on the main page. In Jane's profile she is listed as 'hopeful' and the emoticon displays a smiley face. Presumably, there are a number of connotations of the word 'hopeful' that do not bring the entirely positive sentiment that is presented in the smiley face emoticon. In many cases, conceptualisations of hopefulness are tied to a specific event, e.g. Sue is hopeful she will pass her driving test, I am hopeful she will get through the exam. So what then is Jane hopeful for?

On asking this question the purposes for this mood choice become clear. This is the question that was intended from such a mood selection. The ability to see the *relation* between the emoticon and the word 'hopeful' suggests to the viewer that there is a high potential of a positive outcome of a situation, but the details of what Jane is engaged with are unclear. This prompts an easy opportunity for the question 'how are you doing?'. The reference to the mood conducts the first pair part (FPP) of the sequence. Harvey Sacks and Emmanuel Schegloff describe how such sequence organisation can be achieved through recourse to an 'adjacency pair' (Schegloff and Sacks, 1973). This is a rhetorical device which enables turn taking through a kind of call-and-response structure. It consists of a FPP which is typically met by an established second pair part (SPP). Both the words and images construct the visuality of this relation in a way that promotes the possibility of communication through building a FPP into the design of the page. This could also be understood through another conversation analytic technique, that of 'try-marking' (Sacks and Schegloff, 1979; Schegloff, 1996). Try-marking refers to the way sequencing is initiated when the speaker is unsure of the recipient's response. Different interactional markers attempt to recruit the receiver's reference form. The posts to a public MySpace page are similarly intending to try a range of interactional markers to enlist communication from a range of other users.

Urcommunication relies on continual try-marking through the introduction of textual and visual FPPs on the MySpace page. For example, in her 'blurb', Jane describes herself in the following way:

I guess im just a pretty normal girl, like hanging out with my mates whether its out drinking and dancing the night away or just chilling watching a film.

The use of the phrase 'pretty normal girl' could be seen as an example of conversational 'minimisation' (Pomerantz, 1986; Edwards, 2000). These devices construct Jane as just like everybody else, and in essence, a typical MySpace member who likes the same activities as the perceived audience. This can be seen in the background image that is wild and exciting yet organised and controlled. This constitutes Jane for a wide range of communication sources as both a 'party animal' and yet someone who is merely contented with staying in. For Jane, each of these positions offers a potential signal for communication. The profile thereby accomplishes a subtle management of the relationship between the visual and the textual. This duality of communication is shown most vividly in her profile photograph with the daring, almost confrontational direct gaze into the camera lens that is steadied by the sophistication of her body language and attire.

2: Relations between profiles

Consider the following changes made to Jane's profile within two days of the status considered above (see Figure 7.2).

The changes to Jane's profile, although seemingly inconsequential, do represent a significant change to the urcommunicative environment. To begin, the default

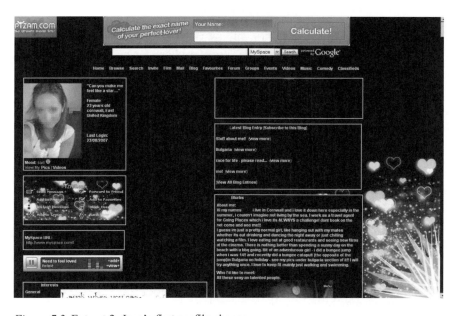

Figure 7.2 Extract 2. Jane's first profile change.

English_Rose   28 Aug 2007 3:07

Hey Jane, How r u? i haven't really spoken 2 u properly since u have

been added 2 my list of friends, Hope everything is cool!!

Take care!

English_Rose x

Figure 7.3 Extract 3. Wall post from English Rose to Jane.

photo has been changed for one that opens the body to the camera and features a more natural setting. However, this sense of naturalness is not easily achieved and requires a certain degree of effort and construction. For example, the blue of Jane's eyes appear to have been matched to the background object and the colour of the emoticon that is present in the mood setting. The mood icon has itself been changed from 'hopeful' to 'sad' and consequently the emoticon also mirrors this change. Can we assume that this sadness means that Jane no longer wishes to communicate?

In fact, it is quite the opposite. At the same time as the change, Jane experiences an increased number of posts to her wall, many of which are related to the changes to her page (see Figure 7.3). It appears that merely being 'hopeful' does not generate communicative response to the profile. However, the switch from hopefulness to sadness, where the former is the noise against which this new signal distinguished itself, appears to provide better urcommunicative possibilities. Notice that English Rose (in Figure 7.3) does not refer to the recent profile changes and offers Jane instead some good news; 'haven't really spoken 2 u properly since u have been added 2 my list of friends'. The extended use of exclamation marks in the post from English Rose can be read as an affective use of paralanguage that attempts to bridge the gap between the statement 'hope everything is cool' and the plausible interpretation of the profile where everything is not 'cool'.

Further support for the urcommunicative shift in the profile can be seen in the display name modification from 'you hold me like you should so im gona keep on dancing' to 'Can you make me feel like a star…'. Both lines reference the specific role of the other in facilitating Jane's happiness, but the latter seems to take a more direct approach. The second display name was better able to reduce the 'noise' and communicate the message more successfully. In light of the other changes to the page, the display name may have prompted the audience to act quickly. Profile changes not only encourage communication with other people, but they also make use of conversations with our (own) selves.

3: Relations between the visual and the textual

The second change to the profile is more drastic than the first (see Figure 7.4). Most notably, the background has been substituted for an entirely new style of

Figure 7.4 Extract 4. Jane's second profile change.

'electro' colours that dart around her profile photograph. Again, it appears that the visual representation of Jane's mood has changed as she is now portrayed as 'happy'. In the new profile photograph Jane appears provocative, up-close and seductive. This is reflected in her body language and her choice of clothing.

We can read this change as a sequentially organised response to the messages from English Rose (in Figure 7.3) that communicates a movement back to a happy emotional state through the visual layout of the profile. The textual is acknowledged through the visual, words answered with pictures, colours and typographic shifts. Of particular note is that the profile name has changed from 'Jane' to 'JaNe'. What might be the reason for the new capital letter in the middle of the name? This is no typo – to make this change it would have been necessary to enter into the profile editor and select 'change display name'. What the use of JaNe does is to make a distinction between the current profile and its previous iterations. The current profile is presented as signal – that which is relevant, of interest, acknowledgement – by setting itself against the noise of the previous versions of the profile, which are now to be understood as irrelevant, uninteresting and no longer requiring a response from others.

However, the use of the JaNe formulation accomplished a variety of things. The introduction of just one capital letter affects the way we read the profile photograph. The new tag line also reads 'can you make me feel like a star???' JaNe has simply added three question marks to the tag line from the previous profile page, but this has significant effects on the framing of the visual elements. In the new photograph JaNe can be read as provocative and seductive. This is certainly different to the second profile photograph, with its appearance of relative passivity and a certain sense of naturalness. Slight changes in textual elements can have enormous effects on the way we perceive the visual elements and vice versa.

The new JaNe has also added more to the 'blurb' and 'about me' section of the page. Of note, the introduction of lines like 'I fucking hate spiders' seems to connote a strong sense of femininity that is conjured up around possible conversations around male courage in gallant battles with unsuspecting arachnids. This buttresses the performance of the particular version of femininity that defines the new JaNe. The visual and the discursive lend their form to mapping out the ever-changing interests and concerns of the user.

Reflections

It is a commonplace and banal critique which levels the charge at contemporary communicative practices, such as those on MySpace and other social networking sites, of being narcissistic, self-obsessed faux acts of communication which border on the 'obscene' (as Baudrillard would have it) in their desire to put the minutiae of one's private life on display. We hope to have demonstrated that this misses the complex urcommunicative work that goes in to designing and maintaining profiles. It is no less commonplace to treat the visual as an ornamentation that is merely there to fill in the gaps of discourse, to provide a support for discourse rather than as an object for analysis in its own right. We have treated textuality and visuality as equivalent elements in a pattern or matrix that composes an individual profile page which together sets up an open series of urcommunicative possibilities.

There are, nevertheless, certain elements which appear to have critical roles within this matrix. In each of Jane's profile changes, for instance, it appears that the default photograph was changed when there was a switch in the urcommunicative sentiment as a whole. The appearance of the photograph seems to have a special relationship with the rest of the page. It serves as a kind of relational nexus that has a significant weight in the organisation of the profile, acting as a kind of centre of gravity for urcommunicative transitions. Jane's move from a sad to a happy profile was accomplished primarily through a new profile photograph that appropriated other objects to align with the new message, and rendered previous iterations of the profile as noise against which this new signal could be grasped. The new photograph shifted the meaning of everything else on the page and the entire sense of the previous version of the profile.

The networks of elements on a MySpace page are in a continual state of appropriation as new elements are inserted. With each new element, the relation shifts such that there is a transformation in the urcommunicative organisation of the profile. The meaning of words and images are locked in a fluid state of interpretation where meaning is continually re-enacted. Unintentional juxtapositions between visual elements and textual elements result in a powerful array of possible foundations for communication. This relation creates an urcommunicative environment that is always highly dependent on the situated position from which the profile is read. The distributions of signal and noise are always reversible in the hands of a reader (e.g. JaNe's 'can you make me feel like a star?' can be read as more noise from a failed hope rather than a clear signal of changing mood).

Visuality and textuality disappear as distinct elements on a MySpace profile. They form an urcommunicative whole – one which could easily be interpreted as narcissism, but is actually a continuous and ongoing effort to forge acknowledgeable messages in the infinite amount of background 'noise' made up by the colossal number of profiles jostling for attention across the entirety of the site. Each MySpace profile is encountered as a set of visual and textual elements that hang together in a perpetual state of readiness. It is in this space that we find the complex, multi-faceted relationship between the visual and the textual that is implied by a commitment to foregrounding communication.

References

Baudrillard, J. (1988). *The ecstasy of communication*. Semiotext(e) foreign agents series.

Benwell, B. and Stokoe, L. (2006). *Discourse and identity*. Edinburgh: Edinburgh University Press.

Blonsky, M. (Ed.) (1985). *On signs*. Baltimore, MD: The Johns Hopkins University Press.

boyd, d. (2006). Friends, Friendsters and Top 8: writing community into being on social network sites. *First Monday*, 11(12).

boyd, d. and Heer, J. (2006). *Profiles as conversation: networked identity performance on Friendster*. Paper presented at the proceedings of the Hawai'i International Conference on System Sciences (HICSS-39), Persistent conversation track, January 4–7. Kauhi, HI: IEEE computer society.

boyd, d. m. and Ellison, N. B. (2007). Social network sites: definition, history, and scholarship. *Journal of Computer-Mediated Communication*, 13(1), article 11. Available at: http://jcmc.indiana.edu/vol13/issue1/boyed.ellison.html

Brown, S. D. (2002). Michel Serres: science, translation and the logic of the parasite. *Theory, Culture & Society*, 19(3): 1–27.

Brown, S. D. (2004). Parasite logic. *Journal of Occupational Change Management*, 17(4): 383–395.

Buffardi, L. E. and Campbell, W. K. (2008). Narcissism and social networking web sites. *Personality and Social Psychology Bulletin*, 34: 1303–1314.

ComScore, (2008). Facebook is beating MySpace worldwide. Retrieved 15 January 2008 from: http://news.cnet.com/8301-13577_3-9973826-36.html.

Daft, R. L. and Lengel, R. H. (1984). Information richness: a new approach to managerial behavior and organizational design. In: L. L. Cummings and B. M. Staw (Eds.), *Research in organizational behavior 6*. Homewood, IL: JAI Press (pp. 191–233).

Eco, U. (1987). Semantics, pragmatics and text semiotics. In J. Verschueren and M. Bertuccelli-Papi (Eds.), *The pragmatic perspective*. Amsterdam and Philadelphia: John Benjamins, pp. 695–715.

Edwards, D. (1997). Structure and function in the analysis of everyday narratives. *Journal of Narrative and Life History*, 7(1–4): 139–146.

Edwards, D. and Potter, J. (2005). Discursive psychology, mental states and descriptions. In H. te Molder and J. Potter (Eds.), *Conversation and cognition*. Cambridge: Cambridge University Press, pp. 241–259.

Edwards, D. (2000). Extreme case formulations: softners, investment and doing nonliteral. *Research on Language and Social Interaction*, 33(4): 347–373.

Ellison, N., Lampe, C. and Steinfield, C. (2006). Spatially bounded online social networks and social capital: the role of Facebook. In Dresden (Ed.), *International Communication Association.*

Gackenbach, J. (2006). *Psychology and the Internet: intrapersonal, interpersonal, and transpersonal implications* (2nd edition). London: Academic Press.

Goodwin, C. and Heritage, J. (1990). Conversation analysis. *Annual Review of Anthropology*, 19: 283–307.

Gottdiener, M. (1987). Space as a force of production: contribution to the debate on realism, capitalism and space. *International Journal of Urban and Regional Research*, 11: 405–416.

Herring, S. C. (2004). Online communication: through the lens of discourse. In M. Consalvo, N. Baym, J. Hunsinger, K. B. Jensen, J. Logie, M. Murero and L. R. Shade (Eds.), *Internet Research Annual, Volume 1*. New York: Peter Lang, pp. 65–76.

Jay, M. (1994). *Downcast eyes: the denigration of vision in twentieth-century French thought*. Berkeley: University of California Press.

Joinson, A. (2001a). Self-disclosure in computer-mediated communication: the role of self-awareness and visual anonymity. *European Journal of Social Psychology*, 31: 177–192.

Joinson, A. N. (2001b). Knowing me, knowing you: reciprocal self-disclosure in Internet-based surveys. *CyberPsychology & Behavior*, 4(5): 587–591.

Joinson, A. (2003). *Understanding the psychology of internet behaviour: virtual worlds, real lives*. Palgrave Basingstoke, UK; Palgrave Macmillan.

Kiesler, S., Siegel, J. and McGuire, T. W. (1984). Social psychological aspects of computer-mediated communication. *American Psychologist*, 39: 1123–1134.

Krohn, F. (2004). A generational approach to using emoticons as nonverbal communication. *Journal of Technical Writing and Communication*, 34(4): 321–328.

Lamerichs, J. and te Molder, F. M. (2003). Computer mediated communication: from a cognitive to a discursive model. *New Media & Society*, 5(4): 451–473.

Locke, S. D. and Gilbert, B. O. (1995). Method of psychological assessment, self-disclosure, and experimental differences: a study of computer, questionnaire, and interview assessment formats. *Journal of Social Behavior and Personality*, 10: 255–263.

Malinowski, B. (1923). The problem of meaning in primitive languages. In C. K. Ogden and I. A. Richards (Eds.), *The meaning of meaning*. London: Routledge & Kegan Paul, pp. 296–346.

Marwick, A. E. (2008). To catch a MySpace predator? The MySpace moral panic. *First Monday*, 13(6). Available at: http://www.uic.edu/htbin/cgiwrap/bin/ojs/index.php/fm/article/view/2152/1966.

McGuire, T., Kielser, S., and Siegel, J. (1987). Group and computer mediated discussion effects in risk decision making. *Journal of Personality and Social Psychology*, 52(5): 917–930.

Moreno, M. A., Fost, N. C., and Christakis, D. A. (2008). Research ethics in the MySpace era. *Pediatrics*, 121: 157–161.

Pomerantz, A. M. (1978). Compliment response: notes on the co-operation of multiple constraints. In J. Schenkein (Ed.), *Studies in the organization of conversational interaction*. London: Academic Press.

Pomerantz, A. M. (1984). Agreeing and disagreeing with assessments: some features of preferred/dispreferred turn-shapes. In J. M. Atkinson and J. Heritage (Eds.), *Structures of social action: studies in conversation analysis*. Cambridge: Cambridge University Press, pp. 79–112.

Pomerantz, A. M. (1986). Extreme case formulations: a way of legitimizing claims. In G. Button, P. Drew and J. Heritage (Eds.), *Human Studies*, 9: 219–229.

Potter, J. (2006). Cognition and conversation. *Discourse Studies*, 8(1): 131–140.

Potter, J. and Wetherell, M. (1987). *Discourse and social psychology: beyond attitudes and behaviour*. London: Sage.

Preece, J. and Maloney-Krichmar (2003). Online communities. In J. Jacko and A. Sears (Eds.), *Handbook of human computer interaction*. Lawrence Erlbaum Associates.

Prescott, L. (2007). *Hitwise US consumer generated media report*. Retrieved 3 May 2008 from http://weblogs.hitwise.com/leeann-prescott/2006/11/social_networking_sites_recove.html.

Rosen, C. (2007). Virtual friendship and the new narcissism. *The New Atlantis: A Journal of Technology and Society*, 17: Article 1.

Sacks, H. (1987). On the preferences for agreement and contiguity in sequences in conversation. In G. Button and J. R. E. Lee (Eds.), *Talk and social organisation*. Clevedon: Multilingual Matters.

Sacks, H. and Schegloff, E. A. (1979). Two preferences in the organisation of reference to persons in conversation and their interaction. In G. Psathas (Ed.), *Everyday language: studies in ethnomethodology*. Hillsdale, NJ: Lawrence Erlbaum Associates, pp. 15–21.

Schegloff, E. A. (1996). Turn organisation: one intersection of grammar and interaction. In E. Ochs, S. Thompson and E. A. Schegloff (Eds.), *Interaction and grammar*. Cambridge: Cambridge University Press, pp. 52–134.

Schegloff, E. A. and Sacks, H. (1973). Openings and closings. *Semiotica*, 7: 289–327.

Serres, M. (1969/1982). *The parasite*. Baltimore, MD: Johns Hopkins University Press.

Serres, M. (1980). *The parasite*. Baltimore, MD: Johns Hopkins University Press.

Short, J., Williams, E., and Christie, B. (1976). *The social psychology of telecommunications*. London: John Wiley.

Siegel, J., Dubrovsky, V., Kiesler, S. and McGuire, T. (1986). Group processes in computer-mediated communication. *Organizational Behavior and Human Decision Processes*, 37: 157–187.

Spears, R. and Lee, M. (1994). Panacea or panopticon? The hidden power in computer mediated communication. *Communication Research*, 21: 427–459.

Spears, R., Russell, L., and Lee, M. (1990). De-individuation and group polarization in computer-mediated communication. *British Journal of Social Psychology*, 29: 121–134.

Sproull, L. and Kiesler, S. (1986). Reducing social context cues: electronic mail in organizational communication. *Management Science*, 32: 1492–1512.

Sproull, L. and Kiesler, S. (1991). *Connections: new ways of working in the networked organisation*. Cambridge, MA: MIT Press.

Thelwall, M. (2008a). Social networks gender and friending: an analysis of MySpace member profiles. *Journal of the American Society for Information Science and Technology*, 59(8): 1321–1330.

Thelwall, M. (2008b). Fk yea I swear: cursing and gender in a corpus of MySpace pages. *Corpora*, 3(1): 83–107.

Thelwall, M. (2009). Homophily in MySpace. *Journal of the American Society for Information Science and Technology*, 60(2): 219–231.

Wallace, P. (1999). *The psychology of the internet*. Cambridge, UK: University Press.

Walther, J. B. (1996). Computer mediated communication: impersonal, intrapersonal, and hyperpersonal interaction. *Communication Research*, 23: 3–43.

Yates, S. J. (2001). Researching internet interaction: sociolinguistics and corpus analysis. In M. Wetherell, S. Taylor and S. Yates (Eds.), *Discourse as data: a guide for analysis*. London and New Delhi: Sage, pp. 93–146.

8   Visualising children's credibility

The role of the visual in psychological research and child witness practice

Johanna Motzkau

This chapter explores the role of the visual in legal practice and psychological research, focusing on issues of children's memory and testimony in the context of child abuse investigations. Reporting experiences and findings from a research project that compared child witness practice in England/Wales and Germany (Motzkau, 2007a), the chapter illustrates how the visual asserted itself throughout the research process, emerging as an important and often equivocal arbiter within practices negotiating children's memory and credibility. It is outlined how the effect of the visual ambiguously shapes children's experience of giving evidence and the conditions under which the credibility of their statements is assessed. The chapter focuses in particular on the role of video technology, introduced in the UK as part of special measures to provide better access to justice for children and vulnerable witnesses. Drawing on courtroom observations and data from interviews with legal professionals, it is illustrated how in practice the video asserted itself as a participant, an autonomous proxy-witness with a gaze and an ambiguous voice of its own.

The chapter underlines the importance of considering visual alongside textual data; it highlights the need to reflect about the direction and efficacy of the gaze as mediated through visual technologies; it points to the problem of invisible spaces produced as a result of the use of visual data; discusses how the visual raises questions about the integrity of the data and researchers' own integrity; and examines the way time influences how data are collected, interpreted and viewed. In the context of the analysis, the chapter reveals a constant slippage between what is visible and what can be said about the visible, a disjunction between seeing and speaking (Deleuze, 1986/1992). In this context, it is suggested that the work of Deleuze (1986/1992) about Foucault could play an important role for consolidating the theoretical framework of visual research in psychology.

Introduction

Children have traditionally held a problematic position as witnesses in courts of law, historically facing a deeply rooted mistrust about the reliability of their memory, and their capability to comply with the laws of evidence (Spencer and Flin, 1993; Ceci and Bruck, 1995). Still, as a result of growing awareness of child sexual abuse since the 1970s, courts across Europe and Northern America began to amend the law enabling children to be admitted as witnesses more frequently. Yet, following a number of high profile miscarriages of justice that hinged on children's evidence (Ceci and Bruck, 1995; Bull, 1998), there was renewed wariness about the reliability of children's testimony. Psychological research has helped to better understand children's testimony, generally affirming children's ability to give reliable accounts (cf. Goodman and Clarke-Steward, 1991). Yet, research also cast further doubt on children's reliability, variously highlighting their vulnerability to suggestion and their potential problems understanding and conforming to the requirements of legal procedure and the laws of evidence (Ceci *et al.*, 1994; see also Motzkau, 2007b, 2009).

Since the early 1990s legislators in England and Wales have introduced a range of special measures (e.g. the police video records witness interviews so they can be played later on in court) designed to protect child witnesses by accommodating their perceived needs, while at the same time ensuring the admissibility of their evidence in court (Motzkau, 2007b; Westcott, 2008). This positive effort stands in contrast to the fact that conviction rates for cases of rape and sexual abuse in England and Wales have dropped from 32 per cent in 1977 to a continuous low of around 6 per cent in 2005/2006 (Kelly *et al.*, 2005; Feist *et al.*, 2007). Additionally researchers in the field point to persisting problems with the prosecution of rape and child sexual abuse (Westcott, 2006; Plotnikoff and Woolfson, 2004).

It is against this backdrop that I conducted a research project that compared child witness practice in England/Wales and Germany, looking particularly at cases of alleged sexual abuse and the impact of psychological research and expertise on legal practice (Motzkau, 2007a). The empirical part of the project combined an ethnography (Latour, 1987) of English/Welsh and German legal practice with the analysis of data collected in semi-structured interviews. In both countries, I observed criminal trials including child witnesses, attended police interview training, and psychological expert practice, and conducted interviews with a total of 35 researchers and practitioners (police officers, judges, barristers, social workers, psychological experts and researchers). One of the main objectives was to examine what constituted the concrete conditions of children's credibility in each country's practice. It focused particularly on the special measures put in place to see how practitioners dealt with the problem of giving children a voice in legal proceedings while remaining wary about their reliability as witnesses and their ability to comply with the legal 'call to truth'.

Methodologically the project was situated within a critical qualitative framework combining tools related to discourse and conversation analysis (Wetherell and Potter, 1992; Potter and Wetherell, 1987), with an analytic approach following what Parker termed 'critical discursive research' (Parker, 1992), to inform the analysis of the historical and socio-political context of child witness research and practice.

At the outset the project had no specific focus on the visual, nor was there a plan to employ visual methods or analysis. However, early on during data collection, and particularly in relation to the new special measures implemented in England and Wales, the visual emerged as a distinct feature, posing a number of perplexing questions. For example, while attending a police training course, where officers learn how to conduct video-recorded interviews with children and vulnerable witnesses, I was surprised by the amount of time spent by officers discussing, and worrying about, the impact and nature of what could be *seen* on the video, and how this 'visibility' could variously affect what could/should be said by the interviewer and the child. I had expected officers to focus much more on what is *said* during interviews, as this is what the rules of evidence and the training guidelines are concerned with (e.g. explaining questioning techniques, conversational rapport and how to avoid suggestion).

Officers' preoccupation with the visible is interesting because witness interviewing or the reliability of an account would usually be associated with conversational issues, i.e. the quality of the questions asked, or the consistency and quality of detail provided in the witness statement. Throughout my data collection however it became clear that the visible played a distinct, and often ambiguous, role for the way children experienced giving their evidence, and for the way their credibility was viewed; a role that could not be subsumed under, or grasped via, the textual or spoken aspect of the practice. Hereby special measures also highlighted an unexpected disjunction between evidence/testimony as 'spoken', and the nature of what the visual would add to this evidence and the perception of its reliability.

In the following I will briefly sketch the role of the visual in legal practice, outlining how some of the questions raised resonate with visual research. I will then return to the findings of my research and give a detailed example of the efficacy of video technology as a measure to improve child witness practice.

Child witnesses and the visual in legal practice

Legal practice and qualitative research in psychology have very different agendas. Still, legal practice is a site where complex institutional, societal and psychological discourses come into play while concrete questions of experience, memory and truth are negotiated with real-life consequences for those involved. Hence the law can be seen to operate as an epistemological practice that encounters and deals with specific methodological problems of evidence and experience, some of which resonate in an interesting way with issues faced by researchers using visual methods in psychology. It is interesting to look at the visual in contemporary legal practice because it seems the English/Welsh legal system is undergoing a 'turn to the visual' not unlike the one seen in qualitative research in psychology. Legal practice thereby encounters and illustrates some of the issues the visual raises.

In the past, the visual has often played a rather problematic role for legal practice, as it invokes a 'naïve empiricism' reflected in the widely held assumption that visual media render objective accounts and thus provide a 'visual truth', as Banks (2001: 42) highlights, '... Euro-American society has constructed photography – and in due course, video tape – as a transparent medium, one that unequivocally renders a visual truth'. Banks (2001) points to Mirzoeff's analysis of CCTV footage used in the case of James Bulger (the grainy footage shows

James Bulger being led away from a shopping mall by two young boys). Mirzoeff (1999) emphasises the symbolic value this footage acquired as proof of the defendants' guilt despite the fact that it did not actually show any of the acts of violence they were convicted of. Another example for the problematic role of the visual in law is the use of images in expert testimony. Research demonstrated that the presentation of random fMRI images alongside meaningless or circular statements about brain functioning, dramatically increased the likelihood that participants considered the statements to be relevant and valid, rather than recognising them as meaningless and rejecting them (which the majority did in the absence of fMRI images) (Scolnic Weisberg, 2008). These issues resonate with a recent critique by Buckingham (2009) who reviews creative visual methods in media research, highlighting that the apparent immediacy of the visual means that it is often taken too literally, introducing a 'naïve empiricism' into research.

In this context, attempts at visualising children's evidence highlight a particularly disconcerting analogy between assumptions about the benefits of creative visual methods held in legal and research practice. Guided by the assumption that children are less able to speak, or indeed less reliable in their speaking (which, as outlined earlier, has a long tradition in legal practice), it was at some point thought they might find it easier to provide evidence about traumatic experiences through drawings. A similar sentiment is expressed in visual research, when researchers highlight the potential of the visual to provide a voice for those who are often not heard when speaking, or are less literate and capable of expressing themselves in language, e.g. children (Reavey and Johnson, 2008; Frith *et al.,* 2005). While this is a valid point, it inevitably also carries and perpetuates the negative implication of visual accounts being just as 'immature', 'irrational', and 'inferior' in their expression as those who are seen to benefit from using them, i.e. they are 'childish' types of expression (Lynn and Lea, 2005; Burman, 2008). In this sense they might not just inadvertently devalue children's accounts, but in turn also perpetuate the implicit sense that children indeed cannot speak and/or are not worth listening to (Buckingham, 2009).

This is reflected in the tragic history of such methods in legal practice where they were used for children who were suspected victims of sexual abuse. During the mid and late 1980s when awareness for child sexual abuse increased (Haaken, 1998) and more children were heard as court witnesses, there was a widespread assumption that particularly children struggled to speak about traumatic experiences such as sexual victimisation. In this context the idea emerged that one could access children's potentially repressed memories, unavailable to language, by interpreting children's drawings (existing ones, or drawings children were encouraged to create). This method was considered a valid means of diagnosing sexual abuse in children who were suspected victims but had not disclosed (or actively denied anything had happened). Painting and drawing are used routinely in therapy, and undoubtedly many children (and adults) find it helpful in the process of working through or disclosing traumatic experiences. However, the coercive and unprofessional way in which such techniques were used in investigative contexts in the late 1980s and early 1990s, was highly problematic. Motivated by good intentions but driven by an exaggerated assumption of the epidemic proportions of sexual abuse, investigations were based on biased interpretations that vastly overestimated the sexual implications of drawings, contributing to a number of high-profile miscarriages of justice with tragic consequences for families and children involved (cf. Bull, 1998; Steller, 2000). (For a broader discussion of the use of visual devices for detecting sexual abuse see also Wakefield and Underwager, 2006.)

Within a research context, visual methods are often considered to offer a richer, 'more powerful way of capturing emotions associated with it [the image] that can be far removed from verbal articulation' (Gillies *et al*., 2005: 201), thus grasping more 'fully', or deeply, our embodied experiences, potentially giving participants the opportunity to 'speak to the often un-speakable', as Reavey and Johnson (2008: 311) put it. While these are valid points, the overgeneralised way in which children's drawings were sometimes interpreted for investigations in the late 1980s is a striking reminder that the uncritical assumption of a direct link between an inner 'un-speakable experiential truth' and a drawing can have rather problematic implications. The example highlights that visual researchers need to remain wary about lapsing into naïve empiricism. We should remain sceptical about suggestions that visual methods could in and of themselves empower research subjects by apparently overcoming 'the rationalistic or logocentric tendencies of verbal approaches, [...] [allowing] subjects of research to express their views more directly, and with less interference or contamination' (Buckingham, 2009: 633), or by seemingly providing more authentic accounts of an embodied 'inner self'. Still, looking at this example around children's drawings, it is also clear that the problem rests not so much with the image, or the visual itself; the problem rests with the institutional and societal discourses driving the interpretative operations that establish a specific alignment between what can be said and what can be seen (in this case taking various features of drawings to be expressions of traumatic experiences).

First, this underlines that the discursive plays a crucial role alongside the visual, and thus must not be neglected in analysis if naïve empiricism is to be avoided. Second, the way the drawings operate in legal practice also exemplifies the disjunction between the visible and the spoken. The drawings as such, before their meaning is linked into the dominant concern for sexual abuse, can invoke multiple interpretations; hence the visible entertains no definite relationship to what can be said about it. This disjunction causes what is often referred to as the polysemic nature of the visual (Gillies *et al*., 2005). I will trace this further in the next section when looking at my research findings and examining special measures and child witness practice in England and Wales in more detail.

Video technology in child witness practice in England and Wales

The special measures introduced in England/Wales since the 1990s for children, vulnerable and intimidated witnesses (see for example Criminal Justice Act 1991, Home Office 1991; Youth Justice and Criminal Evidence Act 1999, Home Office

1999) include the video recording of testimony given to the police, which can later be played in court as evidence; cross-examination of a witness via CCTV-link from outside the courtroom; removing lawyers' wigs and gowns or using screens to hide the witness from the defendant. Additionally, special guidelines and training have been introduced for police officers conducting witness interviews (Motzkau, 2007b; Westcott, 2008). Most of these special measures engineer changes to the visual field of the courtroom. They mediate absences and presences, and manipulate visual immediacy in a way that is designed to preserve the rights of the accused, thus guaranteeing a fair trail, while at the same time facilitating children's testimony by reducing the potential for them to feel intimidated or confused. It is hoped that this will provide conditions under which children are more likely to provide accurate and detailed accounts, thus creating circumstances under which they can give better, less ambiguous, evidence and that allow the jury to assess their credibility more objectively.

The CCTV-link, for example, mediates visual and textual presences across space. During cross-examination, rather than being in the courtroom, the child will be in a small CCTV room, sitting directly in front of a television screen, with a video camera focused on his/her face. For the child this means that the court personnel (defence barrister, prosecutor and judge) are replaced by the television screen the child is looking at, where their faces will appear or vanish depending on who is addressing the child. In turn, the measure allows for the child to be absent from the courtroom, by transmitting the child's televised image onto a television screen in the courtroom. So in a sense the television screen takes the child's physical place in the witness box, as a proxy-witness that is perceived as less ambiguous by the court and the jury, because the child is affected less by what goes on in the courtroom.

Throughout my research, however, it emerged that the way in which the CCTV-link mediated children's experience of giving evidence did not have a straightforwardly protective effect. Practitioners reported that child witnesses have been known to get very distressed about the fact that the video link will expose them to the gaze of an unknown and (to them) invisible group of strangers (in the courtroom). This was particularly unsettling because it meant the defendant would be able to see them on screen, while they were unable to look back at the defendant. This illustrates that, even when mediated, the effect of the gaze is always reciprocal, it goes both ways, and being 'on display' while not being able to reciprocate the gaze can cause anxiety and feelings of loss of control (see also Lee, 2001). This underlines ethical issues with visual data researchers need to bear in mind, as similar problems could emerge in relation to video-recorded data and images.

A further concern I encountered throughout my research related to the way this practice mediates the perception of children's credibility. Practitioners and researchers worried that the 'televised' image of the child is too indirect, too remote ('antiseptic'), not allowing the jury to experience the physical presence of the witness, meaning the jury would be less likely to find the child's account credible. For example a judge commented that in his experience many surprising acquittals could be related to the use of CCTV. He suspected that children's credibility is undermined by CCTV-links, because most people are 'anodised'[1] against empathising with a witness over CCTV-link, because they are used to seeing terrible things on television. Contrary to this, legal practitioners also mentioned the concern that mediating children's presence via a CCTV-link could emphasise children's vulnerability. This, it was feared, would appeal to jurors' general desire to protect them, in turn encouraging jurors to subsume the defendant's dangerousness and thus guilt. In summary, following one interpretation, the CCTV-link underlines children's credibility, as it is seen to highlight their preciousness and vulnerability as victims; while following the other interpretation, the televised image undermines children's credibility, because it is seen to deprive the jury of immediately experiencing children's physical presence, introducing a distance that, as practitioners suspect, makes it difficult to resonate with the child's distress and to sense their sincerity.

These examples illustrate that the CCTV-link can constitute a rather unreliable proxy-witness; one that, rather than transparently mediating the witness account, adds problematic effects to the witnesses' experience and that generates an ambiguous voice of its own to the expression of their evidence in court. Just as in the previous example relating to children's drawings, we can see that there is a friction, a disjunction, between what is said (testimony) and what is seen (screened image). And where court practice previously only had the live statement of the child, the introduction of a visual mediation invokes an equivocal, polysemic set of readings and effects that resonate in contradictory ways with different assumptions about how presences and absences support or discredit the credibility of children's testimony.

In my research this was even more evident in the use of video-recorded evidence. Following this measure, the police will video record the investigative interview they conduct with the child, and in case of a trial this video will be played in court as the child's 'evidence in chief'.[2] Similar to the CCTV-link, this video poses as a proxy-witness on the child's behalf, but the video does not just mediate the child's image/presence and statement across space, but also across time. It preserves his/her image and statement at the initial interview and transports it to the time of the trial, in a sense allowing the two time zones to overlap. This is meant to ensure that the child's account is collected as early as possible, before he/she forgets information, and to preserve it on tape making sure it does not alter or is contaminated in the meantime (the time between reporting and trial can be in excess of 10 months). So by recording the video the officers aim to create a stable forensic exhibit that can be stored and later presented in court, directly transmitting the account from one time zone into another, while also displaying the evidence more predictably than the child would do in person. In Motzkau (2007b) I have analysed the problems resulting from this practice in more detail. To illustrate the ambiguous role of the visual as it emerged in this research, I would like to revisit the three main themes of that analysis, and examine them with a focus on the visual and the disjuncture between the visible and the spoken. The three themes are *total visibility*, *integrity* and *time*.

Video and total visibility

Traditionally, police officers would have interviewed a child witness, recording his/her statement literally or paraphrasing it in writing for the file. Hence the trail of evidence would have been entirely textual, leading up to further testimony given (and cross examined) verbally in court. With the introduction of video-recorded evidence a sense of total visibility, of complete, unadulterated footage has now been introduced to the trail of evidence, and thereby to the work of the police officers. By offering an extremely detailed visual account of the interview itself, the video also highlights the relative lack of visibility everywhere else in the process. This heightens the sensitivity and demand for transparency and accountability. This is, for example, reflected in a section of the police's interviewing guidelines ('Achieving Best Evidence') that instruct officers to accompany a child out of the interview room to the toilet to make sure he/she does not speak to anybody during comfort breaks (Home Office and Department of Health, 2007). This instruction became the centre of an intense discussion at a police training course I attended.[3]

EXCERPT 1

1	*TO:*	[...] but why do we do it? It's this issue about whether they've been what? (.) conduced
2		cajoled (1) threatened that's the issue (.) ((PO1: *hmm*)) if they'd been conduced (.) cajoled
3		(.) or threatened it's likely to be by (.) the person that we've brought with them as their
4		witness supporter (.) ((PO1: hmm)) another family member who happens to be at the
5		police station (.) or a policeofficer (.) ((PO1: *yea*)) ok (.) which can happen at anytime (.) it
6		can happen before they arri::ve at the p'lice station (.) as they arrive at the p'lice station
7		after they le:ave the p'lice station (.) s::o (.) y'know I find that (.) the fact that they say that
8		you gonna do this and that (.) but I find that (3) a little bit a bit a bit you know (1) it it it's
9		a:::lmost like saying like you are (.) hhffff taking this person into custody [...]
10	*PO2:*	if the tape's running whilst they go to the toilet (2) you're gonna be seen on the tape
11		anyway (1)
12	*TO:*	you're gonna be seen?
13		(1)
14	*PO2:*	if the tape's still running (.) while they nip out to the toilet (.) ((TO: yea)) you stay in the
15		interviewroom (.) (TO: yea) you're gonna be shown (.) on there anyway
16	*TO:*	you're gonna be seen?
17		(1)
18	*PO2:*	you're gonna ruin the rapport
19		(1)
20	*TO:*	you're gonna ruin the rapport? by going to the toilet with them?=
21	*PO2:*	Yeah I think so it's quite intimidatin'
22	*TO:*	I think it's potential to offend them

The training officer criticises this requirement and notes that it is almost "like you are (.) hhffff taking this person into custody" (line 9). He also points out that this requirement exclusively focuses on, and thus highlights, potential misconduct by the police during the interview. Yet, if a witness was 'conduced, cajoled or threatened' (1–2), the training officers underlines, this could not just happen during an interview break, but it could 'happen at anytime (.) it can happen before they <u>arrive</u> at the p'lice station (.) <u>as</u> they arri::ve at the p'lice station after they <u>le:ave</u> the p'lice station' (5–7). Still, as we can see, with the introduction of video interviewing the attention is firmly focused on the interview, casting doubt on those activities that are now visibly 'off camera'. The further discussion then reflects the officers' confusion as to whether the video is a neutral witness on their behalf, confirming their good conduct as they are 'seen on the tape' (14–16) doing nothing untoward; or whether the video is actually a surveillance device eying the officers' activities suspiciously. The latter is expressed poignantly at the end of this discussion, where one officer added resignedly, and to the other officers' bemusement, that 'next thing an' we'll have cameras in the toilets' (Pol2: 863–866). He thereby illustrates the effect of an idea of total visibility as implied by the video, because ultimately this would imply that only seeing/recording everything that goes on would really suffice. The officer's remark is likely to have been uttered in jest, as this kind of total surveillance seems unrealistic. Still, the way in which the video suggests the need for 'total visibility' and the problems this brings, is interesting to consider for visual researchers, who might find themselves in a similar position, implicitly creating and then having to account for the invisible spaces around their data.

Video and integrity

Looking at excerpt 2, a passage from the same discussion quoted above, we can see that officers come to the conclusion that what is at stake here is their own integrity as police officers. So regardless of their training officer's critique of the guidelines, the officers see it as paramount to follow this requirement to the letter, as it is the only way they can preserve their own integrity. And this is considered crucial, despite the fact that accompanying a child witness to the toilet might frighten the child, thus ruining the rapport and consequently undermining the collection of reliable and detailed evidence (excerpt 1, 18–22).

EXCERPT 2

1   *POI*:   but effectively your integrity is supposed to be intact isn't it because if anybody else=
2   *TO*:   <u>why</u>? 'cause you'r a policeofficer?=
3   *POI*:   yes <u>absolutely</u>
4   (2.5)
5   *TO*:   yea ok I I'm you know (1) it's horses its its what the the the=
6   *POI*:   I think you can stand up in court and answer all the questions that they're asking you
7   and you'll say no they weren't interfered with no this didn't happen that didn't
8   happen ((TO: yes)) [umm]
9   *TO*:   [all the time] they were with me
10 *POI*:   yes
11 *TO*:   I can say that nothing untoward occurred=
12 *POI*:   your <u>honour</u>

Preserving their own integrity, the officers find, will also protect that of the interview, and thus support the credibility of children's evidence. This also means that if necessary they can later on stand up in court to again assert that integrity. We can see how, via the video, children's credibility is directly tied to the officers' integrity, which in turn is challenged by the video's presence. So, paradoxically, the video is not a reliable witness on behalf of officers' integrity, but it is the video that, by extending visibility, first introduces the ambiguity that makes integrity a specific issue. Before the introduction of video recording, the textual practice of recording evidence was organised around the principle that police officers were reliable recorders of evidence by virtue of being police officers, by virtue of being part of the investigative legal machinery. And while, at times, there may have been doubt about the integrity of their practices, it was not expected for them to routinely display and assert their integrity in relation to practices of recording evidence. But as soon as the video allows us to see what they are doing, their routine performance becomes a central matter for concern, exposing it to multiple interpretations, while fostering a demand for even more transparency. Hence officers now have to actively and routinely produce their integrity, and potentially affirm it again by performing it verbally in court, as the exchange in lines 6–12 (excerpt 2) illustrates in an almost stage-like fashion.

Again we can see that the visible, here illustrated through the use of video, is not a mere addition to the spoken, it is not just an additional channel that doubles and confirms what is being said. On the contrary, it seems notoriously ill-aligned with what is said, it opens up a space for multiple interpretations and adds ambiguity that now needs to be tackled. Visual researchers face a very similar problem. This example highlights that researchers' integrity, the integrity of the data, and the way in which the analysis aligns what is visible with what is said about the data, needs to be considered with great care.

Video and time

The example of video-recorded evidence illustrates further problems emerging around the fact that the officers are operating in one time zone (the interview) but as a result of video mediation are expected to simultaneously perform in another, future, time zone (that of the trial, where the video will be viewed). Further excerpts from the training course show that officers are aware that certain aspects of their interview, which at the time of conducting the interview would be considered as supporting the credibility of a child's statement (e.g. a challenge may be needed to clarify a point in the child's account), might have the opposite effect later, when the video is seen in the courtroom. Here a jury might take an officer challenging a child witness to mean that the officer thought the child was lying, thus 'implanting a seed' (excerpt 3, line 5) of doubt in the jury members' minds.

EXCERPT 3

1 *TO:* Is it so urgent to challenge a witnesses evidence at that point in time?=
2 *PO1:* well it could be that's the thing couldn't it [[...]]
3 *TO:* (...) if it is one interview that is played before the court we've already particularly if
4   the jury get to see that aspect of it we have already ahm (.) we're implanting a seed in
5   their mind that we actually don't believe it [...] which is ammunition for the defence.

This illustrates that the video's future efficacy is difficult to control, even for those who plan and record it. The officers have to fear it might perform as an unpredictable, potentially fanciful proxy-witness, later on presenting the child's account in a different, potentially unfavourable light. Further, this example illustrates how the gaze of the video cameras, trained on the interviewing officers, is also channelling the unpredictable gaze of a potential future jury back in time, into the interview room, where it injects uncertainty into the officers' planning and conducting of the interview. It thereby undermines the officers' confidence which in turn can be detrimental to the quality of the evidence the child is able to give.

In legal practice it is assumed that officers should conduct the interviews following the guidelines ('Achieving Best Evidence'), without concerning themselves with issues surrounding the potential later impact of the evidence, but my research showed that the way this practice is set up makes it difficult for officers to evade the gaze and efficacy of the video technology once it is in place. We could see that much of police officers' concern, and consequently effort, was directed at tackling the multiple interpretations that threaten to emerge from the video, while it remained impossible to anticipate how what is visible on the video will be seen later on, as what is visible seems to stand in no fixed relationship to the statements made on it.

It is interesting to consider how these problems resonate with the process of planning and recording data for visual research. Clearly, as researchers we are also exposed to the gaze of our potential future audience (which might include research participants). This gaze is cast back in time onto the process of data collection and analysis. Furthermore, by displaying videos or images collected during research, we are creating an overlap of time zones similar to the one police officers produce. In doing this we potentially face similar ambiguity in the way our data are perceived by viewers, for whom they might open up further interpretations, or for whom they might even refuse to support our own analysis (see also Ashmore *et al.*, 2004). In this context, the specific problems raised by the visual and enduring nature of [the] video as it operates across time and space, highlights once more the peculiar phenomenon facing visual research in particular: the disjuncture between the visible and the articulable.

This is further illustrated in the account of a prosecutor I interviewed, who outlines how helpful the police's video recordings are for assessing whether to prosecute or drop a case. The prosecutor said the video helped to see what the witnesses were like and thus how they would come across to the jury. She outlined that some children might look somewhat shifty and would thus be perceived to be less credible. The prosecutor's account highlights that, while children's verbal account's are important, the video has introduced a new emphasis on the visible elements of the evidence for assessing credibility. The prosecutor illustrates this by giving the example of a case where the credibility of a very young child, a girl whose statement might have been difficult to bring to court due to her young age, was effectively bolstered by her doll-like, appearance, and the way her 'innocence shone through on the video'. Yet, the prosecutor mitigates this account by adding that children might look shifty, less doll-like, or uncomfortable, not because he/she is lying, but simply because being interviewed by police about traumatic experiences is as such awkward and uncomfortable. However, by adding this comment, the prosecutor implies that visible shiftiness could not just be an indicator of an untrue statement, but it could also be considered as visible proof of a true statement, in the same way as 'radiating innocence' is, thereby re-introducing the ambiguity her example about the doll-like witness had initially eliminated (for a detailed analysis see Motzkau, 2010). This example shows once more how the visible proves polysemic, ambiguous and appears disparate from what is said.

The visible and the articulable in research and legal practice

Child abuse investigations are always delicate and complex, and with this analysis I do not wish to imply that the use of video technology is generally detrimental. The introduction of special measures is clearly a positive move and there are many cases where the use of video technology has helped to facilitate prosecution and to achieve just convictions. This is why my research seeks to help support their effective application. In this spirit, the examples discussed here are meant to create awareness of the efficacy of the visual, and the potential ambiguity added to this practice as a result of the constant slippage between the visible and the articulable. It is this disjunction between seeing and speaking that creates the impression the video was an autonomous proxy-witness with a gaze and a voice of its own. This phenomenon is corroborated by visual researchers who point to the polysemic nature of visual data that makes it difficult to pin down or agree on interpretations. Gillies *et al.* (2005) describe this as the experience of a constant slippage of interpretations as they tried to negotiate the meanings of images they had created themselves in the context of a research project. Temple and McVittie (2005) report a similar experience when describing the unexpected autonomy visual objects and images, created during therapy, gained during the therapeutic process, invoking complex investments and ambiguous relationships with clients, that could not easily be controlled or resolved. It is variously suggested that such issues could be approached by adopting a thoroughly reflexive position in research (Reavey and Johnson, 2008; Lynn and Lea, 2005; Buckingham, 2009). While this is a valid point, researchers remain vague as to what exactly such a reflexive position entails. In this context further examination of the theoretical and practical framework of visual research is needed.

I would suggest that it is one of the most important contributions of visual psychologies to expose the issue of the disjunction between speaking and seeing, and to make it available to systematic analysis. Still, a clearer theoretical framework is needed to support the exploration of research that examines diverse modes of data within and beyond discourse (see also Motzkau, in press). In this spirit I would like to offer a brief theoretical outlook, pointing to theoretical resources that could prove useful to the development of a reflexive and critical version of visual psychologies.

Visual psychologies: a theoretical outlook

Deleuze (1986/1992) finds the question of the relationship between the visible and the articulable to be at the heart of Foucault's exploration of formations of knowledge and his analytic distinction between the discursive and the non-discursive. According to Deleuze, Foucault based this distinction on the fundamental finding that 'There is a disjunction between speaking and seeing, between the visible and the articulable: "what we see never lies in what we say", and vice versa' (Deleuze, 1986/1992: 64). Here Foucault does not insist on a primacy of speaking, but upholds the specificity of seeing, of the visible, asserting that neither speaking nor seeing are reducible to another. Crucially, as Deleuze outlines, Foucault marks these as two distinct ontological formations, i.e. forms of 'there is', a light being and a language being. This in turn means, according to Deleuze, that there is no principle, law or pattern that determines their relationship, as their relation is essentially a non-relation. Deleuze illustrates this strange type of phenomenology by drawing on Foucault's commentary on Magritte's famous painting of a pipe presented above the written words 'Ceci n'est pas une pipe' ('this is not a pipe'). According to Deleuze, Foucault points to the

> little thin band, colourless and neutral', separating the drawing of the pipe from the statement 'this is a pipe' to the point where the statement becomes 'this is *not* a pipe', since neither the drawing nor the statement, nor the 'this' as an apparently common form is a pipe: 'the drawing of the pipe and the text that ought to name it cannot find a place to meet, either on the black canvas or above it.' It is a non-relation.
>
> (Deleuze, 1986/1992: p. 62)

This assertion of the autonomy of the visible resonates with the apparent unwieldiness of the visual and its evasiveness to interpretive capture observed in my own research about child witness practice, as well as in other examples of visual research mentioned above (Gillies *et al.*, 2005; Temple and McVittie, 2005). Developing such theoretical resources could provide a better grasp of what this non-relationship, and the resulting interpretive slippage between the visible and the articulable means for visual psychologies (Motzkau, in press). This would contribute to research that exploits the benefits of visual methodologies alongside textual modes of analysis while avoiding the pitfalls of naïve empiricism, or a dominance of the visual over the textual.

Conclusion

This chapter has illustrated that, where children become witnesses their memory, testimony and the perception of their credibility is intimately linked to the workings of visual technologies. These have a significant effect on intensifying or multiplying visibilities or channelling the impact and direction of children's and spectators' gazes. In this sense my research underlines the value of developing distinctly visual psychologies that employ visual methods and explore the role of the visual for core psychological questions such as memory, credibility, agency and subjectivity. Yet, it also emphasised that we must not neglect the discursive textual modes of data and analysis. These need to be employed alongside visual methodologies, as the articulable forms an entity distinct from the visual. The disjuncture between the visual and the articulable raises intriguing theoretical and practical questions the analytic value of which needs to be explored further.

The chapter illustrated that, even though research and legal practice differ dramatically in their agenda and the potential consequences for those involved, legal practice as an epistemological and social practice offers an intriguing backdrop for reflecting about visual methods in research. This backdrop provides evocative reminders that we should be sceptical about claims that visual data could provide absolute 'experiential immediacy', or could by default offer participants an empowered voice. It highlights that we need to reflect critically on the direction and efficacy of the gaze mediated through visual technologies (in relation to participants, ourselves as researchers and our audience); that we should be aware of the invisible spaces visual data produce; and that we must be alert to the specific ways in which the visual raises questions of integrity and time.

Notes

1 Interview with Judge 2: 588–628. All data quoted in this chapter were collected by the author in 2004/2005 for Motzkau (2007a).
2 'Evidence in chief' is the initial evidence given by a witness under the guidance of the lawyer who called them. It forms the basis of the subsequent cross-examination which, for children and other vulnerable witnesses, will be conducted via CCTV.
3 Data set – Pol2: 720–866. 'TO' = training officer and 'PO' = participating police officers. The excerpts were edited with omissions indicated by square brackets '[...]', but the overall character of the exchanges is not altered. The transcript notations used are a simplified version of Jefferson (1984): Pauses appear in rounded brackets indicating seconds: '(1)' or less '(.)'; speaker emphasis: 'underlining'; overlapping turns: '[square brackets]'; minimal acknowledgement tokens by other speakers: '((double rounded brackets))'; words drawn out: 'col::ons'; a turn interrupted by a take up of another speaker: equals sign '='; rising intonation: question mark '?'.

References

Ashmore, M., Brown S. D., and MacMillan, K. (2004). It's a scream: professional hearing and tape fetishism. *Journal of Pragmatics*, 36, 349–374.
Banks, M. (2001). *Visual methods in social research*. London: Sage.
Buckingham, D. (2009). Creative visual methods in media research: possibilities, problems and proposals. *Media, Culture, Society*, 31(4), 633–652.
Bull, R. (1998). Obtaining information from child witnesses. In A. Memon, A. Vrij, and R. Bull (eds.) *Psychology and law. Truthfulness, accuracy and credibility*. London: McGraw-Hill.
Burman, E. (2008). *Deconstructing developmental psychology*. London: Routledge.
Ceci, S. J., and Bruck, M. (1995). *Jeopardy in the courtroom*. Washington, DC: American Psychological Association.
Ceci, S. J., Huffmann, M. L. C., Smith, E. and Loftus, E. F. (1994). Repeatedly thinking about a non-event: source misattributions among preschoolers. *Consciousness and Cognition*, 3, 388–407.

Deleuze, G. (1986/1992). *Foucault.* Minneapolis: University of Minnesota Press. English translation published 1992.

Feist, A., Ashe, J., Lawrence, J., McPhee, D., and Wilson, R. (2007). *Investigating and detecting recorded offences of rape.* Home Office Online Report 18/07. Retrieved 24 November 2010 from http://rds.homeoffice.gov.uk/rds/pdfs07/rdsolr1807.pdf

Frith, H., Riley, S., Archer, L., and Gleeson, K. (2005). Editorial: imag(in)ing visual methodologies. *Qualitative Research in Psychology*, 2, 187–198.

Gillies, V., Harden, A., Johnson, K., Reavey, P., Strange, V., and Willig, C. (2005). Painting pictures of embodied experience: the use of non-verbal data production for the study of embodiment. *Qualitative Research in Psychology: Special Issue on Visual Methodologies*, 2, 199–212.

Goodmann, G. S., and Clarke-Steward, A. (1991). Suggestibility in children's testimony: implications for child sexual abuse investigations. In D. L. Doris (ed.), *The suggestibility of children's recollections.* Washington, DC: American Psychological Association, pp. 92–105.

Haaken, J. (1998). *Pillar of salt. Gender, memory and the perils of looking back.* London: Rutgers University Press.

Home Office and Department of Health (2007). *Achieving best evidence in criminal proceedings: guidance for vulnerable or intimidated witnesses, including children.* London: Her Majesty's Stationery Office.

Home Office (1991). *Criminal Justice Act.* Available from http://www.legislation.gov.uk/ukpga/1991/53/contents

Home Office (1999). *Youth Justice and Criminal Evidence Act.* www.opsi.gov.uk/acts/acts1999/19990023.htm

Jefferson, G. (1984). Transcript notation. In J. M. Atkinson and J. Heritage (eds.) *Structures of social action: studies in conversation analysis.* Cambridge: Cambridge University Press.

Kelly, L., Lovett, J., and Regan, L. (2005). *A gap or a chasm? Attrition in reported rape cases.* Home Office Research Study 293. London: Home Office Research, Development and Statistics Directorate.

Latour, B. (1987). *Science in action.* Cambridge, MA: Harvard University Press.

Lee, N. (2001). Becoming mass: glamour, authority and human presence. In N. Lee and R. Munro (eds.) *The consumption of mass.* Oxford: Blackwell.

Lynn, N., and Lea, S. J. (2005). Through the looking glass: considering the challenges visual methodologies raise for qualitative research. *Qualitative Research in Psychology: Special Issue on Visual Methodologies* 2, 213–225.

Mirzoeff, N. (1999). *An introduction to visual culture.* London: Routledge.

Motzkau, J. F. (in press). Picturing the truth? Seeing and speaking in psychological research and legal practice.

Motzkau, J. F. (2009). 'Exploring the transdisciplinary trajectory of suggestibility'. *Subjectivity*, 27, 172–194.

Motzkau, J. F. (2010). 'Speaking up against justice: credibility, suggestibility and children's memory on trial'. In P. Reavey and J. Haaken (eds.), *Memory matters. Contexts for understanding sexual abuse recollections.* London: Psychology Press.

Motzkau, J. F. (2007b, January). Matters of suggestibility, memory and time: child witnesses in court and what really happened [42 paragraphs]. *Forum Qualitative Sozialforschung/Forum: Qualitative Social Research* [online journal], 8(1), Art. 14. Retrieved 22 August 2009 from http://www.qualitative-research.net/fqs-texte/1-07/07-1-14-e.htm

Motzkau, J. F. (2007a). *Cross-examining suggestibility: memory, childhood, expertise.* Unpublished doctoral thesis, Loughborough University, UK.

Parker, I. (1992). *Discourse dynamics: critical analysis for social and individual psychology.* London: Routledge.

Plotnikoff, J., and Woolfson, R. (2004). *In their own words. The experience of 50 young witnesses in criminal proceedings.* London: NSPCC.

Potter, J., and Wetherell, M. (1987). *Discourse and social psychology: beyond attitudes and behaviour.* London: Sage.

Reavey, P., and Johnston, K. (2008). Visual approaches: using and interpreting images. In C. Willig and W. Stainton Rogers (eds.), *The Sage handbook of qualitative research in psychology* (pp. 295–314). London: Sage.

Scolnic Weisberg, D. (2008). Caveat lector: the presentation of neuroscience information in the popular media. *The Scientific Review of Mental Health Practice* 6(1), 51–56.

Spencer, J. R. and Flin, R. (1993). *The evidence of children. The law and the psychology.* London: Blackstone Press.

Steller, M. (2000). Forensische Aussagepsychologie als angewandte Entwicklungs- und Kognitionspsychologie. *Praxis der Rechtspsychologie,* 10(1), 9–28.

Temple, M. and McVittie, C. (2005). Ethical and practical issues in using visual methodologies: the legacy of research-originating visual products. *Qualitative Research in Psychology: Special Issue on Visual Methodologies,* 2, 227–239.

Wakefield, H., and Underwager, R. (2006). The application of images in child abuse investigations. In J. Prosser (ed.), *Image-based research: a sourcebook for qualitative researchers.* London: Routledge.

Westcott, H. L. (2006). Child witness testimony: what do we know and where do we go? *Child and Family Law Quarterly,* 18(2), 175–190.

Westcott, H. (2008). Safeguarding witnesses. In G. Davies, C. Hollin, and R. Bull (eds.), *Forensic psychology.* London: Wiley and Sons.

Wetherell, M., and Potter, J. (1992). *Mapping the language of racism: discourse and the legitimation of exploitation.* Chichester, NY Columbia University Press.

9   The video-camera as a cultural object

The presence of (an)Other.

Michael Forrester

Introduction

The emergence and rising significance of qualitative methods in psychology is coterminous with the introduction and advancement of recording technologies (both audio and visual, and analogue and digital). It is likely that part of the reason for this is the apparently less interpretative nature of technologically reproducible 'factual' documents, that is in comparison to earlier methods such as diary studies and ethnographic field notes. Across the discipline there are many examples which exhibit that close and particular integration of theoretical development, methodological innovation, data-collection practices and the associated conventions of interpretation, all coalescing around the record – the documentary evidence produced by audio and video techniques and technologies (Ochs, 1979; Zuengler *et al.*, 1998). Observational methods in developmental psychology and discursive approaches found in social psychology are two example domains difficult to imagine developing in the way they have without the corresponding availability of recording devices and techniques. The aim in what follows is to consider, and place into context, video-recording as a research practice in what is often described as a naturalistic or an 'everyday' setting, particularly when one of the participants also has the dual role of researcher/participant. The focus is on understanding something of how participants orient towards, accommodate or otherwise respond to the video-camera as a cultural object particularly when it is used regularly in an everyday context (family mealtime recordings).

In order to locate the focus of the material reported in this chapter, something should be said regarding the background to these opening comments. Having carried out experimental/laboratory research in the late 1980s and 1990s into the development of young children's conversational skills (Forrester, 1988, 1992), the costs, constraints and challenges presented by developing and extending this particular line of research within a laboratory context seemed out of proportion to the insights that might be gleaned from the results. In contrast, the opportunity afforded by being able to study in detail, over a long period of time, one particular child as she was learning how to talk appeared more fruitful given the insights that can emerge from the longitudinal single-case study. In developmental psychology there is a long history of studies, informing work in such areas as language acquisition and the development of musicality (Brown, 1958; Papousek and Papousek, 1981).

The research that forms the background to the extracts discussed in this chapter employed a single-case longitudinal design, so as to examine the developing conversational skills of one child during an important period of language development during pre-school years, from 12 to 41 months. This child was my youngest daughter Ella, aged one year at the time I began the study, and I was very fortunate in my immediate family giving their permission, and agreeing to participate in this extended piece of research. At the outset the aim of the work sought to understand what is involved in a child learning how to talk and thus become a member of a particular culture. A second objective of the work was to describe in detail the socialisation processes whereby the child learns, and begins to produce, discourses relevant to successful participation in the context he/she inhabits (certain aspects of this work have been documented elsewhere; Forrester, 2002, 2008).

The question of what constitutes the 'natural' or the 'real' in psychology and other social sciences has a long and distinguished history. The discipline, especially in those sub-topics and areas with a close methodological allegiance to the hypothetic-deductive framework(s) of natural science, has a particular suspicion of theoretical over-interpretation and speculation, and going beyond the facts or record (James, 1890; Cooper *et al.*, 2008). This is not the place to enter into a discussion regarding the epistemological or pre-theoretic presuppositions and assumptions underlying different theoretical frameworks in psychology. Many others have done so with considerably more insight than what might be accomplished here (see Edwards, 1997; Burr, 2003). Instead my aim is simply to raise some questions or concerns regarding the procedures and practices we bring into play when we set out to video-record the 'normal', the 'natural' or the spontaneously 'real' when studying human interaction.

Some time ago Hall (2000) drew attention to the fact that social scientists seem peculiarly reticent to consider in detail their own 'activities of collecting, watching, or interpreting video as a stable source of "data" for research and presentation purposes' (p. 647). Hall (2000) outlines four observations relevant to the collection of video records, suggesting that video-recordings,

(a)   reorganise the tasks and experiences of research participants,
(b)   serve different research interests by selectively attending to different aspects of human activity,
(c)   reinforce or break open traditional boundaries between researchers and their study participants, and
(d)   provide both limited and privileged access to aspects of human interaction.

In what follows I would like to refer to these comments when considering extract examples taken from the corpus described earlier, and specifically, moments when the target child displays an orientation to the video-camera as an object.

There are a number of reasons why such examples provide us with opportunities for re-considering or at least articulating pre-conceived ideas we may have regarding video-recording, especially video-recordings of everyday normal or natural interaction. Notice, the focus is not necessarily on the child and how she (may/might have) gradually become aware of the camera, subsequently learning how to 'perform' for it; the original work was solely directed at documenting the child's emerging conversational skills. Further, the question is not one of the veridicality of the 'record' as a record of the true or 'real'. Nor is it a secondary analysis of the processes one might initiate in order to best ensure that interactions being recorded are as natural as they could be, whatever that might mean, if the camera had not been present. Instead by simply substituting 'video-camera' for 'video-recording', Hall's (2000) comments can serve as a entry point into the analysis and discussion of examples.

Methodological approach

Before turning to the extract examples, something needs to be said regarding the methodological approach adopted here, best described as ethnomethodologically informed conversation analysis (CA). The analytic approach adopted for the initial analysis is ethnomethdologically informed, in that (a) the selection consisted of events where there was evidence in the sequence of the interaction itself that participants displayed some orientation to the event as noticeable for some reason, and (b) detailed extracts employing the conversation analytic approach were produced so as to highlight certain aspects of the interactional sequences. This approach is particularly concerned with an examination of the fine-detail of talk-in-interaction, close attention being paid to the unfolding sequence of talk using a transcription orthography that serves to highlight fine-grained aspects of what is going on.

CA originally emerged as a specific method aligned with an approach in sociology known as ethnomethodology. Ethnomethodologists focus on people's own ideas and understandings about whatever it is they are doing, and it is these understandings which guide the analytic enterprise. Ethnomethodology has been described as 'the study of the common, everyday, naturally occurring, mundane methods that are used by people to produce and manage the common, everyday activities of the everyday social world' (Livingston, 1987: 10). Ethnomethodology involves a rational analysis of the structures, procedures and strategies that people themselves use when they are making, and making sense of, their everyday world.

CA itself aims to show how meanings and representations in discourse are produced through the structures, procedures and practices of talk. Conversation analysts have been principally concerned with classifying and describing the structures and general procedures employed by people in understanding and taking part in conversations (Hutchby and Woofit, 2008; Psathas 1995). These include turn-taking, closing conversations, introducing topics, asking questions, making requests and other related features of talk. It is important to recognise that the question of whether or not people perform naturally or not whenever a camera is recording their behaviour, is of no particular theoretical or methodological concern to the ethnomethodological perspective. Instead ethnomethodology/CA is simply concerned with understanding the methodic sense-making reflexive social practices people engage in and produce within *any* social context (Garfinkel, 1964; Livingston, 1987).

Data extract examples

The extract examples considered here come from a series of video-recordings (31) of the author's daughter, Ella. This child was filmed during meal-times as she was interacting with her father, mother, and/or older sibling, Eva (aged 8 at the beginning of the recordings), and for the most part was positioned in a high-chair in view of the camera (as in Quay, 2008). The recordings of the target child were collected from age 1 year to 3 years 5 months. The length of the recordings range from 10–45 minutes (average 35) with the total recording amounting to around 11 hours. Following completion of the recordings, transcriptions using conversation analytic conventions were produced (following Psathas, 1995). Additional transcription notations relevant for child language analysis were also produced (McWhinney, 2000) and the resulting data corpus can be viewed through the web-data feature of the CLAN software (CHILDES, 2008).

The available data corpus was examined in detail and all examples where participants showed some explicit or implicit participant-oriented interest in the camera were noted for further analysis. Across the full detail set the number of instances was 15 in total, all relatively brief (as in the extracts below). Given that there are around 12 hours of recorded material transcribed and documented one might surmise that for these participants, in this context, the video-camera was not necessarily of particular interest or note. We can turn first to the earliest example where the principal participant, that is the target child in the research project, explicitly referred to the video-camera.

Extract 1: Child age – 1 year 5 months

Context

The child is sitting in a high-chair, eating, and the father has only recently switched the camera on. This is the 9th recording in the sequence of 31. During this brief extract the mother enters the room. The video-camera is a small portable digital camera on a tripod in a corner of the room (kitchen).

Summary exposition of extract

In this extract we find one of the first examples where the child explicitly refers to or notices the camera. From the outset there are also indications that the child's father displays an orientation to the fact of being video recorded for research purposes. The mother makes an explicit comment about the video and a brief discussion around this takes place between the adult participants.

EXTRACT 1. CHILD AGE – 1 YEAR 5 MONTHS

```
 1 FAT:   I kn↑ow Mummy's singing a s↑on↓g
 2        (0.4)
 3 FAT:   is she↑              ((spoken as he walks past child))
 4        (1.6)
 5 FAT:   ↑singing a ↑so::ng to us?   ((child looking in opposite direction))
 6        (2.2)                       ((during pause sits down))
 7 FAT:   ((coughs))                  ((looks towards/beyond the camera))
 8        (3.0)
 9 ELL:   ((turns towards father and looks towards camera during turn))
10 MOT:   [xxx xxx ]xxx [xxxx]        ((M singing))
11 FAT:              [sniff]
12        (5.3)                       ((father adopts 'frozen' gesture))
13 MOT:   °it's nearly half xxxx°
14        (0.1)
15 FAT:   alright darlin=
16 MOT:   =coffee first actually      ((child looking at camera))
17        (0.9)
18 ELL:   d[a !]   ((E points to the camera))
19 MOT:    [exx clement↑]             ((spoken while entering room))
20        (0.2)
21 MOT:   ↑ooh are you videoing?
22        (0.3)
23 FAT:   ye↓ah                       ((body posture still 'frozen'))
24        (2.5)                       ((father slight smile at mother))
25 MOT:   °m° bleur:: ↓               ((towards child who puts finger far into her mouth))
26        (0.2)
27 FAT:   hhh
28        (0.4)
29 MOT:   °m° bleur::
30        (0.6)
31 MOT:   that's why you're so calm and relaxed darling isn't it?
32        (0.3)
33 FAT:   ((smiles glumly and looks at camera))
34 MOT:   hhh
35        (0.5)
36 FAT:   ((looks towards mother with quick smile))
37        (3.0)                       ((child looks towards father))
38 FAT:   I kn↓ow ↑I do feel calm and relaxed
39        (0.6)
40 FAT:   don't I googlin(g) it       ((family pet name for child))
41        (0.6)                       ((moves away from table))
42 MOT:   hhh ↓hou::se Daddy hou::se=
43 FAT:   = ↑kno:↓w
```

The extract begins not long after the video-camera has again been set up and switched on. As the father is moving around the room he comments to Ella that her mother (in the next room) is singing and then, at line 6, sits down near the child in view of the camera. Between lines 6 and 13, while the child is eating, and not always looking towards her father, he appears to adopt a somewhat curious posture (around line 12), saying nothing and doing little, that is apart from looking past the child and 'side-on' to the camera.

At this point, line 13, in the adjoining room, the mother quietly comments about the time, which, for these particular participants, presupposes a series of actions regarding what is going to happen next (the mother leaving the child in the care of the father, and going off to prepare for the day). This is indicated in his reply, however as he stops speaking she comments that (before continuing) she will make some coffee.

Our attention is drawn to the next short sequence, from lines 17 to around 24 for a number of reasons. First, the child herself turns towards, looks at, and simultaneously points towards the camera and produces an utterance (line 18). Notice she does this precisely at the point her mother is entering the room and, as far as one can tell from the video, the mother is not aware of or looking at the video-camera. Second, the mother indicates surprise at the fact that the camera is on (line 19). Heritage (1998) and others have documented the significance of the 'oh' comment or response in conversation, indicative of an addressee recognising or understanding something that was not immediately apparent. Third, neither the mother nor the father reply to the child or appear to notice that she has pointed at the camera. Fourth, we can note that between, and through, lines 23–25, the father, although maintaining the body posture mentioned earlier, does two things, (a) he replies with a minimal 'yeah', spoken with a noticeable downward intonation, and (b) looks towards the mother and then produces a slight ambiguous smile. We might ask, who is this smile for, and what might it indicate? The father, occupying a somewhat ambiguous role as both participant and as researcher is concerned with recording the natural and normal everyday behaviour of the child (and her family), and yet it would appear, keenly aware of a potential 'sometime-in-the-future' audience presupposed by the very fact of the production of the record and the collection of data.

Continuing with the analysis, the mother makes a comment (line 25) precisely at the point where Ella places her finger in her mouth while still eating her banana. At line 29 she repeats this phrase, while still looking at the child, and then, displays a specific orientation to the fact that the father appears to be having difficulty in 'doing being natural' while the camera is on (line 31) by producing an ironic comment. His response is noteworthy and may be indicative of precisely the question or rather challenge surrounding the 'capturing' of natural, spontaneous, everyday family behaviour. He produces a curiously 'glum' smile, looks very briefly towards the camera, and noticeably, as he does so, his hand on the back of his chair, falls or rather 'droops'. Sustaining a performance of 'doing being ordinary', as Sacks (1992) has pointed out, always involves effort, and in this instance it is the somewhat stilted and unnatural nature of his attempts at ordinariness that are being explicitly referred to. Explicit reference to such a 'performance' has undermined the very attempt at naturalness.

The final section of this extract again provides us with some indications of the complex role of the camera, or rather, the recording of natural behaviour for academic/research purposes, particularly where the researcher is also a participant in the interaction. In response to the suggestion that he is not 'calm or relaxed' and thus accountably not 'doing being natural', his response is instead to treat the ironic comment in curiously 'literal' terms and, through doing so, transforms the topic or trajectory of the conversation along lines of an agreement. However, it may be worth noting that immediately after saying this, he then (a) acts as if he is addressing the child – using a pet family name for her – and (b) moves to leave the table. One interpretation of this might be the taking of a position such as; 'no, look, I'm just going to carry on and act as if everything is fine and normal'. The mother then changes the topic of the conversation.

Taking into account Hall's (2000) comments above, the events described here certainly accord with the suggestion that the presence of the video-camera re-organises the tasks and experiences of research participants. Here, the father's task re-organised into one of 'being the adult participant' in the task of collecting research data. But notice, this 're-organisation' is subtly embedded in the fabric of the sequence of the interaction. This also draws our attention to the notion of the camera as involved in the breaking of traditional boundaries – raising the question of, in this case, the position of the father as 'insider participant' in the research, including the analysis of the data.

Moving on, and turning to a second extract, recorded when the child was 15 months older, we have an instance where her recognition of, and orientation to, the video-camera is both more marked and possibly more complex than in the first.

Extract 2: Child age – 2 years 8 months

Context

The context is the same as the above, however this is the 23rd recording in the series. During this brief extract the father leaves the room briefly and then returns.

Summary exposition of extract

In this short extract the child, on finding herself alone for a brief moment at the kitchen/breakfast table, looks towards, non-verbally addresses and performs 'for' the camera.

EXTRACT 2. CHILD AGE – 2 YEAR 8 MONTHS

```
 1  FAT:   look there's a big hu::ge bit
 2         (1.8)
 3  FAT:   you can't eat ↓that↑
 4         (0.4)
 5  ELL:   yea::eaoh            ((hands on head – sticks tongue out when speaking))
 6         (3.1)
 7  ELL:   oh
 8         (3.4)
 9  FAT:   mmhhmm
10         (2.1)
11  ELL:   >I can eat<
12         (0.4)
13  ELL:    a::lll by myself
14         (0.1)
15  FAT:   a::wh >that's pretty good↓<        ((turns and makes to leave table))
16         (0.5)
17  ELL:   ye::h all by myself          ((as she finishes speaking father leaves room))
18         (1.6)
19  ELL:   when daddy wasn't coming here I'd be a::::ll al::: ↓one↑
20         (1.0)                  ((during line 19 looks at camera then at toy monkey))
21  ELL:   ((during pause holds hands and looks down))
22  FAT:   well daddy be back in minute ((voice heard from adjoining room))
23         (12.2)         ((see text for detail on activity))
24  FAT:   I am back
25         (11.6)         ((both participants resume eating and eating/reading))
26  ELL:   this tri::angle shape and look
27         (0.9)
```

The earlier extract highlighted how an adult-participant researcher attempts to deal with the challenges and ambiguities surrounding recording 'normal' interaction in an everyday context. In this second extract we are provided with some indication of how the youngest participant orients towards the camera as a significant object, doing so in a manner that presupposes her recognition of its 'presence' or rather something/someone who is 'present'.

The first part of the extract (lines 1–14) involves the father and child discussing the toast she is eating, how this toast is quite large, and her positioning herself as somebody who can nonetheless manage to eat it. We might notice the manner in which, after her father has suggested she couldn't possibly eat all the toast (line 3), she emphasises how she (alone) will manage to eat it by herself by stretching the sound she makes when saying 'all' in line 13.

What happens next draws our attention to how this child orients towards the presence of the camera in a situation where she suddenly finds herself in the room on her own – a situation she marks quite explicitly as something undesirable or negative. Around line 15, the father replies to her assertion that she can indeed eat all her toast by herself, by speaking quickly in a positive tone, and yet simultaneously getting up from the table and walking into an adjoining room. At this point (line 17), Ella produces a receipt of his statement, commenting that, yes indeed, she will eat all the toast herself. However, as she finishes speaking he has already got up from the table, and as he leaves the room she produces the extended utterance at line 19. As she is doing so, at the point where she says 'here', she turns and looks directly at a soft toy (her pet monkey) which is placed opposite her on the table.

Leaving aside the child's mistaken use of 'coming/gone', the utterance itself is interesting as there may be a curious 'slippage' or association between the positive – assertive – use of 'all' which she has just said in line 17 (with some emphasis) and the long-stretched-out plaintive use of 'all' in line 19. The switching from positive to negative or at least from assertiveness to 'sad' or problematic is marked in the particular manner in which, as she speaks, she draws her hand together, and looks downwards (see Figure 9.1a). Immediately after she is saying/ doing this 'performance' we hear the father (line 22) responding to her comment from an adjoining room and displaying an orientation to what she is saying (notice his use of 'well' and mirroring of 'daddy').

We then observe, during the pause in the extract at line 23, a very specific and marked orientation towards the camera by the child which warrants our attention. After the father stops speaking (line 22), she raises her head, and after approximately 3 seconds, looks up and towards the camera (see Figure 9.1b) [and not at her favourite toy]. Following another short pause (2 seconds) Ella then begins to 'interact' with or perform for, the camera (see Figure 9.1c). She begins to sway, move and dance in her chair, adopting a pursed smile while continuously looking towards the camera. She does this [(Figures 9.1(c)–(e))] for the remaining 5 or 6 seconds until the father returns to the room to sit beside her once again.

At the very least her response presupposes her recognition of something/ someone watching. We can ask, and again with reference to camera presence re-organising the tasks or experience of participants, how are we to understand the nature of the child's smile – who is it for and why is it expressed in the manner it is? Certainly there are grounds for suggesting that she displays an awareness of 'being watched'. There is however, and again with regard to earlier comments on video-recordings and privileged access to hitherto unrecorded aspects of human interaction, the question of whether and in what way this momentary interplay between child and camera is potentially somehow private or confidential. A psychoanalytically informed interpretation of the child's response in this instance might draw our attention to children's use of the 'smile' or fixed grin when encountering danger or feeling anxiety. It is difficult to ascertain whether the child appears to draw on the presence of the camera as a resource to assuage her 'being alone' or, in contrast, whether it is the camera itself which initiates her use of a smile as a defensive gesture. The ethical and moral dimensions underpinning research conducted with researchers' own children are not necessarily realised in legislative parameters outlined by bodies such as the British Psychological Society or the Economic and Social Research Council. In other words, the protocols and guidelines regarding what is deemed

Figure 9.1 Video-recording accompanying Extract 2. (a) Ella draws her hands together, and look downwards; (b) Ella raises her head and after a short delay looks up and towards the camera; (c) Ella 'interacts' with the camera; (d) and (e) Ella sways, moves, dances in a chair while looking at the camera.

both acceptable and appropriate will reflect the prevailing cultural conventions regarding children's rights. What might be seen as entirely appropriate in a UK context would not necessarily be acceptable in a Norwegian (Solberg, 1996) or Danish (Qvortrup, 1993) research context. Certainly the recognition that a researcher cannot second-guess any potential future use of research data in an unanticipated manner is often glossed over in established ethical guidelines (King, 2010).

In the next short extract, recorded when the child was a few months older, we find a more clear-cut case of the camera being oriented to as 'something that watches' or records. Here, and in addition to the indications that Ella may view the camera as someone/an entity that can be communicated with and/or appealed to when seeking solace, we have an instance where the camera is viewed with suspicion and/or negatively.

Extract 3: Child age – 2 years 11 months

Context

The father has prepared breakfast for the child and is busy in the kitchen – awaiting her eventual completion in order that they can go to work/nursery. The child is playing with her toys at the breakfast table and does not appear to want to eat her breakfast.

Summary exposition of extract

The child looks towards the camera while engaging in a behaviour which is generally prohibited in this context (using a pacifier/dummy instead of eating food), and before her parent has recognised that she is engaging in such behaviour.

(a) (b) (c)

Figure 9.2 Video-recording accompanying Extract 3. (a) Ella reaches for her 'pub' and puts it into her mouth; (b) Ella reaches for the second dummy and looks at the camera; (c) Ella moves one of her toys around in a circular movement.

EXTRACT 3: – CHILD AGE – 2 YEARS 11 MONTHS

1	*ELL:*	°xx xxx so°
2		(1.2)
3	*FAT:*	have you ↑tried your porridge ↓now
4		(2.3)
5	*FAT:*	has it cooled down for [you?]
6	*ELL:*	[↑I'm] only cutting this kiwi fruit up
7		(.) and [I'll] eat it
8	*FAT:*	[alright]
9		(1.9) ((child cuts toy fruit and one part flies off))
10	*ELL:*	eh but ↑I like my <u>fruit</u> be:::↑es[t]
11	*FAT:*	[you] do don't you
12		(3.5) ((sound of father starting toaster))
13	*ELL:*	°I miss my xxx° (.) xxx xxxx xxxxx
14		(17.9) ((puts dummy in mouth and looks at the camera))
15	*ELL:*	mmmhhhmmmm
16		(7.1)
17	*ELL:*	°mmmmmhhmm°=
18	*FAT:*	=↑a::::W >come on darling< don't put your [pubs in]
19	*ELL:*	[I wann com xxx I'm gonna <u>wait</u>] °for it° =
20	*FAT:*	=well it <u>is</u> cooled down now darling you're not eating i:::↑t
21		(0.2)
22	*FAT:*	>d'you want me< to take it away then?
23		(0.9)
24	*FAT:*	cause you're not eating any and you've not even tried it and you put
25		your pubs back in
26		(3.7)

Around line 3 we hear the father asking Ella whether she has tried her food, and on not receiving a reply then asks whether in fact it has cooled down now. Indications of upcoming disagreement between the participants may be apparent at line 6, when the child both interrupts/overlaps her father's second question, and in doing so uses the qualification 'only' when offering an explanation why she has not yet started eating. This account is accepted as reasonable by the father (line 8). The child however, again after a pause, then makes the suggestion that (rather than eating porridge) she 'likes her fruit' best, doing so with a stress and emphasis on the latter parts of her utterance. The father (who is talking from another part of the room) then simply agrees to what she has said, and it remains ambiguous whether there is any engagement on his part with the ongoing topic (the disagreement over what is being eaten/ or instead played with).

What then happens next again provides us with evidence regarding the status of the camera as a cultural object for this participant. About 3–4 seconds after the end of the quiet utterance in line 13, she looks quickly towards the porridge, then towards her 'dummy' (this/these have the pet name 'pubs' in this family), and putting her head on her hand/arm on the table reaches for her 'pub' and puts it into her mouth (see Figure 9.2a). Then, after a 5 second pause, she first reaches for a second dummy on the table, and after lifting it to her face, then turns and looks at the camera. This 'look' is sustained (4–5 seconds long) without any change in her facial expression (Figure 9.2b). She then looks away before spending another 9–10 seconds moving one of her toys around in a circular motion (Figure 9.2c). And then at line 18 we observe the father returning to the table and on doing so (line 18–24) displaying annoyance at the fact that she is not eating her food, is now sucking her dummies instead and asserting that she has not 'even' tried her food.

Certainly when we consider and compare the manner of these looks towards and actions in front of the camera (Extracts 2 and 3), the earlier example, although highlighting the child's recognition of the camera's presence, nonetheless leaves her experience and responses somewhat difficult to interpret. In Extract 3 in contrast, the looks she directs at the camera happen at a particular point in the sequence where (a) she is being asked to do something she does not wish to, (b) her response towards the food indicates she has little intention of carrying out the adult's request, and (c) instead engages in a series of actions which, in this particular family, are recognised as inappropriate and prohibited in this context (using her pacifiers). The length of the 'look', its manner and the specific moment in time that it occurs lend credence to the suggestion that she displays a recognition of being watched and is possibly being held accountable in some way (i.e., in the sense that somebody is watching you 'being naughty', and you notice that the watching is happening).

In the final extract for consideration, and recorded when the child was 4 months older, Ella's understanding and perception of the video-camera in the context of her everyday life becomes both a topic for specific comment by herself and others, and also an object that elicits particular kinds of behaviours and responses. The extent to which she seems to treat the camera both as a presence (an entity to interact with) and as something akin to a 'mirror' (showing what 'it' can see) seems to initiate an interesting series of gestures and actions by the child. Again, we also observe how the father/researcher is treating the camera as a particular kind of object.

Extract 4: Child age – 3 years 3 months

Context

As before, the recording context is meal-time (breakfast) and on this occasion, following the meal, the father is reading a book on the table (not interacting with the child). Ella is playing with a collection of large alphabet cards in front of her on the table and one of her soft toys is placed nearby.

Summary exposition of extract

On this occasion the child treats the video-camera (when the view-finder/display is visible to her) in a manner not dissimilar to responses children often exhibit when in front of a mirror.

EXTRACT 4. CHILD AGE – 3 YEARS 3 MONTHS

```
 1  ELL:   sun sk:::y              ((child singing across the next few lines))
 2         (1.2)
 3  ELL:   bethlehem
 4         (0.3)
 5  ELL:   ↑bethlehem xxx
 6         (2.4)
 7  ELL:   xxxx xxxx come for you xxx
 8         (7.8)
 9  ELL:   it's not coming ↑U::p        ((looking at camera))
10         (0.8)                        ((child continues pointing – moving index finger))
11  FAT:   what's not coming up darlin =
12  ELL:   =that thing
13         (0.1)
14  FAT:   the camera?
15         (0.3)
16  ELL:   °n:: ↑:o↓°
17         (0.7)
18  FAT:   ((coughs twice))
19         (0.4)
20  ELL:   can you turn it round?
21         (1.3)                        ((father moves from the chair))
22  ELL:   cant see it
23         (1.3)
24  FAT:   [((coughs))]
25  ELL:   [°an turn an xxx it°]  ((child holding hand up and doing 'turning' motion))
26                                ((F turns the display viewer on the camera around))
27         (5.4)                  ((on seeing her own image, child smiles))
28  ELL:   a::::w =
29  FAT:   =a::w awawa
30         (1.1)
31  FAT:   now we can see grommit           ((name of soft toy on table))
32         (4.1)
33  FAT:   grommit's looking quiet isn't he
34         (0.6)
35  FAT:   he he (.) ·hhh
36         (2.2)
37  FAT:   ((coughs))
38         (14.4)
39  ELL:   he had his breakfast (.) and now he's coming to play like a bi::g (.) big (.) big
```

```
40          ↓doggy
41          (3.2)
42  ELL:    and he ate all his breakfast
43          (1.5)
```

The extract begins with the child playing with large cards on the table (the father reading) and quietly singing to herself. During the quite long pause at line 8, during which it appears that she is trying to rub something out of one of her eyes, she looks across to her father, then turns and looks briefly towards the camera and then turns back towards her father again (who continues reading). She then turns again towards the camera, and as she utters line 9, raises her hand, points at the camera, and on finishing speaking, continues to look while moving/wiggling her finger as she holds her hand in the pointed position.

At line 11, and in reply, the father turns towards her, glances at the camera, then moves towards and close to the child, looking at her (not the camera) when he asks his question. When he replies with his question (after the briefest of pauses), he also turns towards the camera. Her quiet response to this question is noteworthy in that it is very quiet, is not in the affirmative and accompanied by a pitch/ intonation contour indicative of communicating "no, it is not" (coming up).

Leaving aside the possibility that his 'cough' that then follows might indicate his recognition/reminder that they are being filmed, Ella then, at line 20, asks if the view-finder/display attachment can be 'turned around'. As he moves from the table to alter the video-camera, she says very quietly something that sounds like 'and turn and see it', while at the same time holding out her hand in front of her and 'simulating' the turning motion of the display part of the video.

What happens next is striking and not dissimilar to the responses young pre-school children exhibit when placed in front of full-length mirrors (Vyt, 2001; Bard *et al.*, 2006). Just before her utterance at line 28, she first smiles bringing her hand to her face in a posture Goffman (1979) describes as a 'cant' (a head or body posture of subordination). As she continues her gaze/smile the father immediately imitates/repeats her 'aw-isn't that nice' sound and, as he returns to sit at the table, comments that now she can see her soft toy. Notice he doesn't say, 'now you can see yourself' or 'oh look, I can see you'. His comment may indicate his efforts at maintaining a 'researcher/professional' perspective on this sequence of events. Instead he says, 'now we can see grommit' (the toy sitting on the table). Of course, an alternative reading is that the adult, given that he was busy reading and not interacting with the child, simply did not wish to be disturbed and produced this comment so as to increase the likelihood that the child would play with the soft toy, leaving him to read.

What is of interest here, and again with reference to how the child participant understands the presence of the camera, is what happens next. The child (line 32), maintains a close studied gaze towards the camera/mirror and, after 4 seconds, the father suggests that the soft toy is not saying very much. Notwithstanding the possibility that this comment is related to the fact that the child is not saying very much at this point, at line 38, after a brief cough, the father returns to reading the book on the table. At this point, we observe an elaborate and detailed set of responses or performed interactions in front of/with the camera/ mirror by the child. While continuously looking at the video-sequence of herself in the view-finder, she first waves the large card in her hand; then puts the card under her chin, strokes her own body with the card, places it down, and although continuing to look at her image, then moves towards the soft toy, gives it a cuddle while still looking, and finally after this somewhat 'plaintive' performance, finally moves away and makes a comment about the soft toy. The father then turns around and looks again at the child.

Consider for a moment how the child responds to the camcorder view-screen, keeping in mind that she requested to see it in the first place. It is difficult to know what is going on here, and how we are to understand the series of actions and gestures initiated following the moment when the view-screen is turned around. The sequence of her gestures, actions and comments move from offers 'to the camera/self-image', touching the card against her body, face and head, while continuously looking, and then performing 'with' and 'comforting her toy dog'. This complex sequence of responses and actions is likely to be an expression of the child's own self-positioning, self-image recognition and the playing-around with image manipulation that children often engage in at around this age. At the very least we can say that the view-finder/camera object is now oriented to, and used by, the child in a manner which highlights something of the multiple associations it brings into play simply by its presence in this kind of context. The video-camera is a cultural object of a particular kind and for many children during the early years, experienced within and through discursive contexts which predicate the significance not so much of the image (photograph) but of the film or video-sequence – the video-clip of the first day at school, the week-end holiday break, the school play and all the self-recordings of everyday play between children. We are only beginning to understand how children themselves understand and orient to such practices.

Concluding comments

At some risk of stating the obvious, there is of course a close interdependence between technological development and changing research practices. Conversation analysis is unthinkable without the development of cheap, reliable, portable recording and playback of talk. The video-camera and associate recording techniques and practices have similarly initiated emerging orientations, perspectives and specific practices, which serve to add to the study of naturalistic everyday human interaction. Notice for example, in discussion and explication of extracts in CA publications (Schegloff, 1992) the referencing of the original recording of the event. One reading of such practices might be something along the lines of 'well, if you don't agree with the analysis, have a look at the video-sequence yourself, and you'll see what I mean'. It is the predicating of the significance or the 'very obviousness' or 'realness' of the associated recording that should draw our attention to the difficulties involved in the analysis of video-recordings. In a way reminiscent of Roland Barthes's (1982) comment that every photograph is a certificate of presence (*Camera Lucida*, p. 81), the video-sequence unfolding-ly making available to us, this, then that, then the next thing. This makes it increasingly difficult to recognise, in the process of analysis, the interrelationships between event selection, interpretation and the subsequent production of the extract/video-clip as analytic object. When the selection, capturing, recording and production of the event is itself a result of an 'insider participant' researcher's own agenda, then matters can indeed become both more complicated and potentially ambiguous.

The extracts examined above may also highlight certain hitherto unrecognised issues regarding the participant's own recognition and orientation to the video-camera in situ. Through documenting one child's changing responses to, and interaction with, the camera we are able to see that, for her, the camera as a cultural object has a particular and occasioned status within family life. Initially these responses are minimal and maybe of little remark, but increasingly it would seem the camera plays a somewhat ambiguous role – potentially a source of comfort and redress (Extract 2) or something more akin to a 'presence' which presupposes accountability (Extract 3). Certainly towards the end of the research study, the child's recognition and orientation towards the camera appears intertwined with the documenting of records, and indeed, her own self-positioning and self-image-play (Extract 4).

We also noted that the researcher himself has a somewhat peculiar relationship or orientation to the camera, envisioned not only on those occasions where the recognition or at least projection of 'possible audiences' in the future becomes clear (Extract 1), and needless to say, in the contribution that constitutes this chapter. The traditional boundaries between participant and researcher, as Hall (2000) intimated, do indeed become somewhat amorphous when engaged in 'insider participation' research concerned with documenting and analysing the everyday world of human interaction.

The analysis of the extracts in this chapters remind us of the challenges and complexities surrounding the recording and analysis of whatever constitutes everyday naturalistic interaction. Within social science, and in particular psychology, there remains a certain suspicion and scepticism over the interdependence between interpretation and the object of analysis. To some extent this reflects the particular emphasis on the experimental laboratory in the discipline such that observational methodologies themselves were traditionally viewed as belonging to the qualitative end of the methodological spectrum. In fact, developmental psychology, and particularly those branches concerned with documenting naturally occurring interactions (e.g., Smith and Connolly, 1980) adapted and extended techniques and procedures from ethology into sophisticated protocols for observational sampling (Altmann, 1974). The initial coding of an event as an instance of a coding category remains the starting point of this form of observational analysis and an important element of such procedures was the development of reliability procedures for establishing, measuring and assessing inter-observer reliability (e.g., the kappa co-efficient index). With the gradual introduction and spread of audio and then video technologies alongside the focus on procedures and practices concerning the documentation of the record of what 'has truly happened', computer-based video technologies have, if anything, increased the focus on quantification (e.g., the Observer Video-Pro system, Noldus *et al.*, 2000).

It is against this background that researchers in psychology using visual methods and adopting qualitative approaches in the study of human interaction have established and developed interpretative approaches from varying perspectives, e.g., ethnomethodological, discursive, ethnographic and social-semiotic. The examples above may help contribute to these recent developments through seeking to understand more of what the presence of recording equipment, and being recorded, might mean to people. How, we might ask, are the various technologies integrated into people's everyday sense-making practices? What forms of analysis might we use which draw out the subtle nature of the interdependence between the document record itself and the conditions within which such records are produced and made realisable? The participant-orientation focus of ethnomethodolgically informed conversation analysis certainly highlights the reflexive nature of everyday sense-making practices in situ. The status of being an 'insider participant', that is when a researcher straddles the boundaries between being 'object of analysis' and 'interpreter', does however draw our attention to the ongoing challenges central to the interdependence between the production of analytic objects (the video segment, the transcribed extract) and corresponding interpretation.

Appendix 1: Conversation analysis orthography

Table A9.1 Conversation analysis: transcription conventions

Transcription element	Meaning	Transcription element	Meaning
↑or↓	Marked rise (or fall) in intonation	:::	Sounds that are stretched or drawn out (number of :: indicates the length of stretching)
underlining.	Used for emphasis (parts of the utterance that are stressed)	[ ]	Overlaps, cases of simultaneous speech or interruptions.
UPPER-CASE LETTERS	Indicate increased volume (note this can be combined with underlining)	° word °	Shown when a passage of talk is noticeably quieter than the surrounding talk
.hhh	A row of h's with a dot in front of it indicates an inbreath. Without the dot an outbreath	=	When there is nearly no gap at all between one utterance and another

(comment)	Analyst's comment about something going on in the talk	(·)	Small pauses
> word<	Noticeably faster speech	(1.4)	Silences (time in seconds)
<word>	Noticeably slower speech	(xx)	Untranscribed talk

Source: Adapted from Forrester (2010).

References

Altmann, J. (1974). Observational study of behavior: sampling methods. *Behaviour*, *49*(3/4), 227–267.

Bard, K. A., Todd, B. K., Bernier, C., Love, J., and Leavens, D. A. (2006). Self-awareness in human and chimpanzee infants: what is measured and what is meant by the mark and mirror test? *Infancy*, *9*(2), 191–219.

Barthes, R. (1982). *Camera Lucida*. London: Jonathan Cape.

Brown, R. (1958). *Words and things*: New York: Free Press.

Burr, V. (2003). *Social constructionism*. London: Routledge.

CHILDES (2008). Childes Overview System – Basic. Available from http://childes.psy.cmu.edu/media/Eng-UK/Forrester

Cooper, H., Maxwell, S., Stone, A., and Sher, K. J. (2008). Reporting standards for research in psychology: why do we need them? What might they be? *American Psychologist*, *63*(9), 839–851.

Edwards, D. (1997). *Discourse as cognition*. London: Sage.

Forrester, M. A. (1988). Young children's conversation monitoring abilities. *First Language*, *8*, 201–226.

Forrester, M. A. (1992). *The development of young children's social-cognitive skills*. Hove, UK: Lawrence Erlbaum Associates.

Forrester, M. A. (2002). Appropriating cultural conceptions of childhood: participation in conversation. *Childhood*, *9*, 255–276.

Forrester, M. A. (2008). The emergence of self-repair: a case study of one child during the early pre-school years. *Research on Language and Social Interaction*, *41*(1), 99–128.

Forrester, M. A. (Ed.) (2010). *Doing qualitative research in psychology: a practical guide*. London: Sage.

Garfinkel, H. (1964). Studies of the routine grounds of everyday activities. *Social Problems*, *11*, 220–250.

Goffman, E. (1979). *Gender advertisements*. London: Macmillan.

Hall, R. (2000). Video recording as theory. In D. Lesh and A. Kelley (Eds), *Handbook of research design in mathematics and science education*. Mahwah, NJ: Lawrence Erlbaum Associates, pp. 647–664.

Heritage, J. (1998). Oh-prefaced responses to inquiry. *Language in Society*, *27*(3), 291–334.

Hutchby, I., and Woofit, R. (2008). *Conversation analysis*. Cambridge: Polity.

James, I. A., and Allen, K. (2004). A post-hoc analysis of emotions in supervision: A new methodology for examining process features. *Behavioural and Cognitive Psychotherapy*, *32*(4), 507–513.

James, W. (1890). *The principles of psychology*. New York: Holt.

Jefferson, G. (2004). Glossary of transcript symbols with an introduction. In G. H. Lerner (Ed.), *Conversation analysis: studies from the first generation* (pp. 13–31). Amsterdam and Philadelphia: John Benjamins.

King, N. (2010). Research ethics in qualitative research. In M. A. Forrester (Ed.), *Doing qualitative research in psychology: a practical guide*. London: Sage.

Livingston, E. (1987). *Making sense of ethnomethodology*. London: Routledge and Kegan Paul.

McWhinney, B. (2000). *The CHILDES Project: tools for analyzing talk* (Vol 2, 3rd ed.) Mahwah, NJ: Lawrence Erlbaum Associates.

Noldus, L. P. J. J., Trienes, R. J. H., Hendriksen, A. H. M., Jansen, H., and Jansen, R. G. (2000). The Observer Video-Pro: new software for the collection, management, and presentation of time-structured data from videotapes and digital media files. *Behavior Research Methods, Instruments, & Computers*, *32*(1), 197–206.

Ochs, E. (1979). Transcription as theory. In E. Ochs and B. Schiefflein (Eds), *Developmental pragmatics*. London: Academic Press.

Papousek, M., and Papousek, H. (1981). Musical elements in infant's vocalisations: their significance for communication, cognition and creativity. *Advances in Infancy Research*, *1*, 163–224.

Psathas, G. (1995). *Conversation analysis*. London: Sage.

Quay, S. (2008). Dinner conversations with a trilingual two-year-old: language socialization in a multilingual context. *First Language*, *28*, 5–33.

Qvortrup, J. (1993). Societal position of childhood: the international project Childhood as a Social Phenomenon. *Childhood*, 1(2), 119–124.

Sacks, H. (1992). *Lectures on conversation*. Oxford: Blackwell.

Schegloff, E. (1992). Repair after next turn: the last structurally provided defense of intersubjectivity in conversation. *American Journal of Sociology*, *97*, 1295–1345.

Smith, P. K., and Connolly, P. K. (1980). *The ecology of pre-school behaviour*. Cambridge: Cambridge University Press.

Solberg, A. (1996). The challenge in child research: from being to doing. In M. O'Brien (Ed.), *Children in families: research and policy*. London: Routledge.

Vyt, A. (2001). Processes of visual self-recognition in infants: experimental induction of 'mirror' experience via video self-image presentation. *Infant and Child Development*, *10*(4), 173–187.

Zuengler, J., Ford, C., and Fassnacht, C. (1998). *Analyst eyes and camera eyes: theoretical and technological consideration in 'seeing' the details of classroom interaction*. Retrieved 20 October 2009 from http://cela.albany.edu/analysteyes/index.html

10 Girls on film

Video diaries as 'autoethnographies'

Maria Pini and Valerie Walkerdine

We want you to picture a scene on screen:

> A young black woman sits on her bed, adjusting the video camera which she has
> balanced in front of her. 'I'm literally whispering now 'cause the walls in my house
> have ears' she says into her hand-held mike. 'This is quite private. It's quite personal,
> 'cause I don't really talk to anyone, about this sort of thing, in my family. So most
> of the time, they don't know what I'm thinking or what I'm planning or anything.
> So I got to keep it down' she says, gradually lowering her voice.

The above describes an extract taken from a video diary made by Rose. Rose's
admission to camera (and within a video diary which she believes may well end
up being broadcast on national television) that she has to whisper, because what
she wants to say is very personal, brings up some of the issues addressed by this
chapter. Centrally, we want to focus upon some of the questions which arise both
in relation to treating the video diary as 'research data', and in terms of notions
about 'empowering' the research subject to 'tell her own story' so to speak. What
do we (or more precisely what do we – as social researchers interested in questions
of subjectivity) get from the video diary, if not some kind of 'innocent', more
'authentic', or 'uncontaminated' (by the research process) representation of self?
How do we interpret such representations, and what do such data give us that a
more traditional research method does not? This chapter argues that when treated
in ways which resist treating this material as 'innocent', 'transparent' or as closed
to re/interpretation, the video diary can provide a particularly rich site for the
investigation of situated subjectivity; being as lived within a complex network of
social relations. In particular, we are drawing, in making our case, upon some of
the work done by Catherine Russell (1999) on experimental ethnography and in
particular, her work on autoethnography.

Birth of a video diaries project

The video diaries project from which Rose's diary comes was the last phase of a
longitudinal study of two groups of young British women who were, at the time
of making their video diaries, aged either 16 or 21 years old. Both groups (one

working and one middle-class) had been studied at various different earlier stages in their lives, and by means of a variety of more traditional data-collection methods. The 21-year-olds were studied for the first time when they were 4, and the 16-year-olds, when they were 6. The initial research aims were to examine how social class came to inform these different women's life trajectories. In the final phase of the project, the original research team (Walkerdine, Lucey and Melody; see Walkerdine *et al.*, 2001) asked the women to produce a video diary. Of the 30 young women originally involved in the study, 23 produced a video diary, but because all of these women were white, a further sample of six black and Asian women was added at this point.

Although it is important to remain critical in interpreting the video diary data produced by these young women (and we move onto this shortly), this material undoubtedly adds a rich body of fresh data to the project. This added depth comes primarily (albeit not unproblematically) from the fact that the research subjects can, and often did, appear to be more open and spontaneous in presenting themselves. This is partly connected to the absence of a figure of authority and to a figure who can 'talk back'. The camera (however much it might *signify* a researcher, a study or an observer) remains inanimate and silent. And this can make it a particularly rich surface for a subject's own projections. In one way, then, the camera functions as a blank page of a diary. Indeed, in an interview conducted when the project was over, several diarists did liken the practice to that of keeping a written diary. As one subject recalls:

> It was like my diary. You could say anything about your feelings or whatever and no one would ever say 'you're not allowed to do that', or 'you've got to be in by 10' or any of that. Whatever you wanted to say or do and wherever you wanted to take it, that was alright. It was someone to talk to that would never answer back.

For many subjects, then, the camera was treated as a trusted confidante; a good friend who listens but doesn't pass judgement. For many, it provided an 'ear' when a diarist felt no one else was listening to her. Rose's extract provides a particularly clear example of this.

From academe to television

The original research team had a number of reasons for wanting to pilot the video diary as a research method within this final phase of their project; the 'transition to womanhood' phase. Principally, the idea arose in thinking about a way of collecting data which might be somehow less 'invasive'. The team wanted, that is, to develop an observational method which did not depend upon the presence of what might be experienced by subjects as a 'surveillant' outsider, and which might also be understood by these subjects as a somehow 'empowering' experience – an opportunity for them to tell their 'own' stories, so to speak. Given the many well-documented problems associated with researching 'youth', and because of the numerous critiques made of the power relations produced within the traditional research setting, getting research subjects *themselves* to produce data seemed to suggest one way forward. Not only did this method constitute a seemingly less 'invasive' means of gathering data, but it also provided a way of working with a medium with which young people were becoming increasingly more familiar and comfortable. Plus, in this study at least, it was found that some of the working-class girls were not always particularly confident about their literacy skills and here video seemed to suggest a way of producing diaries (as personal records of subjectivity) without involving any writing. The research team were interested, then, in piloting a research method which gave the researcher a seemingly more marginal role, thereby affording research subjects a greater degree of control over the data produced.

Such ideas about empowerment and access (giving these girls the means by which to represent *themselves*) echoed not only a long-established feminist interest in the production of what can be called 'counter-fictions' of femininity, but it also echoed moves within British broadcast television of the time. The Video Diary genre was developed by the BBC's Community Programme Unit, and came about as a response by broadcasters interested in 'access TV' (non-professionals making TV programmes) to the proliferation of Hi8 then DV camcorders in the 1990s. As Tony Dowmunt (2001) explains:

> Although cheap, portable, user-friendly video cameras and recorders had been available for the previous 20 years, the coming of Hi8 was the first time that the image quality they offered passed the minimum quality threshold of the broadcast TV engineers, and an industry quick to cut production costs quickly adopted the camcorder in a wide range of factual programming.

As Dowmunt points out however, the advent of the video diary genre within UK television cannot be understood purely in technological or economic terms. It was not simply the case that cheap-enough and good-enough cameras were now available to 'Joe Bloggs'. The move towards 'real people television' within the UK also reflected far broader ideological shifts marking the development of postmodernism. In Dowmunt's words, the growth in 'real people television':

> ... also both reflected and deepened an ongoing post-modern crisis of documentary authority. Whilst the globalisation and centralisation of media power has continued apace it has been accompanied by a seemingly contradictory fragmentation of cultures and political systems. The fragmentation has been reflected by the proliferation of subjective media forms such as camcorder video, which have served to undermine the citadel of objective realism ... the sudden infusion of camcorder truth into the mass media domain reflects wider cultural developments. Subjectivity, the personal, the intimate, as the only remaining responses to a chaotic, senseless, out of control world in which the kind of objectivity demanded by the grand narratives, is no longer possible.

The 'transition to womanhood' research team was inspired by the work of the Community Programme Unit and, having identified girls willing to produce a diary, the team approached the Unit with the idea of a collaborative project. The BBC offered some training in video diary production, but it was Channel Four television which actually contributed funding to buy Hi8 camcorders on the understanding that they could broadcast any programmes which might result from the material. Four years later, in 1996, the team returned to Channel Four with the results, 175 hours of diary material having been recorded.

By this point however, there had been significant changes in personnel within the Independent Film and Video Department at Channel Four, and in the philosophy of the department as a whole. The research team had originally wanted to make a series of one-hour documentaries that would reflect the depth and breath of the diaries and highlight what these said about class and femininity within contemporary Britain. It was quickly obvious however, that the new regime at Channel Four was not interested in this. Where the team had envisaged a collection of 'serious' documentaries, Channel Four wanted a focus on, in their words, 'the feisty dynamism of the girls'. At this time, a proliferation of popular cultural discourses was coming to cohere around the concept of 'Girl Power'. Channel Four's desired focus has to be understood in this context. Eventually for television, the material became *Girls, Girls, Girls*, a series of ten 3-minute programmes shown in *The Slot*, a three-minute strand at 7.55 pm after the news. As Dowmunt puts it in explaining the situation:

> ... the serious, analytical and issue-based documentary form was increasingly being eclipsed at the time by the ratings-grabbing docu-soap. And the concept of 'access TV' was by then completely out of fashion'.

The video diary project began at a very particular time, then. As Dowmunt argues, the situation had changed by the time the bulk of the data had been gathered. The project started against a backdrop of belief in the potentially 'empowering' nature of the video diary. Not only did 'access TV' promise a new public visibility for previously marginalised groups, the video diary suggested the production of something more of the subject's own making, and therefore something which was in some ways more 'pure', or less 'mediated' by another's gaze, be this the gaze of a television production team or that of an academic research team.

Of course, it is easy to understand the original team's beliefs about what they were doing. Aside from the general post-modern crisis of representation which Dowmunt discusses, the diary format has a long history as a record of personal experience. It is easy to believe that what we are getting with the video diary is something more 'authentic'. As Lucey (1997) puts it:

> The testimonial or confessional character of the diary promises a site of veracity and authenticity originating in the diarist's experience.

Indeed, the camera became for many of these young women a 'friend' who accompanies them on their various outings; who sits listening to them late at night and who shares secrets that, in Rose's words, 'not even the walls can hear'. This intimacy becomes most obvious in the close-up piece to camera which, in Dowmunt's view, is a technique which enables the diarist to present herself as an individual with her own agency. This is also what makes the video diary, for any viewer, such a powerful and immediate statement of the maker's subjectivity. As Mark Reid (1999) has put it:

> Being challenged by the face of the author maybe demands that they have a voice, and introduces an ethical dimension to interpretation. The notion of representation is predicated on the subject represented as other and alien which has the unfortunate effect of silencing them as agents.

For Reid, the up-close presence of a diarist's talking face works to upset representation. The video diary guarantees a sense of subjective truth. In so many respects, the diaries come framed in the promise of the 'authentic'. Not only are these young women seemingly telling and showing their *own* stories, but the video diary speaks such a familiar language of realism. The diaries often deal with the domestic, the mundane, the everyday, the seemingly inconsequential, with the passage of real time and with a diarist's often quite disorganised 'streams of consciousness'. They have the appearance of truths spoken from the heart. It is in relation to this that Dowmunt has argued that the video diary challenges representation, because it is self-expression rather than representation. 'These' he argues, 'are presentations of self' rather than re-presentations of prior existing selves'.

The concept of authenticity has remained a central theme in anthropological explorations and discussions around the development of film and video as a research tool. Because video diaries have managed to do away with both elaborate technology and a film crew, they can make seductive claims to authenticity. We can very easily get drawn into thinking that because there is no film crew, people act as though they were not being watched or as though the camera weren't actually there, and that what we consequently get, is something less 'mediated'. All of this, of course, is based upon the notion that what subjects might say about themselves is necessarily more 'pure' and also more 'valid' than what someone else might say about them.

The inevitable limitations of expression and visibility

Clearly, some of the initial beliefs underpinning the development of this phase of the project were based on fictions which are obviously very problematic. For one thing, all of this material is subject to a manifold process of editing. From the condensation of a complicated body of material down into the 'feisty dynamism' displayed within the three-minute *Girls, Girls, Girls* programmes, to the self-editing done by the girls who erased before submitting their tapes, to the diarist who very obviously sets the physical stage for her piece, any notion of, or concern for, 'authenticity' is redundant.

Furthermore, although the diaries may appear to hold truths 'spoken from the heart', the makeup of this 'heart' needs to be rethought. The way Dowmunt addresses it, it is as though the essence of this self-expressing voice is somehow beyond its cultural make-up; unmarked by a whole host of stratifying classifications including, in this case, class and ethnicity. Certainly, with these diary data, it very quickly became obvious that to see this exercise as somehow 'empowering' the research subjects was naïve. Although in *one* sense, in the absence of a physical observer, the diarist *can* feel less surveilled, this is by no means straightforward. The physical observer may well be absent (and this clearly has its advantages) but very often she is brought back into play through the diarist's own projections onto camera – which is often addressed as 'you'. But more than this, many of these women make it very clear that they are *intensely* aware of being watched – and not by just anyone, but by research-psychologists in particular. Within the diaries, we frequently encounter diarists referring to the longitudinal study itself. One particularly clear example is given in Chloe's diary. In the following, Chloe (a white, middle-class diarist) is videoing her friend, who sits in front of the camera, smoking a cigarette as she addresses Chloe:

> 'What's it all for?' she asks the invisible cameraperson, who does not, at first, respond. The woman continues. 'It's all a bit voyeuristic this, you know. Being watched I feel quite …'. She hesitates. 'Quite looked at?' the cameraperson suggests. 'Yes' the woman replies. 'Well' the cameraperson replies, 'I've been studied since I was four, you know. They've given me this camera to make a video diary of myself. It's a longitudinal study of social class and femininity in the nineties and I'm supposed to film myself every day. They want to understand how middle-class and working-class girls live differently in nineties Britain. When I was four, I had a microphone attached to me and they were interested in how our mothers – middle-class and working-class mothers – treated us differently. They're still studying those kinds of questions.' The cameraperson pauses and the young woman nods, saying 'it's interesting'. 'Yes' continues the cameraperson, 'but it's not very objective, is it? I mean, they've explained it all to us and we know exactly what they're looking for'. She pauses for a while before continuing. 'But I suppose that's what they want, you know. See, they're not really interested in those kind of science models of research. So they don't mind that we know exactly what they're looking for.'

For Chloe, we (as researchers), our questions, our project's foci and even our methodology, are ever-present within her video diary. This is not about something produced away from the research 'gaze'. What is produced is always done so in response to the perceived focus of the project. The diarist always produces herself as a *particular* kind of subject in response to this focus. For this reason, what we watch as researchers is not simply a representation of subjects constituted within particular class and gender relations, but also in relation to a particular focus. The particular technology of representation is crucial and the (albeit materially absent) audience is ever-present. These subjects are constituted within a particular 'to-be-looked-at' situation and Chloe is by no means alone in making an ever-present awareness of this obvious. Often, an explicit (and sometimes critical) reference to psychology and to the research gaze in general, is evident. We therefore encounter frequent reference to what is obviously seen to be a normative psychological gaze – with many of the diarists talking about not wanting to appear 'weird', or being concerned about appearing 'normal'. Indeed, concerns about appearance (about appearing respectable and 'normal') are rarely absent from the diaries. Often, such concern takes a particular form with the white, working-class girls – who in several instances appear very aware of how their homes and their accents, for example, might mark them out as 'different'. The black and Asian diarists, having been recruited to the project at a much later stage, are somewhat different in this respect. These women *knew* from the beginning of their involvement that their diaries might well be broadcast on national television. So for these women, this project always involved the possibility of their being visible to a far wider audience.

An awareness of the signifiers of accent (a clear indicator of one's social class position within Britain) signals itself in a variety of ways for the working-class white girls. In one diary, for example, the diarist's grandmother very obviously adopts a 'posh' accent every time she believes that she is being filmed. On several such occasions, in a clearly affected upper-class accent she says 'the rain in Spain falls mainly on the plain', a famous line repeated by Eliza Doolittle in *Pygmalion* the play/*My Fair Lady* the film, as part of her elocution training.

Other diarists, too, refer quite explicitly to a kind of voyeurism which they associate with the gaze of the researcher, saying things like 'see, this is how people like us behave' or 'see this is what black people do'. To return to Rose's diary, another section of this shows a scene wherein a room full of young black people are gathered chatting at a social get-together. Rose appears on screen among her friends and a male voice is heard behind the camera. This male friend is doing the videoing. As he pans those gathered, zooming into smaller groups and particular faces, he adopts the voice of the 'television anthropologist', giving a running commentary as he films. 'See the jungle', he announces, adopting a slow, deep, David Attenborough-like voice. 'Here, this one's from Central Africa' he says as he zooms into one woman's face. He then zooms out and pans further, before zooming into the couple sitting next to her and saying 'here's a couple from the depths of darkest Africa'.

The above example illustrates very clearly one of the most important aspects of the diary data as a whole: the video diary is *always* produced with an audience in mind. The (imagined) interpretative gaze of the researcher is always a reference point. In the above extract, this gaze is being played with or 'mocked'. A very similar approach to this gaze is evidenced within an extract from Jane's diary. Here, Jane and her friend have dressed up and have set a table with plates, flowers, glasses, a filled fruit bowl and a bottle of champagne, in staging what they call an 'average, everyday breakfast'. Music is playing in the background as the girls joke and speak in 'posh' accents, toasting the camera and feeding each other strawberries. The humor of the scene is very clearly structured around the perceived focus of the project. This is a 'middle-class breakfast' 'middle ... "spoof"'.

If imagining that the video diarist feels somehow less surveilled is mistaken, then so too is thinking that actually making a diary is a necessarily 'empowering' experience for these young women. Clearly, what can appear as 'empowerment' within one situation – for example, the camera enabling Rose to tell a story which not even the 'walls' of her house can hear – can appear within another as something quite different. Again, some of the working-class, white women, often gave the impression of having experienced this exercise as, in some ways, another way of being subjected to the surveillant and normative gaze of the (middle-class, usually white) researcher. In later commenting upon how they had experienced the exercise, many of these women spoke of not really having enjoyed this, and some mentioned videoing out of a strong sense of obligation rather than out of enjoyment. As indicated, some also spoke about hating their accents because these make them appear 'common'. And although they were asked not to, several of the working-class girls signalled a certain 'resistance' to the project by actually wiping much or all of their diary before handing in their tape.

Many of the research team's initial assumptions have, then, been shown to be rather naïve. Although there are clearly advantages with being able to gather research data without a researcher being physically present, it is important not to read the data gathered as somehow 'uncontaminated' by the research gaze. In many ways, this physical absence actually makes very little difference. Aspects of the same interpretative mechanics are seen to be at play.

Video diaries as autoethnographies

When assessing the usefulness of the video diary as data, then, one first step involves letting go of any easy over-simplistic notions of 'authenticity', 'access' and 'empowerment'. One way to do this is through turning to moves made within postmodern and postcolonial ethnography, towards the use of film and video in the development of a 'visual ethnography'. Analysis of this data moved, then, towards considering the diaries in relation to Russell's discussion of recent experimental ethnography – to thinking about the diaries as 'auto-ethnographies'. This provides a far more useful set of questions from which to move forwards. In some ways, this is a problematic move, we know, because after all, these diarists are not actual film makers, and Russell focuses primarily upon the work of artists and theorists who are formally involved in the production of avant-garde or otherwise experimental autobiographical film work. Nevertheless, these video diaries can be usefully considered in parallel to such practice. As Russell (1999: 276) explains:

> Autobiography becomes ethnographic at that point when the film – or video – maker understands his or her personal history to be implicated in larger social formations and historical processes. Identity is no longer a transcendental or essen-tial self that is revealed, but a 'staging of subjectivity' – a representation of the self as performance.

Despite the fact that these diarists are not intentionally or formally setting out to conduct 'visual ethnography', they are nevertheless on an ethnographic journey.

They are invited to take a particular 'ethnographic' position in relation to themselves and their situations. Furthermore, they *do* understand themselves to be 'implicated in larger social formations and historical processes'. They know that this is a study about class and femininity within the Britain of the 1990s. They know that they are the subjects of this study. They are therefore invited to recognise themselves in-situation, in-history and in-culture. Chloe speaks openly about having been a research subject since the age of four. Rose's friend takes up the position of 'anthropologist' as he films the party of young black friends at her house. Like all of the diarists, these two, when addressing the viewing 'you', are situating themselves in relation to the foci of this project.

These diarists are, then, invited to take up a dual position of both observer and observed. They move through an 'in between', situated partly as authors of their own stories and partly as subjects of this story. Because of this dual situation, argues Russell, the autoethnography inevitably produces a representation of self which is unambiguously a performance – which rather than being a sign of coherence, is in fact about multiplicity. As she puts it:

> Autoethnography produces a subjective space that combines anthropologist and informant, subject and object of the gaze under one sign.

One interesting aspect of this multiplicity to emerge from the present data comes through seeing the diarists' illustrations of the diverse positions they occupy within their own circumstances. In simple terms, within a single diary, the diarist can be friend, daughter, sibling, student, and worker; each position demanding a somewhat different performance of self. Usually, before friends, a diarist will often present a very different self than that presented before parents. And when alone, before the camera, a different self again.

The video diarist verbally addresses and visually displays the general sense of multiplicity and fragmentation constituting her situation. The viewer is made party to the make-up of selves as these are situated within, and move between, different contexts. A particularly clear example of this is shown when a diarist comments retrospectively to camera about something videoed earlier. There are, for example, a number of instances where a diarist will film herself along with friends within one context and later comment on this footage. Within her initial footage, she might appear as confident and happy for example. But later, when alone and doing a piece to camera, she can present a very different reading of what was going on; of how she was feeling whilst videoing. Diane, for example, presents as a confident, funny, young woman whilst in a scene where she is videoing with friends at a picnic. Later, however, when alone and reflecting on the day's events, she speaks to camera about having felt 'left out' by the group. She thus offers a very different reading – one which highlights the multiplicity and fragmentation constituting subjectivity. These examples highlight how the video diary deals with *situated* subjectivity.

Clearly we have long passed simple questions about 'authenticity', coherence and straightforward 'empowerment'. Instead, what this diary material forces is a recognition of multiplicity and fragmentation. The video diary opens a space within which, in the process of both embodying and representing self, gaps, contradictions and difference are made visible.

Inauthentic subjectivities: using video diaries in a study of class and femininity

> Autoethnography is a vehicle and a strategy for challenging imposed forms of identity and exploring the discursive possibilities of inauthentic subjectivities.
>
> (Russell, 1999: 276)

In analysing the video diary data, with a focus upon the initial research team's questions about social class and femininity, it soon becomes clear that in many ways this material upsets classifications. It is much harder than it might be with an audio-taped interview or with a questionnaire to keep categories such as 'working-class' or 'woman' in place. Here, we are dealing with data which, above all, highlight the multiplicity and fragmentation involved in the constitution of subjectivity. In Russell's terms, reading such data begs an exploration of the discursive possibilities within these categories. Although we can draw broad conclusions about general differences between the diaries produced by the working-class and by the middle-class diarists (and these are drawn out in brief shortly), hard-and-fast distinctions are made impossible. These data include diaries illustrating 'confident' middle-class girls; 'camera-shy' working-class girls; 'confident' and 'creative' working-class girls; less 'confident' middle-class girls and so forth. A single diarist can display moments of 'confidence', moments of apparent 'shyness' and moments in which she is simply ridiculing the whole diary exercise. The categories of class and gender simply cannot contain in any hard-and-fast way, this material. They cannot say *all* that there is to say about a given diarist or about any group as a whole. Although this is *always* the case with the analysis of subjectivity, by means of *any* methodology, the visual component here makes classification even more difficult. The data forces an engagement with the *specific*. These diarists, in producing detailed visual illustrations of their situations, highlight not simply their conformity to any general rules about class and gender, but importantly, to their *individual* negotiations of these classifications. As Russell (1999: 276) puts it in addressing ethnicity, anthropology and autoethnography:

> One's body and one's historical moment may well be the joint site of experience and identity, and yet, they don't necessarily add up to ethnicity as an anthropological category. Autoethnography is a vehicle and a strategy for challenging imposed forms of identity and exploring the discursive possibilities of inauthentic subjectivities.

At the start of analysing these data, a long time was spent attempting to neatly fit the different diaries into class 'boxes'; to find general rules about class location and differences in diary-making. Inevitably, much time was wasted. If anything, these data challenge such imposed classifications and, although we now illustrate several of the more obvious points to emerge in thinking about social class differences and diary-making, we stress that to collapse any given diary into this frame simply does not do justice to the complexity of the material.

To return to the question of social class and diary-making, then, we close with several diary extract descriptions, chosen because they illustrate something of the different material, linguistic, social and also interpretative resources which these different (and differently situated, in terms of social class) diarists seemingly have access to in fabricating a visual fiction of self. We bring together extracts from Susan's diary, Ann's diary, Rose's diary and Penelope's diary in order to highlight one important aspect of the project's findings. In short, the extracts arguably highlight the different storytelling opportunities available to the working-class and the middle-class diarists. To reiterate, however, these extracts do not say *all* that there is to say about the subjectivity of their makers and we return to this in our final comments.

Susan is one of the working-class diarists. In this extract, Susan is sitting on her single bed. Behind her a number of rosettes hang on the wall. Susan remains seated in the same position throughout this eight-minute piece. Her voice is quiet throughout, at points becoming almost inaudible. She checks the camera, and begins a short piece-to-camera:

> 'I've been with my boyfriend, Mike, for three years and one month at the end of this month. So it's quite a long time. And we met in a pub. My mum used to go there with her friend. And Mike's mum used to know my mum's friend and I met him and then I gave him a letter. And he said 'yes'. And we started going out and that's it really.'
> She pauses and looks around her room seemingly considering what to do next.
> 'And we've been going out about three years or something, So it's quite a long time and ... well, so ...' Again, Susan pauses.
> 'I went to two schools and um ... I left in June 1990, and that was it really. And Mike's coming later so you'll be able to meet him and I'll be able to show you him. And my friend Sally. She's coming later and ... that's about it really.'. Again, Susan pauses.
> 'My mum works in the local launderette which is about five minutes' walk down the road, so that's ok. And my nan's just come out of hospital 'cause she's just had her hip done. And my sister's just got a new job in a security company and my dad's got about five weeks off work. So that's about it really.'

This extract illustrates a story very much based within a local, family-based setting. As Susan puts it on several occasions, 'that's it really'.

The second extract comes from a particularly short diary produced by Ann, another working-class diarist. Ann herself does not appear within this piece. Instead she carries the camera as she videos the people gathered within her flat. The extract begins in Ann's kitchen where she is videoing her boyfriend taking a beer from the fridge. The man turns and spots her with the camera:

> 'Oh no, I hate that' he says to Ann. 'Don't. 'Cause I'll get the hump' he tells her, walking away. Ann follows him into the front room and continues to video. He is

clearly annoyed and lifts his hand to cover the camera-lens. The screen goes blank. 'No Chris, don't' Ann shouts. He drops his hand and Ann continues to move around the flat and videoing the other friends present. Two women are seated at a table and smile to the camera as Ann videos them.

She continues into the front room where two men, one of them Chris, are watching television. The men ignore her. Seemingly directed at the men, Ann, still videoing announces 'I'm recording all over what I did today'. This gets Chris' interest and he answers 'I should think so too. Who'd wanna listen to you?' he mumbles.

Ann's very short diary constitutes a particularly clear example of one aspect to emerge from the data; the seeming limitations and constraints facing the working-class diarists. Ann erases most of her video diary and is told by her boyfriend Chris, that it's a 'good job'. Like Susan, although for different reasons, she appears at a loss to find material with which to fill her diary.

The third extract is taken from Penelope's diary. Penelope is one of the middle-class diarists. The extract begins with Penelope playing the violin as she stands reading a music score which rests on a stand in front of her. As she plays, she does not face the camera and has obviously got the camera mounted on a tripod. She finishes the music and still holding her bow, turns to the camera.

'This is actually completely typical' she says, walking around the music stand. 'I've got this Guild Hall deadline to meet by Friday. I've got a philosophy essay to write by Thursday. I've got a folio to prepare for Saturday, with five pieces and I've only got two'. As she says this, Penelope paces the room and uses her fingers to tick off each of her tasks as she lists them.

She continues 'and I'm babysitting tomorrow and I'm babysitting on Thursday. And I'm having to spend all this time … Come home today, eat some dinner because I'm going to the cinema, so I can't eat later … so I've got two and a half hours and I've just done forty five minutes of practice and I've already done two hours practice this morning. Then I have maybe and hour to write a composition and put it in my folio and …'. Penelope rubs her eyes as she lists all of the things that she has to do. She continues, 'And I'm not going to do my English essay, and everyday all I'm doing is practicing every single day.' Penelope pauses and looks around her. 'It's going to be a really, really bad week.' She pauses again and begins to move around the room, seemingly lost in thought. The scene is quiet for a while. 'Actually not only that', she continues sighing, '… I'm giving a talk tomorrow night. I've got to go to the Performing Arts workshop on Friday because there's no other time I can go and ... so that's two hours at home on Friday to do my practice and to do my folio and Thursday I've got to be in school because …' she says facing and addressing the camera directly. 'This is really weird – taking to the camera.' She pauses briefly before continuing. 'Oh and it's Reading Week and we have people coming to talk to us so I can't do my homework on Friday lunchtime either which is … this is completely ridiculous.' Penelope pauses looking at something off-screen. 'Oh I've just spotted The Bell Jar.' She disappears to follow her gaze. Seconds later she reappears with the book in her hand. She puts it close to the camera lens. 'Yes, we're supposed to read this for English' she says as she walks, once again holding her violin. '… Along with the seven other books I've got on the list to read.' Penelope once again begins playing the violin.

Penelope's entire diary is filled with a host of outings, events, deadlines and pieces-to-camera covering the many things happening within her life, including her fears, aspirations and her dreams. Hers is a particularly long and detailed diary. The contrast which emerges from bringing together Penelope's diary with those produced by Susan and by Ann is stark.

Indeed, in relation to all of the data, the working-class diarists tended to produce shorter diaries and they often tended to display less 'confidence' in presenting themselves and their stories. Where Susan's five-minute piece to camera involves details of what is going on within her immediate family and two mentions of how long she has been with her boyfriend, Penelope's covers a whole host of involvements in a world far beyond her family. She appears almost breathless in her attempt to fit everything into her video. Where Susan repeats 'that's about it really', Penelope gives the impression that she could talk for hours. Where Ann erases much of her material, Penelope produces and submits tens of hours' worth. We might say that the diaries of the working-class girls suggest a far more limited range of storytelling resources. These tend to be shorter and tend to be concentrated around the world of home, family and friends. Following this line of argument, we might say that, in many ways, the middle-class girls somehow have it 'better'. Indeed, the video diary phase of this project reinforces many of the findings gathered within previous phases of the project and by means of other research methods. In terms of academic achievement for example, the best qualified of the working-class girls is less educationally qualified than is the lowest academic achiever from the middle-class group. The video diary data adds a further illustration of such differences.

It is, however, extremely important to resist being drawn into any straightforward or over-simplistic reading of the middle-class girls from the sample as being necessarily 'better off'. Perhaps one of the most valuable aspects of these data is that they illustrate so clearly that all of these diarists' stories have *more* than one side to them. To reiterate, they highlight the complexity and multiplicity of these stories. Although, read in one light, Penelope appears to *have it all*. She is a confident, successful young woman. However, the above extract can be read in a very different light; she is stressed and having 'a completely typical …. Bad, bad week'. Indeed, at a later point in her diary, Penelope videos herself speaking about a particular 'exam dream' she has had. As she speaks, she becomes quite emotional, wiping tears from her eyes as she recounts the dream. In this, her A Level exam results are not good enough to allow her entry into the university of her choice. This particular section of her diary sits in stark contrast to a particular section of Rose's diary where, again, the diarist is talking to camera about her academic situation. Rose is, at the time of making her piece, doing a BTEC course in Nursery Nursing. Rose videos this particular part of her diary after she has received an especially pleasing mark for a piece of college work. This thirty-minute extract is entirely taken up by a demonstration of Rose's pride in the piece of work. In great detail, she recounts what her tutor has told her and as she holds each page of her work close up to the screen, she tells of her absolute delight in scoring so much better than many of her classmates. On one level, Penelope is in a far better position academically than Rose. She is already far better academically qualified than Rose, and has aspirations far more closely associated with traditional notions of 'success'. She plans to go to university. Rose, on the other hand, is studying for a diploma, with the aim of working within a nursery. On one level, she has less reason for such an animated display of pride.

But the above contrast speaks of more than simply the relativity of 'success'. Bringing these two extracts together illustrates how the video diary as a research tool forces an engagement with the complexity and multiplicity of subjectivity. This is by no means to say that the data do not allow for any positive conclusions to be drawn about the subject in question; class and femininity within Britain. Rather, it is to recognise that one of the key advantages of using the video diary material in a study of this kind is that it forces a recognition of the variety of different cultural discourses, be these sexual, racial, and/or class based making up the subject. In other words, subjectivity is staged here as a site of different discursive pressures and articulations; individual diarists as negotiators of these conditions.

Conclusions: the value of the video diary within social research

In this chapter, we have sought to suggest some of the advantages of the video diary method in researching subjectivity. We would argue that the primary factor here involves the depth of the material produced. Not only are we presented with subjects' verbal accounts of their situations, but we are also confronted by visual displays of these. Aspects which escape or exceed what a diarist might *say* about herself are revealed for interpretation. A diarist may claim to be a confident, relaxed and happy young woman, but the fact that she has produced a particularly short diary and that she rarely appears personally within this, choosing instead to film others, suggests something quite different. Furthermore, the fact that she can present herself very differently when amongst friends, amongst family and when alone to camera enables the researcher to speak about the multiple faces of subjectivity. The video diary is, we are arguing, perfectly suited to a study which recognises the complexity and multiplicity of subjectivity. Not only does the subject register herself with *voice,* but with *body* and *context* too. The video diarist is always a *situated subject.*

References

Dowmunt, T. (2001) *Dear camera ... video diaries, subjectivity and media power.* Paper presented at OurMedia Conference, Washington, DC.

Russell, C. (1999) *Experimental ethnography.* Durham and London: Duke University Press.

Lucey, H. (1997) *Video diaries: developing a visual method for youth research.* Paper presented at Goldsmiths College, Seminar Series.

Walkerdine, V., Lucey, H. and Melody, J. (2001) *Growing up girl: psychosocial explorations of gender and class.* London: Palgrave.

11 Visual identities

Choreographies of gaze, body movement and speech in video-based mother–midwife interaction

Helen Lomax

Introduction

The aim of this chapter is to explore the potential of a video-based methodology for theorising identity. Drawing on the theoretical and analytical framework of conversation analysis (CA) and video-based research on mother–midwife interaction (Lomax, 2005), the chapter will explore the role of the visual in mediating social interaction and in the discursive construction of identity. Drawing on sequences of interaction in which mothers talk with midwives about their recent birth experiences, the chapter will examine how particular normative professional and patient identities are accomplished locally and sequentially through co-ordinated gaze, body movement and speech. Mothers and midwives story-telling activity can be understood as a dance through which each subtly displays, through their talk and visual attention to the other, their acknowledgement of, and shifting affiliations to, institutionally defined and wider cultural understandings of birth and mothering and through which particular maternal and professional identities are 'talked into being' (Heritage, 1984).

The chapter will also focus on sequences of interaction in which I, as the researcher, am observably drawn in to the on-going interaction through the mother's visual interaction (gaze, gesture and facial expression) to outline an empirically based reflexive approach which moves beyond 'confessional' reflexive positions (Finlay and Gough, 2003) in order to enhance research practice and methodology. Analytic focus on these sequences makes visible the significance of the visual and its pivotal role in the construction of preferred patient identities while also making explicit the role of the researcher and video camera in the construction and mediation of video-based data.

The research context: problems and possibilities

A common theme across the corpus of academic and professional literature, including some feminist literatures, is the promotion and prioritisation of a model of midwifery which claims to support and empower mothers' ways of knowing through an 'emotionally connected supportive relationship' (Wilkins, 2000: 38). Underpinning this perspective is the view exemplified, to varying degrees, in sociological and psychological accounts in which mothers and midwives' priorities are meshed together as the common-gender-based concerns of women (Campbell and Porter, 1997; Martin, 2001). Despite its limited empirical basis, the ideology of woman-centred midwifery underpins much recent professional literature and debate (Hyde and Roche-Reid, 2004; Page and Sandell, 2000; Leap, 2009) and has been a key influence on policy development in which midwifery care is politicised as a means of re-gendering and transforming woman-focused services (Department of Health, 1993, 2004, 2007). However, the suggestion that mothers and midwives locate the same ideological and emotional space is increasingly contested. Research on doctor–patient and nurse–patient relationships highlights the incompatibility of gender-based service provider–user affiliations with professional hegemonies. These works suggest instead a mis-match between clients' gender-based expectations and practitioners' psychological defence against anxiety (Menzies, 1998) and ideas about professional and work-based identities (Brooks, 1998). While, within the sociology of midwifery, work by Sandell *et al.* (2001) on the impact of team-based midwifery on midwives' work practices, found that midwives' needs as both workers and women may be subjugated to mothers' needs through unfriendly work practices and mothers' expectations about service provision.

At a theoretical level, the idea that mothers and midwives are uniquely connected through a shared epistemology has been vigorously attacked by Annandale and Clark (1996). Their post-structuralist analysis provides an authoritative critique of what they see as the essentialist gender-based alignment of mothers and midwives. As they argue, the assumption that because mothers and midwives are biologically female they necessarily share common interests results in the conflation of a set of putative feminine ideals perpetuating an essentialist myth of womanly sameness (and difference from men) which ultimately mitigates against and undermines women. Further, in conceiving power as 'male', it glosses over the way that women may exert power, including over other women (Bowes and Domokos, 1998; Fink and Lundqvist, 2010). Annandale and Clark's position is supported by Foucauldian analysis which questions the unique pairing of gendered discourses of empowerment with midwifery (and medicalised discourses of control with medicine), highlighting the ways in which normative discourses may operate across gender categories (Arney, 1982; DeVries and Barroso, 1997; Pitt, 1997; Williams, 1997). Drawing on documentary analysis (Arney, 1982) and oral history methods (Pitt, 1997), they expose the fluid nature of professional discourses, suggesting that midwives, like their medical counterparts, may draw on 'male/medical' discourses (which prioritise 'science', 'rationality' and birth as 'normal in retrospect') and 'female/midwifery' discourses (which valorise 'femaleness', 'nature', 'intuition' and birth as 'natural') and caution against:

> arguments about the "male take over" of childbirth (which) need to be framed *very carefully* .... professionals of both sexes need to consider how their *practices set up particular relationships of power with the pregnant woman.*
>
> (Pitt, 1997: 228–229, my emphasis)

However, absent from these accounts is an empirically drawn analysis of the ways in which these relationships are managed in practice, including how cultural, professional and institutional discourses are invoked, embraced or resisted in interactions between mothers and professional care-givers, including midwives. In order to answer these questions, a more sophisticated methodological approach capable of capturing and analysing the details of interaction, including its visual dimension, is required. Such a methodology is provided by the theoretical and analytical framework of ethnomethodological conversation analysis (CA; Sacks *et al.*, 1974). CA is a well-established approach to the study of talk-in-interaction which, through an analysis of the detailed organisation of people's talk, and increasingly their gaze and deportment (Goodwin, 2001; Heath *et al.*, 2010; Ruusuvuori, 2001), makes visible the everyday methods that people use to make meaning. CA's focus on 'ethnomethods' (Garfinkel, 1967) makes explicit the ways in which social order is accomplished through 'talk-in-interaction' (Schegloff, 1968). As Antaki and Widdicombe (1998: 1) elaborate, 'social life is a continuous display of people's local understandings of what is going on', an activity which is accomplished by their 'elegantly exploiting the features of ordinary talk.' In this way, identity categories (including gender-based categories), institutional priorities etcetera are viewed, not as independent of members' practical action, but as embedded in and accomplished through their situated interactions. The participants themselves (rather than the analyst) display, orient to and make relevant these meanings.

Within psychology, these analytic concerns have been taken up by scholars of identity including feminist scholars (Kitzinger, 2000; Speer, 2005; Speer and Stokoe, 2009) in their elaboration of the value of CA for making visible the ways in which identity is constructed in everyday interactions and, increasingly, in health and social care-service encounters (Finlay *et al.*, 2008) adding to the body of sociologically informed CA in this field (Heath, 1986, 1997; ten Have 2001; Drew and Heritage, 1992). Within this body of work, Kitzinger's (2000) feminist CA has been of central importance in providing an empirically drawn critique of essentialist feminist perspectives on sex-based identity helping to shift academic feminism away from the binary thinking which constructs such differences as a priori natural facts. As she explains:

'Rather than seeing language use as marking a gender ... identity which exists prior to the act of speaking, we can understand language use as one way of understanding iden- tity ... Instead of "how do women and men talk differently?" we can ask *how particu- lar forms of talk contribute to the production of people as "women" and as "men"*.
Kitzinger (2000: 170, my emphasis)

In articulating gender identities as locally and sequentially accomplished in everyday interaction, Kitzinger's work has resonance for feminist understandings of the mother–midwife relationship which are premised on gender-based assumptions of empowerment and sameness. Rather than seeing gender categories as pre-existing, it is possible from the perspective of CA to explore how the participants themselves orient to their statuses as women, mothers, midwives etc. and how these identities might be displayed and encouraged, refused or resisted in their situated interactions. Further, drawing on recent theoretical and methodological developments within visual methods, it is possible to extend this analysis to systematically consider the role of the visual in mediating interaction. As Goodwin (2001) elaborates:

> A primordial site for the analysis of human language, cognition and action consists of a situation in which multiple participants are attempting to carry out courses of action together while attending to each other, the larger activities that their current actions are embedded within and relevant phenomena in their surround. *Vision can be central to this process. The visible bodies of participants provide systematic, changing displays about relevant action and orientation.*
>
> (Goodwin, 2001: 157, my emphasis)

The development of increasingly sophisticated video technology including video-data handling packages which assist in the inspection of the coordinating role of seen phenomena (gaze, facial expression, eye-movement and gesture) has advanced research practice in this area, enabling analysts to attend to the significant role of the visual in mediating talk and activity including in the co-constitution and display of understanding, disagreement and resistance (cf. Finlay *et al.*, 2008; Goodwin, 2001; Ruusuvuori, 2001).

Research questions and methods

The aim of this research was to empirically explore the potential of video-based methodology for theorising identity and to contribute to the emerging body of literature examining the role of the visual in mediating interaction. Drawing on the theoretical and analytical framework of CA, the research aimed to explore how particular normative professional and patient identities are accomplished locally and sequentially through an analysis of the ways in which midwives and mothers themselves attend to visual phenomena (gaze, facial expression and gesture) and their relationship to the accomplishment of speech and activity. The fieldwork, which involved video-taping midwives' routine home and hospital-based consultations, generated over 30 hours of video-tapes of 22 mothers and 17 midwives (Lomax, 2005). In addition to an analysis of mother–midwife interaction, these data enabled me to reflexively examine my own position and that of the recording device in the generation of data and analysis, something that I have come to see as essential in ethnographic work (Lomax and Casey, 1998; Lomax and Fink, 2010). However, before I discuss this I will briefly describe the methods of data transcription and analysis.

Transcription and analysis

Data were transcribed and analysed according to the system developed within conversation analysis which continues to evolve and encompass visual interaction

(Flewitt *et al.*, 2009; Goodwin, 1981, 2001; Heath, 1986, 1997; Heath *et al.*, 2010). Within the chapter, excerpts from the video-tapes are presented in both verbal and visual format. These transcripts follow closely the original video tape, detailing the interaction of the participants as expressed through their speech, gaze and body-movement. Data are presented, not as isolated utterances but as sequences of talk which display the sequential, turn-by-turn accomplishment of interaction, the primary unit of analysis within conversation analysis. Within the transcripts, midwives are represented as 'M', mothers as 'C' and myself as 'H'. In order to differentiate readily between the two principal speakers, midwives' utterances are presented in bold format and lines of transcribed talk are numbered for ease of referencing. In addition, visual data are presented in one of three forms. For space and ease of reading I have indicated eye and body movement by describing it in parenthesis on the verbal transcript. Elsewhere I have used aspects of the system devised by Goodwin (1981) and modified by Heath (1986) in which visual elements are mapped onto the verbal transcript according to where they occur in relation to speech and silence. As the data extract 7.10 (page 162) displays, the gaze of the current speaker is transcribed above the talk and that of the co-participant, beneath it. A description of the symbols used is contained in the appendix. Additionally, still photographs from the video are used to illustrate analytic points concerning respondents' gaze and deportment. Their relationship to the talk is indicated with captions from the transcript.

Video-based methods and reflexivity: analytic implications of researcher–participant interaction

> Visual images are, at best, 'problematic and tentative statements rather than reflections of truth'.
>
> (Harper, 1998: 138)

In this section I want to draw attention to aspects of the management of the video-taping, suggesting that the ways in which video-based fieldwork is practically managed and analysed has important implications for the status and meaning of visual data. Systematic analysis of the ways in which research participants respond to the video-based research process, provides important insight into the role of the visual in the discursive construction of patient, professional and researched identities. However, my argument for a reflexive methodological approach was not something I had envisaged at the outset of this project. Rather, it emerged as a result of contingencies of fieldwork and, in particular, my growing awareness of the need to both practically manage and account analytically for the research process as a social interaction.

Although, within the broader ethnographic literature, reflexivity is encouraged and advocated as an important means of situating qualitative approaches (cf. Finlay and Gough, 2003; Forrester, 2010; Alvesson and Sköldberg, 2009) within the theoretical framework of ethnomethodological conversation analysis and

158   *Lomax*

video-based conversation analysis, there is a strong positivist tradition such that the ways in which data are collected and the ways in which research subjects position themselves and respond to the research process are frequently overlooked (although see Heath, 1986; Speer and Hutchby, 2003; Mondala, 2009 for important exceptions). There is a dearth of literature describing how to practically manage video-based fieldwork and what is available strongly suggests that researchers maintain a low profile in order to avoid contaminating the data. From this perspective, I had little to draw on when presented with research participants who, despite my efforts, responded to and commented upon the experience and process of being video-taped and did so visually, audibly, and on camera. Not only did these experiences necessitate my having to re-think how to respond to and manage myself and the recording equipment, they also disrupted the idea that data can be extracted, pristine, from the social world (Harper, 1998). Rather, I was confronted with the empirical evidence that video-taped data are both technologically and socially mediated. As Schnettler and Raab (2008: 12) describe, 'every video factually encloses constructive aspects (or "footprints") of those operating the camera'. Video-based data are the product of the technology (the choice of camera, microphone etcetera) and the processes of its production (the camera operator's decisions about how and when to film the event).

Of particular interest to me are the ways in which social actors respond to these technologies and processes. Rather than eschewing this empirical position, I want to propose a methodology which embraces video's unique capacity to preserve the ways in which participants respond to and negotiate the research process; their orientations to the video-camera and to me are important elements of the research process and provide critical analytic insight. This is illustrated with reference to the concept of 'other-directed gaze' which, as the CA literature elaborates, is an important means by which subjects co-ordinate entry into talk, signal enthusiasm for and manage topic closure (Ruussuvuori, 2001). Correspondingly, in these data, the asymmetrical, question–answer format of birth stories is shaped by particular choreographies of talk and gaze through which midwives display, through their situated visual orientation and body alignment, the appropriateness of mothers' contributions. Mothers, in turn, use their own gaze to determine appropriate next action in the bodies of midwives and actively change the structure of their talk and bodily alignment in response to what they see. Mothers' responsiveness to midwives' interactional initiative in this context is an important means by which a clinically focused, partial birth story is initiated and maintained, power relations are mediated and professional and patient identities embodied. However, as I will now explore, the specific contribution and relevance of participants' shifting visual engagement and, specifically, its absence from sequences of talk in which mothers' displayed difficulties in maintaining interactional engagement with midwives, was highlighted through the analysis of sequences of interaction in which, paradoxically, I was troubled by my own visibility in the on-going interaction. This is exemplified in the following sequence in which a mother, 'Hilary', invites a response from me about the noisy fish tank at line one:

DATA EXTRACT 5.11: COMMUNITY MIDWIFE AND HILARY (S27)

```
        (30.0) ((midwife is writing in the notes))
        ((mother starts to smile))
1   C   (You'll be looking at this) and saying what's
2       that noise in the background  on that video
        ((mother looks over at fish tank))
                          [              ]
3   M                     yes it's the fish tank in' it
4   C   Ahahah (you'll be goin') *what's=
          [                  ]
5   M     (that's) noisy in it
6   C   =that noise* ahaaha
7   H   Aha
        ((Midwife resumes note writing. Mother continues
        smiling to herself))
        (4.5)
8   M   *Right then so::* ((murmured to self))
          [                  ]
9   H   They're tropical aren't they?
10  C   'Aven't got a clue..........
```

Whilst initially I felt uneasy about this sequence, unable to quite shake off the view that such examples are evidence of data contaminated by the research process, I began to explore where and in what form respondents sought to elicit my involvement and what this might mean for the status of the data and for the analysis as a whole. This analysis was enlightening. It became apparent that mothers (it was more often mothers) invited me to take part in the interaction (for example, by gazing in my direction or making a specific comment about the camera) in those parts of the visits where interaction with the midwife was temporarily suspended, notably, when midwives were observably busy reading and recording the clinical details of the visit. These issues are clearly evident in extract 5.11 in which the mother's initial utterance at line one 'You'll be looking at this and saying what's that noise in the background on that video' is embedded in a lengthy period of silence (30 seconds) during which the midwife is noticeably occupied writing in the mother's notes and during which she can be observed gazing into the middle distance (illustrated in video fragment 5.4; see Figure 11.1). Following this pause, the mother can be observed to smile, glance briefly at the midwife and, finding her gaze un-met, issue a remark about the noise that the fish tank is generating. Initially the midwife responds to the mother's utterance, briefly breaking off from her paperwork activities to comment about the fish tank in lines 3 and 5 (and which I also acknowledge with a laugh at line 7 in response to the mother's shift in gaze and laughter at line 6). A pause of 4.5 seconds then occurs during which the midwife resumes her record-keeping activities and the mother adopts a middle-distance gaze while continuing to giggle quietly to herself. The mother's continued visible amusement combined with a further gaze in my direction produces a verbal response from me at line 9 to which the mother immediately responds, generating several turns of talk on the topic of fish-keeping.

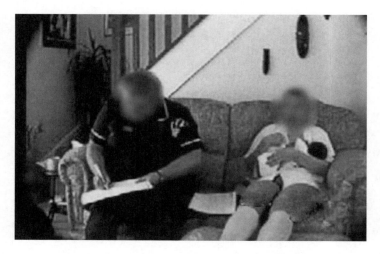

Figure 11.1 Video fragment 5.4: 'Noisy fish tank' (S27, 'Hilary'), from sequence 'You'll be looking at this and saying what's that noise in the background on that video'.

As I have argued earlier with Casey (Lomax and Casey, 1998), the mother's comment here (and my response) is interesting rather than contaminating. The mother's proffered topic at line 1 centres on a 'noticing' (Bergmann, 1990; Sacks, 1995) which is one means by which participants manage interactional unavailability and the social discomfort from silence generated by the midwives' clerical activities. While midwives may be observed, on these occasions, to be predominately oriented to the paperwork, mothers, by contrast, may be seen to be gazing at a non-gazing recipient, a situation which is 'dis-preferred' in the normative order of conversation (Goodwin, 1981, 2001). However, where I am also present a dis-preferred silence can develop in that potential speakers are unaccountably silent, a situation which the mother resolves through gazing and speaking activities which solicit my interactional involvement. In other words, these sequences can be understood as a means by which mothers (and researchers) manage interactional awkwardness.

This analysis is significant for several reasons. First, it makes explicit the ways in which the research process inevitably intrudes upon the activities of research subjects, demonstrating that these activities are part of the situated and on-going interaction and attend to the contingent requirements of the setting. In this way, rather than interpreting researcher involvement as inevitably contaminating, analysis demonstrates that it is both necessary, in terms of maintaining fluent social interaction, but also transparently available on the video-tape for inspection. Second, analysis of these sequences makes visible the significance of other-directed gaze as it is made subtly relevant in the minutiae of the mothers' and midwives' interaction. Systematic analysis of these sequences which are characterised by midwives' visual disengagement reveals occasions of interactional trouble in which mothers attempt to restore the normative order of conversation and midwives resist, prioritising a consultation format scripted by clerical activity and choreographed by visual in-attention. The ways in which this game of repair and resistance is managed are of significance for the construction of professional and maternal identities in these encounters as I shall now explore with reference to sequences of interaction in which mothers talk with midwives about their recent birth experiences.

Scripted identities: birth stories, asymmetries and visual disengagement

Within the home visits, midwives can be observed to accomplish a great deal of clerical work. Indeed, they have a professional responsibility to maintain records of care given and observations made (Nursing and Midwifery Council, 2008). However, reading and writing these documents presents a potential dilemma in that midwives are unable to give mothers their full attention and maintain interactional involvement. One of the ways that midwives appear to manage this is to make explicit their unavailability with comments about 'all this paperwork' and 'pieces of paper everywhere'. Additionally they may invite mothers to talk about their recent birth experiences. However, as I will illustrate, the management of this topic in this visually compromised context has important consequences for the nature and shape of mothers' contributions. Analysis demonstrates that these sequences are asymmetrically organised. What mothers can say within the interactional architecture is strongly determined by midwives' possession of the interactional initiative in which midwives through ownership of the first position in talk are strongly placed to steer talk to a 'factual', clinically oriented agenda and to circumvent mothers' attempts to describe emotional and experiential aspects of birth. While mothers, in response to the conditional relevance (Schegloff, 1968) imposed on them by midwives' questioning strategies, can be observed to restrict their talk to the narrow focus conditioned by the previous turn construction, there is considerable evidence that they prefer to talk about more than just the clinical details. However, their efforts are largely unsuccessful within this asymmetrical structure.

Midwives' orientations to clerical activities contribute to and reinforce these verbal asymmetries in a recurring pattern in which mothers can be repeatedly observed gazing at a non-gazing recipient. This is observable in these visits as interactional 'trouble' (Jefferson, 1984). While studies of mundane conversation have demonstrated that this situation is usually successfully resolved by the speaker engaging in practices such as pauses or restarts in order to secure the gaze of a co-participant (Goodwin, 1981, 2001), these data indicate that this is managed in non-normative ways by the midwife attending minimally to the mother (for example at turn completion points) and the mother, in response to the midwife's visual alignment, shifting her attention away from the midwife's face towards the paperwork. Thus, in this way, and in order to maintain co-operation and engagement with midwives, mothers can be seen to engage in practices which are ordinarily associated with interactional disengagement (i.e. non-looking at a co-speaker) but in this context are the preferred engagement format. This is one of the ways in which mothers must modify their talk and activity, and a particular maternal identity which attends to midwives' definition of what is appropriate in this context is talked into being. These issues are immediately evident in the opening sequence of Jenny's story (extract 7.10), which exemplifies a typical birth story in these data.

DATA EXTRACT 7.10: COMMUNITY MIDWIFE AND JENNY (S8)

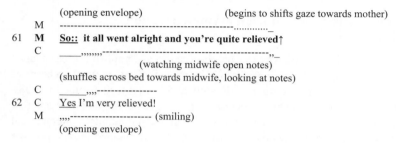

As extract 7.10 displays, the midwife's visual attention during the production of her invitation at line 61 is directed not at the mother but at the envelope which she is simultaneously opening (indicated by ----- in the transcript). As the CA literature makes clear, not looking at an addressee in this way is ordinarily dis-preferred. However, the midwife at this juncture is minimally attentive to the normative order of turn-taking. As the transcript reveals, moments before the completion of her utterance at the end of 'quite', she re-establishes eye-contact with the mother (indicated by ..... in the transcript) so that by the completion of her turn and the production of 'relieved' she is gazing at the mother, an activity which is required for smooth speaker exchange. In this way, her actions facilitate turn-taking and maintain interaction, but they do so minimally. The mother, in response, actively displays co-operation in a number of ways. She answers the midwife immediately, which is the preferred turn-construction (Sacks *et al.*, 1974) and her answer is produced as an agreement which mirrors the midwife's in both emphasis and expression (repetition of 'relieved' and increase in pitch at the completion of the turn). In addition, the mother's co-operation is reinforced posturally. During the midwife's production of the invitation at line 61 she moves physically closer to the midwife and can be seen to align her gaze in response to the midwife's direction of gaze. This subtle shift in orientation is captured in video fragments 7.5 and 7.6 (see Figure 11.2 and 11.3, respectively). Fragment 7.5, taken immediately before the production of 'so', shows the mother gazing at the midwife, while fragment 7.6 illustrates her postural and visual shift towards the paperwork on the midwife's lap. In this way, as the transcript and fragments display, the mother attends verbally and visually to the midwife's interactional initiative. On finding the midwife's gaze directed not at her but at the paperwork, the mother – in a choreographed organisation of talk, posture and gaze – re-orients her attention to the notes. However, she remains attentive to potential shifts in the

Figure 11.2 Video fragment 7.5: Taken immediately before the production of 'so' (line 61); mother gazing at midwife; the preferred engagement format in the normative order of the conversation (S8, home visit).

Figure 11.3 Video fragment 7.6: Taken from line 61 'it all went alright and you're quite relieved'. Mother aligning posturally and visually to the paperwork in a non-normative engagement frame in response to the midwife's visual and postural in-attention (S8, home visit).

midwife's direction of gaze, monitoring the midwife's movements in order to be able to perform the relevant next action (Sacks *et al.*, 1974). In this way mothers can be seen to actively monitor their speech and activity, changing their visual orientation and bodily alignment in response to what they observe in the embodied action of midwives.

A further example of the powerful mediating factor of the visual and mothers' responsiveness in the context is illustrated in the following extract from Gail's story. As with the previous example, this sequence displays features of mothers' and midwives' talk which are typical of those seen across the data set as a whole.

DATA EXTRACT 6.7: GAIL (S20)

```
18   M    So what time did
19        you actually deliver in the end?
          (1.5)
20   C    (.h) Um:: (0.4) it was ten past eleven
          (1.1)
21   M    Ten past eleven
22   C    yeah
23   M    So what time did you
24        actually go into hospital then?
25   C    Well I left it a bit late I didn't -I wanted to leave it
          as late as I possibly could unfortunately probably just (.) aha
                 [                  ]
26   M           oh right right
27   C    about managed to get there .h.h  (.) I had a bit of a job sitting
28        down in the car getting in the car (0.4) but I didn't realise that
                                          [                    ]
29   M                                    So what time
30        did you actually go in then?
31   C    Um::
          (1.4) ((Mother looks down))
32        I can't remember
                 [               ]
33   M           Cos I spoke to you I spoke to you about six
34        o'clo::ck (if you remember) yesterday didn't I
                 [                ]
35   C           that's right
```

In this example, in response to the midwife's question at line 18 'so what time did you actually deliver in the end?', Gail's reply makes explicit the emotional and embodied circumstances of her decision to remain at home for as long as possible and the difficult journey to hospital, a response which is shaped by the midwife's determined questioning about the timing of events (lines: 18–19; 21; 23–24; 29–30 and 33–34). As the transcript displays, this questioning does not acknowledge Gail's emotional and experiential contribution and, indeed, is interruptive of it, violating the turn-taking rule that only one speaker should speak at a time (Sacks *et al.*, 1974). Rather, the midwife's question, at line 29 'So what time did you actually go in then?' intrudes deeply into the internal structure of the mother's utterance to assert a factually oriented agenda concerning the precise timing of entry to hospital. Despite its interruptive status and lack of topical projection, Gail suspends her description to provide the required response, an activity which gives her some difficulty. As the transcript displays, her speech is noticeably 'dysfluent' (West, 1984), characterised by hesitations ('um') and a lengthy pause (1.4 seconds).

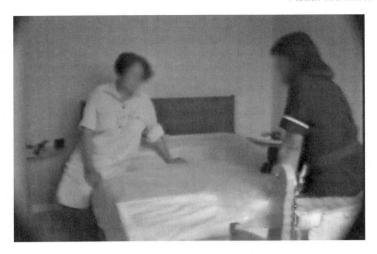

Figure 11.4 Video fragment 6.2: Gail (S20) breaking the visual engagement frame with the midwife and displaying 'remembering' in response to the midwife's interruptive question at lines 29–30: 'So what time did you actually go in then?'

This dysfluency is echoed and reinforced in the mother's body movement. Analysis of the video tape at line 31 shows Gail struggling to remember the time of admission. She temporarily suspends her visual alignment with the midwife, briefly looks down and makes a visual display of 'remembering', running her hands through her hair, an activity which culminates in the adoption of a middle distance gaze away from the midwife (illustrated in video fragment 6.2; see Figure 11.4), and her utterance, at line 32, 'I can't remember'.

In this way, the midwife's verbal interruption results in a fractured non-normative engagement frame which shifts the story to a narrow clinical focus. Moreover, as with the previous example, the midwife's speech and activity and the mother's associated visual and verbal acquiescence, re-asserts the midwife's authority to steer talk and activity and militates against the mother's efforts to provide a coherent account of her birth experience.

Summary and conclusion

The aim of this chapter has been to explore the potential of a video-based methodology for the study of professional and patient identities in the context of a body of literatures which make a priori claims about the nature of mothers and midwives on the basis of shared gender. Analysis of the situated talk and activity of mothers and midwives demonstrates the unique insight that video-based methods can offer. As I have shown, identity-work is accomplished locally and sequentially through co-ordinated displays of speech, body-movement and gaze. Midwives, as hearers of mothers' stories, display – through their situated use of body alignment, speech and gaze – the appropriateness of mothers' contributions in this context, preferring responses from mothers which have a narrow clinical focus and an engagement frame which is co-operative but which has the printed page as its focal point. Mothers are attentive to the interactional order imposed by midwives and can be observed to momentarily resist and attempt to reinstate an interactional format in which speech, body-movement and gaze are more symmetrically organised and which makes explicit the emotional and experiential aspects of birth. They are, however, largely unsuccessful. Rather, as the visual analysis elaborates, mothers are relatively powerless in this context. Midwives commitment to non-normative engagement frames coupled with their professional record-keeping responsibilities, result in a fractured, clinically oriented birth story and consultation which is problematic for theoretical and policy positions which privilege the gender-based alignment of mothers and midwives.

A second objective of this chapter was to explore the potential of a reflexive analysis of sequences of interaction in which participants make explicit their visual orientation to the research method and to the recorded interaction. As the analysis illuminates, investigation of these sequences makes possible an understanding of these interactions as the contingent activities of social actors and is informative of the analysis as a whole. Rather than glossing over these sequences as examples of spoiled data, CA makes visible the interactional work that is being accomplished. By rigorously exploring such sequences, a reflexive approach, conceptually located within the analytic framework of CA, makes possible an analysis of the situated, visually mediated identity work of social actors as mothers, midwives and research participants in this context. In this way, the video record and analyses make explicit the significance of visual events such as other-directed gaze and the relevance of seen phenomenon for the accomplishment of social action. The visual, but more specifically participants' embodied orientations to seen phenomena, is a powerful mediator of social action through which power relations are embodied and professional and patient identities talked into being.

Appendix: transcription notation

Symbol	Explanation
M	Midwife
C	Mother
H	Researcher
[ ]	Overlap in speakers' talk
.h	Indicates an in-breath
(0.5)	Pause in speech, in this case of 0.5 seconds
(.)	Pause of less than one tenth of a second
-	No pause between speakers
=	Used at the beginning or end of a new line to indicate continuous speech
<u>word</u>	Speaker's <u>stress</u> on a word or phrase

Word	A quietly spoken word or phrase
(word)	Transcriber's uncertainty about what was said
wo::rd	Extension of the sound preceding the colon (the more colons the longer the sound)
word↑	A rise in intonation occurring in the sound preceding the symbol
((raises head))	Contains transcriber's description
_____	A single continuous line above transcribed speech indicates that the person is gazing at the face of the co-participant
,,,,,,,,,,,	A series of commas above transcribed speech indicates that a participant is turning away from a co-participant
--------	Indicates that a participant is looking at an object other than the co-participant. The object is described above or below the symbol
....	Participant is turning towards the co-participant

References

Alvesson, M. and Sköldberg, K. (2009) *Reflexive methodology: new vistas for qualitative research*. London: Sage.

Annandale, E. and Clark, J. (1996) What is gender? Feminist theory and the sociology of human reproduction. *Sociology of Health and Illness*, 18(1): 17–44.

Antaki, C. and Widdicombe, S. (1998) *Identities in talk*. London: Sage.

Arney, W. (1982) *Power and the profession of obstetrics*. Chicago, IL: The University of Chicago Press.

Bergmann, J. (1990) On the local sensitivity of conversation. In Markova, I. and Foppa, K. (eds.) *The dynamics of dialogue*. New York: Harvester Wheatsheaf.

Bowes, A. and Domokos, T. (1998) Negotiating breast-feeding: Pakistani women, white women and their experiences in hospital and at home. *Sociological Research Online*, 3(3), http://www.socresonline.org.uk

Brooks, F. (1998) Women in general practice: responding to the sexual division of labour. *Social Science and Medicine*, 47(2): 181–193.

Campbell, R. and Porter, S. (1997) Feminist theory and the sociology of childbirth: a response to Ellen Annandale and Judith Clark. *Sociology of Health and Illness*, 19(3): 348–358.

Department of Health (1993) *Changing childbirth: the report of the Expert Maternity Group*. London: HMSO.

Department of Health (2004) *Maternity Standard, National Service Framework for Children, Young People and Maternity Services, Standard 11: Maternity Services*. London: HMSO.

Department of Health (2007) *Maternity matters: choice, access and continuity of care in a safe service*. London: HMSO.

DeVries, R. and Barroso, R. (1997) Midwives among the machines. In Marland, H. and Rafferty, A. M. (eds.) *Midwives, society and childbirth: debates and controversies in the modern period*. London: Routledge.

Drew, P. and Heritage, J. (1992) *Talk at work: interaction in institutional settings*. Cambridge: Cambridge University Press.

Fink, J. and Lundqvist, A. (eds.) (2010) *Changing relations of welfare: family, gender and migration in Britain and Scandinavia*. London: Ashgate.

Finlay, L. and Gough, B. (2003) *Reflexivity: a practical guide for researchers in health and social sciences*. Oxford: Blackwell.

Finlay, W. M. L., Antaki, C., Walton, C. and Stribbling, P. (2008) The dilemma for staff 'playing a game' with a person with profound intellectual disabilities: empowerment, inclusion and competence in interactional practice. *Sociology of Health and Illness*, 30(4): 531–549.

Flewitt, R., Hampel, R., Hauck, M. and Lancaster, L. (2009) What are multimodal data and transcription? In Jewitt, C. (ed.) *The Routledge handbook of multimodal analysis*. London: Routledge.

Forrester, M. (2010) *Doing qualitative research in psychology: a practical guide*. London: Sage.

Garfinkel, H. (1967) *Studies in ethnomethodology*. Cambridge: Polity Press.

Goodwin, C. (1981) *Conversational organisation: interaction between speakers and hearers*. New York: Academic Press.

Goodwin, C. (2001) Practices of seeing visual analysis: an ethnomethodological approach. In Van Leeuwen, T. and Jewitt, C. (eds.) *Handbook of visual analysis*. London: Sage.

Harper, D. (1998) On the authority of the image: visual methods at the crossroads. In Denzin, N. and Lincoln, Y. (eds.) *Collecting and interpreting qualitative materials*. California: Sage.

Have, P. ten (2001) *Doing conversation analysis: a practical guide*. London: Sage

Heath, C. (1986) *Body movement and speech in medical interaction*. Cambridge: Cambridge University Press.

Heath, C. (1997) The analysis of activities in face to face interaction using video. In Silverman, D. (ed.) *Qualitative research: theory, method and practice*. London: Sage.

Heath, C., Hindmarsh, J. and Luff, P. (2010) *Video in qualitative research: analysing social interaction in everyday life*. London: Sage.

Heritage, J. (1984) *Garfinkel and ethnomethodology*. Cambridge: Polity Press

Hyde, A. and Roche-Reid, B. (2004) Midwifery practice and the crisis of modernity: implications for the role of the midwife. *Social Science and Medicine*, 58(12): 2613–2623.

Jefferson, G. (1984) On the organisation of laughter in talk about troubles. In Atkinson, J.M. and Heritage, J. (eds.) *Structures of social organisation: studies in conversation analysis*. Cambridge: Cambridge University Press.

Kitzinger, C. (2000) Doing feminist conversation analysis. *Feminism and Psychology*, 10(2): 163–193.

Leap, N. (2009) Woman-centred or women-centred care: does it matter? *British Journal of Midwifery*, 17(1): 12–16.

Lomax, H. (2005) *Mothers, midwives and the interactional accomplishment of the birth story during routine postnatal care*. Unpublished PhD thesis, Department of Sociological Studies. University of Sheffield, UK.

Lomax, H. and Casey, N. (1998) Recording social life: reflexivity and video methodology. *Sociological Research Online*, 3, 2. Available online at http://www.socresonline.org.uk

Lomax, H. and Fink, J. (2010) Interpreting images of motherhood: the contexts and dynamics of collective viewing. *Sociological Research Online*, 15(3). Available online at http://www.socresonline.org.uk/15/3/2.html

Martin, E. (2001) *The woman in the body: a cultural analysis of reproduction*. Boston, MA: Beacon Press.

Menzies, I. (1998) The functioning of social systems as a defence against anxiety. In Mackay, L., Soothill, K., and Melia, K. (eds.) *Classic texts in health care*. Oxford: Butterworth-Heinemann.

Mondala, L. (2009) Video recording practices and the reflexive constitution of the interactional order: some systematic uses of the split-screen technique, *Human Studies*, 32: 67–99.

Nursing and Midwifery Council (2008) *The Code: standards of conduct, performance and ethics for nurses and midwives*. London: Nursing and Midwifery Council.

Page, L. and Sandell, J. (2000) The Third Way: a realistic plan to reinvent the profession. *British Journal of Midwifery*, 8(11): 673–676.

Pitt, S. (1997) Midwifery and medicine: gendered knowledge in the practice of delivery. In Marland, H. and Rafferty, A. M. (eds.) *Midwives, society and childbirth: debates and controversies in the modern period*. London: Routledge.

Ruusuvuori, J. (2001) Looking means listening: co-ordinating displays of engagement in doctor–patient interaction. *Social Science and Medicine*, 52: 1093–1108.

Sacks, H., Schegloff, E. and Jefferson, G. (1974) A simplest systematics for the organisation of turn-taking for conversation. *Language*, 50(4): 696–735.

Sacks, H. (1995) *Lectures on conversation*. Cambridge, MA: Blackwell.

Sandell, J., Bourgeault, I. L., Meijer, W. J. and Schuecking, B. A. (2001) Deciding who cares. In DeVries, R., Benoit, C., Van Teijlingen, E. R. and Wrede, S. (eds.) *Birth by design: pregnancy, maternity care, and midwifery in North America and Europe*. London: Routledge.

Schegloff, E. (1968) Sequencing in conversational openings. *American Anthropologist*, 70: 1075–1095.

Schnettler, B. and Raab, J. (2008) Interpretative visual analysis: developments, state of the art and pending problems. *Forum Qualitative Research* 9(3) Article 31. Available online at http://www.qualitative-research.net/index.php/fqs/index

Speer, S. (2005) *Gender talk: feminism, discourse and conversation analysis*. London: Routledge.

Speer, S. and Hutchby, I. (2003) From ethics to analytics: aspects of participants' orientations to the presence and relevance of recording devices. *Sociology*, 37(2): 315–337.

Speer, S. and Stokoe, E. (eds.) (2009) *Conversation and gender*. Cambridge: Cambridge University Press.

West, C. (1984) *Routine complications: troubles with talk between doctors and patients*. Bloomington, IN: Indiana University Press.

Wilkins, R. (2000) Poor relations: the paucity of the professional paradigm. In Kirkham, M. (ed.) *The midwife–mother relationship*. London: Macmillan.

Williams, J. (1997) The controlling power of childbirth in Britain. In Marland, H. and Rafferty, A. M. (eds.) *Midwives, society and childbirth: debates and controversies in the modern period*. London: Routledge.

Part III

Shared visions

Opening up researcher-participant
dialogues in the community
and beyond

12 Visualising mental health with an LGBT community group

Method, process, theory

Katherine Johnson

Researching LGBT mental health in a community setting

Studying the mental health of lesbian, gay, bisexual and/or transgendered (LGBT) people is not a straightforward issue. In recent years there has been a growing acknowledgement that *some* LGBT people suffer from high levels of mental distress, including anxiety disorders, mood disorders, suicide and self-harming behaviour, as well as substance misuse problems, and that this is related to elevated levels of discriminatory practices including physical and verbal abuse (King *et al.*, 2003a; Warner *et al.*, 2004). Yet, because of the socio-medical origins of 'homosexuality' that led to the pathologising of same-sex activities and the classification of homosexuality as a mental illness, there is a well-placed resistance within LGBT communities to associate with psychological and psychiatric practices. The legacy of pathology is difficult to shake off and studies have pointed to the homophobia and heterosexism that still exists within the mental health services (e.g. McFarlane, 1998). A qualitative account of the experiences of LGB people who had accessed mental health services noted problematic encounters that ranged from 'instances of overt homophobia and discrimination, to a perceived lack of empathy around sexuality issues by the clinician' (King *et al.*, 2003b: 3). Transgendered people have their own ongoing battles as 'gender identity disorders' are still classified within *DSM IV TR* (APA, 2000), thus their identity status is considered one of mental illness, and despite political lobbying psychiatrists still regulate gender reassignment processes (Johnson, 2007a).

This poses two problems for those who wish to understand how LGBT people experience mental health issues and provide appropriate services to meet their needs without reconstructing a pathologising narrative for all. First, to speak of elevated rates of psychological distress or suicide-related behaviour in the LGBT population runs the risk of reinforcing a relationship between sexuality/trans status and mental health issues that might imply that mental health problems are the result of being LGBT. This is not the case. Recent research in the area suggests

Thank you to the participants/artists who produced the exhibition on which this chapter is based and to those who funded the exhibition: Community University Partnership Program (CUPP), University of Brighton; South East Coastal Communities (SECC) Program; Pride in Brighton & Hove.

that mental health problems are related to levels of anxiety created by discriminatory practices and minority stress (Warner *et al.*, 2004). Whether these experiences cause mental health problems is less clear but they would inevitably exacerbate any coexisting mental health issues. The second problem for researchers is to gain access to a research sample willing to take part in psychological research. This is because of the level of suspicion already surrounding the psychological professions coupled with the problem of accessing hard-to-reach and/or hidden minorities. In order to overcome this, my recent research (e.g. Johnson *et al.*, 2007; Johnson, 2007b) has worked within a community psychology approach (e.g. Harper and Schneider, 2003; Nelson and Prilleltensky, 2005; Rappaport and Seidman, 2000) using participatory-action research methods (e.g. Brydon-Miller, 2004; Park, 2001; Silver, 2008) that seek to involve participants within the research process and create a sense of belief in and ownership of the research objectives and outcomes. Community-based participatory research is an internationally recognised framework for developing culturally relevant research and addressing issues of marginalisation, inequality and injustice.

In 2005 I began developing a research programme with *MindOut*, a local community and voluntary sector organisation supporting LGBT people who self-identified as having long-term suicidal distress. Our first project produced a qualitative understanding of suicidal distress and strategies for survival (Johnson *et al.*, 2007) via focus groups and one-to-one interviews. There were many positives to come out of this research in terms of the impact of the findings on local community initiatives and future funding bids of the organisation, however there were some limitations with the research methodology. On reflection, although participants had been involved in designing the research focus and interview questions, there was little in the data collection stage that managed to transgress the traditional dichotomy between the researcher and the researched. In order to address these limitations, in our second project, the group decided to employ a visual methodological approach, specifically photography, to enable participants to reflect on their everyday experiences of living with and managing their mental health. As Frith, Riley, Archer and Gleeson (2005) suggest, visual research methods can enhance psychological inquiry in three distinct ways: accessing information that is hard to reach through other forms, such as interviews; changing the 'voice' of the research by using participatory-action research principles to enhance the agency of the participant in the research process; enabling research findings to reach a wider audience by presenting them in both a visual and verbal format.

Photography, 'photo-elicitation' and the 'photovoice' method

The use of photography in social, cultural and community studies is not new. Collier (1967) is credited with being the first to use photography as part of the research interview (Loeffler, 2004; Castleden *et al.*, 2008) and it has been used in a number of studies to facilitate how participants make sense of their identities and everyday life experiences (e.g. Clark-Ibáñez, 2004; Pink, 2007). Photo-elicitation method has grown in favour with critical psychologists who are interested in embodied experience (e.g. Frith and Harcourt, 2007; Radley and Taylor, 2003) as the use of visual methodologies can open up participants and researchers to alternative modes of experience, more so than the heavily mono-modal approaches that dominate textual qualitative analyses (Reavey and Johnson, 2008). Photovoice has more recently emerged in community-based research as an innovative approach to facilitate the participation and empowerment of those who are marginalised, and as a means to promote social change through engaging marginalised groups in dialogue with those that have the potential to transform opportunities and inequalities, often including policy makers (e.g. Wang *et al.*, 1997). These projects have been used with diverse groups such as homeless adults (e.g. Radley *et al.*, 2005), indigenous communities (Castleden *et al.*, 2008) and black gay men and lesbians in post-apartheid South Africa (e.g. Graziano, 2004). However, to date, most of the engagements with photographic research methods emerge out of community-invested research initiatives in health and education (e.g. Killion, 2001; Mitchell *et al.*, 2005; Wang and Burris, 1997) with few projects developed in the area of mental health (for one recent exception see Fleming *et al.*, 2009).

This does not mean to say the arts- and culture-based initiatives have not been singled out for their potential value in promoting better psychological well-being in political agendas that aim to tackle social injustice. Prior to the current global financial crisis, the left-leaning government think-tank, the *Institute for Public Policy Research*, produced its first publication that sought to put the arts and culture at the heart of a social change agenda, with then Director, Nick Pearce, stating in the Preface: 'the arts and culture go to the heart of what it means to be a fulfilled, active citizen. They have the capacity to touch and inspire us as individuals, and to challenge as well as cement our social norms' (Cowling, 2004: i). In this short collection of essays mental health is highlighted as one of the three targets for the arts, alongside education and offender rehabilitation, and two chapters are dedicated to promoting the importance of art-based initiatives arguing that art projects have the potential to tackle negative public attitudes towards people with mental health problems (White, 2004) and, if targeted at specific groups of people with mental health problems, that it is 'intuitively appealing that engaging in artistic activity may prevent mental ill health and, indeed, may promote recovery and prevent relapse in people who have already developed mental disorders' (Geddes, 2004: 64). It was with these hopes in mind that we entered into the spirit of our second research project and clarified our aims in relation to understanding LGBT mental health and challenging societal stigma.

Aims

- To use photographs and textual extracts to explore how group members view themselves, their feelings and the world around them, as well as the practices and techniques that help or hinder in the daily management of their emotional well-being.

- To provide an innovative photographic exhibition showcasing the experiences of lesbian, gay, bisexual and transgendered people living with and managing mental health issues.
- To develop a sense of ownership and achievement over the research process for participants.
- To raise awareness about mental health and challenge stigma by promoting a dialogue between the photographers and audience.
- To invite the audience to comment on the exhibition and become part of the research process.

Method and process

As with our previous project, the initial stages of the project focused on discussion and building a secure relationship with the mental health service users. The group facilitator and eleven people from Out of the Blue@MindOut invited me to attend one of their closed meetings to discuss the photographic project, sharing ideas and concerns. We discussed in detail the process by which we would work, including what type of camera we would use (disposable or digital), who and what might be in the images, issues of confidentiality and anonymity and how these might be addressed, a time period for taking the photographs and subsequent interview with myself, and ideas for the final exhibition including what space we would like to have the exhibition in and who might help fund the expenses. After this initial discussion seven people decided to take part and I drafted a research design taking into account key concerns of the group, and wrote a detailed ethics proposal for the University Faculty Research and Ethical Governance Committee. The central tenets of this process are summarised below:

- Participants were to use the camera to take photographs to represent and reflect on their mental health and their experiences in relation to their sexuality and/or transgender identity.
- Participants would use a digital camera rather than a disposable camera because they were concerned about creating unnecessary waste and because some wished to use the timer feature which was not present on disposable models.
- Participants were to take no more than 15 photographs in order to keep some boundaries around the timeframe for the interview, 35–55 min.
- Participants would have access to the same model of camera. Two cameras were distributed and each participant had the camera for a week.
- Participants were free to take photographs of themselves and other people. If they wanted to take photographs of other people and discuss them within the project because of the relationship they had with them they were to ask the person to sign a consent form, first to take their photograph, and second, to display the photograph in a public forum. It was agreed that there was no need to request consent from 'background people' who might appear in a more general shot if they were of little relevance to their personal narrative.

- Interview data were to be treated as confidential while photographs would be shared with the group, and offer the potential for further discussion.
- Short extracts from the interviews would accompany the photographs in the exhibition in order to contextualise the image and these were to be agreed by participants.
- The group agreed that they would like their first name to accompany the photographs in the exhibition.
- After the interview each participant chose three favourite photographs and these formed their contribution to the exhibition.
- A comments box was left in the exhibition space for the audience to become part of the project through their own textual reflections.
- The exhibition was called *Focusing the Mind*.

The photographic exhibition: representing data

The exhibition took place in the Gallery Foyer, Grand Parade, University of Brighton (24 July–2 August 2008). The space is located in the university building but accessible to a broad spectrum of the local and wider community as numerous external events are held in the hall it surrounds. Although we have no formal record of the number of viewers, in the time of the exhibition display we can estimate that at least 300 people would have had the opportunity to view it, including passers by and specific visitors. People who passed by included attendees at external conferences, music events, film events; arts students; attendees at the hip-hop graffiti exhibition that was running in the next-door gallery and a multitude of university staff attending the retirement party of the Registrar. The display material for the exhibition was professionally produced by a local photographic laboratory and included 21 images printed in matt and mounted on aluminium. The exhibition was hung with the assistance of a gallery technician. The photographs ranged in their representational content, stylistic approaches, conceptual engagements and aesthetic value. Hanging the exhibition was an early stage in the process of analysing the images as we discussed whether to organise the images 'thematically' or by 'photographer'. Although there were some immediate themes that ran across the chosen images, attempting to present the work in this way produced an uneasy visual experience. It became apparent that the individual style of each participant was expressed across their three photographs even down to the colours they attended to. For example, one set of three photographs was bathed in a pink glow that clashed terribly with another set of photographs, and a second set that sought out the fresh green of rolling hills and woody grasslands took a while to place where it complemented rather than overpowered surrounding images. The decision was thus made to organise the exhibition aesthetically, with any attempt to synchronise overall meaning or provide an interpretative framework left to the viewer, with some assistance from the brief qualitative extracts presented alongside each image.

In addition, the exhibition served as a second data collection point. As one of the aims was to promote a dialogue between participants and the potential audience, a feedback box was left in the exhibition with paper and pens so viewers could comment on the exhibition. In total, 39 comments were left in the box and these were added to the data set.

Constructing an analytic approach

Analysing visual data according to the principles of 'photovoice' (Wang and Burris, 1997) requires a large group discussion in order to pick the 'best' photographs followed by group codification of key issues, themes and theories and for these to be presented to policy makers and others who may be able to facilitate social change. In this tradition it is 'story telling' that is emphasised with the visual playing an important role in accessing particular stories of the marginalised and providing a means by which to communicate concerns in a way that might be more readily noticed than through written reports. Key features can therefore be discerned as classification of community concerns, dialogue, connection and social change. Like others (e.g Castleden *et al.*, 2008), this project followed a modified approach to 'photovoice' as our data consisted of seven detailed individual interviews that discussed all the photographs and not just those participants picked as 'best' for the photo-exhibition. In addition, our data set also includes 39 responses left in the comments box. Our goal was also to promote dialogue, connection and social change, but the central element of producing a photographic exhibition prior to explicitly coding the data into themes and categories blurred the analytic process. While participants picked out three photographs and began to recognise similarities across their experiences, the analytic process was primarily left to myself, with their goal to represent their feelings in a public domain that viewers from all backgrounds might connect with. In addition, the exhibition enabled us to promote the status of the visual above a thematic and conceptual understanding of the content of participants' images or narratives, which has further implications for the types of interpretations we can make from the data. We are currently left with a large data set that incorporates both visual and textual material and raises certain challenges in terms of making sense of the data as a whole, while attending to the specificity of individual experience, and attending to the broader social justice goals expressed in the original aims of the project. For the purpose of this paper, I will discuss three broad themes that encompass the exhibition photos, before moving on to reflect on the audience engagement with these, and how we might make sense of their comments in relation to the initial aims of challenging stigma and transforming social attitudes towards LGBT mental health.

Embodied representations of affective states

A key theme across the data was attempts by the participants to represent and discuss affective states. Images depicted and texts supported feelings of 'anxiety', 'distress', 'frustration', 'grief' and 'fragility'. These were not simply communicated in a descriptive form, but the image/text format enabled the viewer to experience how these are lived through the body. For example, the image "Uphill battle" presents a steep, grassy slope covered in dandelions that rises up to a bright blue sky. On its own it could be interpreted as 'spring-like' and 'uplifting' but the text draws us through the metaphor of life as a struggle, as a battle, and as a hill that has to be climbed. This embodied sense of weariness is found in other images that communicated a longing for alternative embodied states such as the desire for 'peace' that is found in 'I wish I could be like that'. Here the participant has taken an image of a giant sculpture of a sleeping man, resting barefoot on lush, green grass in a woodland glen. The text that accompanies this states:

> …I've been really agitated and not sleeping and constantly feeling so over-emotional and overwhelmed, I just wanted to… he looked so peaceful, and that's what I wanted.

In terms of understanding the affective states presented I propose that while the extracts provide us with a textual description the images amplified the words, drawing us in primarily through our own affective response which is then enhanced or challenged when we read the small extracts printed by their side. For example, the spatial landscapes and scenes of nature depicted in "Horses", "Bleak" and "Trucking on" communicate something beyond the textual descriptions that accompanied them. As we will see when examining audience feedback comments, rather than simply offering a conscious rational understanding of what is represented the viewer is either 'touched' or 'moved' as some of the images trigger uncanny feelings of recognition and familiarity, or they are 'repelled' by them.

Figure 12.1 'I wish I could be like that'.

Weight gain and medication

A second key theme that came out in most participants' images and narratives related to the side-effects of medication and in particular weight gain. In "Side-Effects" the participant illustrates the complexity of managing her mental health regimen with bottles and boxes of tablets arranged around her medication box that lists days of the week and times of day, including morn, noon, evening and bed. The boxes are displayed for us on a wooden table. They are not pristine, rather battered, bent and crumpled at the edges, illustrating a familiarity that comes with the routine of everyday use, like a well-read book. The extract supports this but also reveals something else:

> I've been on some of those medications for years. In fact, all of those medications for years. And I've had seriously bad side effects from them. I've ended up in hospital more than once from low sodium levels ... so that signifies for me the fact that my psychiatrist was, in my opinion, poisoning me ... I want to complain about it ... he kept prescribing the same tablets with the same side effects.

In the extract we sense more acutely the participant's sense of frustrated hopelessness, underpinned by a quiet anger at the perceived risk she has been put at and that her complaints have not been heard. One question for this project is whether the use of the camera has enabled her to 'voice' her complaints and whether the appropriate audience will hear them. For me, as one possible reader, I return to the deferment in her verbal contextualisation where she states "in my opinion" followed by the accusation of poisoning. To me it stands as a deferral to the better knowledge of the 'experts', the psychiatrists who have kept her on certain medication despite the side-effects, and it is only via the image/text interface that she is able to represent her long and frustrating encounter with medication, where the battered pile of boxes can be interpreted as a seemingly necessary but maligned element of managing mental health.

This participant also discussed her diet and need to focus on what she ate because of large swings in weight as a result of medication (something that also triggered eating disorders). This theme came up for a number of participants and was represented in the exhibition particularly in two images. "Doughnuts" appeared on the wall nearest to the café in the gallery space and it was possible to see people on their way to and from the eatery drawn to the picture of the enticing, sugary cakes. The image of four doughnuts in a tray attracts the viewer in but then startles them with the contrasting text that accompanies it:

> I have an issue with food, and to try and deal with my pain I feed, or to deal with whatever's going on for me, I use food to try and help me cope with life, although it damages me. And it looks nice, but its very damaging for me too ... because I would probably eat four of those.

Affectively this has the potential to raise different emotions in the viewer, from shame and disgust to admiration for her honesty about her eating in a culture that denigrates over-eaters and the 'fat' female body (see Murray, 2008). In a second picture, 'Everything I consume in a day', the participant carefully organises a conceptually and aesthetically striking image depicting all she puts into her mouth and her attempts at regulating her eating through 'being healthy' (fruit) despite 'cravings' (Peperami) and concerns about her weight gain. The image also shows the regulation of her medication through the box that is opened to reveal the day, and shows the effort in the creation of the image through the laying out of an entire day's food and the pre-rolling of cigarettes. It is these that frame the image. Textually, her account that accompanies the image in the exhibition is brief and indicates humour, but the grounding of the image comes through her more daunting challenge of managing the identity shifts that she has undergone since rapidly gaining weight: 'My medication has made me put on weight and I'm just constantly thinking about food and wanting to eat … But, I also have a Peperami addiction (laughs)'.

The images discussed here demonstrate the dramatic effect medication can have on an embodied sense of self, yet the way these concerns are communicated through everyday images of food enable multiple readings from the viewer in terms of their own concerns with diet, body weight and the contemporary cultures of food and consumption.

Figure 12.2 'Everything I consume in a day'.

Support and emotional connections

A third theme that can be read across the images relates to the formal and informal support networks participants draw on for their mental health. Across all the images people took photographs of a family member (Dad), pets (cats, dog, horses) and organisations (GP surgery, online support network). In the exhibition this theme was developed through a photograph of ornaments given to one participant by a friend, called "Treasured Possessions", and physical activity as shown in "Climbing" demonstrating the trend to acknowledge the benefits of physical activity in relation to mental health and substance misuse. In terms of a more detailed analysis for this theme I focus on the photograph 'Alcohol'. This is a striking image. The vibrant primary blue colour instantly stands out amongst images that are darker in context and colour. The picture illustrates the Alcoholic Anonymous (AA) sign stuck on the inside of a glass door with a large blob of Blu-Tack.® The clarity of the image means you can almost trace the imprinted finger ridges of the person that adhered the sign to the window. Focusing on the round, blue symbol we see, in the reflection, the participant. She is holding the camera across her face in order to take the picture, which surreptitiously maintains her anonymity. She is therefore both visible and invisible, as we cannot identify her. There was no planning in the process of taking this picture, unlike the detailed preparation that went into 'Everything I consume in a day'. Instead, this picture

Figure 12.3 'Alcohol'.

emerged from a snapshots design, a literal interpretation of the request to show things that help manage her mental health. Yet, the contingent coalescence of sunlight and the glass door makes for us, the viewer, a terribly clever picture. Here she stands, an anonymous outsider at the heart of the image. The light and colour reflect her and the possibility of recovery as she stands with the world passing by behind her, the glass door allowing her to see into another world, on the first step of an AA recovery process. As the participant states in the text that accompanies the image:

> That is the sign of Alcoholics Anonymous. I've recently become a member and it means a lot to me because I've gained friends and they are very, very helpful. I've got an alcohol problem and they're being ever so helpful at trying to get me off the alcohol … it's become part of my life.

Audience engagement with the exhibition

While some have written elegantly of the relationship between the aesthetic and politics in visual forms of social activism (see Radley, 2009 for an excellent account), few comment on the process of wider audience engagement. An innovative factor of this exhibition was endeavouring to incorporate the audience within the research process by asking them to leave their comments and reflections. Of course this is not an objective or systematic evaluation, as only 39 comments were left from a much larger audience, but it does allow us to say something about the process of communication between the exhibitors and the audience.

As one might expect, in the 39 comments left in the box we found a variety of responses to the project, although most were positive. In terms of facilitating connection, many members of the audience left comments that suggested we had been successful in communicating with people through an affective dimension. For example, some left broad comments about how the exhibition as a whole had made them feel:

> I felt very emotional looking at these photos and reading. I was laughing and crying at the same time. It touches me to think we are not alone. Thanks for a great exhibition!

> Wow. What an amazing moving exhibition. So personal and universal. Moved to tears – strange as the space is full of graduation people buzzing around but that's great coz at least some are looking at the pictures and not immediately turning away. Uncomfortable viewing for some who want to pretend we are all ok. I love this – it's beautiful – thanks. Well done.

Certainly it seemed that the audience were able to connect because of the way the images, aided by the text, *moved* them. It was their own embodied experience and relation to affective states that enabled the facilitation of a dialogue that we had hoped might be part of the process of challenging stigma about LGBT mental health. What was interesting here, though, was the way that sexuality and gender identity faded into the background, both in participants' images and the responses of the audience, despite it being publicised as an LGBT project. Looking over the entire content of the participants' images, only one person provided any symbolic form of representation of queer life in their images. This was not a purposeful image taken to demonstrate identification with the LGBT community, but rather a chance symbolic representation revealed by a background item in a photograph. The symbol was indicated by a business card depicting the rainbow flag that happened to be left lying on a desk that was photographed to represent using the computer to communicate with other mental health service users (a representation of support gained from an online bi-polar user forum). This suggests, much as Bourdieu (1990: 7) claims, that when photographing the everyday, identity is not 'proclaimed' as an explicit intention, but rather deciphered through surplus meaning that 'betrays' our belonging to particular social groups (in this case the business card). In the exhibition itself there were no visual representations that would 'betray' the group's belonging to the LGBT community. The only revelation of a same-sex orientation could be found in a textual extract that accompanied the image "Phoebe makes me happy", where a female exhibitor used the term 'girlfriend' to describe why she had taken a photograph of her girlfriend's dog. Other than the signage that advertised the image as an "LGBT mental health project", the only other specific mention of sexuality was found in the comments box. One comment was left from a viewer who also experienced mental health problems and it proposed that mental health stigma is more prevalent than that of sexuality. This is presented in full below:

> There's a stigma about mental health, it's more of an 'issue' for other people than sexuality. You have to be brave to express how you feel to other people, but I think being open is the best thing – seeing how other people feel the same as me makes me feel so much better. This is an excellent exhibition. I really empathise with everyone involved and wish them all the best.

This is interesting, but it appears that in the context of this exhibition the importance of a non-normative gender or sexual 'identity' moved to the background with the primary goal being to connect through affective dimensions.

Other members of the audience left comments that related to specific images, rather than the exhibition as a whole, highlighting the specificity of individual experience and how we might be moved by different images and stories, rather than all moved in the same way. Again, here the connections transgressed sexual orientation and gender identity, with the audience leaving comments about how images reminded them of friends, parents and family members. For example:

> I found the exhibition extremely moving and sad. P's photo of 'coping mechanisms' reminded me of my dad who died a year ago and who was an alcoholic. Even the medication is the same. I feel angry at how he was treated by the mental health services in Brighton. I think this project is invaluable in highlighting mental health problems and the effect they have on people. This project humanizes the issues of poor mental health. I think that those who took part are very brave and only wish my dad had been able to have such support that the group offers.

The final sentence here does something to acknowledge the role of the LGBT support group and the general lack of support for people with mental health problems in the community at large. Finally, it should be clarified that not all comments left were positive or supportive, and not all viewers were moved in an empathetic or sympathetic manner. Two of the shortest examples include:

BOO-FUCKING-HOO

W T F??? How enlightening?!![1]

Trying to reflect on what these might indicate is purely speculative. We do not know whether they are responses to the images, whether they were written after lengthy consideration of the exhibition as a whole, or whether they were left to be purposefully polemical. What they do show, though, are less sympathetic cultural responses to psychological distress, which in itself reminds us of the stigma that still surrounds mental health. These comments were received in good humour by the mental health group, in fact they made most of us laugh. There was something shocking in their short, sharp dismissal, relief that they were not homophobic assaults, and their very existence confirmed the purpose of the exhibition. These comments showed that we had created a dialogue with a range of viewers and that the need to challenge and respond to various cultural stereotypes about mental health is ongoing.

Witnessing, wit(h)nessing and social activism: some theoretical reflections on the transformative possibilities of participatory visual methodologies

Participatory research, although commendable in the types of values it promotes for working with marginalised groups, is often criticised for producing a-theoretical understandings (Silver, 2008). In my own endeavours within the field (e.g. Johnson, 2007b), most papers focus on the 'process' element of the methodology, reflecting on experiences of working with groups with less space targeted at producing empirical findings, less on the types of transformations that take place, and even less at the theoretical implications of such engagements. In this final section I want to embed some of the insights discussed so far on the relationship between the photographers and audience in a deeper theoretical framework that considers the concepts of witnessing and wit(h)nessing in the aesthetic field and its possibility for personal and social transformation.

In his work on images of illness, Alan Radley (2009: 81) discusses the position of 'the aesthetic of witness' that arises when an artist forms a relationship with individuals who are willing to engage with their work. For Radley, this relationship is experienced in the affective realm and 'lies in a confirmation by the reader or viewer of a semblance of illness that the work is able to show forth'. Thus, the recognition that the viewer brings to the work 'resides in ideas-with-feeling evoked in the reader or viewer, for whom the work illuminates something previously in shadow, or names something that was previously inchoate'. I would like to argue that it is this type of process that the viewers of this exhibition struggled to describe in their accounts of 'feeling moved' or 'touched' by their viewing experience. Bracha Ettinger's (2006) theory of the 'matrixial borderspace' offers us a similar insight into the affective realm of feelings of togetherness and 'wit(h)nessing' that can be prompted, for her, through the aesthetic field of painting. Her theory is a complex, dense, looping development of Lacanian and Freudian psychoanalysis, which does not seek to replace the notion of the phallic order, rather indicate that there is an alternative form of connection that we all emerge from. For her, we are born into trauma and loss, a loss of connection to the (m)other and we are driven towards linking with the Other. This desire has been repressed, but through art we are opened to a partial memory: a partial memory that we are always already in togetherness, always already in relation to the other; a partial memory that can move us to tears without our knowing why we are moved. Within her account, there is little consideration of other forms of artwork than painting, and perhaps like others considering the relation between psychology and art (e.g. Arnheim, 1986), she would be sceptical of photography as an artform. That said, many of her observations in relation to terms such as com-passion, wit(h)nessing and metramorphous (via Freud's account of the Uncanny) resonate with my observations of the processes at play in this visual participatory project. There are many provocative extracts from her writing that would make for suitable reflection, but this I hope captures some of the transformative, intersubjective, affective adventures in relationality that can emerge when engaging with a participatory visual research project.

> In (the) artwork, traces of a buried-alive trauma of the world are reborn from amnesia into co-emerging memory. The potential for partially sharing this memory in the transferential borderspace offered by the artwork is the condition for its apparition. Such uncanny anxieties allow and accompany the contact with the gaze with-in/ through a work of art. ... The matrixial gaze thrills us while fragmenting, multiplying, scattering, and assembling together the fragments. It turns us into what we may call participatory witnesses to traumatic events, at the price of diffracting us. It threatens us with disintegration while linking us and allowing our participation in a drama wider than that of our individual selves.
>
> (Ettinger, 2006: 152–153)

Conclusion

Visual participatory projects are predicated on the assumption that they will facilitate social and personal change by demonstrating community needs and focusing on broader processes of 'empowerment'. However, when embarking on a visual participatory project it is useful to be aware of certain limitations to their transformative possibilities. First, no one who took part in the project had some miraculous recovery in terms of his/her own mental health, although some reported a sense of personal achievement from taking part. Second, not all the participants found taking part a rewarding experience. The original premise was that having a camera increased people's control over what they revealed, and some reported an almost therapeutic benefit in terms of using the camera to freeze their negative and spiralling thoughts. Others, however, reflected on the difficulties of focusing on their mental health and sense of identity, and some only produced a very small number of photographs and stated that they would not want to take part in another similar project. Thus, we must be cautious in celebrating visual methodologies on the basis of increasing participation or user involvement for marginalised groups. Finally, participatory visual approaches cannot be seen as some rationalist project that will enable the transformation from situation A to situation B: we did not know beforehand how we or the audience would be affected by partaking in or viewing the project (we did not know even if we would be able to put an exhibition together). What our photographic exhibition revealed, then, is that we can be transformed (even momentarily) by our viewing, that connections do sometimes occur, but that we cannot predict in what form this may take: there is always a 'risk' in the types of affective responses that may be experienced by both those participating in the project and those who view; we do not know exactly how, when or if we will be affected. When coupling this with the multi-modal form of representation available to visual methods; the possibility for numerous interpretations, readings, affective responses and connections is significantly amplified.

Note

1 WTF??? Colloquial text speak for What the fuck???

References

American Psychiatric Association [APA]. (2000) *Diagnostic and statistical manual of mental disorders 4th ed. Text revision.* Washington, DC: APA.
Arnheim, R. (1986) *New essays on the psychology of art.* Berkeley, CA: University of California Press.
Bourdieu, P. (1990) *Photography: a middle-brow art.* Cambridge, UK: Polity.
Brydon-Miller, M. (2004) Using participatory action research to address community health issues. In M. Murray (ed.), *Critical health psychology.* Basingstoke, UK: Palgrave (pp. 187–202).
Castleden, H., Garvin, T. and Huu-ay-aht First Nation (2008) Modifying photovoice for community-based participatory Indigenous research. *Social Science & Medicine, 66,* 1393–1405.
Clark-Ibáñez, M. (2004) Framing the social world with photo-elicitation interviews. *American Behavioral Scientist, 47*(12), 1507–1527.
Collier, J. (1967) *Visual anthropology: photography as a research method.* New York: Holt, Rinehart & Winston.
Cowling, J. (2004) *For art's sake? Society and the arts in the 21ˢᵗ century.* London: Institute for Public Policy Research.

Ettinger, B. (2006) *The matrixial borderspace*. London: University of Minnesota Press.

Fleming, J., Mahoney, J., Carlson, E. and Engebretson, J. (2009) An ethnographic approach to interpreting a mental illness photovoice exhibit. *Archives of Psychiatric Nursing*, *23*(1), 16–24.

Frith, H. and Harcourt, D. (2007) Using photographs to capture women's experiences of chemotherapy: reflecting on the method. *Qualitative Health Research*, *17*(10), 1310–1350.

Frith, H., Riley, S., Archer, L. and Gleeson, K. (2005) Editorial: imag(in)ing visual methodologies. *Qualitative Research in Psychology*, *2*(3), 187–198.

Geddes, J. (2004) Art and mental health: building the evidence base. In J. Cowling (ed.) *For art's sake? Society and the arts in the 21st century*. London: Institute for Public Policy Research (pp. 64–74).

Graziano, K. J. (2004) Oppression and resiliency in post-apartheid South Africa: unheard voices of black gay men and lesbians. *Cultural Diversity and Ethnic Minority Psychology*, *10*(3), 302–316.

Harper, G. W. and Schneider, M. (2003). Oppression and discrimination among lesbian, gay, bisexual, and transgendered people and communities: a challenge for community psychology. *American Journal of Community Psychology*, *31*, 243–252.

Johnson, K. (2007a) Transsexualism: diagnostic dilemmas, transgender politics and the future of transgender care. In V. Clarke and E. Peel (eds.) *Out in psychology: lesbian, gay, bisexual and trans perspectives*. Chichester, UK: Wiley Press.

Johnson, K. (2007b) Researching suicidal distress with LGBT communities in the UK: methodological and ethical reflections on a community–university knowledge exchange project. *The Australian Community Psychologist*, *19*(1), 112–123.

Johnson, K., Faulkner, P., Jones, H. and Welsh, E. (2007) *Understanding suicidal distress & promoting survival in the LGBT communities*. Brighton: Brighton & Sussex Community Knowledge Exchange Project.

Killion, C. (2001) Understanding cultural aspects of health through photography. *Nursing Outlook*, *49*(1), 50–55.

King, M., McKeown, E., Warner, J., Ramsay, A., Johnson, K., Cort, C., Wright, L., Blizard, R. and Davidson, O. (2003a) Mental health and quality of life of gay men and lesbians in England and Wales: controlled, cross-sectional study. *British Journal of Psychiatry*, *183*, 552–558.

King, M., McKeown, E., Warner, J., Ramsay, A., Johnson, K., Cort, C., Davidson, O. and Wright, L. (2003b) *Mental health and social wellbeing of gay men, lesbians and bisexuals in England and Wales*. London: Mind Report.

Loeffler, T. (2004) A photo elicitation study of the meanings of outdoor adventure experiences. *Journal of Leisure Research*, *36*(4), 536–557.

McFarlane, L. (1998) *Diagnosis: homophobic – the experiences of lesbians, gay men and bisexuals in mental health services*. London: P.A.C.E. Retrieved 30 November 2010 from http://www.pacehealth.org.uk/Resources/PACE/Gallery%201/diagnosis_homophobic.pdf

Mitchell, C., Delange, N., Molestane, R., Stuart, J. and Buthelezi, T. (2005) Giving a face to HIV and AIDS: on the uses of photo-voice by teachers and community health care workers working with youth in rural South Africa. *Qualitative Research in Psychology: Special Issue on Visual Methodologies, 2*, 257–270.

Murray, S. (2008) *The 'fat' female body*. Basingstoke UK: Palgrave Macmillan.

Nelson, G. and Prilleltensky, I. (eds.) (2005) *Community psychology: in pursuit of liberation and well-being*. Basingstoke, UK: Palgrave Macmillan.

Park, P. (2001) Knowledge and participatory research. In P. Reason and H. Bradbury (Eds)

Handbook of action research: participative inquiry and practice. London: Sage, pp. 81–90.

Pink, S. (2007) *Doing visual ethnography.* London: Sage.

Radley, A. (2009) *Works of illness: narrative, picturing and the social response to serious disease.* Ashby-de-la-Zouch: InkerMen Press.

Radley, A. and Taylor, D. (2003) Images of recovery: a photo-elicitation study on the hospital ward. *Qualitative Health Research, 13,* 77–99.

Radley, A., Hodgetts, D. and Cullen, A. (2005) Visualizing homelessness: a study in photography and estrangement. *Journal of Community and Applied Social Psychology, 15,* 273–295.

Rappaport, J. and Seidman, E. (2000) *Handbook of community psychology.* New York: Kluwer Academic/Plenum Publishers.

Reavey, P. and Johnson, K. (2008) Visual approaches: using and interpreting images in qualitative psychology. In C. Willig and W. Stainton Rogers (eds) *Handbook of qualitative research in psychology.* London: Sage.

Silver, C. (2008) Participatory approaches to social research. In N. Gilbert (ed.) *Researching social life* (3rd ed.). London: Sage.

Wang, C. and Burris, M. (1997) Photovoice: concept, methodology and use for participatory needs assessment. *Health Education & Behavior, 24*(3), 369–387.

Wang, C., Burris, M. and Ping, Z. Y. (1997) Chinese village women as visual anthropologists: a participatory approach to reaching policy makers. *Social Science & Medicine, 42*(10), 1391–1400.

Warner, J., McKeown, E., Griffin, M., Johnson, K., Ramsay, A., Cort, C. and King, M., (2004) Rates and predictors of mental illness in gay men, lesbians and bisexual men and women. Results from a survey based in England and Wales. *British Journal of Psychiatry, 185,* 479–485.

White, M. (2004) Arts in mental health for social inclusion: towards a framework for programme evaluation. In J. Cowling (ed.) *For art's sake? Society and the arts in the 21st century.* London: Institute for Public Policy Research (pp. 75–99).

13 Tribal gatherings

Using art to disseminate research on club culture

Sarah Riley, Richard Brown,
Christine Griffin and Yvette Morey

One of the advantages of using visual methods in research is that the immediate and evocative nature of images can be used to increase the accessibility of research findings to a wider audience. There are a variety of ways in which the visual can be used in dissemination, and in this chapter we explore one form by describing the processes we engaged in when producing an art exhibition. This chapter is therefore not about using visual methods to produce data or answer research questions, but the processes involved in our attempt as psychologists to create an innovative form of dissemination by working with an artist to produce mixed media material that communicated our academic work.

Our art exhibition aimed to disseminate aspects of work from a larger study that explored relationships between leisure, identity and participation, entitled 'Reverberating Rhythms'.[1] Social theorists have argued that leisure activities have become increasingly important indicators of identity and may be sites for new forms of social and political participation (e.g. Giddens, 1991; Maffesoli, 1996). However, empirical work on these ideas is limited and scattered. Reverberating Rhythms aimed to address this paucity using electronic dance music culture (EDMC) as an example. EDMC involves socialising and dancing to electronically produced music, often under the influence of stimulant and hallucinogenic drugs and/or alcohol. EDMC was chosen because it is now a significant leisure activity for many young people and in its 20-year history it has been analysed in contradictory ways, both as a site for alternative forms of subjectivity and political participation, but also as a subculture that provides its participants with a form of apolitical escapism that reproduces traditional social stratifications (in relation to taste, class, income and gender). (For further discussion of EDMC please see Riley *et al.*, 2008; Riley, Morey *et al.*, 2010; and Riley, Griffin *et al.*, 2010.)

Reverberating Rhythms employed a range of methods; namely, interviews, focus groups, participant observations, questionnaires and photography, with two case studies – of an urban 'drum and bass' scene and of a rural 'free party' scene, chosen to reflect some of the heterogeneity of EDMC. To briefly describe the difference between the two: drum and bass is characterised by fast tempo broken beat drums with heavy and often intricate baselines. Drum and bass originated as urban, industrial, working-class and black-oriented music although at least some aspects of the music have been commercialised and incorporated into wider popular culture. In contrast, 'free parties' are unlicensed parties held in rural areas or urban settings, such as empty warehouses. Typically one or more sound systems are set up over a weekend, often, although not exclusively, playing techno or acid-techno. These forms of electronic music are fast and use a regular 4/4 beat. Acid-Techno has had little commercial impact. In our participant observations for both case studies the participants were white (90–100 per cent) and male (60–75 per cent).

Participants were recruited at club and party nights for later participation. Thirty-one interviews, two focus groups and ten participant observations were conducted (divided between the two case studies). Twenty-two males and nine females participated, with an age range of 20–41 years; of whom 82 per cent were 'white', 11 per cent 'mixed ethnicity', and 8 per cent 'black'. Fifty per cent were employed, 21 per cent unemployed, 4 per cent were in college and 25 per cent categorised themselves as 'other'[2].

The art exhibition aimed to disseminate an aspect of Reverberating Rhythms that examined a particular theory of social organisation called neo-tribalism (Maffesoli, 1996). Neo-tribal theory argues that in contemporary Western culture people move between a variety of small and potentially temporary groups or 'neo-tribes' to which they are members. These neo-tribes are distinguished by shared lifestyles, values and understandings of what is appropriate behaviour. Neo-tribal theory points to leisure as an important site for neo-tribal formations, arguing that such groups are potentially political because they allow participants to create moments of sovereignty over their own existence. Important concepts within neo-tribalism include sociality, proxemics, belonging, hedonism, vitality and sovereignty. The objective of our art exhibition was to articulate these concepts of neo-tribal theory and show how they were reflected in our participants' talk and experiences of EDMC. By using an art exhibition to address this objective we aimed to reach a wider audience than we would with traditional academic dissemination and to do this in an accessible and vibrant way.

Art exhibitions have the potential to (re)introduce vitality into the way we present and experience our research since they can disseminate ideas through a range of forms of knowing. This 'extended epistemology' may include personal, practical, emotional and experiential knowing, as well as rational, cognitive understandings with which we are more familiar. An extended epistemology therefore allows the audience to engage with exhibits from multiple standpoints, creating more dialogical relationships between academics and their audience (Denzin and Lincoln, 2002; Gergen, with Walter, 1998; Reason and Riley, 2008; Sparkes, 2002). Working with an artist to create an exhibition allows psychologists to benefit from the training artists have in the conventions, bodies of knowledge and practical skills in working in this medium (Frith *et al.*, 2005). However, few psychologists have done such collaborative projects. A notable exception is Ken Gergen, who with Walter created an exhibition that employed poetry, painting and social science writing to articulate some of the concepts of a social constructionist model of the self. They argued that using these different media enabled them to produce an evocative work that allowed their audience to actively engage with complex and thought-provoking ideas. In doing so they aimed to use their exhibition to blur the boundaries between knower and learner and disseminate research ideas to a wider public (Gergen, with Walter, 1998).

Little has been written on the processes involved in producing exhibitions that bring together artists with researchers. A notable exception is an article by Liz Lee (2002), a General Practioner (GP) who, with artist Susie Freeman, produced a widely exhibited Pharmacopoeia exhibition. Pharmacopoeia aimed to get people to consider the ubiquity of pharmaceuticals in our society and in doing so also reflect on their own use of drugs and medicines. Lee and Freeman created textiles that produced visual narratives about people's relationships with pharmaceuticals. Taking advantage of the ambiguity and multiplicity of visual symbolism, they encouraged their audience to engage in a dialogue with their works that sometimes brought very different readings to the same piece. The subject of Pharmacopoeia came from a shared interest in exploring the medical world – Lee through her career as a GP and for Freeman through an invitation from a gallery to address this subject using a technique she had developed in working with textiles. Freeman's technique enabled small objects to be knitted into transparent nylon pockets, creating a material that could be used to make clothing that displayed objects such as pills, vials or sweets. In her 2002 paper, Lee discussed their collaboration processes, noting that as friends they had a long history of discussions around the issues they subsequently worked on and that their professional relationship was enhanced by a mutual desire to learn from each other and a sense of equality in the relationship. Their work was on-going, so that one piece could provide ideas for subsequent work. Lee (2002) also noted that their working relationship developed as they produced more artefacts with each gaining confidence to contribute ideas that had previously been in the other's area of expertise. In the present chapter we aim to develop Lee's paper on the processes of collaboration to provide a framework for others wanting to communicate academic theory and analysis through art exhibitions. To do so we use the proceeding chapter to discuss the processes involved in the production of our event, evaluate it and provide a 'Practicality check list' for those considering doing an art exhibition of their own.

Processes and production

The team involved in the exhibition was artist Richard Brown and academics Sarah Riley, Christine Griffin and Yvette Morey. Richard brought to the group experience in curating art and museum exhibitions and of working in a range of materials, both conceptually and figuratively. He had a degree in Fine Art and Sculpture and experience of working in graphic design. The academics were social psychologists who shared an interest in identity from a social constructionist perspective. They were experienced qualitative researchers with some previous experience and training in using visual methods. For example, Yvette had used videos in her PhD work on young people, identity and appearance (Morey, 2006); Chris had used photo-elicitation on a study of young people and Sarah had supervised various student projects that had used visual methods, as well as attending several courses on using new media.[3]

At the time of the exhibition the academics had been working together for over a year, forming personal and professional relationships with each other and also with Richard, as he was Sarah's partner. The ability to communicate, organise and listen with respect had therefore already been put in place. In addition we already had relationships with our funding partner, as we had applied successfully for ESRC Festival of Social Science funding to create the art exhibition as a form of dissemination.[4]

To address the first objective of the exhibition, sharing key concepts of neo-tribal theory, the academics of the team had formed a reading group for the book *The Time of the Tribes* (Maffesoli, 1996). *The Time of the Tribes* is an in-depth exposition of neo-tribal theory, but is a conceptually complex book and not always written in an easily accessible style (Maffesoli, 1996). Our first step was to identify and develop our own understanding of the key concepts of neo-tribalism and then to communicate these ideas to Richard, who had not read the book nor had a psychology background. His degree did, however, give him a familiarity with the concerns of psychology, as many of the academic aspects of arts degrees cover shared topics, such as identity, the body, and postmodernism.

To share *The Time of the Tribes* with Richard, Sarah used ideas and notes made during the reading group to produce a 36-page summary, which she then précised further, creating a 12-page document. Although she considered this an achievement, she was not that surprised when Richard returned it to her with the request to make it more manageable. The academics then produced a third summary document, which took the form of 7 pages. Each page represented one theme from neo-tribalism and contained approximately 10 lines of text, namely: the title of the theme, a brief description of the theme and 2–3 quotes from *The Time of the Tribes* that seemed to most clearly articulate the theme. These themes were 'proxemics', 'puissance, vitalism and unicity', 'sociality and belonging', 'family and mutual aid', 'hedonism', 'freedom and politics' and 'the social divine'. We then added 2–3 quotes from our participants' interview and focus group data that acted as examples of participant's talk that reflected these themes. For example, one of the themes was 'Sociality and belonging' and a quote from our participant that reflected it started with the line 'it's nice to have a sense of belonging isn't it?'. Finally, we searched through our photograph data bank looking for images that in some way reflected the theme. Our photograph data bank comprised photographs taken at participant observations; at other relevant events during the project data collection period (e.g. EDMC festivals); and during the focus groups, where participants had been invited to bring in objects that were related to their experiences of EDMC, which the researchers had photographed. The image we used for 'sociality and belonging', for example, was of two young men in hoodie tops standing together on the top of a hill looking down on a large gathering of people, vehicles and sound systems that made up a free party in Wales. The picture evoked both the intimate and large nature of social gatherings that are part of 'belonging' to free party culture.

In choosing the words and images for each theme we produced our final summary document, which Richard accepted as something he could work with.

Our training as academics was obviously useful here as the cyclical process of summarising notes down and identifying key quotes drew on skills honed in exam revision and qualitative data analysis. However, this experience also highlighted a key difference between the academics and the artist: as academics we were much more comfortable with large amounts of prose. The lesson from this exercise was that if we were going to meet our third aim of the exhibition and communicate to a wider audience we were going to have to find ways of being less 'wordy'.

The final summary document allowed us to discuss and clarify our ideas on neo-tribal theory; how it might be being expressed in our participants' experiences of EDMC; and how these ideas may best be represented in the exhibition. Richard suggested that for this type of exhibition we use both art and graphics because they do different kinds of work. The aim of graphic design (often referred to as 'commercial art') is to create images and text that form a distinctive unified style in order to clearly and effectively communicate a set of ideas/concepts. In comparison, art is not required or expected (either historically or culturally) to follow such a literal interpretation. Instead, art works are produced through a loose interpretation of ideas and concepts, from which the artist may think tangentially and so create new and diverse perspectives that may seem remote from the original source material.[5] By employing both graphic design and art we aimed to communicate ideas in different ways (literal and conceptual interpretations for example), as well as through different mediums (e.g. print, photographs, paintings and music). We hoped that employing these different media and approaches to representation (graphic design and fine art) would allow us to communicate our ideas through an extended epistemology, thus allowing our work to be vibrant, evocative and accessible to people engaging with it from different standpoints.

In creating works that enabled literal and conceptual interpretations of neo-tribalism we wove a range of simple and complex ideas into different media that either reflected or re-worked the key themes we had identified. This use of both graphic design and fine art principles allowed us to produce an exhibition that assumed a level of intellect in its audience, while being entertaining for those who didn't feel like using theirs at the weekend. It also helped us to avoid creating an exhibition that felt alienating, patronising or bland, problems Richard had noted artists can struggle with when producing work for the wider community. Addressing these concerns by using mixed media, graphics and art allowed us therefore allowed us to create a conceptually strong exhibition while remaining accessible to a wide audience.

Our processes were first to focus on the graphic design element of the exhibition. We concluded that the six-page summary document we had produced from our reading of *Time of Tribes* could be easily developed into seven banners, with each theme having its own banner. Each banner would follow the same format, in which the theme was introduced and then elaborated on using text and images. Each banner was headed with the name of the theme, followed by a dictionary definition of the theme, a brief description of the theme that used either a quote or key phrases from *Time of Tribes*; a quote from a participant that articulated the theme in relation to EDMC and an image from our photograph data bank. See Figure 13.1 for an example.

SOCIALITY & BELONGING

Sociality; [s_shee áil_tee] the tendency to form social groups or live in a community,
Belonging; [bi láwnging] Acceptance as a natural member or part:/ sense of security in friendship.

The self is exteriorised and transcended through collectivity.
Neo-tribalism is a society based on a family-clan-sect
structure in which we choose the collectivities to which we
belong. These clans represent a "re-enchantment with the
world." Society is not moving towards greater individuality,
but to "participation in the mystical sense of the word …
keeping warm together … a re-actualization of the ancient
myth of community" (Maffesoli, 1996)

It's nice to have a sense of belonging isn't it? There's pleasure in being part of a group.
There's no cliqueyness, everyone's welcome and anything's welcome, so then you
know it's really nice, because it's like a sense of warmth. (Lu-Lu)

Figure 13.1 'Sociality and Belonging' – one of the banners from the exhibition.

Combining headings, dictionary quotes, Maffesoli quotes, participants' talk and images from club/party culture allowed us to create a 'resonance' of meaning in which the texts and images worked to illustrate, reiterate, reflect or play with each other, what Gergen calls 'a synergistic advantage through juxtaposition' (Gergen, with Walter, 1998: 112). Written text was therefore still important in our attempt to communicate our ideas. The different 'voices' of the texts and images allowed us to do different things. For example, the quotes from *The Time of the Tribes* allowed us to introduce Maffesoli's style of writing, which employs a dense prose that may be experienced as intellectual or impenetrable, depending on one's standpoint. Since Maffesoli himself argues that his book may be too dense and complex for some academics, it was likely that alone his words may have alienated a non-academic audience. Our brief description of the theme that went with the *The Time of the Tribes* quote plus the participants' quotes provided other ways to think of the subject matter, acting to both make a link between theory and practice and to allow academic and 'everyday' speech to reflect each other. For example, in the banner 'Proxemics' the theme was explained as

> In sharing a space and an activity we gain a sense of being-together and an emotional attachment to the group. We value the group that we are physically (symbolically or virtually) close to. Proxemics is the glue that binds people together and enables puissance – a will to live.

and in the participant's quote

> when you go out clubbing or when you're going to a party or just standing in a queue or just in a load of cars or something there is that kind of sense of community, even if it's just for a moment. I feel it kind of builds up and there's always a certain point it where it kind of comes up and then it drops off again – sometimes you're lucky and it kind of stays there for a while sometimes you've got to hunt around to find it again.

These multiple voices thus gave the audience 'academic' and 'everyday' ways of thinking about each concept, allowing us to set up a dialogue between the two different worlds of social theory and EDMC.

We used the photographic images to illustrate some aspect of EDMC (e.g. the kinds of places free parties are held in), provide a sense of atmosphere, and to both reinforce and challenge the narrative in the text. The images were therefore multi-purpose, since the ambiguous, intertextual and layered aspects of images can enable playful or subversive disruption, contradiction or reinforcement with accompanying text (Barthes, 1980; Frith *et al.*, 2005; Pink, 2001). For example, the text in the Proxemics banner was supported with an image from a club night in which people stood, danced or walked near each other in a room that had activity, but was not excessively busy. This image both illustrated the concept (people sharing a space in order to practice a particular set of values and behaviours) and had the potential to open up an interesting dialogue between the words and image used (since in silhouette the relationships between the people were ambiguous, reflecting a sense of the temporary, fluid and dynamic nature of neo-tribal social organisation). We hoped that the interaction between the images and the texts would allow for a conceptually strong exhibition since the dialogue with the texts and images invited the audience to engage with the overall message of the banner (e.g. the role of proxemics) while also making multiple readings that could draw on a wider shared visual culture or their own personal associations.

While the process of choosing the images was long for some of the banners, for others it was so fast as to feel intuitive – we 'knew' this was the right image, we just had to work out why. An example of the latter was the photograph of a cluster of white flags fluttering in the breeze, taken at a festival, which seemed an obvious image to represent our banner 'FREEDOM and pOLITICS' – the 'everyday politics' (hence the small 'p') of participating in something alternative that you believed in, but which was the antithesis of official organisational governance. The image was of a group of fluttering flags that were identical in not having a logo, symbol or text, suggesting a coming together of people who either rejected official organised governance or who rejected the notion of having anything to say about organised governance. This implicit challenge to traditional political engagement could then be read as a sign of 'freedom', but in being white, the flags also evoked alternative readings, such as surrender.

From a graphic design perspective the aesthetic of the images was important. We chose images that could be cropped in a similar way and which shared a similar colour scheme and tone, creating a harmonious aesthetic that linked them together. For the same reason, the typography needed to be consistent and both the text and images needed to be of sufficient resolution that they could withstand enlargement, since in 'real life' the banner would be forty times larger than the computer screen image of it on which we were working. To create banners that employed consistent typology it was essential to proof read the banners several times before taking them to the printers. Proof reading involved not just checking language but also all aspects of typeface formatting, including text size, font, style and spacing.

The banners became the central set of pieces of the exhibition. We then focused on creating art works that engaged conceptually with aspects of neo-tribalism. Some were ideas waiting to have a focus – as in the central piece 'Divine'. 'Divine' reiterated one of the banners, entitled 'Social Divine', which focused on what Maffesoli calls the 'enchantment' of social gatherings. Divine was a two-metre-long, one-metre-high board of gold sequins that sparkled in a breeze created by a fan, in which the word 'Divine' was written in blue sequins in a script that was evocative of the 1970s (see Figure 13.2). Divine was made specifically for the exhibition – it represented the opulence and splendour of something Divine – however, the idea to 'write' in sequins had been in Richard's mind for some time. Other pieces were produced as we developed our ideas – one of the photographs we didn't use for a banner was blown up as a photograph in its own right, unaccompanied by written text, to illustrate the gathering of people living out hedonistic values. It showed a large gathering of people dancing, illuminated by fire and under an inflatable red star - it was a vivid image evoking Bacchanalian revelry in a modern party context.

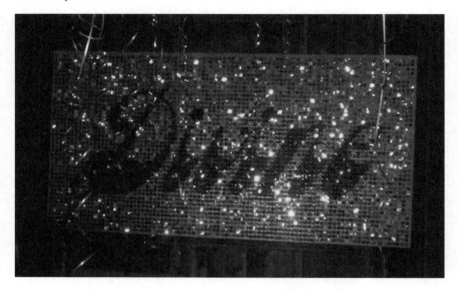

Figure 13.2 'Divine'. Image produced with kind permission of Richard Brown.

Other pieces played with sub-cultural symbols. For example, in 'Everyday Politics' we painted a large canvas with a reproduction of an image of a riot policeman that had originated from 1968 and which had subsequently been used in various civil disobedience literatures including those against the Criminal Justice Act[6]. We used this iconic image of youth culture and politics to make a large imposing painting that created an emotional response in the viewer, resonated with other cultural images, and interacted with written text so as to pose a question to the viewer. We wanted to use the piece to introduce a controversial aspect of neo-tribal theory (the relationships between 'everyday' and traditional politics) and so supported the image with a short piece of text that asked the viewer to consider these relationships (see Figure 13.3).

A total of 15 pieces were made, these included the six banners, Divine, two paintings, the 'Red Star' photograph, a suggestions box (where the responses fell into a wastepaper basket), vinyl lettering on the floor that introduced the exhibition and a TV/video installation. In addition we made badges, a handout and had various ESRC promotional materials available. The development of the pieces was cyclical, with ideas being generated and developed between the team with Sarah co-ordinating this aspect of the work.

At production stage, Richard took over the co-ordination, doing or supervising any in-house production (as in Divine and Everyday Politics) and using Word and Photoshop programmes to produce any graphics that were subsequently taken to a professional printer. Both development and production required a range of skills and a lot of time. The development of ideas was aided by regular scheduled meetings between various members of the team, as well as clearly set, agreed

Figure 13.3 'Everyday Politics'. This was accompanied by the following text: 'Maffesoli argues that people are turning away from traditional "modernist" politics and towards "everyday politics" – a society full of lifestyle groups protected from state intervention by the fact there are too many to focus on. But what happens when the authorities do focus on you, name you and criminalise you? In 1994 the Criminal justice Act made rave the first youth subculture to be prohibited by law.'

individual tasks. Skills and time were drafted in from supportive friends; some worked for free, others for a bottle of whiskey (something we did not attempt to charge to the ESRC).

Producing the pieces was only one aspect of curating the exhibition; we also had to make decisions on how to arrange the works so while individual pieces were meaningful in their own right, a narrative was also produced as one walked around the exhibition space. One of the advantages of using alternative forms of dissemination, such as an art exhibition, is that it can free researchers from the linear argument structure that characterises most academic writing. Employing different narrative structures changes the 'voice' of research, in doing so it can (re) introduce vitality into academic work by opening up the possibility for new forms

Practicality check list

- Find adequate and relevant funding.
- Consider what each of the team brings in terms of skills, relationships and materials. For example, a strong understanding of the subject, previous experience of curating exhibitions and of working with each other.
- Consider the equipment, materials or training you need.
- Work with people whose previous work you like.
- Organise a series of formal and informal meetings. Ideas may be best developed though a cyclical process. Different members of the team can take on different roles or be responsible for particular aspects of the work, e.g. writing, painting, organising, but keep in regular contact to check on and develop a shared vision. A regularly updated and referred to timeline of required activities is useful.
- Give time and value to building relationships and ideas through discussions, this will help you develop a shared sense of aesthetics as well as depth to your work.
- Have a clearly defined aim and concept. Consider how to 'story' your concept for your chosen audience(s).
- Consider articulating your ideas through a range of media in order to communicate the concept in different ways through different modalities.
- Visit the site and plan with the space you have in mind. Try to find a space that has a central location or is easy to access. Be aware that exhibition spaces are often booked up years in advance.
- Identify a wider community of people and resources who may be able to help.
- Focus on promotion – use a range of mediums and ways to communicate to your chosen audience(s). These may include fliers, banners outside the exhibition space (see Figure 13.4), press releases, contacting listing magazines, sending emails via your own and other's lists. Consider who can help you, e.g. University press offices.
- Delegate where you can.
- Accept you have to give up a lot of personal time (you don't have to marry the artist but it can help).

Figure 13.4 Outside banner advertising exhibition.

of dialogue between the researchers and their audience. These forms of dialogue are produced through the multiple readings that are enabled by the various standpoints that members of an audience will bring with them. Although we are most familiar with linear narrative, other formats are available in our culture. For example, electronic dance music often uses audio samples or, in relation to music videos, visual images, that employ a 'looping' narrative, in which sound samples/ images will be repeatedly returned to. These acts of repetition work to develop the relationship between the music/image and the audience by, for example, creating a trance-like effect or articulating a message, such as a celebration of technology (e.g. Hexstatic) or a political critique (e.g. Banco di Gia). In our exhibition we arranged the pieces in a way that allowed several forms of narrative to be read. The banners were lined up along one wall, which, if followed from the main entrance, led to the centre piece, Divine. This order produced a linear narrative, with Divine being the conclusion to the story told by the banners. However, the banners worked as stand-alone pieces too, each telling its own story (for example, of the importance of belonging) and, when looked at as a group, also contained 'looping narratives', both in the text (such as emphasising sociality) and through the similar colours and tones of the photographic images.

The pieces described above formed the main part of the exhibition. However, an early site visit showed that part of the space could be sectioned off with blackout curtains; we decided to turn this area into a club, installing record decks, DJs, dance music videos projected onto a white screen and a UV cannon light (a large UV light, kindly lent to us by a friend). On opening night it also had a bar and, as people danced, the space became its own dance culture neo-tribe. We used the UV cannon to create other forms of interactivity and participation. Leaving a heavily annotated copy of *The Time of the Tribes* and some UV pens by the cannon, we invited people to peruse the copy, find their favourite quote and write it on the wall. In doing so, we allowed people to see how academics engage with books (highlighting, annotating etc.) and in giving them direct access to *The Time of the Tribes* we encouraged them to act as academics themselves, exploring the content and style of the book to find passages that said something meaningful to them. To counteract the 'heaviness' of Maffesoli, we set this task in a playful way, evoking being naughty children writing on walls, with ink that was only visible in the club context of UV lighting.

Performance & post-script[7]

With one member of the public already at the doors, we opened an hour later than advertised and over the course of a weekend 242 people attended the event. The ESRC provided a feedback questionnaire and the responses on these showed that many of those who attended were not academics, demonstrating that we had met our aim of reaching a wider audience. The audience consisted of people who had an interest in EDMC – including some of the Reverberating Rhythms participants and clubbers/partiers who had seen the promotional material; there were also academics, ESRC staff, and passers by with an interest in art exhibitions. The way people responded to the exhibits, in terms of spending significant time at the exhibition; talking with us about their interpretations; their comments in the suggestions box (some of which were long, many of which thoughtful); the careful copying of Maffesoli quotes onto the UV wall (as well as drawing silly pictures); and the dancing on the opening night, all gave us a sense that we had produced a conceptually strong presentation – since people engaged intellectually with our work – and in a way that was accessible and vibrant – after all it's not often that people dance during academic dissemination.

There were some responses we hadn't expected. For some the exhibition was a powerful experience – one couple spent three hours circulating around the exhibition space, engaging with each piece as they went, telling us how much they loved it and choosing to write 'cheese' on the UV wall ("because I like cheese and I knew that it would be ok for me to write that). At the other extreme, a colleague with a background in clubbing spent less than ten minutes with us – the space seemingly failing to resonate. For us, this was a sign that the exhibition was successful, a good exhibition will have a particular aesthetic and this will not be to everyone's taste. That it resonated for a significant number of people is a sign that we were not bland, or patronising; but reaching a wider audience successfully does not mean pleasing everyone.

We felt we had succeeded in representing our work in a way that was more 'engaged' than traditional academic outputs and that this voice enabled us to bring vitality into social science dissemination. However, we wonder how seriously the exhibition was taken by other academics – we had hoped to use the exhibition as a way of networking with other academics working in our area and to this end Sarah had sent personal emails to a range of academics working in four local universities in psychology, sociology, geography or arts departments. As far as we can tell, none of these people came, although some did send their postgraduate students. And while their students were enthusiastic, the lack of attendance by academic staff suggests that many academics may not consider this kind of dissemination important or relevant to themselves.

From the suggestions box two challenging issues emerged. First, that some people had different expectations. For example, one visitor had hoped to participate by bringing his/her own photographs although there was no suggestion of this in our promotional material. This comment reminded us that we only ever have limited control over the expectations people bring to events. The second set of comments could be interpreted as concerns around the right to exhibit rave culture in relation to losing the spontaneity of events if one pins them down or the right to communicate rave culture to the wider world. The latter comment was of concern for us because we realised we had assumed we had that right, particularly as the exhibition could easily be read as a celebration of the culture – allowing positive comments to be made that could act as a counterpoint to the fairly consistent folk devil status of clubbers (except when money is needed for city centre regeneration). Overall, however, the participants of the event were enthusiastic and celebratory about the event.

We conclude our chapter by noting that art has gained ascendancy in popular culture recently. The implication of our event is that psychology can harness this popularity to create accessible, attractive and interesting forms of dissemination. We suggest that successful events that merge psychology with art are likely to involve a genuine collaboration between artists and psychologists. Such collaborations require time, a focus on relationship building, an expectation for iterative processes in idea generation, and the need to respect the artist's visual literacy. For qualitative psychologists, this is likely to mean severely cutting the number of words we want to use. It is also essential to consider how to create different forms of knowing through your work; what the needs, wants and expectations of your audience(s) are; how to make your exhibition aesthetically pleasing; and the different narratives that may be played out across your exhibition space. As a discipline, psychology is still deeply wedded to a naturalistic science model of clear, objective, parsimonious communication. To embrace multiplicity, ambiguity, intertexuality and a lack of control over your 'take home message' may move many of us out of our comfort zone but, as action researchers note, this is often where the best work is done.

Notes

1 Reverberating Rhythms: Social Identity and Political Participation in Clubland was funded by the Economic and Social Research Council (ref: RES-000-22-1171).
2 These figures are rounded up.
3 This was part of an ESRC project (ref. R000239287) entitled 'Consuming Identities: Young People, Cultural Forms and Negotiations in Households' that ran from 2001 to 2005.
4 This is an annual competition with a maximum grant of £2000 to be used to disseminate social science research.
5 For an introduction to the role of graphic design and Fine Art the following links are useful: http://www.cl.cam.ac.uk/~ig206/oak_tree.html
   http://www.cl.cam.ac.uk/~ig206/oak_tree.html
6 The Criminal Justice Act included legislation that directly targeted raves. CJA is available at: http://www.publications.parliament.uk/pa/cm200203/cmbills/008/2003008.pdf
7 For more details on the exhibition pieces see http://www.aber.ac.uk/en/psychology/staff/rileysarah

References

Barthes, R. (1980). *Camera Lucida*. London: Flamingo.
Denzin, N. and Lincoln, Y. (Eds.) (2002). *Handbook of qualitative research*. Thousand Oaks, CA: Sage.
Frith, H., Riley, S., Archer, L. and Gleeson, K. (2005). Editorial: imag(in)ing visual methodologies. *Qualitative Research in Psychology*, 2(3), 187–198.
Gergen, K. J. with Walter, R. (1998). Real/izing the relational. *Journal of Social and Personal Relationships*, 15(1), 110–126.
Giddens, A. (1991). *Modernity and self-identity: self and society in the late modern age*. Stanford, CA: Stanford University Press.

Lee, L. (2002). Pharmacopoeia – A collaboration between the textile artist Susie Freeman and the general practitioner Liz Lee. *Feminist Review*, 72, 26–39.

Maffesoli, M. (1996). *The time of the tribes: the decline of individualism in mass society.* London: Sage.

Morey, Y. (2006). *Looking for/at clothed selves: performativity, visuality and the construction of clothed subjects.* Unpublished PhD thesis, University of West of England.

Pink, S. (2001). *Doing visual ethnography.* London: Sage.

Reason, P. and Riley, S. (2008). Co-operative inquiry: an action research practice. In J. Smith (Ed.), *Qualitative psychology: a practical guide to methods.* London: Sage Publications.

Riley, S. Griffin, C. and Morey, Y. (2010). The case for 'everyday politics': evaluating neo-tribal theory as a way to understand alternative forms of political participation, using electronic dance music culture as an example. *Sociology*, 44(2), 1–19.

Riley, S., Morey, Y. and Griffin, C. (2008). Ketamine: The divisive dissociative. A discourse analysis of the constructions of ketamine by participants of a free party (rave) scene. *Addiction Research & Theory,* 16(3), 217–230.

Riley, S., Morey, Y. and Griffin, C. (2010). The 'pleasure citizen': analysing partying as a form of social and political participation, *Young* (Special Issue on 'Emerging forms of youth engagement: everyday and local perspectives'), 18(1), 33–54.

Sparkes, A. C. (2002). Autoethnography: self-indulgence or something more? In A. Bochner and C. Ellis (Eds.), *Ethnographically speaking: autoethnography, literature, and aesthetics.* New York: AltaMira.

14 Risk communication and participatory research

'Fuzzy felt', visual games and group discussion of complex issues

Angela Cassidy and John Maule

Introduction

Psychological research has shown that the general public often perceives and acts in the face of risk in ways that are very different from those responsible for assessing, managing and communicating these risks (see, e.g., Fischhoff, 2009 for a review). Powell and Leiss (1997) interpreted these differences in terms of two languages of risk: a 'public' language grounded in social and intuitive knowledge (see also Tulloch and Lupton, 2003) and an expert or 'scientific' language grounded in scientific, specialised and statistical knowledge. 'Public' risk language takes account of qualitative aspects of the threat (e.g. the amount of control people perceive they have; how familiar/unfamiliar it seems) whereas 'scientific' risk language is founded on formal models that define risk as the product of the likelihood of some event and the impact, value or utility of its outcome (French *et al.*, 2009). These differences have important implications that have, until comparatively recently, been largely ignored by risk communicators. On the one hand, public audiences often have difficulty making sense of the specialised, statistical basis of professional risk assessments, so tend to ignore communications based on them, or draw conclusions that are different from those intended. Until recently, risk communicators have aimed to resolve such problems by investigating how people interpret statistical risk information, and then sought to improve the presentation of this information accordingly (e.g. Berry, 2004; Gigerenzer, 2002). On the other hand, such communications often fail to address issues of concern to the multiple and varied 'publics' they address,[1] so are thought to be irrelevant and are ignored, contributing to problems of mistrust and miscommunication between experts and publics (see, e.g. Wynne, 1995).

A potential solution to these difficulties can be provided by replacing this one-way 'sender to receiver' model of information transfer with a model of communication as a two-way process, in which audiences take an active role in constructing the meaning of a message (Lewenstein, 1995; McQuail, 2005). This also leads to recognition of the need for partnership and dialogue between experts, policy makers, wider publics, and stakeholder groups with particular interests in the issues of concern (e.g. Fischhoff, 1995). A key focus of this work has been the development of methods and processes for enabling public and stakeholder participation in risk management and decision making, such as citizens' juries and decision-making workshops (Rowe and Frewer, 2005). A potential benefit of this approach is that it facilitates greater dialogue and understanding of the issues for all those involved and has the potential to improve communications by taking into account the different conceptualisations of risk. However, comparatively little attention has been paid to the question of how to apply this 'partnership' model, and the outputs of participation exercises, to develop more effective and sensitive communication of risk issues.

A notable exception to this lack of interest in partnership models is provided by the Mental Models Approach (MMA) (Morgan *et al.*, 2002). This approach builds upon the idea that people internally represent the world in terms of small-scale 'mental models' of external reality and the actions that they might take (Craik, 1943). The act of comprehension is thought to yield a mental model (Johnson-Laird, 1975) and, once established, models are used to simulate behaviours and their possible outcomes (e.g. Schwartz and Black, 1996). Importantly for the MMA this body of work also confirms that experts and novices often have different models for understanding the same issue (e.g. Gentner and Gentner, 1983). With this body of work in mind, the MMA to risk communication involves eliciting and comparing 'expert' and 'lay' mental models of a hazard to identify misunderstandings and errors in lay understanding. Comparing the identified mental models allows the researcher to then construct risk communications that rectify these shortcomings (Morgan *et al.*, 2002). The advantages of this approach are that it has a sound theoretical base in psychology, is user-centred and that it has successfully been applied across a variety of domains (e.g. Cox *et al.*, 2003; Niewohner *et al.*, 2004).

However, the traditional cognitivist view of knowledge which the MMA operates upon cannot take account of the ways in which even expert risk knowledge is contingent, partial and socially constructed, as a broad range of psychological research on risk has shown (see for example, Funtowicz and Ravetz, 1992). Therefore we have developed and adapted the MMA, integrating it with a social representations model of risk knowledge (Breakwell, 2001). Unlike mental models, which are seen as held solely in the individual's mind, social representations theory can account for how risk knowledge is built, held and communicated collectively, allowing greater potential for a partnership model of risk communication (Joffe, 2003). Since risk knowledge exists at both individual and social levels, our approach assumes that both perspectives are necessary to gain a comprehensive understanding of risk knowledge and communication (Cassidy and Maule, under review).

Working from this modified approach, and taking a more nuanced approach to expert/lay differences, we have adapted the MMA to investigate how risk across the food chain is conceptualised by a range of stakeholders.[2] These groups included scientists and risk policy managers; farmers; NGO (nongovermental organisation) campaigners; food industry workers; and 'interested publics' for food risk.[3] In contrast to the MMA, we have sought to avoid privileging 'expert' perspectives on risk – either those of risk experts or our own.

However, our initial attempts to elicit and compare the mental models of these highly diverse groups ran into difficulties. We ran pilot in-depth interviews and focus groups on the topic and found that lay groups, and to some extent expert groups, generated outputs that were very limited in content. All groups found it hard to develop a model of the food chain and discuss the relevant risks at the same time, particularly the novice groups who were not used to organising their knowledge and talking about food risk in this way. Thus, the data generated were impoverished and failed to reflect how our participants thought about the issues involved. Thus, we needed to find a satisfactory method for eliciting the mental models of these diverse groups that could manage the very different types and degrees of experience and expertise in food chain risks that each had. To overcome this problem we developed an innovative and what proved to be highly productive visual research method for use in group interview situations.

This chapter outlines the development of this method, and demonstrates its value when investigating how different groups of people conceptualise complex situations such as risks in food production. We begin by describing the broader case study which our work contributed to, alongside our central research questions and the challenges we encountered in attempting to answer these questions. We then outline the potential of visual methods to meet these challenges, and describe the development of our approach (the 'fuzzy felt method'). We discuss participants' interactions with the method, speculate on why using images may have helped them engage with our research topic, and discuss some of the problems we encountered. Finally, we outline avenues for further enquiry in risk research and visual methods, and explore potential applications of the method in domains beyond psychological and social research.

Case study

The research was carried out as part of a larger multidisciplinary project addressing natural and social scientific approaches to managing and communicating food-chain risks (Shepherd *et al.*, 2006; Shepherd, 2008; Barker *et al.*, 2010).[4] As described above, our research focused specifically on participatory risk communication, but in line with the wider project we employed a case-study approach, looking at the food chain for two specific foods – apples and chicken. Our central research questions were:

i How do different stakeholder groups understand the risks associated with the production, distribution and consumption of food?
ii What risks would they identify in the food chain and where would they place them?
iii How do they think such risks should be managed and mitigated?

These questions could be rephrased as: what are the differences and similarities between different stakeholders' mental models of food chain risk?[5] Our interests in the social aspects of risk knowledge and inter-group comparisons led us to conclude that group interviewing would be a viable option: as well as the more general benefits of focus group research (Barbour and Kitzinger, 1998), it seemed that in a group of known peers, participants would be more likely to reflect frankly on the sometimes sensitive risk issues we were interested in.[6] The group context would also help mitigate the sense of putting participants 'on the spot' about their knowledge of food risk, and lessen any felt pressure to give the 'correct' answers.

Therefore we ran several pilot interview groups, addressing our research questions. As indicated above, it became apparent that the group discussions rapidly moved away from our central research questions about risk in the food chain. This was due in part to lay participants' unfamiliarity with systems of modern food production. However, we also found that both lay and some 'expert' participants had difficulty engaging with the extreme complexity of these systems and identifying and talking about interactions between different parts of them. It seemed that groups needed a great deal of intervention from the facilitator in order to stay 'on topic', which was extremely problematic for our commitment to avoid researcher framings of the interview process. To overcome these problems we explored the possibility of using visual research methods, which we believed had the potential to engage with these kinds of difficulties.

Potential of visual methods

The use of visual methods in social research is becoming increasingly common, although at present the work is scattered across many research fields and specific areas of study, leading to little methodological or intellectual coherence in how they are employed. Visual methods are probably best established in anthropology (Banks, 2001) and educational/developmental research with children (Prosser and Burke, 2007), however, as the contributions to this volume attest, they are becoming increasingly popular in general psychology research. Broadly speaking there are three main approaches to visual research: analysis of (previously produced) images, use of preselected images in interviews or focus groups to elicit discussion, and participant production of images (Prosser and Loxley, 2008).

As described above, our research on food chain risks needed a method which would:

i   draw out participants who regarded themselves as unfamiliar with food production and risk issues;
ii   enable participants to think about and explore in depth the complexities of the modern food production systems;
iii allow an equal basis for comparison between participants with different degrees of familiarity, experience and expertise with food risk issues;
iv   not frame the research in terms of 'expert' understandings of food risk;
v   contribute towards a participatory approach to risk communication.

Asking participants to produce their own images (through drawing, model-making, photography or video), either prior to or during an interview situation, is a research technique which we felt had the potential to fulfil these requirements for two major reasons.

First, many visual research methods work by helping participants to structure or develop their thoughts in some way. At a basic level, images provide a simple 'elicitation' role in interviews by providing a stimulus for discussing the research topic. Participant-produced images can also be helpful when working with people who are less articulate, such as young children (e.g. Dove *et al.*, 1999), or when broaching particularly sensitive subjects (Wakefield and Underwager, 1998). Gauntlett (2007) argues that the creative process can help participants to reflect more deeply on topics that they may not have thought a great deal about beforehand (which is often the case with food risks). Drawing can also help people structure and organise their thoughts more systematically, and such images can in turn play an elicitation role in group discussion. Research in this vein has used drawing to explore people's understanding of how ideas connect together, through the creation of 'concept maps'. This idea has been used extensively in educational practice (e.g. Buzan, 1995), as well as in management research, where the resulting 'rich pictures' are used to understand organisations better and therefore identify how to make them more efficient (French *et al.*, 2005). Therefore, it seemed possible that asking participants to create images of the food chain and of food-chain risks might help them explore the issue at greater depth than we had managed previously.

Second, some researchers argue that visual-based methods are inherently less directed and not filtered through researcher's expectations, because the creative activity acts in the place of researcher questioning and prompts. For this reason, these methods are also frequently utilised by practitioners of participatory research who aim to increase the meaning, validity and 'ownership' of social research for the participants themselves, which can in turn aid participants in organising collectively to effect social and political change (Kesby, 2000). Therefore, we anticipated that a visual method would help us in our stated goals of avoiding 'expert' framings of the research topic, and of working towards a participatory approach to risk communication.

Development of the 'fuzzy felt method'

As described above, we had run several pilot interview groups designed to elicit participants' mental models of food-chain risks, but had run into difficulties in engaging with the research topic, and in particular with exploring the complexities of contemporary systems of food production. From reading the literature on visual research methods, it seemed that using images, and in particular asking participants to draw while thinking about food-chain risk, might help us overcome these problems. Therefore a second pilot study was run, in which small groups (2–4) of participants were presented with a piece of A3 paper and asked to draw an image of the food chain for a particular item – the series of connections any food goes through on its journey from 'farm to plate'. Five trial groups were run, each with a different type of participant (farmers; food scientists; green campaigners; young professionals; parents of young children). Once the picture was complete, participants were then asked to use red pens to identify and locate what they thought the main risks were on that food chain, and finally to use green pens to identify how and where those risks could be managed.

We found this approach to be partially successful: the task helped participants focus on our central issue of enquiry (risk in the food chain), and supported them in a process of 'thoughtful reflection' about the complex issues at hand (Gauntlett and Holzwarth, 2006: 84). The resulting images were complex, interesting and 'rich' in their content (see Figure 14.1 for an example; detail given in Figure 14.2) and group discussion was longer, more developed and much more focused on the research topic than in the earlier pilot. Crucially, we also found that *very little intervention* was required from the interviewer, aside from the central prompts asking for an image of the food chain, and for the key risks and mitigations present. However, we found that participants' interactions with the drawing task were variable, both within and between the groups: while some took to the idea well, drew lots and talked more, others seemed wary and were reluctant to engage in the drawing activity. There were two primary reasons for this reluctance: participants expressed embarrassment at doing something 'artistic' without considering themselves to be talented at that activity, especially in a group context; and confusion/scepticism at how the task comprised a valid piece of research. In addition, once engaged in the task, the degree to which people used drawing/ images was highly variable, with some choosing to mostly talk, others to write 'labels' but not use images, and others to draw pictures. This variability presented problems for how representative the data were of all group members, as well as raising concerns for how to analyse validly and interpret the data across groups in order to answer our primary research questions.

We did, however, notice some consistency in the images produced – all the groups created some sort of interconnected network to represent the food chain, with specific elements, usually objects, places or processes (e.g. tractors; chickens; warehouses), at the node points of these networks. Inspired by this and the child's game, 'Fuzzy Felt' – which involves arranging a series of pre-cut felt shapes onto a textured board to create larger 'scene' pictures – a version of the game was developed for use in our group interviewing.[7] This involved sticking icons of the food chain elements onto a large piece of paper and connecting them with hand-drawn lines. As with Gauntlett's (2007) research using Lego™ figures to explore identity issues, we anticipated that such an activity would help people engage with food risks in a creative, but less challenging, more 'playlike' fashion. In addition, we hoped that this would help address some of the problems we had encountered with freehand drawing. By providing the activity with some structure, we hoped to overcome participants' reluctance to draw, and to make the resulting data on their mental models of food-chain risk a little clearer and more easily comparable.

In order to ensure that this framework remained participant generated, the freehand drawings from the pilot study were used to generate a list of food chain elements (see Table 14.1), which in turn were converted into a series of 'clipart'-style images (mostly publicly licensed images obtained from the Internet, with a few researcher-generated images in the same style).[8] The revised interview

Figure 14.1 Example freehand food chain drawing. 'Red' pen (risks) appears as light grey; 'green' pen (mitigations) appears as dark grey.

Figure 14.2 Detail of freehand food chain drawing.

Table 14.1 List of participant-generated food chain elements

Food chain element		
General	*Apple food chain specific*	*Chicken food chain specific*
Farm	Apple	Slaughter
Garden/allotment	Drink	Chicken (live)
Factory	Apple tree	Chicken (meat)
Warehouse		
Lorry		
Car		
Ship		
Plane		
Farm machinery		
Kitchen preparation		
Kitchen storage		
Processed product		
Plate		
Supermarket		
Small shop		
Catering/restaurant		
Market		
Wholesale		
Blank		

procedure went as follows. Small groups of peers (2–6 members) were presented with a piece of A3 paper on a drawing board, with the food-chain elements arranged around the edge in the form of labelled, printed pictures on small pieces of paper mounted on Blu-Tack®. Several 'blank' images were also available so that groups had the option to create new elements if they wished. Each participant was given black, red and green pens. As with the earlier freehand pilot, the group was asked to work together to create an image of the food chain (either apples or chicken), using the provided 'element' pictures and the black pens. Once they agreed that this was complete, they were asked to use the red pens to write down the risks they thought were involved in their food chain, locating them in the image. Once this exercise was complete, they were asked use the green pens to identify possible risk management actions that could and should be taken to mitigate the risks they had already identified. As a closing question, participants were asked about sources of information about food risk (Where did you find out/hear about these things? Where would you go to find out more?).

As in the pilot study, it was made clear to participants that we were interested in 'what *you think* happens', rather than what participants might know for sure. Discussions amongst the group while they worked on this were recorded and transcribed, and these transcripts were analysed alongside the images produced during the interview session. An example of the type of image produced in this second version of the task is reproduced below in Figure 14.3 (detailed in Figure 14.4). Thus the resulting images provide an effective way of capturing how

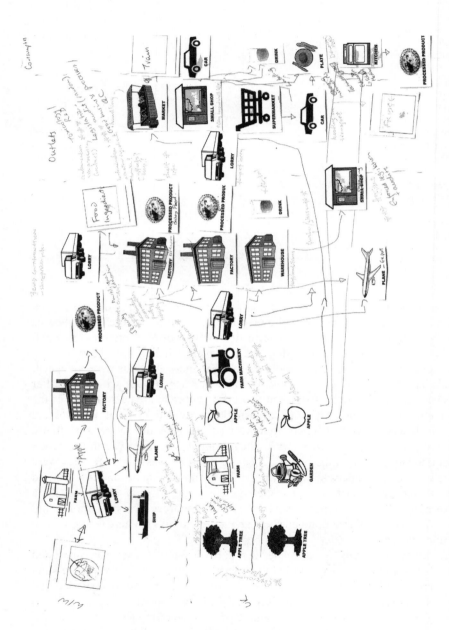

Figure 14.3 Example 'fuzzy felt'-style food chain image. 'Red' pen (risks) appears as light grey; 'green' pen (mitigations) appears as dark grey.

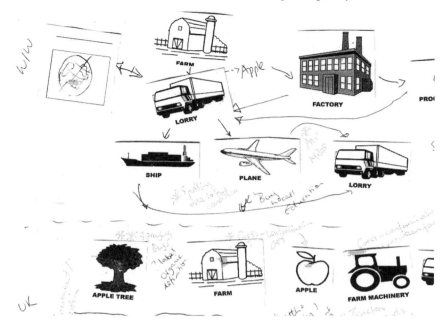

Figure 14.4 Detail of 'fuzzy felt'-style food chain image.

particular stakeholder groups conceptualise the food chain, the associated risks and how these risks may be mitigated. As such they not only embody some of the defining features of mental models, e.g. the principle of iconicity stating that a mental model has a structure that corresponds to the known structure of what it represents (Johnson-Laird and Byrne, 1991), but also fulfil the needs of the MMA by providing a method for capturing and comparing the mental models of experts, the public and other key stakeholders.

Interpretation and analysis

Since the method had been designed primarily to facilitate group discussions of food-chain risks, it was paramount that transcripts of the group interview sessions were analysed directly alongside the images produced by the groups. The analysis comprised a two-stage process, each asking different questions of the data, which we will describe as the 'descriptive' and 'interpretive' stages of data analysis. The initial 'descriptive' analysis was designed to answer some of our more basic research questions, i.e. what, where and how our stakeholder groups defined risk, and risk management in the food chain. To do this, we carried out a simple content analysis on transcripts and images alike, coding for relatively straightforward features (what risks, what mitigations, where in the food chain?). As an adjunct to this content analysis, the images were also coded for various structural features of the food chains that had been produced (e.g. the ratio of 'risks' to 'mitigations', the number and type of icons, the number of linkages between icons) and the overall 'shape' (e.g. the number of routes and branches).

However, we felt that such an analysis on its own could not hope to fully answer our research questions, as it could not access more complex issues surrounding the meaning of the kinds of risks identified, how the groups negotiated definitions of what constitutes 'food risk'; their broader attitudes to different modes of food production; to risk management and responsibility; what they considered to be 'good/bad' food; and their relationships and attitudes to the other stakeholders in food production. Therefore, a more conventional, in-depth, qualitative 'interpretive' analysis of the interview transcripts was carried out, addressing the above questions as well as drawing out the major themes of discussion in the interview groups. This second stage of analysis focused more upon the textual rather than visual data, although coding was carried out in close reference to the visual images. In part this was due to the limitations of the qualitative data analysis software in use (NVivo), but also because we felt that the 'standardised' nature of the images (i.e. the use of clipart) meant the visual data was not sufficiently 'rich' (i.e. complex and open to the same level of interpretation as the transcripts) to warrant qualitative analysis at this depth.

Presentation and interpretation of our findings lies outside the scope of this chapter (see Cassidy and Maule, in preparation, for a full description of these). However, the analyses showed that all stakeholder groups were aware of a broad range of processes and procedures that take place between the farm and the point of consumption. Groups conceptualised the food chain, and the risk issues involved, in strikingly different ways. For example, environment/food campaigners and members of the public tended to divide food production into two food chains, mainstream and 'alternative' (organic, fair trade, locally sourced) production, associated with very different levels of risk. In contrast, scientists, farmers and food industry representatives tended to see food production as a unified system, incorporating all modes of production. Also, participants had very different understandings of what constituted 'risk' in the food chain. For scientists and risk managers, food risks were defined exclusively as factors that cause harm when ingesting a foodstuff. However, other stakeholders included broader risk issues relevant to their own interests and values, such as economic risks (farmers and food industry representatives) or environmental issues (NGO campaigners). Finally, we found that food industry 'insiders' (scientists, risk managers, food industry representatives and farmers) understood food risks in the context of risk mitigation systems (good management, regulation, inspection and assurance schemes), while other stakeholders showed little awareness of such systems.

Discussion

Running small group interviews structured around a 'fuzzy felt'-style activity proved to be significantly more productive and useful, not only in terms of our research objectives, but also, it seemed, for the experiences of the research participants themselves. While we found that participants were often initially puzzled or wary of the task they were asked to undertake, the majority quickly warmed to it as they became engaged in the activity. At times, it was palpable that participants were actively enjoying the chance to 'play' in a situation they had obviously expected to be quite formal.

M1: also it could go to wholesale as well down here, with a lorry . . . well it doesn't matter actually, and that can go then to the small shop, wholesale to small shop and catering . . . and this can also go to supermarket and catering up here to really. Sorry, I've taken over here, I love this!
[laughter]
M2: I'll see if I can get you an Etch-A-Sketch!

(Food industry association, 16/10/06)

Other participants directly commented on how the activity was helping them to think about, and focus on, food risks in new and different ways – interestingly this occurred in groups with both low and high levels of familiarity with the issues at stake.

F2: I think for these sort of sources, these risks, that would be from a number of outbreaks, and you can see what causes them. But actually to put the whole chain together is quite difficult, 'cause often you only ever see little bits of it. It's only because you've got experience of lots of different areas that you actually see the whole thing, you know, if you see someone at this end, they just say, well we buy birds from a wholesalers, this is what we do with them.
M1: that's right, yes. What we are also doing, is surmising that there is actually a linkage, a continuum between over there and all the way down through going into somebody's mouth over there.

(Food scientists, 01/03/06)

We speculate that this effect shows how producing an image can facilitate participants' thinking about the issue at hand, helping them to explore their ideas in much greater depth than they may have ever done beforehand. It may also be possible that, particularly with the kind of highly complex system we were asking people to think about, the image acted as a memory aid, providing a record and summary of the groups' thoughts that they could continue to refer back to throughout the interview. It is probable that this is why we found that facilitator intervention could be kept to a minimum.

However, several problems with the method did arise at different stages of the research process. While the majority of participants interacted positively with the 'fuzzy felt' task, there was still a significant minority who did not – either by refusing to fully engage in the drawing activity, or by making it clear that they did not consider it to be 'serious' or authoritative enough to constitute legitimate research. The problems around reluctance to engage in the creative activity of freehand drawing were therefore obviously mitigated, but certainly not eliminated

218 Cassidy and Maule

by the use of the 'fuzzy felt' exercise. Furthermore, we found that sometimes a single person would be nominated 'scribe', either via seniority or willingness to draw, and other group members would only contribute verbally – this may bias the findings towards one individual's viewpoint. As with the earlier drawing stage, we could not see any obvious pattern in how particular groups or individuals interacted with the methodology, an issue which warrants further investigation. We also found the textual data arising from group discussions to be somewhat 'patchy', whereby long periods of very instrumental conversation about creating the image (e.g., 'Let's put this here', 'OK', 'But how does this connect to that?') were interspersed with patches of richer material in which issues such as risk definition were discussed. While this was not necessarily a problem (we did find answers to our research questions), it meant that sections of some of the interview transcripts were not coded. As alluded to above, the imposition of structure upon the research process by using the 'fuzzy felt' method also led to some (probably inevitable) loss of richness in the visual data. Furthermore, although we attempted to use 'neutral' looking images for use in the procedure and to label them as such, these choices would not have been impartial, especially in the case of images we had to produce ourselves.[9] For our study, we considered the trade-off between richness and reliability of data to be worthwhile: however it may not be so for other research. Certainly further work involving freehand drawing of food risks is likely to prove to be a highly productive avenue of enquiry.

Finally, as indicated in the previous section, we encountered some problems while developing a reliable and valid strategy for analysis of the resulting verbal and visual data. We are satisfied that the analytical approach finally adopted was sufficiently robust, but we did find it to be very demanding of researcher time and resources, and speculate as to whether this is a general issue with the analysis of visual data, or visual data in combination with texts/transcripts. Although the method worked well to minimise researcher influence in the interview situation, this of course did not carry through to data analysis, which was as subject to researcher bias as any piece of qualitative research, and was combated in the usual ways, e.g. through inter-coder checking. A potential extension to the methodology which could increase its validity might involve a further research stage in which participant groups reconvene, and the completed and analysed 'fuzzy felt' images are discussed, giving participants the opportunity to offer their own interpretations of the model. In a participatory context, a joint session involving representatives from several different groups, in which the completed images from those groups are discussed, might prove to be a highly fruitful approach to fostering dialogue and mutual understanding between them.

Overall, the 'fuzzy felt' method has considerable potential to be developed into a powerful and flexible research tool for use in group interviewing. As seen in our work on food-chain risks, it provides participants with a support structure around which they can explore their thoughts in-depth about the issue at hand, whilst simultaneously reducing researcher influence upon the interview process. This combination of features means that the method is particularly useful in research situations where a complex system or issue is under discussion; when comparing participants who have differing levels of familiarity or ease with the topic at hand; and when researcher framings of the interview is to be avoided. The method can also be of potential use in contexts beyond the relatively restricted one of social research methodology. For example, colleagues in the RELU-Risk project have developed a computerised version of the 'fuzzy felt' method, designed for use as a communication tool for exploring food-chain risk issues (Zhang, 2007, 2008). 'Fuzzy felt' may also have other applications where its potential as a facilitation aid, rather than data-gathering tool, could be exploited, for example in classroom discussions and public participation events. A potential model for this might be provided by the Democs card games, which use a series of cards with themed images to stimulate discussion in classrooms and small group participatory exercises (Walker and Higginson, 2003; Duensing *et al.*, 2006).[10]

We have carried out the initial development and testing of this unusual new visual method in the context of some very specific research challenges. Although the method has worked well for this particular project, at present not enough is known about how and why it has helped our participants discuss food-chain risks. What is needed next is further research to investigate in detail how 'fuzzy felt' method works (and when it doesn't, why); how it might be useful for research in domains beyond that of food, knowledge and risk; and to further explore its potential for application in other areas beyond research such as risk/science communication practice, education and public participation.

Notes

1 Researchers in public engagement with science generally use the term 'publics' rather than 'the public' to avoid reducing the complex and variable relationships different groups of people have with science to a unitary whole.
2 We would define a 'stakeholder' as anyone with a specific relationship to food risks, from a professional risk manager, up to and including anyone who buys and eats food.
3 'Interested publics' are groups likely to have a particular investment in an issue – for example in our case this included members of parent–toddler groups (see Miller, 1986)
4 The project, known as RELU-Risk (see www.relu-risk.ac.uk), was supported by the UK Research Councils' Rural Economy and Land Use (RELU) research programme (RES-224–25–0090).
5 As described above, we are employing the mental models concept in tandem with social representations theory: we use the term 'mental models' in this piece as shorthand for the combined mental and social representations we have been trying to access in our research.
6 Food risk issues are 'sensitive' not only in personal terms, but can often be commercially and politically sensitive, particularly to campaigning, policy and industry stakeholders.
7 See http://www.fuzzyfelt.com/load.swf for further details of the game.
8 Dillon (2006) has argued that such 'clipart' images have strong continuities with earlier styles of illustration, and may provide a rich seam for researching social representations in and of themselves. As such, our use of this form of image may have facilitated the process of eliciting further mental/social representations.
9 For example, the icon for 'slaughter' created was a neutral box with a live chicken going in one side and a chicken carcass coming out the other. This was commented upon several times as being quite funny, but highlights the sanitised nature of the

choice – outcomes could have been quite different if a more 'realistic' or 'emotive' image had been used.
10 See also the Democs website: http://www.neweconomics.org/gen/democs.aspx

References

Banks, M. (2001) *Visual methods in social research.* London: Sage.
Barbour, R. S. and Kitzinger, J. (1998) *Developing focus group research: politics, theory and practice.* London: Sage.
Barker, G. C., Bayley, C., Cassidy, A., French, S., Hart, A., Malakar, P. K., Maule J., Petrov, M. and Shepherd, R. (2010) Can a participatory approach contribute to food chain risk analysis? *Risk Analysis*, 30(5): 766–781.
Berry, D. (2004) *Risk, communication and health psychology.* Milton Keynes: Open University Press
Breakwell, G. (2001) Mental models and social representations of hazards: the significance of identity processes. *Journal of Risk Research*, 4(4): 341–351.
Buzan, T. (1995) *The mindmap book.* London: BBC Books.
Cassidy, A. and Maule, A. J. Building partnership in risk communication: evaluating and developing the mental models approach. Under revision for *Journal of Risk Research*.
Cassidy, A. and Maule, J. So what do you mean by 'risk', anyway? UK stakeholder knowledge of food chain risks. In preparation for *Health, Risk and Society*.
Cox, P., Niewohner, J., Pidgeon, N., Gerrard, S., Fischhoff, B. and Riley, D. (2003) The use of mental models in chemical risk protection: developing a generic workplace methodology. *Risk Analysis*, 23(2): 311–324.
Craik, K. (1943) *The nature of explanation.* Cambridge: Cambridge University Press.
Dillon, G. L. (2006) Clipart images as commonsense categories. *Visual Communication*, 5(3): 287–306.
Dove, J. E., Everett, A. and Preece, P. F. W. (1999) Exploring a hydrological concept through children's drawings. *International Journal of Science Education*, 21(5): 485–497.
Duensing, S., Smith, K. and Windale, M. (2006) *Just like a bed of roses: Democs and discussion based learning in the classroom.* London: New Economics Foundation. Retrieved 11 November 2008 from http://www.neweconomics.org/gen/uploads/felp dx23mw24ilm35senee4521042006140824.pdf
Fischhoff, B. (1995) Risk perception and communication unplugged: twenty years of process. *Risk Analysis*, 15(2): 137–145.
Fischhoff, B. (2009) Risk perception and communication. In R. Detels, R. Beaglehole, M. A. Lansang, and M. Gulliford (Eds.) *Oxford textbook of public health*, (5th edition). Oxford: Oxford University Press, pp. 940–952. Reprinted in N. K. Chater (Ed.), *Judgement and Decision Making.* London: Sage.
French, S., Maule, A. J., and Mythen, G. (2005) Soft modelling in risk communication and management: examples in handling food risk. *Journal of the Operational Research Society*, 56(8): 879–888.
French, S., Maule, A. J., and Papamichail, N. (2009) *Decision behaviour, analysis and support.* Cambridge: Cambridge University Press.
Funtowicz, S. O. and Ravetz, J. R (1992). Three type of risk assessment and the emergence of post-normal science. In S. Krimsky and D. Golding (Eds) *Social theories of risk.* Westport CT: Praeger.

Gauntlett, D. and Holzwarth, P. (2006) Creative and visual methods for exploring identities – A conversation between David Gauntlett and Peter Holzworth. *Visual Studies* 21(1): 82–91.

Gauntlett, D. (2007) *Creative explorations: new approaches to identities and audiences.* London: Routledge.

Gentner, D., and Gentner, D. R. (1983) Flowing waters or teaming crowds: Mental models of electricity. In D. Gentner & A. L. Stevens (Eds) *Mental models.* Hillsdale, NJ: Lawrence Erlbaum Associates.

Gigerenzer, G. (2002). *Reckoning with risk: learning to live with uncertainty.* Harmondsworth, UK: Penguin.

Joffe, H. (2003) Risk: from perception to social representation. *British Journal of Social Psychology*, 42: 55–73.

Johnson-Laird, P. N. (1975). Models of deduction. In R. Falmagne (Ed.) *Reasoning: representation and process.* Springdale, NJ: Lawrence Erlbaum Associates.

Johnson-Laird, P. N. and Byrne, R. M. J. (1991). *Deduction.* Hillsdale, NJ: Lawrence Erlbaum Associates.

Kesby, M. (2000) Participatory diagramming: deploying qualitative methods through an action research epistemology. *Area*, 32: 423–435.

Lewenstein, B. (1995) Science and the media. In S. Jasanoff, G.E. Markle, J. C. Peterson, and T. Pinch (Eds) *Handbook of science and technology studies.* Thousand Oaks, CA: Sage.

McQuail, D. (2005) *McQuail's Mass Communication Theory* (5th edition). London: Sage.

Miller, J. D. (1986) Reaching the attentive and interested publics for science. In S. L. Friedman, S. Dunwoody, and C. L. Rogers (Eds) *Scientists and journalists: reporting science as news.* New York: Free Press.

Morgan, M. G., Fischhoff, B., Bostrom, A. and Atman, C. J. (2002) *Risk communication: a mental models approach.* Cambridge: Cambridge University Press.

Niewohner, J., Cox, P., Gerrard, S. and Pidgeon, N. (2004) Evaluating the efficacy of a mental models approach for improving occupational chemical risk protection. *Risk Analysis*, 24, 349–361.

Powell, D. and Leiss, W. (1997) *Mad cows and mother's milk.* Montreal: McGill-Queen's University Press.

Prosser, J. and Burke, C. (2007). Childlike perspectives through image-based educational research. In J. G. Knowles and A. Cole (Eds) *Handbook of the arts in qualitative research: perspectives, methodologies, examples and issues.* Oxford: Oxford University Press.

Prosser, J. and Loxley, A. (2008) *Introducing visual methods. ESRC National Centre for Research Methods Review Paper.* University of Southampton, UK: National Centre for Research Methods.

Rowe, G. and Frewer, L. (2005) A typology of public engagement mechanisms. *Science, Technology & Human Values*, 30(2): 251–290.

Schwartz, D. and Black, J. B. (1996) Analog imagery in mental model reasoning: depictive models. *Cognitive Psychology*, 30: 154–219.

Shepherd, R., Barker, G., French, S., Hart, A., Maule, J., and Cassidy, A. (2006). Managing food chain risks: integrating technical and stakeholder perspectives on uncertainty. *Journal of Agricultural Economics*, 57(2): 311–327.

Shepherd, R. (2008) Involving the public and stakeholders in the evaluation of food risks. *Trends in Food Science & Technology,* 19: 234–239.

Tulloch, J. and Lupton, D. (2003) *Risk and everyday life*. London: Sage.

Wakefield, H. and Underwager, R. (1998). The application of images in child abuse investigations. In J. Prosser (Ed.), *Image-based research: a sourcebook for qualitative researchers*. London: Falmer Press, pp. 176–194.

Walker, P. and Higginson, S. (2003) *So you're using a card game to make policy recommendations?* London: New Economics Foundation. Retrieved 11 November 2008 from http://www.neweconomics.org/gen/uploads/4o3vno55cn3lgu55it3n0pau25032004150620.pdf

Wynne, B. (1995) Public understanding of science. In S. Jasanoff, G. E. Markle, J. C. Peterson, and T. Pinch (Eds.) *Handbook of science and technology studies*. Thousand Oaks, CA: Sage.

Zhang, N. (2007) *Interactive food chain tool*. Manchester: University of Manchester. Available at http://wintest.humanities.manchester.ac.uk/Mzyxdnz2/WebApplication1/tools/default.aspx

Zhang, N. (2008). *Evaluation of e-participation*. Doctoral thesis, Manchester Business School, University of Manchester, Manchester.

15 Picturing the field

Social action research, psychoanalytic theory, and documentary filmmaking

Janice Haaken

While videotaping in West Africa many years ago for a research project on women and war, a colleague who was assisting with translations told me a story. 'There was this tourist who was taking photos of a Baobab tree,' she began, explaining how this dramatic tree with its distinctive sculptural form was a standard backdrop in pictures of West Africa. 'This tourist is taking snapshots of the tree and a young local guy approaches her. 'Mama [the term of address for older women], you have deeply offended me and my ancestors', he says. 'My uncle who died long ago has returned as a lizard living in that tree. Now that you have taken the pictures, he must find another tree to settle his spirit.' My friend went on with her funny story, widening her eyes in mocking imitation of the horrified tourist. 'So this clever young guy offers to find a witch doctor to undo this unfortunate disturbance of his uncle's spirit and the tourist gratefully offers to pay the price. She rushes away with her camera, and the young guy rushes off to tell his friends about the silly tourist.'

I began a series of field projects in West Africa much like the anxious tourist, eager to settle my debts as they arose and to avoid colonial habits of exchange. But I found that the ledgers of history extended far beyond the horizons of my project, and that pictures circulate within African social spaces in ways that do not map readily onto colonial and capitalist systems of exchange. Although we learned to negotiate and explain what we were doing and why, sometimes paying people small sums for letting us take their pictures, the debts implicit in our very presence exceeded any available economic register. Yet once women in the refugee camps, the site of much of our videotaping, learned that our aim was to educate students in North America about their views on the Sierra Leonean civil war and the peace process, their responses were consistently welcoming. There was 'use value' in our educational project that went beyond any meager exchange value it might hold for Western markets. As video ethnographers, we were bearing witness to their experiences as women in ways that notes and tape recorders could never achieve. From survivors in refugee camps, traditional healers, to counselors working with child combatants, Sierra Leonean women gathered in beautiful African garb to give expression to collective memories of the civil war through dance, music, and talk. Extending beyond the individual speaker, the wide angle of the lens captured the collective voice and physical presence of the many women gathered.

But what does the camera promise in such contexts and what illusions does it produce? I initially thought of the camera as merely a research tool. My primary concern was to equip myself with tools suitable for the terrain and the data sought. Videotaping captured non-verbal communication in ways that other technologies would not permit, and it allowed for a wider range of options in the analysis and interpretation of field data. As the use of the camera extended beyond the aim of identifying themes, however, it became apparent that working with visual images required specific methodological and theoretical attentiveness, including attentiveness to the projective aspects of field data. For example, many of the students who initially responded to the footage commented that the women 'did not look like refugees.' The creative use of fabric was evident in the lovely garments the women wore, even in the stark environs of the refugee camps. Many of my students' conceptions of refugees were based on images that circulate in Hollywood films – an area that emerged as a focus of critical discussion. For Sierra Leonean activists who saw this same footage, the pictures registered the capacities of these women to hold onto a sense of self, to wrap themselves in the scattered fragments of their culture, even as they were displaced by civil war – a line of analysis that was incorporated into the documentary. Rich visual material such as this footage may be seductively misleading, however, even as it opens a wider lens onto field data. While the documentary form retains a greater fidelity to the phenomena under study than do the transformations through traditional forms of data analysis, this very capacity of the medium fosters the illusion of a direct correspondence between the object and its representation. As Dai Vaughan (1999) puts it, 'The documentary – implicitly – makes two claims: one the one hand, to present us with images referring unashamedly to their sources; on the other, to articulate a statement of which those sources will be the object.' (p. 30). The transformations involved – indeed, the inevitable gap between image and statement – typically are concealed.

A key aim of the chapter is to show how documentary film and video production – with their reliance on visual images–bring into bold relief many of the ethical quandaries of field research more generally. Any research question of social significance carries emotional and social investments and potential ethical conflicts over the representation of findings. Tensions inevitably arise over how to take into account the point of view of the researcher/observer in pictures produced of some aspect of social reality (see Mirzoeff 1999; G. Rose 2007). In the documentary format, tensions emerge over the power of directors/producers to engage in a kind of double projection, on the one hand, in both projecting their own subjectivity onto the external world and transferring this projected world back onto the screen, and to create a fuller record than other media permit of social truths on the other (see Nichols 1991). Indeed, tension between the 'subjective' and the 'objective' demands of the documentary format remain at the center of debate in the field (Vaughan 1999). The politics of representation – often concealed in the abstract language of academic writing – are exposed in the documentary. The accessibility and evocative power of visual media invite broader critical engagement in what is shown and what is omitted and demands on the filmmaker to justify such choices. On the other hand, to the extent that a picture 'tells a thousand words', it operates as a seductive screen in seeming to obviate the necessity of interpretive concepts. Indeed, as documentaries have moved beyond educational films and reached new aesthetic heights, audiences bring many of the conventions of highly produced fiction films to their viewing experiences (Rothman 2009).

A second aim of the chapter is to introduce principles from psychoanalytic theory and social action research methods that inform the Sierra Leonean documentary projects. Although there is a rich history of psychoanalytic film theory, including feminist psychoanalytic film theory (see, for example, Mulvey 1988; Kaplan 1990; Doane 1991; hooks 1994), the documentary film has been relatively under-theorized despite a growing consensus that the line between fictional and non-fictional films can be murky (Nichols 1991; Rothman 2009). Similarly, the traditions of social action and participatory action research, while sometimes drawing on visual data, have not carried the critique of positivist science into the arena of working with visual images. Yet psychoanalytic film criticism and the social action research tradition carry important insights for documentary film, specifically in working through dilemmas in the use of moving images (G. Rose 2007).

The chapter enlists these dual theoretical lenses in discussing visual methods in the *Moving to the Beat* project – the second of two documentaries carried out in collaboration with Sierra Leonean peace activists. After providing a brief history of this project, I deploy a framework routinely introduced in my teams to identify areas of critical reflection. The framework encompasses three sequential and dynamically recurring sites of concern – sites where questions arise over the *premises* behind the project, the *processes* through which it is carried out, and the *products* created through the labor deployed.

The Project

Moving to the Beat grew out of an ongoing collaboration with Sierra Leonean peace activists in West Africa and the United States and came to include 125 university students in the USA and 75–80 youth in Freetown, Sierra Leone engaged in various activities over a 4-year period. The *Moving to the Beat* (M2B) project included the production and distribution of the documentary (a version for television broadcasting and a DVD with special features), a series of music videos, an interactive website and curriculum guide, and a hip-hop activist organization. Although the production of the documentary film was the primary project of the M2B team, students and activists were engaged in the other activities of the project as well. Routine meetings with screenings of work samples and phone conference calls were held, and students assisted in writing grants and organizing conferences. In addition to high school and university M2B conferences, students attended film festivals where *Moving to the Beat* was screened (see www.moving2thebeat.com).

The *Moving to the Beat* project began with the videotaping in Sierra Leonean refugee camps in 1999 that resulted in the production of the documentary *Diamonds, Guns and Rice,* distributed with a curriculum book, *Speaking Out: Women, War and the Global Economy* (Haaken *et al.*, 2005). In the course of filming special features for inclusion in the *Diamonds, Guns and Rice* DVD in 2005, we learned that the next generation of Sierra Leonean youth in Freetown and in Black communities in the USA were enlisting hip-hop to speak out on issues, from post-war trauma and the AIDS/HIV pandemic to poverty and political rights. The *Moving to the Beat* documentary was initiated as a means of both documenting this use of hip-hop among youth on both sides of the Atlantic, and providing a forum for young men and women to speak in their own voices about why they were using hip-hop as a language for social change. The visually performative aspects of hiphop – embodied in expressive forms such as break dancing, gestures, and characteristic modes of dress – were central to the concept of language deployed in the documentary.

From the early project focused on women to the later project centered on youth, we sought to understand the role of music, dance and storytelling in post-conflict healing and reparation. Since many of the women I interviewed in refugee camps along the border of Sierra Leone communicated through song and movement, as well as through verbal language, my interest was in using the camera to capture in a fuller way their experiences. This interest extended into deeper forms of collaboration as the focus on producing a documentary required gathering materials from immigrants and refugees living in the United States, United Kingdom and West Africa. Sierra Leoneans contributed a rich range of materials, from documents, photos, and archival footage – much of which was used in the production of *Diamonds, Guns and Rice*. This process of collecting images of the country and culture prior to the war, as well as images of the war itself, became a form of grief work for many of the participants (see Haaken 2001; Haaken *et al.* 2005). In recovering sustaining images of the cultural past as well as images of the ravaging impact of the war, the documentary project drew on the psychoanalytic assumption that recovering from trauma requires capacities to recover the 'good objects' of the relational past as well as the 'bad objects' (see Haaken 1998, 2010). Editing of both documentaries involved alternating between disturbing and consoling imagery as a means of sustaining a connection with viewers – a line of analysis pursued later in this chapter.

This background of quite extensive involvement in the Sierra Leonean communities, both in West Africa and in the USA, provided the impetus for the *Moving to the Beat* project, continuing the initial focus on embodied forms of protest. Whereas *Diamonds, Guns and Rice* showed how women were using traditional cultural practices to resist patriarchal forms of power, *Moving to the Beat* grew out of an insistence on the part of youth that they were breaking from traditional music and dance and identifying with global youth culture. For Sierra Leonean elders and many of us on the project team, the question of whether youth were engaging hip-hop in a socially progressive or regressive way motivated continuation of our collaborative inquiry.

The visual aspects of hip-hop storytelling confronted us with the constraints of many of our discursive methods of analyzing field data. *Moving to the Beat* enlists the narrative device of the journey – in this case, the journey of a hip-hop group from Portland, Oregon who travelled to Sierra Leone to bring the radical roots of hip-hop to the Motherland. The story tells a broader collective tale of Black youth searching for an identity that encompasses the trauma, ideals, hopes and losses born of their common and differing histories. But for our participants, the story emerged in the form of visual pictures and fantasy images as readily as it did in linguistic forms. For example, many Sierra Leonean youth described their fantasies of America as a 'second heaven' – as a place of sensual gratification and commodified displays of wealth – even as they recognized the illusory aspects of this same fantasy. Their bitter conflicts over the diamond trade, a conflict at the center of the Sierra Leonean civil war, brought home the recognition that the 'bling-bling' of American hip-hop culture was a mirage.

Instead of identifying with the dazzling icons of mainstream hip-hop culture, Sierra Leonean artists, much like youth elsewhere in the world, tended to identify with Tupac Shakur. Tupac was often described as a mentor to hip-hop activists in both Freetown and Portland, idealized in part because his lyrics and movements resonated so potently with the collective pain of the Black struggle (see T. Rose 1994, 2008; Chang 2005). Posters of Tupac were often on display in hip-hop social spaces in Freetown, and the social basis of this identification of many youth with Tupac emerged as a theme in the documentary. The image of this beautiful man, often with his upper body exposed, circulates in some contexts as an object of the white gaze – exploited much as are fetishized female objects of the male gaze (see, for example, hooks 1992). But images of Tupac were deployed in *Moving to the Beat* through the interpretive gaze of Black youth who identified with this defiant figure, with his characteristic proud pose, bare chest, chains, and loose 'prison pants,' markers of a shared history of violent oppression and political resistance (T. Rose 2008).

Just as the *Moving to the Beat* documentary traces a journey where Black youth struggle to find common ground, the process of making the documentary involved entering this same rocky terrain. With crews working in two cities and production members reaching across race, age, gender, and class divisions, as well as differences in immigration status, the project itself needed to find its unifying beat. The lead team in Portland included Caleb Heymann, a young Euro-American man (also my son), who was director of photography, co-director, and editor; Abdul Fofanah, a young Sierra Leonean American man who was co-director and narrator; P. C. Peri, a middle-aged African-American man who was a cinematographer and co-producer; and myself, a middle-aged Euro-American woman who was producer. In addition to this lead crew, the three Rebel Soulz, three African-American young men, participated in the M2B group meetings, as well as contributing to conferences and fundraising events. The team in Freetown, all of whom were young Black Africans, included Sam Dixon, assistant director, and 25 production assistants and artists who worked on the project over a period of 4 years.

Premises

Field projects involve the organization of human labor much like other forms of productive human activity. The labor process includes the forces of production – the technologies, resources and tools deployed in the purposeful transformation of nature – and the relations of production – the social organization of human activity in carrying it out. This attentiveness to the material conditions of field projects constituted an organizing frame and site of critical reflection at various stages of the documentary, beginning with the premises that guided its development (see Burman 2004; Whitehead and McNiff 2006). The premises behind a project include the personal histories and assumptions that participants bring to the activity, as well as the theoretical and methodological frameworks invoked in striving for a common language. The *Moving to the Beat* team took up readings ranging from literature on hip-hop (e.g., T. Rose 1994, 2008; Clay 2003; Chang 2005), to video ethnographic and documentary theory (e.g., Nichols 1991; Haaken 2005), to social action research (e.g., Argyris *et al.* 1985; Lykes 1989; Fine and Torres 2006), psychoanalytic-feminist film theory (e.g., Mulvey 1988; Doane 1991), and cultural theory (e.g., hooks 1992; Foucault 1995; Hall *et al.* 1996; Hall 1997; Fanon 2004).

As a social justice activist as well as an academic, my interests in film criticism and film production are grounded in understanding cultural forces that shape everyday forms of consciousness and processes of social change (see Haaken 2001, 2005). In moving from teaching courses on the psychology of film to actually producing films, my aim was to create products of social knowledge that are both educational and entertaining, both intellectually demanding and aesthetically satisfying (also, see www.queensofheartdoc.com; www.guiltyexcept. com). The recent availability of high-end consumer cameras and editing equipment opened the field for projects such as *Moving to the Beat* – projects that would have been far more difficult to carry out just a decade prior.

In beginning the collaboration with an explicit feminist focus, specifically centered on bringing the perspectives of women into discussions of war and the peace process, the decision to turn to hip-hop seemed at first glance to be counter to feminist principles. Students and conference participants where work samples were presented routinely condemned hip-hop for its sexism and challenged us on this point. As a research and production team guided by activist commitments, our aim was to bring gender into the analysis of the dynamics of hip-hop and to understand how women were positioning themselves in relation to this form. We also drew on feminist frameworks that stressed the historically dynamic and multilayered dimensions of gender identity (see Segal 1990; Crenshaw 1994; Layton 1998; Collins 2000). As women were entering the field of hip-hop performance, we were interested in understanding how they were taking up the aggressive style of this cultural language, as well as the multiple expressions of masculinities produced through hip-hop. Before each of the three trips to Freetown for intensive shooting, the production team discussed ways of engaging women artists and activists and bringing their experiences into view.

Our aim throughout this project was to use the power of visual media to capture the gripping dramas of oppressed and marginalized people, caught in historical and social forces not of their own making. Images of Africa brought to American audiences tend to alternate between brutally violent, tragic and exotic. Narratives often follow a formulaic Western storyline that centers on either a talented individual (or few individuals) that survive and escape their miserable lot, or portray a hopeless state of senseless violence and misery. The *Moving to the Beat* team sought to bring a more complex reading of African politics and culture into view, and to work through a series of dilemmas in the use of visual media – an area where the accessibility of the medium may readily conceal its problematic cultural cargo. Although fiction films carry these same potentials, with the documentary, 'the image is perceived as signifying what it appears to record' (Vaughan, 1999: 58). The cultural codes embedded in the construction of the signifying system of the documentary film are often eclipsed by the evocative power of the image itself.

In calling for researchers to leave their laboratories and enter the field of real social problems, Kurt Lewin (1975, c1951), the founder of social action research in psychology, quipped that 'there is nothing so practical as a good theory' (p. 169). His program of research was oriented toward practical problems but action research also depended on good theory – ways of seeing and understanding how things may fit together within some explanatory framework. Indeed, without a theoretical frame, interpretations of data are inevitably structured by conventions in the culture that work their way into the program of inquiry. *Moving to the Beat* drew on this same ethos in exploring how hip-hop was enlisted by youth as a language for protest and social change. A key premise behind social action research – one that similarly informs psychoanalytic approaches to field work – centers on the idea that researchers are deeply embedded in the phenomena of interest (Argyris, *et al.*, 1985; Fine and Torres 2006; Fine 2006).

Although psychoanalytic and social action researchers mutually emphasize the subjective side of science, psychoanalytic researchers emphasize the role of unconscious anxieties and defenses not readily accessible through methods of self-reflection, for example, through field notes, journaling, and analyses of power relations that structure the research process. Psychoanalytic researchers make use of techniques such as free association, where space is allowed for exploring past experiences that come to mind in relation to the project (see Burman 2004; Hollway 2004). In the research context, this means reflecting on personal and collective forms of transference – for example, how intense feelings that may seem inappropriate or infantile, whether anger, fear, competitiveness, or forms of desire, are part of human experience but may be heightened when crossing cultural borders (Obeyesekere 1990; Molino 2004; Haaken 2010).

An example from the *Moving to the Beat* project team illustrates this dynamic tension. One of the students – a white woman – was perpetually unable to carry out her assignments. We met repeatedly to review instructions and to clarify the nature of her tasks but to no avail. A very bright and capable student, she nonetheless seemed to forget what she was supposed to do and was unable to even understand her notes after our review sessions. She was doing well elsewhere in her studies and confused that a project team she had sought to join would also be the site of her most defeating moments as a student. One principle we had discussed in the research team concerned this tendency to bring hopes and ideals to field projects that make them intense sites of anxiety and disappointment. The idea of working on a research team that was also making a movie seemed particularly seductive. Yet much like other research teams, the work of this team included tedious tasks, from transcribing, shotlogging and coding footage to taking field notes and carrying out library research.

For my distressed stuck student, the dilemma seemed to center on what was happening in the field. So we began to talk about her experiences as a production assistant on shoots at the clubs and houses where we were videotaping hip-hop artists and activists. As we talked about her experiences, she recalled how upsetting it had been when some of the young Black men at the clubs snubbed her. She felt that they were prejudiced toward her because she was white, noticing that they were quite friendly toward the Black members of our team. Although they were not physically threatening, these young men had a hostile edge that made her uncomfortable. As we talked about her reactions, we returned to the concept of transference that we had taken up in our research seminar (Wachtel 1993). For my student, understanding that she evoked a history of associations for these young men, just as they did for her, allowed a vital degree of emotional distance.

Carrying out research across cultural borders, and particularly across borders forged through a history of racist violence and trauma, requires some capacity to weather the intense affects that emerge. Just as psychoanalysis teaches that the therapeutic encounter revisits ancient conflicts in the form of the transference, so, too, does the documentary encounter.

Presenting findings in the format of documentary films, with their evocative power and potential to invite projection and identifications with the images produced, tends to heighten such effects (Nichols 1991; G. Rose 2007). Indeed, presentation of footage at academic conferences inevitably stirs more intense audience responses than those expressed at conventional academic conferences. As a form of socially produced *memory*, the moving image evokes a distinctive splitting in consciousness: the subject is both palpably alive and registered as a ghostly absence. Because of the direct exposure and vulnerability of subjects on the screen, audiences express, perhaps unconsciously, distress and hostility if they perceive that the filmmaker has not ethically justified his/her use of these images.

Drawing on feminist-psychoanalytic film theory, we attempted to unpack the concept of the camera as a 'phallic' form of power (see Mulvey 1989; Doane 1991). Through this critical theoretical lens, the phallus is conceptualized as a defensive structure, organized around infantile fantasies of omnipotence and narcissistic control. Psychoanalytic theory brings to theorizing the visual an emphasis on pleasure in looking, *scopophilia*, as constitutive of subjectivity. This pleasure also carries infantile anxieties projected onto the world, whether in the form of powers associated with the gaze, or looking, just as there are anxieties and defenses associated with looking away (J. Rose 1986). This displacement of vision and turning away from the frightening object was central to Freud's concept of the masculine fetish, a concept taken up by feminist film theorists in working with the politics of spectatorship (see G. Rose 2007). Feminist theorists draw on psychoanalysis in emphasizing the anxious, conflicted and ambivalent currents in masculine identity in patriarchal societies (Penley 1988; Ehrens 1990). The feminine object – as a fantasy or an object in the visual field – serves as repository for disavowed or repressed masculine anxieties. This focus on the dynamic instability of such psychological processes opens the ground for cultural interpretations oriented toward social change. Women, as well as men, may deploy the gaze in exploitive ways, even as women may also suffer excessive inhibitions in relation to the aggressive aspects of looking.

Political premises included discussion of how feminist portrayals of gendered violence may inadvertently perpetuate racist stereotypes (see hooks 1992). In *Diamonds, Guns and Rice*, debate had centered on how to incorporate graphically violent images into the documentary. The most readily available photos and video footage available to us supported the view that young Black men were largely responsible for the carnage. Many of the Sierra Leonean women sought to place at the center of the documentary gruesome images of mutilated bodies with young men – part of the Revolutionary United Front and various militia groups – fleeing triumphantly. In taking up this difficult issue of which images to include, we spent considerable time talking about what the images meant to the various participants in our group. Many Sierra Leonean activists in the group pressed to include these graphic images to break through the Western wall of denial and indifference. But I had grown increasingly wary of shocking images of third-world trauma as they captivated Western audiences, arousing as they often do fleeting feelings of self-righteous moral outrage. I voiced my concern that images of violence circulate all too readily in Western culture and that they often stir voyeuristic fascination, or feelings of despair and depressive withdrawal from political situations portrayed as hopeless. For if everything has been destroyed and victims rendered utterly impotent, why care enough to understand the situation more deeply? Our aim was to show that in spite of the civil war, people are still living and connecting with one another, and they hold insights into political and existential concerns beyond the borders of their own crisis. Nonetheless, I wondered if my investment in downplaying visceral displays of violence was overdetermined by my uneasiness in displaying the horrifying destruction. Even as I may have been defending against my own impulse to withdraw out of a sense of hopelessness and despair, the sustained efforts required in creating a concrete and publically accessible product provided a vital holding ground between the manic and depressive poles of our project.

From the perspective of psychoanalytic film theory, we are as concerned with the *missing object* and the *repressed object* as we are with those objects dominating our field of vision (J. Rose 1986). Images of racially inflected violence routinely circulate in Western media, often masking less visible actors. Many of the dynamics behind the Sierra Leonean civil war were *out of view,* located, for example, in the sanitized and remote worlds of the International Monetary Fund, the World Bank, and the diamond industry. This same dynamic, where broader societal influences may be less readily accessible to empirical observation, remains a pervasive problem in psychological research more generally (Prilleltensky 2003).

This interest in the unconscious of the film – those images referenced that remain out of view – draws on the premise that visual culture develops around the management of human conflict and anxiety. Action films, for example, project phallic images of power, where the helpless maiden serves as the repository for disavowed male feelings of helplessness and vulnerability (Kaufman 1996). In producing a documentary film that centers on Black young men and violence, spectators carry conventions of Hollywood films into their viewing experiences. At the same time, the documentary mode implicitly offers viewers the promise of seeing 'how it really is' and 'what is really going on.' Anxiety over viewing massive destruction is often managed in conventional films – both documentary and fiction films – through enlisting audience identifications with the survivors. The highly acclaimed documentary *Born into Brothels* (Briski and Kaufman 2004) is one such example. Much like the prototypical action film, the resolution of the danger at the center of *Born into Brothels* resolves through the deliverance of exceptional individuals from a situation of collective misery. In addition to reproducing ideas about art as a magical process unrelated to schooling, the documentary invites identification with the talented few that are spirited out of their desolate situation. Images of the mothers of these destitute children – women who work as prostitutes – conform in the film to conventional prototypes of passive victims. While they are not demonized, they are cast as standing helplessly by as the filmmakers engage in the rescue work at the center of the story. The actual political organizing of prostitutes in Calcutta remains outside the frame of the documentary. In *Moving to the Beat*, our aim was to work against such conventions and to create a complex representation of collective trauma, reparation, and resistance, with hip-hop as the shared language for global dialogue on issues affecting marginalized youth (see Bloustien 2007; Watts and Flanagan 2007; Rose 2008).

Processes

Social action and psychoanalytic researchers share an emphasis on the relational side of knowledge production – how findings emerge through working alliances and taking into account the varying subjective registers of any given phenomenon. Psychoanalytic fieldwork extends this notion of socially situated knowledge to how group members may learn to correct for the unconscious blindspots of one another (Burman 2004; Hollway 2004). Many forms of critical self-reflection stir defensiveness in ways that occlude the frame. Indeed, areas where insight is most important can be areas of severe blindspots (Argyris *et al.* 1985). For example, graphic images of battered women – often taken up in feminist campaigns concerning violence against women – stir relatively little debate, often because the images seem to establish so incontestably the moral weight of the critique (see Morrison and Lacour 1997; Haaken 2010).

In its focus on conflict and ambivalence as central to human development, as well as an impetus for growth and social change, psychoanalytic concepts offer critical tools for thinking through group dynamics in field projects (Haaken 2010). These tensions – and the transferences from past experiences onto the present encounter – may be particularly pronounced in research across cultural boundaries. White researchers in minority or oppressed communities may feel the ghosts of the colonial past inhabiting the encounter – always present in the room as that 'third term' of history.

In contrast to field researchers who generate data from surveys and retreat to a laboratory to analyze their findings, the approach adopted in this program of inquiry requires sustained engagement in field settings. Findings that matter to people often emerge slowly over time within a space that allows for some freedom of thought and genuine dialogue. The footage provided this space where representations of experience could be presented and negotiated over time. As we worked though the questions that arose at meetings and screenings of work samples of *Moving to the Beat*, interest in understanding social identity took center stage. Rather than simply asserting the importance of hip-hop as an identity and a language, we wanted to understand its dynamics and what it meant to the various participants. Although these are the kinds of questions researchers typically ask, the impetus for *Moving to the Beat* came from the participants themselves and their interest in combining interviews, dialogue, lyrics, and hip-hop performance. As one Sierra Leonean artist commented, 'When we come together to understand something, we do it through music rather than holding a conference.' This same sentiment motivated the documentary. Or as Isadora Duncan was thought to have said, 'If I could say it in words, I wouldn't have to dance to it' (cited in Nichols, 1991: 276).

In the course of this collaboration, many conferences *were* held, however, in bringing academics, peace activists and artists together to discuss the questions to be taken up in the documentary. We also sought to breach the wall between academia and everyday life. Hip-hop emerged as a rich site for this convergence of interests. There is a flourishing scholarly literature on hip-hop as both an artistic genre and social movement (Clay 2003; Chang 2005; T. Rose 2008), but very little of this work makes its way into hip-hop culture.

There are many styles of documentary production with their varying aesthetic, political, and intellectual sensibilities. Much of the discourse in the academic literature centers on four prototypical styles: the *expository*, the *observational*, the *interactive*, and the *reflexive* modes of documentary. Although *Diamonds, Guns and Rice* and *Moving to the Beat* included elements of the expository style, with its focus on presenting an analysis of a social problem, and the observational approach, which involves extensive shooting to capture a world in as unobtrusive a way as possible, *Moving to the Beat* drew on more theoretically informed discussions of these various approaches. The observational approach characterizes many vérité-style films, where there is little or no narrative arc, as well as ethnographic films – an approach developed early on by anthropologists (see Nichols 1991). Ethnographic films follow from intense engagement in a setting and sustained contact with informants – with participants who assist the filmmaker in translating and interpreting the activities or practices documented. The contemporary movement toward *reflexive* approaches grew out of challenges to the observational style, and particularly its tendency to conceal the motives and interventions of the filmmakers. The reflexive documentary brought the process of producing images to the center of the film project, whether in bringing the director into the frame itself or through editing techniques. The reflexive tradition strives to expose the concealed operations of the film and to display rather than suture over the production process. The aim here is to disrupt the spectator's fantasy of accessing a world that can be mastered through the medium of the camera (for examples, see Rothman 2009).

In selecting a style for shooting and editing, we discussed these various approaches and their implications for carrying out the aims of the project. One aim was to draw on some of the principles of direct or observational cinema, with their emphasis on allowing the story to 'emerge' from the footage, but we also were convinced by many of the critiques of this approach. Although the principle of 'show don't tell' pervades contemporary documentary film production, particularly in breaking from the didacticism of the 'educational film,' facts or images also don't speak for themselves. As Gilberto Perez (2009: 14) points out,

> It's a posture, a trope, for an author to hide behind his or her own fiction, to conceal the hand that constructed these characters and incidents, the mind that intended them to have a certain meaning and effect … It's ironic for the author of a story to pretend that the story says it all and that he or she has nothing to say.

It also has become a conventional trope in reflexive approaches to bring the filmmaker into the frame, as though his/her visible presence is sufficient to expose such effects. Although one of the co-directors served as the narrator and guide in *Moving to the Beat*, we also sought to employ editing techniques that broke from the realism of some observational cinema. Our reflexive method centered chiefly on the participatory mode of developing the content. Following in the tradition of Paulo Freire (1972/2004), we sought to understand hip-hop as a form of social identity and a political language from the perspectives of hip-hop artists/activists. Rather than recording their lyrics and analyzing them from a distance, we enlisted the youth in interpreting their own lyrics and identifications with hip-hop. After the shooting in Sierra Leone, the team pursued the same questions with an African and African-American hip-hop community in Portland, Oregon. The Portland group held a deep affinity with the Sierra Leonean hip-hop group, both in their mutual interest in political hip-hop and their identifications with the radical roots of American hip-hop.

Products

Scholars and documentary filmmakers are routinely required to clarify their intended audiences, whether other academics or specific demographic groups, but such queries often presuppose that intellectual rights have been worked out in advance. Similarly, ethical issues are negotiated in advance, for example, through human subject review procedures. Uncertainties attached to the fate of the final product in documentary field projects, however, require an ongoing process of negotiation. In this sense, they never permit the ethical dissociation of scholarly questions from ongoing commitments to the context of inquiry. After producing a series of work samples, trailers, and writing grants to fund the final editing process, the National Black Programming Consortium, in conjunction with the Corporation for Public Broadcasting, funded the *Moving to the Beat* documentary to air on national public television in the United States. This time-limited licensing of the documentary leaves open, however, ongoing issues around rights and responsibilities for the products of this shared activity.

Just as hip-hop pushes the boundaries of intellectual property rights, with sampling as one key site of controversy, *Moving to the Beat* raised some of these same political and legal issues concerning who owns and controls the project. From the beginning the decision was made to divide any proceeds from sale or distribution between the Portland and the Freetown M2B organizations, with two-thirds of the revenue to the Freetown group. At the same time, ongoing issues required negotiation over dvd distribution and music videos that were produced, as well as how to work with the tension between the activist mission of the project and the individual aspirations of participating artists.

Having identified a series of themes that had emerged from the footage and discussions, informed by phone consultations and exchange of work samples with the group in Freetown, the Portland team proceeded with editing the final version for public television broadcasting. As activist filmmakers, we were interested in themes related to resistance and rebellion, but we also wanted to portray these insurgent elements of youth identity in complex and nuanced ways. Whereas some social science literature approaches hip-hop as a forum where the rebellious or aggressive energies of marginalized youth may be safely 'channeled' (Dimitriadis 2009), we sought to critique this same concept. Although the youth sometimes spoke of 'putting down the gun and taking up the mic', they also talk in the documentary about how politicians and commercial forces often authorize sanitized forms of hip-hop as a means of managing youthful rebelliousness.

Even as African and American artists shared identifications with radical traditions and disdain for commercial hip-hop, they brought differing under-standings of what hip-hop identities carried. A key dilemma in editing the final product centered on reconciling aesthetic conventions cultivated in Western cinema, conventions that often build the drama around an individual story, and our commitment to represent a collective experience. The National Black Programming Consortium appreciated this dilemma but also asked that we draw out more of the individual story of Abdul Fofanah. Our methods of developing our character of Fofanah, as the guide and narrator, were through his memories of the war, using cuts to war imagery he had seen on television and fades to images of food markets in the streets of Freetown, to represent his struggle to find the 'good objects' amidst this destructive imagery. Abdul also was often in dialogue with others in groups and positioned as a bridge between worlds, reinforced by the visual alternating between scenes that drew out the beauty of public spaces where poor people gather in both cities.

A central dynamic of psychological recovery from trauma centers on developing capacities to move into and out of disturbing memories and states of mind. Replicating what Tricia Rose (1994) describes as the elements of flow, layering, and rupture that characterize hip-hop aesthetics, *Moving to the Beat* shifts between the ruptures created by the civil war, poverty, corruption and the AIDS epidemic in West Africa to the layered identity and loose flow of Black global identities at the center of hip-hop culture. The editing style of the documentary includes alternating jump cuts and quick edits with long shots with extended storytelling, and 'reverse time shots' that capture visually the turn-table record scratching effects so prevalent in hip-hop music. Much like rap music itself, the documentary brings a collision of words and images onto the screen.

An additional dilemma in producing the final product centered on how to visually represent key themes, particularly differing conceptions of what it means to identify as a *rebel*. Even as the two groups spoke and rapped about their outrage against the system and their elders, differences emerged in their associations between hip-hop and rebellion. The aggressive elements of hip-hop and its capacity to 'tell it like it is' resonated with youth who described feeling silenced and abandoned by their elders. But associations with the word 'rebel' diverged for the American and Sierra Leoneans. When the Rebel Soulz went to Sierra Leone with our team for the last phase of shooting, the group performed one of their songs, 'Soul Rebel', before an audience of thousands at a stadium in Freetown. As the documentary visually demonstrates, the rowdily enthusiastic audience became notably still during the performance. Co-director and narrator, Abdul Fofanah, offers commentary on this scene, suggesting that the audience may not have understood most of the lyrics but the term 'rebel' aroused disturbing memories of their own rebel war that concluded a few years prior. After the concert, Rebel Soulz members went to the local radio station to talk about what the term 'rebel' meant to them, rapping as well about their vision of non-violent resistance. The documentary follows Abdul and Rebel Soulz members as they talk with hip-hop artists at the Milton School for the blind and learn how the trauma of the war has shaped their uses of hip-hop. These images of blind hip-hop activists advance the idea that we don't hear much of what inspires the music and movement – that vision is just one of many senses for grasping the world. Further, in bringing into view young people who have been traumatized but also remain quite intact and vibrant, the M2B team sought to work against the fetishizing of a very narrow vision of beauty in Western films.

More than their US counterparts, the Sierra Leonean group carried the trauma of violence into their lyrics. They also were using hip-hop to educate older men in their communities about condom use and sexual practices – a subversive use of hip-hop that challenged traditional intergenerational borders of acceptable discourse. Scenes of youth – young women and men – playfully holding condoms and performing condom education, sometimes in parody of their moralizing elders, may be offered as one example of how a 'picture tells a thousand words'. The pictures are no substitute for analysis but they are places where key dilemmas portrayed in the film register in memory. Students often return to this scene in discussions after the film of sexual politics, sometimes commenting that they thought women in Africa had no sexual rights. While this is an area where Sierra Leonean women have been repressed, sexuality also is an area of struggle and female resistance. The images fortify the film's challenge to Western habits of counterposing 'liberated' Western women and those who are cast as completely subjugated elsewhere in the world. Set against the vast academic and policy literature on AIDS/HIV, these scenes in *Moving to the Beat* are more effective because they carry out an important aim of the documentary: to make sayable the unsayable. They also make visible the invisible by bringing images of marginalized groups into view in ways that disrupt Western fantasy images of these same people and their political dilemmas.

Another idea carried into the final editing was to show how social movements hold contradictory elements, both progressive and regressive. They may claim new space for self-development and simultaneously oppress others (Morrison and Lacour 1997; Haaken 2010). We drew on footage where sites of tension and dialogue emerged between female and male Sierra Leonean artists and visually juxtaposed their moments of recognition and misrecognition. Young audiences, particularly, routinely comment on one of the scenes in the *Moving to the Beat* documentary as illustrative of this dynamic. The scene is of Lady Bee, one of the best regarded hip-hop artists in Sierra Leone, performing on a stage and then leaving the stage after the equipment fails. In the after-performance interview, Lady Bee is asked what happened and why she had not finished her song. She comments that it was just a technical problem. The interviewer continues with a probe, however, posing the question of whether it would have gone differently if she were a man. 'If I were a man', she responds with more authority, 'they would have fixed the problem so I could finish my performance.' The interviewer goes on to ask her to say more about the position of female performers in Sierra Leone. In commenting on this scene, memorable because it is so visually evocative, young audiences often note that the probes by the interviewer opened the space for Lady Bee to interpret her situation resistively. The documentary establishes an alliance with her in holding the ground behind the stage, cinematically granting her a larger stage than the one that she was forced to relinquish.

Conclusions

'Keepin it real' is a repeated refrain in hip-hop literature (T. Rose, 1994, 2008). For researchers and documentarists outside of the hip-hop world, the question of how to 'keep it real' carries a double challenge. Rebel Soulz take this up as a mission to 'bring the real America' to the Motherland and to disrupt African fantasies of the American dream. Progressive researchers and documentary filmmakers bring their own fantasies and defenses to documentary field projects and the realities they portray, even as they may be committed to reflective and non-oppressive practices. And they work against powerfully hypnotic notions of 'the real' already circulating in popular culture (Dimitriadis 2009). Indeed, students at screenings of *Moving to the Beat* often comment that these Black youth, with their hip clothes and styles, 'don't look like real Africans'. As they share their associations with 'looking African', stock images from Hollywood films typically emerge as a context for discussion.

Working to portray worlds ruptured by the trauma of history while seeking new forms of recognition inevitably gives rise to forms of misrecognition. And in advancing the urgency and scope of humanitarian crises in places such as Sierra Leone, field researchers may enlist the immediacy of visual media in ways that inadvertently reproduce Westernized ways of seeing – ways that perpetuate the fantasy that however bad things are in the West, the specter of life on the margins of the Empire are infinitely worse. Visual media have the capacity to disrupt habitual modes of looking and to reduce social distance. But they also carry unanticipated freight that require ongoing engagement and capacities to weather conflicts that emerge in producing cultural material while working across cultural borders. Documentary field projects widen the lens for such possibilities and make visible the process of knowledge production and its various blindspots, even as they carry powerful potential for suturing over these same effects.

References

Argyris, C., Putnam, R., and McLain Smith, D. (1985). *Action science*. San Franciso, CA: Jossey-Bass.

Bloustien, G. (2007). 'Wigging people out': youth music practice and mediated communities. *Journal of Community and Applied Social Psychology*, 17, 446–462.

Briski, Z., and Kaufman, R. (Directors). (2004). *Born into brothels: Calcutta's red light kids* [Film]. Calcutta, West Bengal, India: Lionsgate Entertainment.

Burman, E. (2004). Organising for change? Group-analytic perspectives on a feminist action research project. *Group Analysis* 37(1) 91–108.

Chang, J. (2005). *Can't stop, won't stop*. New York: Picador.

Clay, A. (2003). Keepin' it real: black youth, hip-hop culture, and black identity. *American Behavioral Scientist*, 46, 1346–1358.

Collins, P. H. (2000). *Black feminist thought: knowledge, consciousness, and the politics of empowerment* (2nd ed.). New York and London: Routledge.

Crenshaw, K. W. (1994). Mapping the margins: intersectionality, identity politics, and violence against women of color. In M. A. Fineman and R. Mykitiuk (Eds) *The public nature of private violence: the discovery of domestic abuse*. New York: Routledge, pp. 93–118.

Dimitriadis, G. (2009). *Performing identity/performing culture: hip-hop as text, pedagogy, and lived practice*. New York: Peter Land Publishing.

Doane, M. A. (1991). *Femmes fatales: feminism, film theory, psychoanalysis*. London: Routledge.

Ehrens, P. (1990). *Issues in feminist film criticism*. Bloomington, IN: University of Indiana Press.

Fanon, F. (2004). *The wretched of the earth*. New York: Grove Press.

Fine, M. and Torres, M. (2006) Intimate details: participatory action research in prison. *Action Research*, 4(3), 253–269.

Fine, M. (2006). Bearing witness: methods for researching oppression and resistance—a textbook for critical research. *Social Justice Research*, 19(1), 83–108.

Foucault, M. (1995). *Discipline and punish: the birth of the prison*. New York: Random House.

Freire, P. (1972/2004). *Pedagogy of the oppressed*. New York: Continuum.

Haaken, J. (1998). *Pillar of salt: gender, memory, and the perils of looking back*. New Brunswick, NJ: Rutgers University Press.

Haaken, J. (2001). Shallow graves: women and war in Sierra Leone. *Psychoanalyst/ Psychologist*, 21, 26–34.

Haaken, J. (2005, December). What's so funny? Video ethnography and drag performance. *Journal of Psychoanalysis, Culture & Society*, 10, 319–327.

Haaken, J. and Haaken-Heymann, C. (Directors). (2005). *Diamonds guns, and rice* [Video]. Portland, OR: Ooligan Press.

Haaken, J. (2010). *Hard knocks: domestic violence and storytelling*. London: Routledge.

Haaken, J., Ladum, A., Zundel, K., DeTarr, S., and Heymann, C. (2005). *Speaking out: women, war, and the global economy*. Portland, OR: Ooligan Press.

Hall, S. (Ed.) (1997). *Representation: cultural representations and signifying practices*. Thousand Oaks, CA: Sage.

Hall, S., Morley, D., and Chen, K. (1996). *Stuart Hall: critical dialogues in cultural studies*. London: Routledge.

Hollway, W. (Ed) (2004). Psycho-social research. *Critical Psychology: The International Journal of Critical Psychology*, 10.

Hollway, W. (2006). *The capacity to care: gender and ethical subjectivity*. London: Routledge.

hooks, b. (1992). *Black looks: race and representation*. Boston MA: South End Press.

Kaplan, E. A. (1990). *Psychoanalysis and cinema*. London: Routledge.

Kauffman, L. S. (1996). Bad girls and sick boys: inside the body in fiction, film, and performance art. In S. Smith and J. Watson (Eds.) *Getting a life: everyday uses of autobiography*. Minneapolis, MN: University of Minnesota Press, pp. 27–46.

Layton, L. (1998). *Who's that girl? Who's that boy? Clinical practice meets postmodern gender theory*. Northvale, NJ: Aronson.

Lewin, K. (1975, c1951). *Field theory in social science: selected theoretical papers of Kurt Lewin*. Westport, CT: Greenwood Press.

Lykes, M. B. (1989). Dialogue with Guatemalan Indian women: critical perspectives on constructing collaborative research. In R. K. Unger (Ed.) *Representations: social constructions of gender*. Amityville, NY: Baywood, pp. 167–185.

Mirzoeff, N. (1999). *An introduction to visual culture*. London: Routledge.

Molino, A. (Ed.) (2004). *Culture, subject, psyche: dialogues in psychoanalysis and anthropology*. Middletown, CT: Wesleyan University Press

Morrison, T. and Lacour, C. B. (1997). *Birth of a nation'hood: gaze, script, and spectacle in the O. J. Simpson trial*. New York, NY: Pantheon Press.

Mulvey, L. (1988). Visual pleasure and narrative cinema. In C. Penley (Ed.) *Feminism and film theory*. New York: Routledge, pp. 57–68.

Nichols, B. (1991). *Representing reality: issues and concepts in documentary*. Bloomington, IN: Indiana University Press.

Obeyesekere, G. (1990). *The work of culture: symbolic transformation in psychoanalysis and anthropology*. Chicago, IL: University of Chicago Press.

Penley, C. (1988). *Feminism and film theory.* New York: Routledge Press.

Perez, G. (2009). Errol Morris's irony. In W. Rothman (Ed.) *Three documentary film-makers.* Albany, NY: State University of New York, pp. 13–18.

Prilleltensky, I. (2003). Understanding, resisting, and overcoming oppression: toward psychopolitical validity. *American Journal of Community Psychology,* 31(1/2), 195–201.

Rothman, W. (2009). *Three documentary filmmakers.* Albany, NY: State University of New York.

Rose, G. (2007). *Visual methodologies.* London: Sage.

Rose, J. (1986). *Sexuality in the field of vision.* London: Verso Press.

Rose, T. (1994). *Black noise.* Hanover, NH: University Press of New England.

Rose, T. (2008). *The hip-hop wars.* New York: Basic Civitas.

Segal, L. (1990). *Slow motion: changing masculinities, changing men.* New Brunswick, NJ: Rutgers University Press.

Vaughan, D. (1999). *For documentary: twelve essays.* Berkeley, CA: University of California Press.

Watts, R. J. and Flanagan, C. (2007). Pushing the envelope on youth civic engagement: a developmental and liberation psychology perspective. *Journal of Community Psychology,* 35(6), 779–792.

Wachtel, P. L. (1993). *Therapeutic communication: knowing what to say when.* New York: Guilford Press.

Whitehead, J. and McNiff, J. (2006). *Action research, living theory.* Thousand Oaks, CA: Sage.

16 Towards a visual social psychology of identity and representation

Photographing the self, weaving the family in a multicultural British community

Caroline Howarth

Social psychology has long recognised the role of the visual in the development of identity, representations of others and prejudice (Forrester, 2000). The images that others have of us impact on identity as we develop a sense *and a vision* of self. The images and so representations that others have of us sometimes affirm or jar with our own image of who we are (Howarth, 2002). Research within the Social Representations tradition (Moscovici, 1998), for example, demonstrates the ways in which representations produce, extend, threaten and sometimes transform different social identities (see Moloney and Walker, 2007, for a useful edited collection). Yet, methodologically, there are few empirical studies that practically explore the *actual* production of self-images or the contestation of stigmatising representations of particular communities.[1] As Forrester (2000) has commented, 'it is a little surprising that photography has rarely been used in psychology either as a basis for analysing cultural conceptions of the self-display, or as a methodological tool in research exploring the relationship between self-concept and presentation' (p. 168).

In this chapter I examine one community-based arts project that does precisely this: it uses art (photography, painting and weaving) as a medium to examine the images that people hold of themselves and explore how far these correspond to and contest others' sometimes negative images of themselves.

Traditionally, social psychology uses interviews, focus groups or surveys to capture people's sense of themselves and feelings about social stereotypes that relate to them. For example in my first study on identity (Howarth, 2000), I examined how young people living in Brixton in South London felt about the different social stereotypes of Brixton (or social representations of Brixton). In the main, I used semi-structured interviews and focus groups to access how people related to Brixton, how far they developed a 'Brixtonite' identity or distanced themselves from the often racialised and negative representations of the area (Howarth, 2002). These standard methods served the study well and revealed important aspects of the participants' struggle for identity.

However, in this first study, I also analysed a television documentary series about people from Brixton and ran focus groups exploring the images produced in the series and how these could be interpreted by viewers in general. Following Gillespie (1995), I wanted to reveal the 'mediated messages, through the eyes of her informants themselves' (p. 1) and so I asked the focus group participants to consider both the encoding and the decoding of the programme (Hall, 1997). In many ways, the media programme and related focus groups went to the heart of the issue – the very *visual* significance of representations of Brixton, something taken-for-granted and simultaneously avoided as too sensitive or political to discuss. This was the racialisation of people from Brixton, the psychological politics of this and people's collaborative efforts to reconstrue negative representations of Brixton in more positive ways. Hence the visual methods led to an important finding: *identity is both restricted by and liberated by its very visibility*. (Ironically it was harder to publish this work as psychology journals do not accept images.) This early study drew me to visual methods generally, which developed into a commitment to explore the visual politics of identity and the value of using visual methods in psychological research.

Mosaic identities: using visual methods to explore identity.

In this research project I collaborated with MOSAIC, a Black and mixed parentage family group. With funding from *The Arts Council*, MOSAIC set up workshops to provide a context for children and young people to explore mixed heritage, assert positive cultural identities and develop social skills to protect themselves in racist encounters. Together we drew on both a) social psychology to facilitate a clear understanding of the connections between identity, representation and prejudice and b) art – as a means of bringing somewhat abstract concepts to life – such as the gaze, self-image, social representation, narrative and performativity. As other researchers have found (e.g., Banks, 2007; Clark-Ibáñez, 2007), we discovered that visual methods were a useful methodology to engage young people, to build rapport and unsettle the power dynamics of much social research. The workshops provided an ideal context to explore the value and limitations of visual methodologies as a means of examining the (co)production of identities, the diverse nature of identity (i.e. hybridity) and the ways in which identities are acted out or performed (i.e. performativity).

Following an ethnographic approach (Rose, 1982), I worked very much in the capacity of a participant-observer, recording as much data as possible while assisting the children and, where appropriate, participating myself. Each workshop ran over four days in two different groups: 7- to 10-year-old children and 11- to 19-year-old teenagers.[2] Experienced artists ran each workshop, with support from MOSAIC's art education officer and myself. The artists were highly skilled in using art as a means of subverting common stereotypes, encouraging rich narrative and promoting self-reflection. As a whole, the workshops aimed to promote the expression of secure cultural identities through creative and interactive activities that forged a collective sense of cultural heritage and history. We hoped to create a forum for 'community conversations' (Campbell *et al.*, 2007) on identity and a space to develop the social support to overcome experiences of racism, other forms of prejudice, rejection and hostility.

The children and teenagers in the workshops were used to being seen as 'minorities', subjected to stereotypes of otherness and often treated as the object of reifying and racialising representations. As bell hooks (1992) has argued, to be an object of reifying representations is to the lose the power to represent one's self and so to lose the possibility for being recognised as one sees one's self. Creating a space to work with images of the self was important. In the photography workshop, the children and teenagers took photographs of themselves and painted over these – discussing the ways in which they saw themselves and understood others' images of them. In the weaving workshop, family groups told stories of connection, belonging and cultural identity while weaving together fabrics, wools and maps into individual, family and collective weaves. (These activities are discussed in greater detail below.) As other researchers have found, 'making and sharing photographs can be helpful in generating rapport' (Gold, 2007: 145). I found the experience very powerful and the resulting data incredibly rich. The analysed data included the photos and the weaves, cultural artefacts brought in from home, group discussions within the workshops, recorded interviews participants made with one another and focus groups with participants (including children, teenagers and parents).

Interpreting images: connections between representation, identity and power

The best way of conveying the value of visual methods for this research is to give examples that illustrate the textured connections between representation, identity and power. I suggest that it is necessary to ground these connections in practice otherwise research questions and conclusions can literally get lost in words. However, we also need talk, some verbal qualitative data, to see the images collected in the project through the participants' eyes. The verbal data contain individual and collective interpretations of what the weaves, paintings and photos mean and how they can be read. Hence the combined analysis of verbal and visual data gives a much richer and more complex picture of the social encounters produced in the workshops and the connections between identity, representation and power. Here I give four examples, using both visual and verbal data, which illuminate four main aspects of the research project:

1. Representations as the building blocks of identity
2. The psychological violence of representation
3. The creative possibilities produced in 'doing' identity
4. The power of collaboration and collective identities

Representations as the building blocks of identity

Social psychology demonstrates that identity is always produced in relationship and is marked by the particular context in which it is performed (Condor, 2006; Tajfel, 1978). One of the mothers made this point:[3]

Lucie: It (my identity) depends very much on the context – and how other people
see me. I am aware of different parts of myself in different situations.

One of the main objectivities in designing the workshops was to produce a
particular context that would facilitate a rich, multilayered discussion of identity
– focussing on cultural identities, cultural heritage, feelings of belonging,
connection and disconnection. In both workshops this was done unobtrusively by
placing artefacts, books and maps in the room – either simply as a backdrop or as
tools. For example, one activity was to produce a family weave – a small weave
with different colours and textures of wool to symbolise significant family
members. This used a book as the frame on which to actually weave. The artist
brought a diverse collection of books which appropriately reflected different
cultures. These included well-known books (such as Maya Angelou's *The Caged
Bird Sings,* Nelson Mandela's *Long Walk to Freedom* and Jung Chang's *Wild
Swans*) and travel guides (for example to West Africa, India and Hong Kong).
When discussing the weave and showing it to the others, participants discussed
how they ended up choosing particular books that had some connection to their
own cultural histories. Indeed, I found that this was what I had done myself in
choosing a text that highlights my own connection to Africa (see Figure 16.1).
The workshops were managed in such a way that I could work very much as a
participant observer (Rose, 1982) – joining in activities, sharing the stories

Figure 16.1 My family weave.

developed through the art projects and being very open to questions about my own childhood in Kenya and the South Pacific. Some of the other participants had also grown up in Africa or had connections to the Pacific, and this created a considerable degree of connection and warmth. Assumptions about identity, which connections were prioritised and how other people construct 'different' cultural identities quickly and easily became topics of animated discussion.

The very practical, visual and creative nature of the activity brought the role of representations as the building blocks of identity to the fore. Just as Harper (2002) has found, this methodology can 'mine deeper shafts into a different part of the human consciousness than do words-alone interviews' (p. 13). Participants chose colours and textures to identify with, physically wove these together, showed photos and weaves to others, created narratives about what they saw in their art and in work produced by others – perhaps seeing the emerging images through others' eyes and with new insight. While focus group discussions would have revealed some of these aspects of identity, I would suggest that the importance of visibility for identity in terms of how we are seen, how we 'capture' the other in our gaze and how we collaborate to discover alternative visions of both self and culture would not have been so evident without the use of visual methods.

The psychological violence of representation

Evident in both workshops were the very political consequences of visual representations of identity. That is, people, cultures, communities but especially minoritised groups are literally *captured* in a particular way by the gaze – otherness is thereby marked onto their skin, their hair, their facial features and there are certain stereotypes that flow from this act of looking (Fanon, 1952; Hall, 1997; Howarth, 2006). As Foucault has forcefully demonstrated 'visibility is a trap' (1977: 200). Many of the participants gave examples of how this 'trap' affects them, discussing their desire to relax (straighten) hair, have smaller noses and lips, be white – or to proudly assert afros, African features and other visual markers of difference. For example, this is an extract from a discussion with the mothers of the young participants:

Linda: Because Tracey – she never wears her hair down and I'm hoping that might change, you know, as her confidence grows and her own identity, you know, her perception of her own identity. … [When she was younger] Trace was coming home from the nursery in tears because another child wouldn't kiss her because she thought it might be catching, and this is at three years old. And kids weren't using the water fountain after my daughter used it. It is terrible, and some woman, 'Oh, you've got hair just like my poodle'.

Lucie: I was one of the only three black children in the school and immediately people's eyes were on me and it was just – being singled out. I was very shy and I just wanted to hide, and it was somewhere near that time I remembered thinking 'I wish I had straight hair', 'I wish I was white'.

In these extracts and image two (see Figure 16.2) it is possible to see the effects of the psychological violence contained in the politics of representation – as certain representations restrict the ways in which we are seen and so limit the possibilities of self (Howarth, 2002). In analysing image two, produced by Lucie's youngest child Jamelia, it would be an easy assumption that her daughter's identity is in fact damaged by the same negative representations of blackness that equate beauty with 'white' features such as thin lips. Let me explain how this image was produced. In the workshop the artist asked participants to photograph a part of their face that they particularly liked *or* disliked. After these were developed as black and white A3-size pictures, participants were invited to paint on the image and to explain the changes they made. One of the aims of this exercise was to explore how we are seen, how others see us and how we may change or challenge this. Most images were changed a great deal – participants enjoyed spending a lot of time adding various colours and patterns as we can see in image three (see Figure 16.3 below). By contrast Jamelia made a few very simple changes to her photo – she painted her lips bright red but also, significantly, made her lips much narrower. In colour this image is quite shocking. The red stands out dramatically against the black and white, and the narrowing of the lips is less obvious, but when seen it jars with common hopes for and MOSAIC's ambitions of supporting positive and assertive cultural identities.

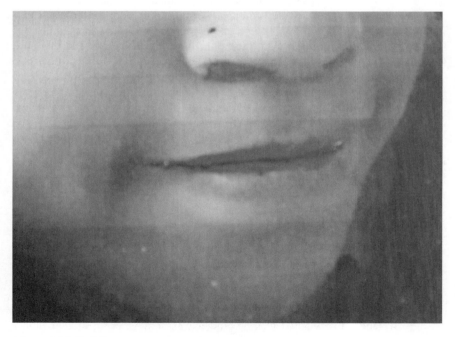

Figure 16.2 Red lips.

From the image alone it is impossible to know what this says about Jamelia's own identity: whether she is revealing a desire to hide her black features and therefore a certain degree of shame and a spoiled identity (Goffman, 1968), or whether she is demonstrating her knowledge of racialised stereotypes and that this in fact is a subversive attempt to challenge assumptions about beauty, femininity and 'race'.[4] From the verbal data as well as discussions with her mum, it seems just as likely that she is very conscious of racialised representations and is making quiet, determined attempts to unsettle easy assumptions about her identity and what she 'should' be like.

The creative possibilities produced in 'doing' identity

Interestingly the other photo that was also barely changed was of someone's hair. When I asked the teenager who took this photo why he hadn't painted it he simply said, 'it's cool like that, no need to change. ... Too many people mess with their hair. "Don't mess with my hair!" [*in a mock angry voice*]'. Hair can be a very political issue as it may assert or contest various representations about African and Caribbean identities (Haley, 1998). The photo itself hints to this significance and the political nature of the connections between how we are seen and how we re-assert identity. The act of taking a photo and then painting over it (or not) was very successful in highlighting the dynamic, creative and provocative aspects of 'doing' identity.

Image three (Figure 16.3) is another example from the photography and painting activity. Initially Akinyi was very resistant to keeping this photo at all; she said she 'hated' the photo and would 'put it in the bin'. Gentle persuasion from the artist and MOSAIC's arts facilitator did not change her mind it seemed and she worked on another image. However, she later came back to the discarded image and spent a good deal of time painting onto it what she described as African colours and textures. At the end of the four-day workshop, she admitted that she 'really, really liked the picture', saying 'you can really express yourself using pictures and art'. She went on:

Akinyi: This was an experience. (*laughs*) I hated this photo – my nose! It looked so ugly. Then I thought - this is my nose, it is an African nose (*laughs*). I shouldn't feel bad about it. So I painted it in a Africany way – the colours of Africa. The hills and valleys of Africa! (*Laughs*)... I like the multicolours too. I mean, it also symbolises I like multicultural – I like living in a multicultural community. I am proud to say that I live in a multicultural community.

Through the workshop as a whole, Akinyi's attitude seemed to change a great deal. She seemed to change how she saw herself, how she dealt with others' representations and expectations of her and this increased her confidence and cultural pride. This parallels a shift from her positioning herself at the centre of her stories, to a focus on the community as a whole. She seemed much more assertive

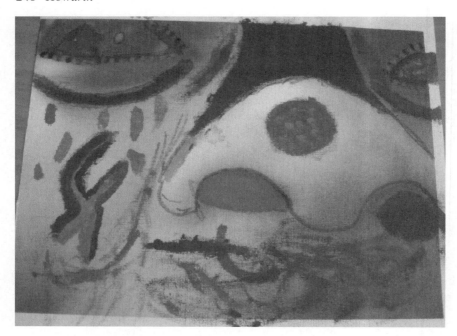

Figure 16.3 The colours of Africa

and connected to the group by the end of the workshop. One of the other activities seemed to elicit these feelings of a new-found confidence to assert proud identities. This was a dressing-up task – where participants choose from a diverse range of clothes, wigs, hats and props that represented different cultures, generations and fashions. Hair again was a common topic – as children and teenagers chose to play with different types of wigs – making them feel 'more African', 'like a girl' and 'happy'. Olive was very enthusiastic about this task – choosing items that reflected what she 'was like before', wearing an ankle-length skirt as she used to in Tanzania but in a style that she described as 'Australian, hippy-ish and super-confident!'. She looked at her image in a full-length mirror and said:

Olive: This gives me a picture of who I can be. Hippy-ish, confident. I used to wear skirts like this. I think this is how Australians are. I will be like this one day. (*pause*) It makes me feel liberated! (*laughs*) Yeah! Liberated! (*Makes a power-to-the-people gesture with her fist*). Yeah, Liberated.

She said this on day one of the workshop. By day four she was even more assertive about her identity and the need to stand up to racism. She told us that she now realised that she has been very much a victim of racism and she had not had the confidence to stand up to racist bullying in the past. She says that the workshop activities enabled her 'to express my feelings and stuff through pictures'. She repeats a story that she told earlier of extreme racism on the school bus, racist chants and jokes told literally on a daily basis. She shares with us that she has realised she has never stood up to racists or asked anyone to help her deal with this. While she recognised this would be very daunting, she seemed to feel less victimised by the situation, realising she has a choice in how to respond. Such reflection was made possible by the particular dynamics of the workshop - with a Freirian emphasis on creativity and criticality as fundamentally *social* processes, achieved in interaction and dialogue with others (Freire, 1973/2005). It must *not* be assumed that Olive should find her own individual solutions to her experiences of racism. Quite the contrary, the workshops showed that understanding the complexities of racism and developing strategies for challenging racism can only be done in dialogue and relationship with others.

The power of collaboration and collective identities

What the analysis above fails to highlight is the very collaborated nature of the workshops, the art produced and the narratives told. Many of the participants commented on the value of having 'a space to stop and think about our cultures', as the mothers said, 'a forum' where they could 'see each others' stories', appreciate differences in cultural experiences and find commonalities in identity-work. Two of the participants talked about what they liked about the workshops:

Karen: The workshops helped me think about myself, and where I am from. It made me want to learn more, about where I am from. It made me understand myself more – which helps. I liked thinking about what my culture is – the smell of mangoes, West Indian food, and the heat! It is hot. And also my English culture – like was grey skies really! (*laughs*) Because the more I understand myself, the easier it is when I have to deal with racism, the better I deal with it the more I know about myself. Because I feel strong, you know, about who I am.

Susannah: I liked finding connections with other people. Like she said she thought of the smell of mangoes – so did I! So we both chose the same colours (*in the collective weave*).

All of the parents and older participants in the photography workshop commented on how much they learnt from each other, especially about experiences of racism. Some of the weaving embodied the collaborative and collective aspects of cultural identities very tangibly – in the production of large collective weaves such as image four (see Figure 16.4, approximately 3 feet by 5 feet).

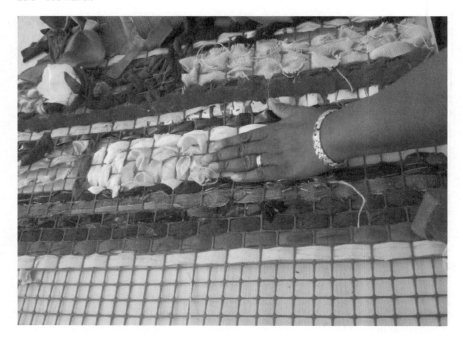

Figure 16.4 Collective weave.

Participants wove together colours and fabrics that held cultural significance for them while telling the story of these pieces to each other. In the making of these group weaves, therefore, there was a real sense of a collective narrative of identity emerging – as people found similar memories of 'home', of food, music and smells, of parents and grandparents, of journeys to other places and connections to Britain. As well as telling these stories to each other, families were also sharing stories, as one of the mothers said:

Lucie: it reminded me of stories you hear about people who are working and making quilts or weaving in Africa. Not necessarily singing, but working and talking and telling stories and passing around stories from centuries ago. It's something about telling your story to your children that keeps it alive.

Everyone in the workshops was in some way 'mixed' – and so, for a change, people enjoyed 'being part of the majority', as another mother said. Being in a minority was a more common experience for the children; one parent said that in her children's school of about 550 children there are only 6 non-white children. Like many of the other parents, she was passionate about the need for organisations like MOSAIC where they not only learnt about cultural identity and mixed heritage but they also learn how to deal with negative stereotypes and racism. As she said:

Nancy: They've got to be able to stand up (for themselves). That's what I want for them.

The very practical aspects of the methods invited the participants to work together, share difficult stories of prejudice and hostility and find ways of supporting each other. This made the workshops feel very empowering and invited both individual and collective forms of agency to develop, as other visual researchers have also found in their use of visual methods (e.g. Clark-Ibáñez, 2007; Banks, 2007).

Towards a visual social psychology of identity and representation

The contextual and relational dynamic of identity has been at the heart of Social Psychological theories on self and identity from Mead's influential lectures on the self and society, Goffman's conceptualisation of the performative self, Tajfel's early studies of social identity and Turner's emphasis of the situation-specific nature of identity, and is also highlighted in powerful critiques of the field (e.g. Reicher, 2004; Wetherell and Potter, 1992) and explicit in recent, innovative work on identity and prejudice (e.g., Ahmed, 2000; Condor, 2006; Phoenix, 2006). Despite these weighty intellectual traditions, homogenising and reifying versions of identity and 'race' still penetrate the field (Howarth, 2009; Stevens, 2003). I hope that the research described here highlights the potential of visual methods for developing a Social Psychology of identity and representation that instead examines the creativity, collaboration and criticality involved in the telling and performing of cultural identities. This is what I hope I have addressed in this chapter: the importance of visibility for identity and the value of a methodology that brings to the fore the ways in which we see ourselves, are seen by others and the psychological politics that this provokes. Through a visual approach to the psychology of identity we can see how identity is both restricted and liberated by its very visibility.

People's sense of self, their fluid, dynamic and collaborated sense of connection and disconnection (to many different social groups and communities) and the negotiated limits to the production of identity is something that is often intensely visual. Being British, being white or Asian, being old, being female, having mixed heritage – these are all aspects of ourselves that are seen, displayed and created. The visual aspect of identity at once highlights the conditional politics of the gaze (we cannot often avoid being *seen* in very particular ways – as brown or white or 'mixed') and the psychological politics of resistance (there are so many ways of asserting/performing/challenging what it is to be *seen* as brown or white or mixed). While this is undeniable in racialised contexts – as we impose 'race' in the very act of looking, I would argue that visual methods are relevant for looking at all aspects of identity – most importantly the relational and restricted aspects of identity (how identity is literally captured in a social relationships with others) and the creative aspects of identity (how we challenge, resist and re-create how others literally see us).

The workshops described here used the visual to great effect to bring out these tensions between representation and identity, highlight stigmatised assumptions and invite collaborative narratives of positive cultural identities. To summarise, we have seen how:

a) creative photography can capture the gaze of the other and the symbolic violence of racism as well as the possibilities for recasting the self in the eyes of others
b) weaving together different threads and fabrics that resonate with cultural associations and social memories can produce shared images and narratives of connection and disconnection, belonging and exclusion.

One of the participants described identity as 'an unfinished project – a work in progress' and this was very evident in the workshops as a whole. Different activities explicitly and implicitly asked the participants to consider how others view them, expect them to be and so impact on their identities. Marcus Banks (2007) has argued that 'the act of looking produces knowledge that in turn constitutes society' (p. 42). The activities worked with this principle – and found ways to encourage the participants to challenge the ways they were often looked at, to challenge the knowledge so produced and thereby to challenge the racialisation of society. For example, the act of taking a photo or producing a weave, consciously reflecting on it and debating this with others somehow seems to unsettle negative representations of identity and 'race'. Hence the visual methods used here portray how *identity is both restricted by and liberated by its very visibility*. Exploring the connections between identity, visibility and possibilities for transformation, as we have done here, brings the essentially social, collaborated and contested element of these processes to the fore. Examining the visual politics of identity demands a rigorously *social* psychological approach - where we examine the interconnections, social categories and social agents, identities as they are imposed and identities as they are collaborated, and the intersection between the social-cultural and the psychological.

Acknowledgements

I would like to thank all those at MOSAIC who contributed to this project, particularly the children, young people and parents who gave of their time and stories so generously. I would also like to thank Monique Forbes-Broomes, Naima Nouidjem, Alinah Azadeh and Poulomi Desai who taught me much about using art in research. I am also grateful to the Arts Council for proving the funding for the workshops.

Notes

1 The main exceptions to this come from photo-elicitation studies (see Stanczak, 2007, for a good collection from Sociology) and social psychological analyses of images of 'others' in a discursive or social representations tradition (e.g. Moloney, 2007). Such

studies have been criticised as they 'may be limited by the researcher's interests' and so miss what is meaningful to the participants (Clark-Ibáñez, 2007: 167). Rarely do studies look at the actual production of images themselves, as we do here, directed by the research participants and produced in collaboration with researchers.

2 As the focus in the weaving workshop was on family heritage, one or two main carers participated alongside their children.

3 All names and some personal details (such as nationalities) have been changed in order to protect the identities of the participants.

4 'Race' is problematised with speech marks in order disrupt its taken-for-granted and often naturalised status in both everyday and academic discourses. This emphasises the socially constructed nature of 'race'.

References

Ahmed, B. (2000). Constructing racism: discourse, culture and subjectivity. In C. Squire (Ed.), *Culture in psychology*. London: Routledge.

Banks, M. (2007). *Using visual data in qualitative research*. London: Sage.

Campbell, C., Nair, Y., Maimane, S., and Sibiya, Z. (2007). Building contexts that support effective community responses to HIV/AIDS. *American Journal of Community Psychology*, 39(3–4), 347–363.

Clark-Ibáñez, M. (2007). Inner-city children in sharper focus: sociology of childhood and photo elicitation interviews. In G. C. Stanczak (Ed.), *Visual research methods: image, society and representation*. London: Sage, pp. 167–196.

Condor, S. (2006). Public prejudice as collaborative accomplishment: towards a dialogic social psychology of racism. *Journal of Community and Applied Social Psychology*, 16, 1–18.

Fanon, F. (1952). *Black skin, white masks*. London: Pluto Press.

Forrester, M. (2000). *Psychology of the image*. London: Routledge.

Foucault, M. (1977). *Discipline and punish: the birth of the prison*. London: Allen Lane.

Freire, P. (1973/2005). *Education for critical consciousness*. New York: Continuum.

Gillespie, M. (1995). *Television, ethnicity and cultural change*. London: Routledge.

Goffman, E. (1968). *Stigma: notes on the management of spoiled identity*. Harmondsworth: Penguin.

Gold, S. (2007). Using photography in studies of immigrant communities: reflecting across projects and populations. In G. C. Stanczak (Ed.), *Visual research methods: image, society and representation*. London: Sage, pp. 141–166.

Haley, A. (1998). *The autobiography of Malcolm X as told to Alex Haley*. New York: Random House.

Hall, S. (1997). *Representation: cultural representations and signifying practices*. London: Sage.

Harper, D. (2002). Talking about pictures: a case study for photo elicitation. *Visual Studies*, 17(1), 13–16.

hooks, b. (1992). *Black looks: race and representation*. London: Turnaround.

Howarth, C. (2000). *'So, you're from Brixton': towards a social psychology of community*. Unpublished PhD thesis, University of London.

Howarth, C. (2002) Identity in whose eyes? The role of representations in identity construction. *Journal of the Theory of Social Behaviour*, 32(2), 145–162.

Howarth, C. (2006). Race as stigma: positioning the stigmatized as agents, not objects. *Journal of Community & Applied Social Psychology*, 16, 442–451.

Howarth, C. (2009). 'I hope we won't have to understand racism one day': Researching or reproducing 'race' in Social Psychological research? *British Journal of Social Psychology*. 48(3) 407–426.

Moloney, G. (2007). Social representations and the politically satirical cartoon: the construction and reproduction of refugee and asylum-seeker identity. In G. Moloney and I. Walker (Eds), *Social representations: content, process and power*. New York: Palgrave Macmillan.

Moloney, G., and Walker, I. (2007). *Social representations: content, process and power*. New York: Palgrave Macmillan.

Moscovici, S. (1998). The history and actuality of social representations. In U. Flick (Ed.), *The psychology of the social*. Cambridge: Cambridge University Press.

Phoenix, A. (2006). 'Centring marginality? Otherness, difference and the 'Psychology of Women'. *Psychology of Women Section Review*, 8, 2–11.

Reicher, S. (2004). The context of social identity: domination, resistance and change. *Political Psychology*, 25(6), 921–945.

Rose, G. (1982). *Deciphering sociological research*. London: Macmillan.

Stanczak, G. (2007). *Visual research methods: image, society, representation*. London: Sage.

Stevens, G. (2003). Academic representations of 'race' and racism in psychology: knowledge production, historical context and dialectic of transitional South Africa. *International Journal of Intercultural Relations*, 27(2), 189–207.

Tajfel, H. (1978). Social categorization, social identity and social comparison. In H. Tajfel (Ed.), *Differentiation between social groups*. London: Academic Press, pp. 61–76.

Wetherell, M., and Potter, J. (1992). *Mapping the language of racism: discourse and the legitimisation of exploitation*. Hemel Hempstead, UK: Harvester-Wheatsheaf.

17 'I didn't know that I could feel this relaxed in my body'

Using visual methods to research bisexual people's embodied experiences of identity and space

Helen Bowes-Catton, Meg Barker and Christina Richards

Introduction

Recent research into bisexuality has tended to use discourse analysis to explore bisexual people's articulations of identity. Such research demonstrates that, although many bi people argue that they experience their identities as coherent and unified, and vehemently reject binary categories of sex, gender, and sexuality as bogus and constructed (Bowes-Catton, 2007), such discourses inevitably creep back into their identity talk (Barker *et al.*, 2008) resulting in 'structurally fractured' articulations of identity (Ault, 1996). Following the 'turn to the body' in sociological and psychological research (Featherstone *et al.*, 1991; Stam, 1998; Reavey, 2008), we argue that an approach to identity research which privileges discourse makes it difficult for participants to articulate identities outside of the prevailing binary categories of male/female, straight/gay, and obscures experiential and material aspects of sexual identity such as embodied experience and performativity. Our research therefore aims to move towards an understanding of the ways in which bisexual identity is grounded in the bodily practices and performances of lived experience. In this chapter, we present preliminary results from the application of visual methods, such as modelling and photography, to bisexual people's embodied experience of space, with the aim of moving towards an understanding of the experience and production of bisexual identity, both in everyday life, and in bisexual spaces such as BiCon, the annual gathering of the UK bisexual community.

The research context

From the late 1990s to the present, the vast majority of qualitative work on bisexuality has focused on the ways in which bisexual people and communities construct their identities through language (e.g. Ault, 1999; Berenson, 2002; Bower *et al.*, 2002; Bowes-Catton, 2007). Generally such work has involved collecting data through interviews, focus group discussions, or existing sources such as bi community materials and bi activist texts, and subjecting these to some form of discourse analysis. Researchers have been particularly interested in the ways in which bisexual people and groups construct and present their identities within a linguistic and cultural context that sees sexuality and gender as dichotomous (gay *or* straight) and leaves little discursive space for bisexuality (Barker and Langdridge, 2008).

Bisexuality is commonly understood to refer to sexual attraction to both sexes, but these discourse analytic studies consistently find that many bisexual people vehemently reject the notion that sexuality can be reduced to binary categories, and express deep ambivalence about the term 'bisexuality' itself, because of the way it reinforces this binary view of sexuality (Bower *et al.*, 2002: 31). Petford (2003), for example, described the preferred definition of bisexuality within the bi communities she studied as 'mutable sexual and emotional attraction to people of any sex, where gender may not be a defining factor' (p. 6). Similarly, Berenson (2002: 13) noted that for her participants, bisexuality was less about 'the inclusion of both men and women in the realm of their possible attractions' than it was concerned with 'a refusal to exclude'.

Despite such explicit rejection of dichotomies, however, these studies find that discourses of bisexual identity, rather than moving beyond binary definitions of sexuality altogether, frequently construct discursive space for bisexuality by recasting these binaries in ways that position bisexuality as normative or natural. For example, Ault (1999: 180), Bower *et al.* (2002: 37), Hemmings (2002: 29), and Bowes-Catton (2007: 64) note that such discourses often dismiss the categories of heterosexual and homosexual as bogus and divisive constructions imposed on a whole and natural bisexuality, or recast the binary in terms of bisexuals and monosexuals, or queers and non-queers.

Notwithstanding these attempts to rework dominant understandings of sexuality in ways that leave space for bisexuality, such studies also demonstrate how very difficult it is for bi people to talk about their sexuality without making reference to the polarities of gay/straight and male/female. While bi people's identity talk often involves the explicit repudiation of these categories, the constraints of discourse mean that it is almost impossible to describe one's sexual subjectivity without making reference to them, resulting in 'structurally fractured identities' (Ault 1999: 173–174).

The findings of these studies were supported by our own discursive research on bi identities, conducted as a discussion workshop at a bisexual community event in the UK (Barker *et al.*, 2008). At the beginning of the discussion, participants unanimously rejected dichotomies of sexuality and dismissed gender as 'irrelevant'. For example, one participant stated:

> When I was slowly realizing that I was bi, the first thing was 'I fancy women' then it was 'I don't think actually gender is that relevant' … it's about as important as something like eye colour.

Another said that being bisexual meant that:

> your desires and your attractions can wax and wane as time goes on. I realized that there was a parallel to gender as well: you don't have to clearly define, you don't have to cast off the male to be female and vice versa.

Later in the discussion, however, participants drew on dichotomies of gender when talking about their own experiences of bisexuality. For example, one said:

> I'm finding myself looking at women more. I've got one [man] and so I don't need any more,

and another noted that their sexual practices varied with gender:

> I'm pretty much sub[missive] to blokes and top [more dominant] to women.

Similarly, participants recounted experiences of being attracted to different features in male or female partners, whilst, at the same time, several expressed discomfort with their habitual attempts to discern a person's gender on meeting them.

Discourse analytic research into bisexual identity, then, consistently shows that binaries of sexuality and gender are simultaneously rejected and re-inscribed in accounts of bi subjectivity, which are 'inescapably marked' by the very binary structures of sexuality they seek to undermine, resulting in indistinct and fragmented articulations of identity (Ault, 1999: 173–174). Despite this, however, bi people vehemently stress the wholeness and coherence of their identities (Bowes-Catton, 2007: 64, 66).

Faced with this contradiction, we began to speculate that our participants were struggling to articulate coherent identities, not because they experienced their identities as fragmented, but because the structural constraints of discourse forced them to locate their accounts of sexual subjectivity within the very binary paradigm they so vehemently rejected. This led us to investigate visual and creative methodologies for studying bisexuality, and other sexual and gender identities, which would facilitate people to talk in new ways about the experience of sexual subjectivity.

In doing this, our interdisciplinary research follows the wider challenging of the privileging of language in qualitative research, and the 'turn to the body' within sociology and critical psychology (Featherstone *et al.*, 1991; Stam, 1998; Reavey, 2008). This involves recognizing that people's lived and felt experiences of the social world take place in embodied material and spatial contexts, and viewing the body not just as a surface that can be inscribed with meaning, but approaching the study of the social world from an embodied perspective. From this perspective, power relations are not just transmitted through discourse, but through the 'dispositions, bodily habits, emotions, and senses that run through the process of thinking and action' (Del Busso and Reavey, in press). Embodied experience is situated in what Del Busso and Reavey call 'socio-spatial contexts, which can facilitate or restrict embodied expression' and our work therefore also draws on feminist and queer cultural geography such as Bell (2006), Valentine and Skelton (2003) and Ingram, Bouthillette and Retter (1997), as well as on theories of the everyday (Highmore, 2002). We agree with Reavey and Johnson (2008) that eliciting visual materials from participants offers one possible way into incorporating such embodied experiences and awareness of socio-spatial contexts. Perhaps most significantly we will draw on the work of the cultural geographer

Clare Hemmings (2002), who has been the only other researcher we know of to date who has explicitly addressed bisexual spaces, although she does not attend particularly to the embodied experience of individuals within such spaces.

By using visual methodologies in the study of bisexual identity, then, we hope to overcome some of the limitations of previous discursive work in this area. We also find that visual methods fit well within the tradition of feminist participatory research (Wilkinson, 1999) in which our work is located, and offer exciting possibilities for research projects whose agendas are set, at least in part, by participants, rather than being imposed upon them by researchers. As Packard (2008) points out, there is of course nothing inherently empowering in the use of visual methods; however they seem to offer the potential for enabling participants, especially those, like bisexuals, who are often marginalized or silenced (Barker and Langdridge, 2008), to gain a voice in research to a much greater extent than traditional positivist methods do (O'Neill, 2008). For example, Reavey (2008) suggests that the use of the visual allows people to show researchers their experiences and their lived spaces rather than simply to describe them.

As queer feminist researchers, we are also committed to producing research that comes from within communities, rather than being imposed upon them (Hagger-Johnson *et al.*, 2006). Visual methods seem ideal for work on bisexuality conducted from this standpoint, because they fit in well with the kinds of activities already being run at bi community events, which often involve the use of art, poetry, music, games, and drama to explore issues of relevance to the community. Community events such as BiCon, the annual UK gathering for bisexuals, also prompt many attendees to create their own artefacts and ephemera such as mix CDs for the disco, badges covered with various stickers and colours to represent different aspects of identity, photographic records of the event, costumes for the Saturday night ball, and memory posts on blog sites. Thus, creative means of identity exploration were familiar to participants within this context.

The incorporation of a visual research project into BiCon 2008, the event where the present studies were conducted, was timely because the organizers had asked two of the authors (Meg and Christina) to extend the usual event with an extra day at the beginning focusing on disseminating and developing research on bisexuality (BiReCon, 2008). This was the culmination of several years of explicit engagement between bi communities and academic researchers which also involved an annual survey of BiCon attendees, workshops and an email discussion group for those interested in helping with research (mostly coordinated by ourselves). Many attendees arrived early in 2008 in order to attend BiReCon, and it formed an opportunity for the lead researcher on the current study (Helen) to run an initial visual methods workshop and to inform attendees about previous research in this area.

Research aims

The aim of this research was to explore the ways in which visual methods of data elicitation can facilitate access to experiential data about embodied experiences in space, rather than purely discursive accounts about identity, producing rich data about the lived, sensorial experience of being bisexual, rather than accounts of 'structurally fractured' identities.

Methods

Bisexual space is not just hard to come by in discursive terms, but also in literal ones. Specifically bi spaces in the UK are few and far between. There are a small number of bi social/support/activism groups around the country, and a couple of regular pub/club nights, but there is not a commercial bi scene in the way that there is a commercial lesbian and gay scene. Bi spaces tend to be temporary, and when they do occur, they draw people from a wide area. Regional events such as the BiFests held in Brighton, Manchester and London each year, draw people from all over the UK.

The main event of the organised UK bisexual calendar is BiCon, an annual long weekend of workshops and socializing that takes place somewhere in the UK every summer, and has been taking place since 1982. In recent years it has tended to take place on a university campus, often with onsite accommodation.

According to the annual questionnaire data (see Barker *et al.*, 2008), between 200 and 300 people attend BiCon each year, 85 per cent of whom identify as bisexual, and the rest made up of allies and other minority group members. Ages range from 17–61, but most attendees are over 30 and under 50. In many ways the attendees of BiCon can be seen as 'the usual suspects' of LBGT communities, with middle class and white people enormously over-represented – 99 per cent of those surveyed in 2004 were white, while 80 per cent had at least one degree. Just under half (47 per cent) of those who completed the survey at BiCon in 2004 identified as female, and just over a third (36 per cent) as male, with 19 per cent identifying as trans or genderqueer (either in addition to, or instead of, identifying as female or male). Thirty-six per cent identified as having significant mental or physical health impairments affecting their daily lives. According to official statistics, 16 per cent of people in the UK have limiting long-term illnesses, and 7.5 per cent are classed as 'disabled', so people with health impairments seem to be well-represented at BiCon. This may be explained by the strong commitment to access within BiCon constitution and organising committees, though our broad definition of 'health impairments' should also be taken into account here.[1] The context in which the current research was conducted was therefore overwhelmingly white and middle class, but with diversity in terms of disability and gender identification.

The research conducted at BiCon 2008 was in two parts. For the first study, 11 volunteer participants were asked to take photographs of their embodied experiences of BiCon, and to make notes on the experiences and feelings that had prompted the photographs. They also completed a similar photo-diary of their embodied experiences of a week in their everyday lives, following Alison Rooke's similar studies of lesbian experience (see Ryan-Flood and Rooke, 2009). They were interviewed about both these diaries between September and December 2008. During the interviews, participants were also asked to draw maps of the BiCon space and talk about their experience of the space.

For the second study, the lead researcher (Helen) ran three workshops at BiCon 2008 itself in which participants were asked to make and discuss models of their experiences of BiCon using Lego™, Plasticine and other craft materials. This modelling work draws on and develops David Gauntlett's (2007) application of Lego™ Serious Play modelling methods to the study of identity, in which he found that giving people the time to reflect on their experiences and make models representing them enabled them to 'present a set of ideas all in one go', and allowed them to articulate clearly things that are usually difficult to express verbally or appear contradictory, thus avoiding some of the problems of discursive research.

The process of transcribing and analysing the data collected in those two studies is still in progress. Thus the data and analysis presented here are only preliminary and should be regarded as exploratory and in its early stages. The data to be analyzed consists of the transcriptions of participants' descriptions of the embodied experiences prompting them to create visual artefacts, rather than the visual images themselves, and thus could be critiqued for continued over-reliance on discursive data. However, we would argue that producing visual materials and using them as the focus of interviews and discussions is a useful way of moving towards a multi-modal form of data collection which allows participants to capture and reflect on particular moments of embodied experience and engage more fully with multiple modalities of experience than a traditional interview or discussion.

We are in the process of developing a poststructural, phenomenological method of analysis for the interviews following Langdridge's (2007) approach, which applies both a hermeneutics of description, and a hermeneutics of suspicion, to the data (drawing on Ricoeur, 1970). This allows for both an empathetic engagement with lived experience, and a critical analysis of the way that narratives of embodied experience are located within power dynamics. The preliminary analyses below thus aimed to present a sense of the participants' lived experience whilst relating it to wider issues of embodiment and socio-spatial context.

Analysis

One of the most striking aspects of the data so far in terms of embodied experiences is the common expression that bisexual spaces are places where participants feel that they can breathe differently. Relating to this, the title of this chapter comes from this comment by a participant in a pilot workshop for this study, describing her first experience of being in bisexual space. Below (see Figure 17.1) is the sculpture that she produced about her experience and her subsequent description of it:

> Um, well I did a two sided collage sculpture and um, I guess this side, um, I picked out a lot of pictures of water and sky and birds and sort of this expanse of feeling which I was just feeling when I was out on the deck (laughs) and just thinking to myself, my God, I have this whole afternoon to be *myself*, and I can just *be* bisexual, and it just felt *so amazing* and I'd never felt that before and it was just like, wow, I didn't know that I could feel this relaxed in my body, and I actually do, because I go around on my bike with my muscles and my body very contracted all the time, and

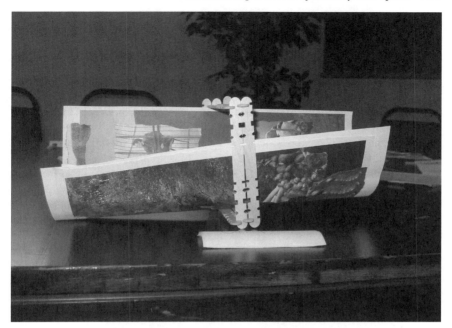

Figure 17.1 Participant sculpture.

it just felt like these *spaces* opening up within my muscles and just like, air, and opening up the spaces, yeah, it just was an incred-(outbreath/sigh) yhaaaaaaa, it feels *good*, you know. So I wanted to express that.

This embodied sense of bi space as an airy place where you can relax bodily, breathe out and 'just *be* bisexual' also emerged in several of the individual interviews. From a phenomenological perspective, this participant appears to be describing a sense of interpenetration by the world, an overcoming of Descartian dualistic splits to experience themselves as body-subjects rather than body-objects (Merleau Ponty, 1945/2002). In this extract, the participant describes how, in bi space, her body felt physically more open and spacious inside, than in everyday life. She experienced 'an expanse of feeling', seemingly expanding out of herself into the space and feeling part of it, the boundary between the world and her body becoming less distinct. This is analogous with the participants in Del Busso's research (Del Busso, 2009), who experienced bodily subjectivity when their bodies were in motion, rather than trapped in the gaze of an other. Just as Del Busso's participants found liberation from constraining discourses of desirable femininity in movement, so this participant reports that, in a bisexual space, she experienced a sensation of liberation from her usual experience of 'going round on [her] bike with [her] muscles and [her] body very contracted all the time', where there is a clearer separation between her body and the world.

It is notable that the participants in the initial workshop that this participant was involved in were actually not asked to produce models of their experience of bi space, but of experiences of *home*. It was anticipated that participants would produce collages depicting their actual homes, but, while many did, many also produced models reflecting their experience of bi community space as home, either by itself or in addition to models showing their experiences of their households. In her analysis of the 1990 National Bisexual Conference in the USA, Clare Hemmings talks about how the conference was explicitly conceived as a 'homecoming' for bisexual people, as a safe refuge from a biphobic outside world (2002: 169). Referring to the sense of 'bisexual home' invoked here, Hemmings notes that, in this sense, 'home' is not simply geographical, but a site of meaning within which one both recognizes oneself and is recognised in return' (2002: 169).

Related to this, the data from several of the interviews and some of the workshops suggests that BiCon is indeed a space in which one is 'recognized', and that bisexuality itself is therefore actually less salient at BiCon than in everyday life. As several participants noted, BiCon is a space where bisexuality is the normative centre and everyone is assumed to be either bisexual or bi-friendly. Indeed it was notable that data collected in the later discussions (where participants were asked to model their experience of being at BiCon) were rarely explicitly about bisexuality. Several participants remarked that they noticed bisexuality more in their everyday lives where it was not 'the norm'. This is illustrated in the model (see Figure 17.2) and accompanying description below:

> Erm well. When I'm in, not at BiCon you feel like um, you feel like, kind of like, you *are* bisexual. And you're kinda like separated from everyone else because they think you're weird or something. And they've got the bi colours on the little people. Erm there's like a few bi people I know but it's kind of a thing of everyone else just

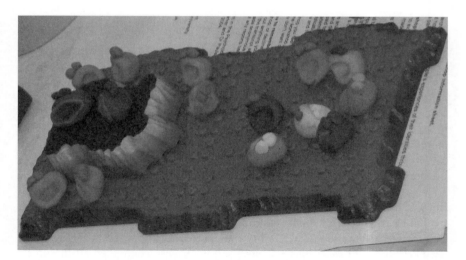

Figure 17.2 Participant model.

thinks you're strange and stuff. But when I'm at BiCon there's loads of different people. And but we don't care we just get on and we like feel normal and stuff. And we don't feel like anything.

Hemmings (2002: 172) describes how the US bisexual conference she studied constructed bisexual group unity through reference to its own internal diversity, positioning difference as the core of bisexual identity. It is interesting how the participant above similarly explicitly refers to there being 'loads of different people' in bi space: people who despite (or perhaps because of) their differences from one another, 'just get on ... and feel normal', whereas in the outside world 'you're separated from everyone else'. The result is that in bi space 'we don't feel like anything', and bi identity is less marked than in everyday life.

Many participants in the photo diary study took pictures on their way to BiCon, and talked about bi space, this 'bisexual home' as a place outside daily life, which had to be literally journeyed to. In the photograph (see Figure 17.3) and excerpt below, the sense of bi space as a place apart from daily life is continued.

Figure 17.3 Photo-diary photograph.

This is the same train station that I go to em, erm, my partner's, one, and then, yeah so it gives always a lovely sort of feeling of, this is *my* station where I get away to bi loveliness and yeah, I just thought, that just *was* part of BiCon, being there. And also just the space, and the nice airiness, the freedom, it kind of just reinforced being free, being able to be self-determined. So yeah, that's why I took these three.

[Interviewer: And that kind of openness, is that about the station, or about...?]

Well I'm usually *reasonably* open, I'm, I said before I'm out at work, which is great, and I try not to sort of like squash bits of meself nowadays, though I know I did very much in the past, but erm I just think I could just re-emphasise, I could just sort of breathe out and there was just all this space and I didn't have to squash meself in or double life there or and it just felt freeing and liberating.

So here we see 'bi loveliness' as something the participant feels that she 'gets away to', separate from everyday life. In describing the experience of being on the train to BiCon later, the same participant describes the experience of 'speeding through the countryside untouched by everyday life'. The railway station is a liminal space that's full of people coming and going, and this fits Hemmings's (2002) description of the bi conference space she studied as a 'space with no actual place', without borders or constituents. The participant above experiences this airy space as a space of possibility and self-determination. Bisexual space is also presented as a place where, even if one is 'out' in daily life, you can 'breathe out' and not be 'squashed' or 'contracted'. The sense of expansion and airiness referred

Figure 17.4 Participant model.

to in the first extract is evident in this account too, and again seems to point to the embodied experience of bi space as involving the dissolution of boundaries between subject and object, self and world (Merleau-Ponty, 1945/2002).

This sense of being free to be oneself in bi space without experiencing oneself as separate from/at odds with the world is also found in the following participant's description of her model (see Figure 17.4):

> I have a sort of the four elements in the middle here. I don't know what they really are but that's what they are for me. Because BiCon feels like five bazillion Pagan festivals I've been to and so like Stella I don't have a sense of 'I'M IN BI MODE NOW' but I'm just in me mode and I can let all those closet doors open. So I can be bi and poly and Pagan and into BDSM and whatever and like it's just I can just be me. I can just breathe and that's what the tree is. It's that breathing deep down to the bottom. Where I don't get to do that during the normal days.

Like this participant, several people in the research referred to having multiple minority identities, and this is reflected in the earlier questionnaire data (Barker *et al.*, 2008) which found that many participants identified with minority genders (e.g. trans, genderqueer), religions (particularly forms of paganism), subcultures (e.g. goth, naturism), and relationship or sexual communities (e.g. polyamory, sadomasochism). The current participants largely saw BiCon as a space where these were recognized and accepted. The identities referred to by this participant are generally reflected in the programmes of BiCons where workshops cover interests such as kink (a flogging workshop), polyamory (workshop on time-management and non-monogamy) and spirituality. As well as reiterating the previously discussed sense of BiCon being a space to breathe, this participant also spoke of BiCon as a space where she could be 'all of me' and could 'let all those closet doors open', tying this back to her experience of her own sexuality.

Preliminary analysis of the data presented here, then, suggests that participants in these studies experienced bisexual space as physically and experientially separate from their everyday lives. Bi space is constructed/experienced as a 'home' space where bisexuality and diversity are normalised or taken as read, where bisexuality itself may be less salient, and where there is a sense of interpenetration between the embodied self and the wider world.

Discussion

In this section, we will compare our use of visual and creative methods in workshop-based research on bisexual identity, to our earlier use of discussion-based sessions, arguing that visual methods have several important advantages over traditional methods, and discussing some of the issues that need to be considered when using visual methods in this context.

The most compelling advantage of using visual methods to research bisexual identity is their potential for disrupting the rehearsal of dominant discourses of identity, which result in the reiteration of 'structurally fractured' identity narratives

(Ault, 1999). The preliminary data presented here suggest that visual and creative methods can be used to elicit rich data about the lived experience of bisexual subjectivities that circumvent the rehearsal of these narratives.

We would argue that this is in part because, as Gauntlett (2007) has pointed out, visual methods give participants time to think before answering the question. Semi-structured interviews, in particular, demand a fairly instant response from participants (within the conventions of conversation). Focus group discussions make it difficult for participants to think because other people are talking (and, likely, influencing their own response). Even with written questionnaires the convention is to respond immediately, rather than to take time considering answers. With visual methods, the process of creating a model, drawing, or set of photographs gives participants time (from 15 minutes to several days) to think about their experiences without much influence from anyone else, and to produce and describe artefacts that enable them 'to present a set of ideas all in one go' (Gauntlett and Holzwarth, 2006) rather than being constrained by the linear modality of speech.

We also found that there was much less attempt at 'consensus building' in modelling workshops than in discussion-based sessions. As we outlined above, in discussion-based research workshops on bisexuality, participants are likely to introduce dominant notions that 'love counts more than gender' (Bicon, 2005), or bisexuality means equal attraction to both genders (see Barker *et al.*, 2008), and then trouble these notions to some extent. However, participants would then quickly move on to trying to find commonalities between their experiences, as if the accepted purpose of such discussions were to come to agreements and/or to divine universal rules. However, this was not the case in the workshops using visual methods. One of the accepted conventions of artistic creation is that it is about self-expression and individuality, and in collage and modelling workshops there seemed to be a tacit acceptance that the objects created might all be different. This opened up the possibility that the experiences or identities expressed in the subsequent discussion might also all be different and that there might well be inconsistencies and contradictions between and within people's stories. Participants often pointed out similarities between their creations and those presented by other people, but it seemed just as common for people to speak up in order to point out how different their creations were. The discussion following this then seemed to flow naturally into drawing out multiple ways of experiencing bisexual identity, some of which were shared between some members of the group and some of which were unique. The methods of modelling and collage allowed people to articulate their own experiences and have them affirmed without people feeling the need to link into their own stories or offer advice, as often happens in conversation.

We have argued thus far that the usefulness of conventional discourse-based approaches to research is limited by the constraints that language places upon participants, and have also noted that participants' understandings of how to 'do' group discussion shaped the data we gathered. Whilst our discussion group participants struggled to coherently articulate their identities in response to interview questions, they were able, when given time and engaged in a creative process, to present a complex and sometimes contradictory set of ideas simultaneously and coherently (Gauntlett, 2007). Visual methods, then, in our experience, are helpful in producing data that overcome these constraints and meet the phenomenological aims of eliciting rich descriptions of lived experience and multiple meanings, rather than universal understandings (Langdridge, 2007).

If visual methodologies remove one set of constraints from data elicitation, however, they add another, and in this final section we briefly outline some issues for consideration when using visual and creative methods in fieldwork.

A key concern in designing our methodology was to minimize the impression that participants were required to produce 'something arty'. We therefore selected methods of artifact production that we hoped would avoid participants feeling constrained by concerns about artistic merit. In a pilot workshop for this project, we provided participants with collage materials, but some participants commented that they had found it difficult to engage with the 'artiness' of the creative process:

> I think it's probably fine for artistic people but I find it very hard to express myself artistically.
>
> (Pilot workshop participant)

Using Lego™ was particularly helpful in addressing this, as participants did not seem to share the same anxieties about their ability to model in Lego™ as they did about their abilities to make a model in plasticine (whose free-form nature felt too much like 'sculpture' to some), or to produce a collage. For most participants, the Lego™ and Plasticine-based workshops seemed to be less intimidating and more accessible than the collage-based workshops, with less expressions of anxiety about not being 'arty', and more positive comments about enjoying fun, playful elements of the workshop.

In both the modelling-based workshops, and the collage-based pilot project, we found that providing participants with some materials which they could use to structure their creations (such as the pre-made Lego™ figures, pictures from catalogues and magazines, and other craft materials such as glitter and lollipop sticks) helped to mitigate fears about being 'artistic', and lent a sense of playfulness to the workshop which encouraged people to be experimental and creative (Gauntlett 2007: 134). Nevertheless, we found that, even with a medium such as Lego™ participants seemed to share common understandings of how Lego™ should be used, such as that blocks should be fitted together, and that like colours should be contiguous. Some participants also commented that, even with this method, they still found themselves worrying about being artistic, or competing to produce the 'best' model:

> I liked the Lego™. Um, (.) I was feeling really, I was feeling a bit self-conscious, because even though I knew, it was one of those things, even though I knew the point of the Lego™ was that people worry less about being artistically able, even so, I was feeling competitive and worried about my artistic ability in front of the group. I was thinking, 'this is stupid, just get on with the bloody Lego™', but it was no, I had to

be best at the Lego™! And yeah, yeah, I was kind of chuckling at my own inability to (.) um, face the fact I might be slightly crap at something even if it was just Lego™, but.

(Interview participant)

Finally, we found that it was important to be clear with participants about the status and purpose of visual products within the research, and to counter received understandings of the diagnostic role of images in psychological research. We found that our participants sometimes assumed that we were interested in analyzing the visual materials they produced in order to discover something about their inner worlds, and were careful to point out inappropriate inferences they felt the models might suggest to us. For example, the participant who made the model below (Figure 17.5) wrote on the workshop feedback form: 'The house would have had an inside and an outside and windows and solid walls with more time – the slightly unfinished bit isn't a reflection of mental state.'

Being careful to be clear with participants about the status of visual products within our research (as techniques to give people a chance to reflect upon their experiences and speak about them in new ways, rather than as diagnostic tools or artistic endeavours) also had the effect of helping participants to feel more relaxed about producing 'imperfect' visual products.

Figure 17.5 Participant's Lego™ model.

Conclusions

Preliminary analysis of the data presented here suggests that participants in these studies experienced bi space as physically and experientially separate from their everyday lives. Bi space is constructed/experienced as a 'home' space where bisexuality and diversity are normalised or taken as read, where bisexuality itself may be less salient, and where there is a sense of interpenetration between the embodied self and the wider world.

Acknowledgements

We would like to thank the many members of the UK bi community who took part in this research. We are particularly grateful to the organisers of BiCon 2008 for providing the space and support to conduct the workshops on which this chapter is based and, more broadly, for encouraging a greater interface between research and the bi community. An earlier version of this paper was presented at the Annual Conference of the British Sociological Association in April 2009, and we would like to thank delegates for their useful comments. Thanks also to Paula Reavey for her invaluable help in supervising the research and providing editorial support through the preparation of this chapter.

Note

1 Participants were asked: 'Do you have a physical or mental health issue which affects your day to day life?'

References

Ault, A. (1996). Hegemonic discourse in an oppositional community: lesbian feminist stigmatization of bisexual women. In B. Beemyn and M. Eliason (Eds), *Queer studies.* London: New York University Press, pp. 204–216.

Ault, A. (1999). Ambiguous identity in an unambiguous sex/gender structure: the case of bisexual women. In M. Storr (Ed.), *Bisexuality: a critical reader.* London: Routledge, pp. 167–185.

Berenson, C. (2002). What's in a name? Bisexual women define their terms. In D. Atkins (Ed.), *Bisexual women in the twenty-first century.* New York: Haworth Press, pp. 9–21.

Barker M., Bowes-Catton, H., Iantaffi, A., Cassidy, A., and Brewer, L. (2008). British bisexuality: a snapshot of bisexual identities in the UK. *Journal of Bisexuality*, *8*, 141–162.

Barker, M., and Langdridge, D. (2008). Bisexuality: working with a silenced sexuality. *Feminism & Psychology*, *18*(3), 389–394.

Bell, D. (2006). Bodies, technologies, spaces: on 'dogging'. *Sexualities, 9*(4), 387–407.

BiCon (2005). Retrieved 27 November 2010 from www.urban75.net/vbulletin/threads/93105-BiCon-2005-The-23rd-Annual-Bisexual-Convention.

BiReCon (2008). Retrieved 4 June 2009 from http://www.bicon2008.org.uk/BiReCon.html.

Bower, J., Gurevich, M., and Mathieson, C. (2002). (Con)tested identities: bisexual women reorient sexuality. In D. Atkins (Ed.), *Bisexual women in the twenty-first century*. New York: Haworth Press, pp. 25–52.

Bowes-Catton, H. (2007). Resisting the binary: discourses of identity and diversity in bisexual politics 1988–1996. *Lesbian & Gay Psychology Review*, 8(1), 58–71.

Del Busso, L. (2009). *Being-in-motion: movement, femininity and space in young women's narratives of their embodied experiences in everyday life.* Unpublished PhD thesis, London South Bank University.

Featherstone, M., Hepworth, M. and Turner, B. S. (1991). *The body: social process and cultural theory.* London: Sage.

Gauntlett, D. (2007). *Creative explorations: new approaches to identities and audiences.* London: Routledge.

Gauntlett, D. and Holzwarth, P. (2006). Creative and visual methods for exploring identities – a conversation between David Gauntlett and Peter Holzwarth. Retrieved 16 September 2009 from http://www.artlab.org.uk/interview-mar06.htm.

Hagger-Johnson, G. E., McManus, J., Hutchison, C., and Barker, M. (2006). Building partnerships with the voluntary sector. *The Psychologist, 19,* 156–158.

Hemmings, C. (2002). *Bisexual spaces: a geography of sexuality and gender.* London: Routledge.

Highmore, B. (2002). *Everyday life and cultural theory.* London: Routledge.

Ingram, G. B., Bouthillette, A. and Retter, Y. (Eds) (1997). *Queers in space: communities/public places/sites of resistance.* Seattle: Bay Press.

Langdridge, D. (2007). *Phenomenological psychology: theory, research and method.* Harlow: Pearson Education.

Merleau-Ponty, M. (1945/2002). *Phenomenology of perception* (trans. C. Smith). London: Routledge.

O'Neill, M. (2008). *Ethno-mimesis as performative praxis.* Presentation at the first Visual Psychologies Conference, University of Leicester, 4 June 2008.

Packard, J. (2008). 'I'm gonna show you what it's really like out here': the power and limitation of participatory visual methods. *Visual Studies, 23*(1), 63–77.

Petford, B. (2003). Power in the darkness: some thoughts on the marginalization of bisexuality in psychological literature. *Lesbian and Gay Psychology Review, 4*(2), 5–13.

Reavey, P. and Johnson, K. (2008). Visual approaches: using and interpreting images in qualitative research. In C. Willig and W. Stainton Rogers (Eds) *The Sage handbook of qualitative research methods.* London: Sage, pp. 296–314.

Reavey, P. (2008). *Back to experience. Material subjectivities and the visual.* Presentation at the first Visual Psychologies Conference, University of Leicester, 4 June 2008.

Ricoeur, P. (1970). *Freud and philosophy: an essay on interpretation* (trans. D. Savage). New Haven, CT: Yale University Press.

Ryan-Flood, R., and Rooke, A. (2009). Que(e)rying methodology: lessons and dilemmas from lesbian lives: an introduction. *Journal of Lesbian Studies, 13*(2), 115–121.

Stam, H. J. (Ed.) (1998). *The body and psychology.* London: Sage.

Valentine, G., and Skelton, T. (2003). Finding oneself, losing oneself: the lesbian and gay 'scene' as a paradoxical space. *International Journal of Urban and Regional Research, 27,* 849–866.

Wilkinson, S. (1999). Focus groups: a feminist method. *Psychology of Women Quarterly, 23*(2), 221–244.

18 Travelling along 'rivers of experience'

Personal Construct Psychology and visual metaphors in research

Alex Iantaffi

Seeking embodied knowledge and swimming along a river of questions

Thirteen years ago I officially became a researcher and an academic. I had just received a studentship to undertake a PhD at the University of Reading, focusing on issues related to social justice in education, and I was faced with a vast sea of dilemmas. I knew that I wanted to research the experiences of disabled women students in Higher Education, but I also knew I had to face two major challenges: what to focus on exactly and how to carry out this study. The latter was the beginning of a continuing journey into, and fascination with, the landscape of research methodologies. Once I decided that my focus would be on the identities, both collective and individual, of women experiencing a wide range of disabilities (physical, sensory, intellectual), then I knew that verbal methods alone would not be sufficient to explore this topic within the theoretical framework that was emerging for my work. Indeed I felt strongly that many of those experiences might not be readily available through language to the participants since their stories had, at that time, mostly remained invisible and untouched (Blackwell-Stratton *et al.*, 1988; Matthews, 1994; Cornwall, 1995; Potts and Price, 1995). During the piloting phase, this was confirmed by the type of written narrative that I received by participants. All the narratives focused on the medical stories (e.g. listing limitations and physical accommodations needed to access classes) that affected their lives as students and which were rattled off with practised ease. Other issues, such as what those experiences meant to them and how they might be shaping their sense of self, remained largely unarticulated and yet just present enough, beneath the surface, such as follow-up conversations, to spur me on.

Several of my methodological, epistemological and research questions started to become entwined. For example, how could I talk about issues of disability and gender with my participants without imposing my own preconceptions, that is my own experiences and understanding of gender or what it meant to be a student in Higher Education? Which theories best reflected my own belief in research as a collaboration, yet acknowledged the power differential between my position as a researcher and PhD student and the position of my participants? What methodological approach would enable me to step back enough for the participants' stories to emerge and how could I pursue further what those stories meant to them, in their own words? How would, or even could, I define disability in a non-pathologising way, if I truly wanted to avoid the pitfalls I could see in the medical model?

I wanted to explore their own journeys, which had led them to become students in Higher Education at the moment of the interview, and to observe whether and how disability and gender came into play, if at all. The idea of using the research process as exploration of those topics, not just for me but for the participants themselves started to emerge. I wanted a participatory model of research that was in line with some of the radical feminist thinking of the time, which rejected 'grand theories', which tried to explain the world (Stanley and Wise, 1993), and rather sought to understand the world (McCarthy, 1996) and even more so individual people in it. The latter approach moves away from the more traditional approach to research, which may seek to uncover universal patterns, and towards a model of research that values context-specific knowledge, promoting a more in-depth understanding of specific issues and leaving the reader to decide how such findings may or may not apply to their own context. Such an approach to research also challenged the dichotomy between theory and practice and I became fascinated by the idea of praxis, that is the application of theory to a particular task, in this case research, as a way to synthetise different epistemological and methodological approaches for a purpose (Siraj-Blatchford, 1994). What I was after was embodied knowledge because that was the site of my participant experiences of both disability and gender. By embodied knowledge I mean the lived experiences of their lives, which unfold in a dialogical and relational manner, rather than being crystallised in time or place (Shotter, 1997). As such this type of knowledge is also an outcome of the relationship between researcher and participant as it emerges from the joint reflection on a topic of interest to the former and the life of the latter. It seemed to me that uncovering this embodied knowledge also required new tools, which could tap into those constructs that had not yet been verbalised. Initially I thought I would use metaphors, because of the rich, often visual landscape they could offer and then realised that I needed another step before reaching a more crystallised verbal image, which could be captured in a metaphor. This step would be one that would allow me to co-create shared meaning with my participants and, in doing so, to see them as co-researchers in this process, albeit temporarily (Fromm, 1992). This is also the step, and the tool, that I seek to share in this chapter: the river of experience. I developed the latter over the years as both a research and a teaching tool. However, before I can go on to explain more fully what this tool is and how it works, I need to ask you to travel a little further with me along the current to frame this tool within the theoretical framework from which it was born, that is Personal Construct Psychology (PCP).

Big ideas from a small (theoretical) island: a whistlestop tour of PCP

After exploring various theoretical and methodological approaches to qualitative research, I realised that I wanted a framework that allowed me to enter into a dialogical relationship with my participants, so that I could meet them 'on the intersubjective level, which makes understanding possible' (Habermas, 1974: 11) and that also allowed a non-verbal exploration of issues that may not have previously been talked about by the participants. At the time, my 'working theory' was born from the firm belief that each one of us, throughout our lives, generates theories from our beliefs, experiences, attitudes and other facets of our being. These theories are usually a mixture of original, individual traits and social, collective ones, and we use them to make sense of the world and of ourselves. I soon found that my working theory was well reflected in Personal Construct Psychology (PCP), a theory that seems to have a loyal, if somewhat small following of clinicians, researchers, educators, health and business professionals and academics dispersed across the globe. Since the tool here described was developed within this framework, it seems opportune to provide a brief tour of this approach to understanding people.

The theory of personal constructs, more commonly known as PCP, was elaborated by George Kelly (1955) and offers tools [see Pope and Denicolo (2000) for a more complete description of PCP methodologies] which can be used to dialogue with other people on a one-to-one basis, interacting in a way which could be meaningful and enriching for both them and the researcher. PCP, in fact, sees other people's constructs as their way of making sense of the world around them, and of themselves, and does not view some constructs as superior to, or better than, others. Science, in this context, does not hold the monopoly on valid thinking, and not even on itself, since 'every man [sic] is, in his own particular way, a scientist' (Kelly, 1955: 5). Although developed within a clinical framework, Kelly's approach is extremely flexible and highly suitable for researching various fields, because of its open approach and recognition of the personal dimension of construing ourselves and the world. As Salmon noted 'personal construct theory, grounded as it is in ordinary human experience, seems to represent that rare thing – "nothing so practical as a good theory" ' (Salmon, 1988: 13), since it not only includes an understanding of how people may operate in the world, but also how this understanding can be uncovered both in clinical and research settings, through tools such as the repertory grid or laddering up/down interviews. It is also a theory that leaves room for other theories as well, since it strives to understand the person as a whole. For example, some writers in the field have connected PCP to Merleau-Ponty's phenomenology of the body (1962) as well as Bateson's ideas on systems (1972).

'Human experience' can be seen as the heart of PCP and it is through exploring people's own constructs that the PCP practitioner strives to achieve an understanding, rather than an explanation, of it. Construct systems, that is the collections of experiences, ideas and beliefs that may be organised around a central theme (e.g. what it is like to be a student in an English University), are what each one of us uses to understand, learn, make choices, and ultimately organise our lives around. Constructs are the complex combination of our beliefs, attitudes, experiences, feelings, thoughts and decisions and, as such, the spectacles through which we look at ourselves, others and the world. Our systems are not static, but change continuously through life and the experience of living and interacting with both our inner and outer worlds. Those systems do not exist in isolation, but in relation to other people's systems, which allows room for social and political analysis of construct systems within PCP, as Bannister (2003) has clearly shown in his writing and life. One of the most appealing and possibly political statements made by Kelly, in my opinion, is that we do not need to be victims of our biographies (Kelly, 1955: 21–22). This is due to the fact that, within PCP, we construe our own identities and interpretation of events and, therefore, we have agency over our own construct systems, beliefs and identities.

Within Kelly's framework, we are given the freedom to change ourselves, our understanding of and beliefs about other people and the world, without having to necessarily be who we are expected to be. To the young academic that I was, this most certainly seemed an emancipatory approach to research praxis, where the researcher and the participants can work together to negotiate not solely meaning, but also change, by claiming the ability to live consciously and having agency on an individual level, which in turn affects the collective level. Change is, of course, never simple, but the hope of its possibility is often a vital part of our enthusiasm towards life, and therefore essential and central to any existence. The appeal of PCP lay, for me, in the promise of that possibility, the freedom to become our most authentic selves and to see that as a constantly evolving process of change and creativity. The reflexive aspect of the theory was also another strength that attracted me to this theory. The contemplation of, and reflection on, myself, and the contemplation and reflections of others can, in this framework, be seen as valid research as we attempt to construe and re-construe ourselves and others, reclaiming our stories as part of a wider web of meaning. It is by travelling along those currents, on such a wider web, that I came across the methodological tool of the 'snake', which then became the 'river of experience'. If, in fact, we understand constructs to be more than mere verbal labels but rather complex representations of our inner worlds, than verbal language can be limiting to both researcher and participant when trying to reach a common understanding of the topic explored. PCP offered more than methods based on linguistic interactions as it encompassed other ways of representing our inner worlds, such as drawing, which, for example, was used extensively by Ravenette (2003) in his work with children. As such, PCP offered me the opportunity to widen my methodological repertoire as a young PhD student and realise the possibilities of exploring people's constructs visually as well as verbally.

Wading through many waters: exploring the rivers of experience

A belief that guided me as a researcher early on in my journey is that we can never truly know our participants and their worlds but only their perceptions of it, filtered through our understanding. This is, in my opinion, also the case for observations, since even then all that we can truly know is the meaning that we give to that which is being observed. Nevertheless, as researchers using qualitative methods, we can create spaces between ourselves and our participants, where, through dialogue and reflection, we can inhabit a shared portion of our worlds, at least during our fieldwork and often beyond, if we involve our participants in latter parts of our studies, such as data interpretation. This process creates what we call data as well as, hopefully, shared meaning. The latter then enables the participants to have a more authentic voice in the findings that are usually presented by the researcher(s) alone. The challenge, however, is how can we create shared meaning and explore the participants' worlds of experience without constraining them within a path so narrow that we, as researchers, might miss what we were not planning or expecting to find? For example, if I had chosen an entirely verbal form of interviewing, I might have missed the significance of early experiences of schooling on my participants' current experiences of Higher Education. Instead, by asking them to draw their river from any point they chose to in their lives, I realised how many participants started from a significant experience in elementary schooling. As well as choosing a more visually-guided interview method, I also chose to ask only two questions (What led you to become a student in Higher Education? Could you draw, or describe, an image that sums up your experience of being a disabled woman student in Higher Education?) Starting from the first question, I asked the participants to not answer it verbally but rather to reflect on it whilst drawing a river, which I would then use as a map for our interview. The river of experience is a different name developed for an expansion of the 'snake technique'. The latter was first used, within a constructivist context, as a research tool for exploring participants' career stories by Denicolo and Pope (1990: 158– 159). The snake technique is described in the following quotation.

> They [the participants] were asked to reflect in private, visualising and drawing their lives as a winding snake in which each 'twist' in its body represented a change in direction of, or intention for, their career. Brief annotations were to be included, for each twist, about the experience or incident which precipitated the change. No instruction was given about when in their lives to start considering whether experiences influenced career.

This tool, created just for a specific research study, turned out to be a powerful way of inviting people to connect threads of their stories and weave them together in their own way, using their own words. Over time, the analogy of a river of life or river of experience started to be preferred by Denicolo, Pope and their doctoral students, including myself. Rivers of experience started to take a range of different directions and to be used in a variety of contexts. Personally, I chose to describe this technique as a river of experience because the imagery lent itself to a richer metaphor. To begin with, I would ask participants to think of their life as a river and to imagine each bend in the river to be a significant moment, person or object (e.g. a book or film) that had an impact on how they came to be a student in Higher Education, in this particular example. At this point I also reassured them that the scope of the drawing was not to be 'artistic' and that they could make it as simple or as complex as they wished. In the case of one participant, who was physically unable to draw, I asked her to describe the river to me and gave her the option to have me draw it or to describe the picture created in her head in as much detail as possible. By using the metaphor of the river, I could also invite them to reflect in their drawings not just the main flow of the river but also what tributaries there might be, what currents may be present in different parts of their river and where any confluences may be. Further, participants would be able to imagine their own particular river, which might have waterfalls, rapids and all sorts of features deemed to be relevant to the participants' stories. Although the drawings tended to be fairly simple, as can be seen in the two figures below (see Figures 18.1 and 18.2), the descriptions that the participants used during the interview provided a far richer visual imagery, bringing their sketches to life. For example, they might describe how they navigated particular bends in the river, whether they felt they were 'swimming along' or were 'swept along' or were 'cruising' comfortably.

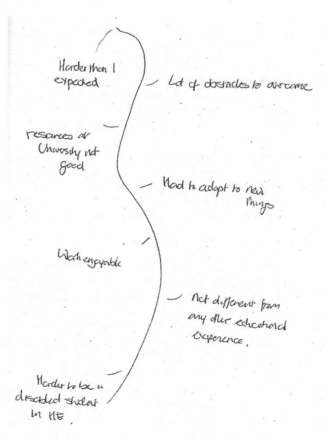

Figure 18.1 Example of river of experience – participant F.

Asking the participants to start from a simple question (what led you to become a student in Higher Education) and imagine their life as a river, enabled me to create a far more unstructured, yet clearly mapped, dialogue with each participant. Something that, I believe, I could not have done through a traditional, purely verbal interview. First of all, it allowed the participant to start at any chronological point, as well as to set the pace and the extent of the dialogue. In turn this gave me the opportunity to elicit each participant's individual constructs whilst also looking out for common milestones, such as the use of terminology similar to that of other participants. I could then delve deeper into both individual and collective meanings

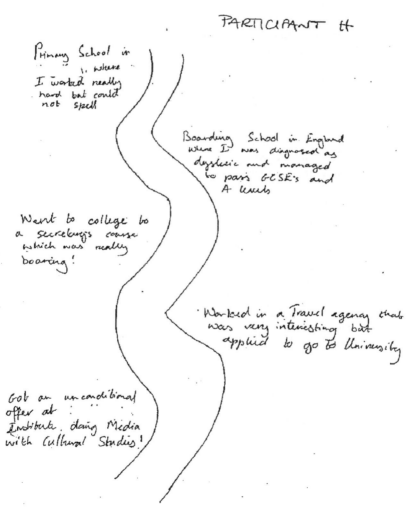

Figure 18.2 Example of river of experience – participant H.

by asking follow up questions, once the participants had given me a 'verbal tour' of their drawings. In those interviews, the rivers became the shared space that the participant and I could inhabit during the research dialogue. In one case, when a participant's mobility restrictions did not allow her to draw the river herself, this sharing became literal, as she asked me to draw the river for her, whilst she talked me through it. This, and similar experiences, also showed me that this technique can be effective beyond the physical ability to draw, since it allows participants to create a visual landscape and, with it, wider possibilities, regardless of whether such landscape is captured on paper or not.

Following my PhD, I realised that the metaphor of the river could be explored even further. What kind of river were the participants thinking of? How did it connect to the larger landscape around them? This could be seen as the wider context of their individual lives or their individual lives in relation to a social context. Where were they in relation to the river described? Swimming, drowning, walking alongside it, washing themselves in it, navigating its waters in a canoe, sailing or speeding along in a motorboat? What kind of relationship did they have with the stories chosen for each bend of the river? I also realised that I could ask them to reflect those questions in their drawings, rather than just asking those questions verbally, leading to far richer visual metaphors than were possible in my first, simple use of this technique. This seemed to be important, as, even when the participant chose just one word to describe a particular point in the river, there was usually another story unfolding around each curve, between one point and the next. Furthermore, the imagery of the river provided the opportunity to look at stories as journeys. Participants then had the choice to think of their lives, or portion of their lives, as rivers of experience along which they travel. The metaphor of the journey opened further opportunities to explore constructs over periods of time and in a variety of contexts. This meant that neither the participants or myself had to believe that the stories we shared were the whole picture or even a static one. Research dialogues could indeed be a process of which written findings are but a snapshot and the process itself could be made transparent by describing it, creating yet another shared space, this time between participants, researcher and readers.

One of the concerns I had when I first started using this technique was that I wanted it to be accessible for as many people as possible, particularly as I was exploring the experiences of disabled women students in higher education I soon realised that, as already stated earlier, the rivers could be highly flexible. I could describe to the participant what I wanted of them, that is to think about their lives as a river of experience, and then offer a variety of possibilities. I could draw their river under their guidance, they could draw their own river or they could simply think about what their river would be like and talk me through it. I always do this with all participants, regardless of their apparent abilities, as I want to make sure nobody feels pressured into an activity that they are not comfortable with, for whatever reason. In another project, on peer doctoral supervision, I asked participants to prepare their river of experience before having a constructivist interview with them. At times, I have also used the technique after the first interview, in order to provide an opportunity to reflect on the stories told before further phases of the study. The most important message I like to give participants is that this is but a tool to facilitate a participant-led reflection on aspects of their lives.

The fact that this technique requires little input, beyond mere explanation on the part of the researcher, can be, for some researchers, slightly disconcerting at first, especially if they have previously experienced more researcher-led approaches. However, in my own research, participants have often commented positively on the use of this tool, as can be seen from the following quotes from my PhD research (Iantaffi, 1999).

> It [the river of experience] was quite interesting, it really made you think about how the whole idea about the route to Higher Education. I thought it was an interesting idea, to explore rather than, bang, now you're here. I think when I thought about it at first I thought, Oh help, but when I thought about it more deeply and then I started writing about things, these thoughts came up ...

Of course, some of the characteristics of this tool, which can be seen as advantages, can also create constraints in research. The personal dimension of the rivers created by the participants does mean that the data are unique but also diverse. There are no guarantees of homogeneity across a set of data elicited from a variety of participants. They could all come up with individual, unique constructs, which is something that needs to be considered at the onset of a project. The singularity of the rivers and the stories being told by participants in their own way, using their own words, rather than being prompted by the researcher, contribute to creating a tool for research that is participatory and compatible with epistemological paradigms (e.g. radical feminist theory, social constructionism) that value authenticity, that is, congruence between research narratives and lived experiences, over objectivity. Nevertheless, such approaches to research entail a certain level of 'risk', particularly for new researchers who may find it challenging to explore connections, or the lack of, across a diverse data set. Furthermore, although the river of experience has been mainly developed as a research tool, one of its purposes is to encourage a deeper understanding of an individual's constructs and their connections. This means that this tool can be used as a means for reflection by researchers, as a teaching activity by educators seeking to encourage students' reflexivity and by clinicians in therapeutic settings. Within a research context, since this method can entail surprising and sensitive revelations for the participants, as well as the researcher, this technique should always be used with care and attention. Researchers should tread carefully, ensuring that they are not maneuvering participants to reveal more than they are comfortable with, as well as needing to have a plan for further support available to participants, should it be necessary (e.g. local organisations, helplines, further reading).

Before moving on to briefly describing how the rivers can also be used as a teaching and clinical tool, I'd like to say a few words on the relationship between the river of experience and the wider context within which it was developed, that is, PCP. This tool privileges the position of the participant as co-researcher and therefore the idea of the person as scientist as well as highlighting the nature of knowledge as being constructed by individuals within a social network of relationships. It is also based on the premise, stated earlier, that research is an enterprise of co-construction between researcher(s) and participant(s): the river is a weaving of stories told in a particular context to a particular person for specific purposes. The latter statement implies that, in this context, experiences are seen as stories rather than undisputable, objective facts, for which only one account is possible and that constructs evolve over time and in relation to other constructs. As such, the river of experience can be a useful tool to show research participants that transformation is always present in our stories and always a possibility in our futures.

Swept away from the rapids of research: rivers as teaching and clinical tools

As highlighted in the previous section, the river of experience is a powerful technique for research but can also be used in other contexts, such as teaching and clinical work. It is usage in such contexts that I would like to briefly discuss before moving towards some final reflections to conclude the journey shared in this chapter. When facilitating learning around gender and sexuality, either with students in Higher Education or with health professionals, I have found this tool to be invaluable. For example, after introducing some definitions of gender and sexuality, I would describe the technique and ask a group to individually draw a river of experience that depicts how they have arrived to this point, here, today, with their current beliefs about their own gender (and/or sexuality). They are never asked to share their rivers with anyone else in the group but they often share insights gained through the exercise, which is always quoted as helpful in evaluations. I have also used the river in order to encourage students to reflect on their own learning journeys or explore what expectations they might have at the beginning of a new course. Because people are asked to draw their rivers individually, I have found this to be a useful technique with larger groups, as well as smaller groups, as a way of engaging them on a deeper level of learning by making the issues discussed not just personal but also pertinent to their lives. I have also used the latter to highlight the influence that personal beliefs and experiences have on professional values, practices and judgements. For example, what are the stories, people and crucial events that we carry with us when, as family therapists, we work with families. Drawing rivers that reflect on what comes to mind when we think of the word 'family', and then another river reflecting on a particular family with which we work, has proven to be a rich learning experience both on an individual level and when working with colleagues.

The previous example leads me to a brief nod in the direction of the river as a tool for clinical interviews. After some years in academia, I retrained as a systemic psychotherapist and found that being a researcher was a fertile training ground for me as a budding clinician, whilst my later clinical training deepened my abilities as an academic researcher. Both in training and, later, as a registered therapist, I have used this technique with clients. In my experience, it has proven particularly useful when a client, a couple or a family, has come to me with a complex web of stories and events. I introduce them to the technique and ask them to draw a river, either during the session or at home, which stems from the question: what has led you to be here today? In the case of couples or families, they can choose to do this individually or together. For me this has proven effective in punctuating what is important for my client(s) at this particular point in time. When I just ask this question verbally, I might get a brief, and often rather vague answer (e.g. 'it was the right time', 'someone suggested this clinic', etc.). However, when asked to draw a river before discussing the answer verbally, clients seem to be able to access more complex stories as well as to represent complex relations between a range of issues and to communicate layers of meaning, which verbally might take several sessions to be brought to light. From the river we can not only move to conversations about what they would like to focus on or where they would like to go next but also towards creating shared meaning within the therapeutic room. When used with couples or families, this shared meaning is also woven amongst clients and it starts creating a web that can hopefully hold the therapeutic work to come. The river can then become a tool to be revisited, thus offering opportunities for relational reflexivity (Burnham, 2005) in the therapeutic context, that is, moments in which therapists and clients can touch base on how the process of therapy is going for them or reflect on what is happening in this moment, between them. Once again, the visual representation can enable both client and therapist to access a complex picture in a more immediate way and often to access both cognition and affect simultaneously by engaging the person in a kinaesthetic manner.

Ripples and reflections

This seems an apt moment to pause and reflect about what is happening in this chapter. As an author, I hope to have navigated the choppy waters of non-linear thinking and that a picture of what a river of experience is and how it can be used has emerged for you, the reader. Before leaving you free to undertake your own journey in the field of visual methodologies in psychology, I would like to offer some final reflections. I have now used this technique for over a decade, in a variety of contexts and with a diverse range of people. The way I used it as a novice academic and PhD candidate is not the way I use it now and I believe that there is room for this tool to be developed even further. One of the conclusions that I have come to, over the years, is that even when using a tool, such as this, which goes beyond the verbal labels that the spoken word can offer, we, as researchers, teachers or clinicians, are still a long way away from the actual experience of the people we are working with. Drawings, metaphors or any other kind of images or visual representations are still constructs that show us someone's understanding and translation of their own experience. We cannot directly access the latter or generate analyses that are devoid of our own biases and construct systems.

Every time I undertake a river of experience with someone, I am not just entering their own worlds of experience but also my own. I have written elsewhere

(Iantaffi, 2006) about my belief that research is a value-laden process, 'a dialogical adventure undertaken by both researcher and participant' (op. cit.: 225), which is far from hygienic. Using rivers of experience allows me to also reflect on my own positions as a researcher, teacher or clinician by noticing not just my cognitive but also my emotional reactions to someone's experience and to do so by accessing what seems to be a more visual, creative and less linear part of my brain (for further information on right/left brain hemispheres, see MacNeilage *et al.*, 2009). As a writer, it gives me an opportunity to share with the reader the process by which I have reached my conclusions so that they can judge by themselves the validity and applicability of my findings. The river belongs to the person who draws it but my interpretation of it is what is shared with the larger academic community, as that individual river is juxtaposed to others and to the wider context of the research process. Nevertheless, I still believe that the river of experience can also be a tool that allows participants to access a wider vocabulary, both verbal and visual, whilst trying to convey the complexities of their lives and experiences to a researcher. Finally, despite being a tool that appears linear, the river of experience can be used to challenge traditional, linear thinking in research, since it provides us with an opportunity to explore the participants' landscapes further and on a multiplicity of inter-related and simultaneous levels. As stated earlier, we can probe into the landscape surrounding the river, enquire about the pace of the journey, the mode of transport along the river and even delve into what is not on the page as well as the unlabelled curves from one bend to the next. Even though this tool involves drawing, the limit is not artistic skill but only the bounds of our own imagination.

References

Bannister, D. (2003). Personal construct theory and politics and the politics of personal construct theory. In F. Fransella (Ed.) *International handbook of personal construct psychology*. Chichester: Wiley, pp. 181–189.

Bateson, G. (1972). *Steps to an ecology of mind*. New York: Ballantine.

Blackwell-Stratton, M., Breslin, M. L., Mayerson, A. B. and Bailey, S. (1988). Smashing icons: disabled women and the disability and women's movements. In M. Fine and A. Asch (Eds) *Women with disabilities. Essays in psychology, culture, and politics*. Philadelphia, PA: Temple University Press, pp. 306–332.

Burnham J. (2005). Relational reflexivity: a tool for socially constructing therapeutic relationships. In C. Flaskas, B. Mason and A. Perlesz (Eds) *The space between: experience, context and process in the therapeutic relationship*. London: Karnac Books, pp. 1–18.

Cornwall, J. (1995). Psychology, disability and equal opportunity. *The Psychologist*, 8, 396–397.

Denicolo, P. and Pope, M. (1990). Adults learning – teachers thinking. In C. Day, M. Pope and P. Denicolo (Eds.) *Insight into teachers, thinking and practice*. Basingstoke: The Falmer Press, pp. 155–169.

Fromm, M. (1992). Difficulties of asking people what their constructs are. In *European perspectives in personal construct psychology. Inaugural Conference of the EPCA*, York, EPCA, pp. 115–120.

Habermas, J. (1974). *Theory and practice.* London: Heinemann.

Iantaffi, A. (1999). *Lost tales? The academic experiences of some disabled women students in higher education in England.* Unpublished PhD Thesis, University of Reading, UK.

Iantaffi A. (2006). An hygienic process? Researcher and participants construing each other's worlds. In: P. Caputi, H. Foster and L. Viney (Eds) *Personal construct psychology. New ideas.* Chichester, UK: John Wiley, pp. 215–226.

Kelly, G. A. (1955). *The psychology of personal constructs.* New York: W.W. Norton.

Matthews, J. (1994). Empowering disabled women in higher education. In S. Davies, C. Lubelska and J. Quinn (Eds) *Changing the subject. Women in higher education.* London: Taylor & Francis, pp. 138–145.

McCarthy, E. D. (1996). *Knowledge as culture. The new sociology of knowledge.* London: Routledge.

MacNeilage, P. F., Rogers, L. J., and Vallortigara, G. (2009). Evolutionary origins of your right and left brain. *Scientific American Magazine*, July, 60–67.

Merleau-Ponty, M. (1962). *Phenomenology of perception.* New York: The Humanities Press.

Pope, M. and Denicolo, P. (2000). *Transformative education: personal construct approaches to practice and research.* London: Taylor & Francis

Potts T. and Price J. (1995). Out of the blood and spirit of our lives: the place of the body in academic feminism. In L. Morley and V. Walsh (Eds) *Feminist academics. Creative agents for change.* London: Taylor & Francis, pp. 102–115.

Ravenette, T. (2003). Constructive intervention when children are presented as problems. In F. Fransella (Ed.) *International handbook of personal construct psychology.* Chichester: Wiley, pp. 283–293.

Salmon, P. (1988). *Psychology for teachers. An alternative approach.* London: Hutchinson.

Shotter, J. (1997). The social construction of our 'inner' lives. *Journal of Constructivist Psychology*, 10(1), 7–24.

Siraj-Blatchford, I. (1994). *Praxis makes perfect: critical educational research for social justice.* Ticknall: Education Now Books.

Stanley, L. and Wise, S. (1993). *Breaking out again. Feminist ontology and epistemology.* London: Routledge.

19 Psychogeography and the study of social environments

Extending visual methodological research in psychology

Alexander John Bridger

Introduction

In this chapter, I will reflect upon how walking can be used as a visual method, and how experiences of walking, writing narrative accounts and creating subverted maps can all contribute to the study of subjective experience and material environments. This work extends qualitative research in psychology in arguing for a 'turn to place' in psychology. The rationale for this work is to evaluate the extent to which the situationist concepts of détournement and the dérive can be used as strategies for visual research. I will refer to empirical examples from my research at Ground Zero, New York to substantiate the claims made. The aims are not only to interpret environments as social texts and to reflect on our experiences of being in places but also more importantly to question what can often be the taken for granted ways in which we think about and experience the world. It is important to challenge the ways in which we would ordinarily identify or associate with our surroundings so that we can dissociate ourselves in places in order to begin to imagine what environments of the future could look like. Although I, like the situationists, do not aim to map out what future environments would look like, because this is something that would be decided by the people through radical action. I offer my analysis as one possible way to interpret environments but it is important to acknowledge the plurality of ways in which environments can be studied. The situationists aimed to understand social environments as texts in order to envision what non-capitalist cities would look like, although they never stated what these environments would look like. In this work I will reflect on the extent to which this is possible within psychological research.[1]

Methodological resources: situationism and critical psychology

In order to understand the conditions of urban living, it is important that researchers walk the streets and that they study public spaces as political spaces (Hayes, 2003). Our experiences of walking in places can be documented not only with talk and text (for example, narrative accounts, poems and songs) but also with 'paintings, maps and landscapes' (Barnes and Duncan, 1992: 5). I draw on literature from geography (Harley, 1988a, 1988b, 1992; Thrift, 2004), critical psychology (Burnett *et al.*, 2004; Grup de Lesbianes Feministes, 2005; Precarias a la Deriva, 2005; Rose, 1999), cultural studies (Pinder, 1996, 2000, 2005) and urban theory (Harley, 1988a, 1988b, 1992; Joyce, 2003; Sadler, 1998) to situate the basis of this research, which I will discuss in more depth in this chapter. I focus on the French section of the Situationist International from the mid to late 1950s and early 1960s. It was this phase of their work where they questioned the assumptions of urban town planning which they argued to be based on 'the dominant language of capitalism, rationalism, modernization, the "Puritan work ethic", and spectacle' (Sadler, 1998: 96). The word 'spectacle' refers to a concept developed by Guy Debord (1967), whereby society is viewed as a spectacle and people within society are spectators. In the society of the spectacle, spectators are supposed to be duped by the spectacle, whereas the situationists and other radically orientated thinkers are aware of other peoples' oppression and they strive to find the means to completely transform everyday life (Debord, 1967; Vaneigem, 1967).

The situationists referred to a practice called psychogeography whereby they actively disorientated themselves in places to open themselves up to how they experienced and made sense of the environment. The aims were to critique the capitalist gentrification of cities by walking and they documented these walks with stories and poems.

Now I will refer to how the situationist concepts of détournement and dérive can be applied to what is referred to as psychogeographical studies of environments as visual texts. Détournement was an important political concept for the situationists, which referred to the importance of diverting and changing the meaning of words, images and sounds (International, 1959). The situationists challenged dominant discourses of literature, art and television by replacing the dialogue in films and comic strips, writing political articles and pamphlets, creating maps and by intervening and disrupting public events. They were against the capitalist order of things and they sought to create an anti-capitalist mode of living. The situationist concept of drifting, otherwise known as the *dérive*, was applied to how they used walking as a political act. The practice of doing dérives was about 'direct, effective intervention' to create 'new situationist ambiances' which would lead to 'permanent change' (Khatib, 1958: n.p). Debord defined the dérive as:

A technique of rapid passage through varied ambiances. Dérives involve playful-constructive behaviour and awareness of psychogeographical effects, and are thus quite different from the classic notions of journey or stroll. In a dérive one or more persons during a certain period drop their relations, their work and leisure activities and all other usual motives for movement and action, and let themselves be drawn by the attractions of the terrain and the encounters they find there. Chance is less an important factor in this activity than one might think: from a dérive point of view, cities have psychogeographical contours, with constant currents, fixed points and vortexes that strongly encourage and discourage entry into or exit from certain zones.

(Debord, 1958: n.p)

Kotanyi and Vaneigem's (1961) aims were to inspire people to question how they think and act in social spaces. Many people have been inspired by the work of the situationists (Manchester Area Psychogeographic, London Area Psychogeographic, Materialist Psychogeographic Affiliation, Loiterers Resistance Movement and the Bored in the City Collective). They have produced new techniques and practices of disorientation in order to question how environments are experienced and how these types of places are used and could be used. The situationists used dérives to emotionally disorientate themselves in places so that they would be more 'open' to new experiences and how places could make them feel (Debord, 1958). They also used dérives to investigate particular areas of cities. Debord (1958) argued that the aims of emotional disorientation and investigations of particular areas over-lapped. The implications of doing dérives meant that the situationists could demarcate their positions as antagonistic to dominant society.

Situationist methods in practice

I aimed to study Ground Zero by drawing on existing psychogeographical theory and research, by reflecting on my position in the research and by thinking about the extent to which it is possible to disassociate oneself from environments. Debord (1958) specified that the most productive dérives take place in groups of two or more, so individuals can cross-check their findings with others to generate objective statements. I had initially planned to do the dérive at Ground Zero on my own, but decided to cross-check my observations with another person. My brother reflected on his thoughts and experiences by writing in a diary.

In terms of the reflexive considerations of this research, it is important to address how the situationists utilised their reflexive approach. Although the situationists reflected upon the contemporary social conditions that shaped how the 'present' context could be understood, they neglected to examine their own subjective responses to environments. They did not engage with how their personal standpoints would shape their understandings of social environments. This is one reason why it is necessary to mobilise autoethnography as a response to this limitation of situationism. I understand and deploy autoethnography as a means through which to reflect on my position in the research and to use it as an observational method, observing social environments. Autoethnography is different to ethnography in that the latter method does not involve addressing the role of the researcher in the research but, rather, extends to the study of other cultures. Ellis and Bochner (2000) discuss how autoethnographic responses can be documented not just in traditional academic prose, but also through stories, poems, fiction and photographs. Furthermore, Burnett *et al.* (2004) undertook an ethnographical research project in London, where they used diaries and cameras to reflect on their experiences of walking. Their dérive account was written as a narrative account interspersed with photographs to visually represent the places visited. I draw inspiration from how they documented the dérive as a narrative in this work. In autoethnographic research, researchers reflect on their roles in the research as they are the only participants in the research (Ellis, 2000). A key criticism of autoethnography is that it is individualistic (Sparkes, 2000) and entails an over-indulgent reflexive position by researchers (Atkinson, 1997). However, it can be argued that if personal responses are understood as being produced from within particular social, cultural and political contexts (Holt, 2003) and if the personal is understood as being political, then this is one way to tackle potential criticisms that autoethnography is too individualistic and over-reflective.

Having discussed the theoretical framework of the situationists and how elements of détournement and the dérive are drawn on, I will now explain how these concepts can be utilised as part of a visual qualitative method in psychology. Psychogeographical research is different to other modes of psychological research in that the aims are to develop a radical activist dimension to psychological research. Some of the current qualitative and critical psychological research has quite a docile and apathetic conceptualisation of political practice and it is one of the aims of this type of research to revive this radicalism. It is important to revive radical research in psychology by connecting it to psychogeography, situationism and Marxism. In conceptualising how I conduct psychogeographical research, I did not aim to produce formulaic criteria from which to construct the methodology.

The research aims were primarily methodological because I needed to conceptualise how I could apply principles of situationism to a visual analysis of reading places as social texts. It is important to study the impact of regeneration in towns and cities and to think about the impact on the communities that use those places. As all social relations are enmeshed within power relations, it is important to study the concept of power. I draw on the concept of subject positions from discourse analytic work (Hollway, 1989) and reconfigure this as studying how power is spatialised in places as *spatial relations of power*. Moreover, I wanted to deconstruct what maps and places can mean and to consider research as like a situationist game or strategy, with the aims being to re-consider and re-interpret what the site of Ground Zero meant to me. There was scant research in critical psychology in how to analyse social environments (Burnett *et al.*, 2004; Grup de Lesbianes Feministes, 2005; Precarias a la Deriva, 2005). I wanted to think about how walking could be used as a research method to analyse the site of Ground Zero in New York. This particular site was chosen as the original aims of my PhD research were to deconstruct dominant mass media framings of the events of September 11th and the aftermath. I wanted to reflect critically on how words and images were used by the mass media to make sense of the events. During the research process, I became interested in the situationists and their practice of psychogeography and decided to focus the work on studying Ground Zero and how walking could be used as a qualitative method of research in psychology. At this stage in the research it was necessary to do some preparations for how Ground Zero could be studied. I referred to a Lonely Planet Guide to *New York City* and a Lonely Planet map. I used the book and the map to visually orientate myself at the site before visiting. This was an important activity to do beforehand because it is not possible to subvert/détourn a map or a place unless it is known what it is that needs to be subverted/détourned. So I reflected on how the concepts of the dérive and détournement could be applied to the research aims. The situationists had used a map of Paris in London and so I decided to do something similar by using a map of Bangkok to 'anti-navigate' myself at Ground Zero, New York.

It was an important aim of the research to think about the different ways in which the dérive could be documented. I decided that I would use a notepad to reflect on my experiences of being at Ground Zero and to use photographs to remember where we had walked. At this point I anticipated that the dérive would be written up as a narrative account, which would be interspersed with photographs and that notes from the diary would be used to inform the autoethnographical narrative account. What I aimed to do was to draw on situationist practices such as investigating parts of cities which one would feel drawn to, to try to be 'open' to new experiences and encounters and to think about which experiences might be produced by being in particular places. What I did not want to do was to assume to be able to find the true essence or meaning of the city as this would go against the critical relativist position taken in this research.

Having conducted the dérive, I decided that the analysis section would be written up as a reflective autoethnographical narrative account whereby I would cite academic writings and political prose and poetry, which would support the claims made. Photographs of Ground Zero would be interspersed throughout the narrative account to visually document the places investigated but also in some cases to disorientate readers. The account would be written in the first person past tense, similar to other autoethnographical writings (see Ellis, 2000; Ellis and Bochner, 2000). In terms of the particular writing style, I was particularly interested in the work of Burnett *et al.* (2004) which provided an example of what an 'academic' account of a dérive would look like, i.e. a narrative account, which served as a story of what had happened and which was interspersed with situationist theory and research. The second part of the analysis would be represented in the form of a détourned map which would represent places investigated but would also document the disorientation during the dérive. One way to explore the limits of words in documenting the dérive could be done by constructing détourned maps. Maps represent the dominant power relations of place and are reflective of assumptions of particular political systems such as capitalism (Harley, 1988b). It was not my aim to construct a map where people could identify where they were or what they would expect to find at particular sites. The construction of this map was informed by Debord's (1958) arguments on détournement and the dérive. I wanted to use the construction of this map to reflect on my situated experiences of being at Ground Zero. The construction of these détourned maps extends Ellis and Bochner's (2000) arguments on how autoethnographic texts can also include maps.

However, having constructed a détourned map of Ground Zero based on photocopying and pasting together maps from Lonely Planet guidebooks and maps, I encountered a problem. I was not able to show the détourned map in this publication due to a copyright issue. I did contact Lonely Planet to ask if I could modify their maps and use them in published academic research in a manner similar to what they demonstrated in their *Lonely Planet Guide to Experimental Travel* (Antony and Henry, 2005) and they said that they would not license the maps for my use. The situationists produced détourned maps which were meant to contravene copyright laws but clearly, with published research, it is not fully possible to produce détourned maps which are meant to be cut and pasted plagiarised work based on original maps. However, what I have done is to draw what the détourned map looked like, which is featured after the autoethnographical narrative account.

The autoethnographical narrative account of the dérive: memorial space at Ground Zero

My brother and I decided to undertake the dérive shortly after we had arrived so that the effects of acclimatising to the difference in time and our having jet lag would contribute to our sense of disorientation. We wanted to reflexively analyse what Ground Zero meant to us and it was also an aim to think about the extent to which discursive theory could be drawn on to interpret these responses. We looked at the site of Ground Zero and felt shocked and speechless.

It was a vast horizontal expanse of concrete space (Figure 19.1), with a few small cabins dotted around the site. This was a place which I took to be representative of injury and of being wounded. It felt important to me to reflect on what the implications of that injury could be:

> To be injured means that one has the chance to reflect upon injury, to find out the mechanisms of its distribution, to find out who else suffers from permeable borders, unexpected violence, dispossession, and fear, and in what ways.
>
> (Butler, 2004: xii)

Figure 19.1 Photograph 1: Ground Zero.

It was as if the site had been wounded and had not yet healed from the attacks. We wanted to reflect on what this injury meant to us. The above quote by Butler has been used here to explain the importance of thinking about everyone who could suffer from events such as terrorism, war and conflict and to raise questions as to why such events would happen.

Whilst we stood there, several people gathered, probably to offer their respects to loved ones and to mourn what had been a huge international disaster. As I stood there, I thought back to where I was when I had first heard about the terrorist attacks. I had felt shocked and speechless when my brother told me that a plane had crashed into the World Trade Center in New York. Then we decided to walk around Ground Zero. We walked over to a wall where there were several photographs of the World Trade Center before the attacks of September 11th 2001. The Twin Towers were described on a Lower Manhattan Development Corporation poster as 'tough, un-wielding shapes' and there were several proposals for re-development such as to rebuild the buildings, to create even taller buildings, to create a different type of building/s, a monument, memorial and even a park.

Governance of place through Ground Zero

We could not randomly walk anywhere that we wanted to at Ground Zero as it was fenced off and there were guards patrolling. Therefore, we could only walk according to the designated route set out for us, which was a rectangular route. This was far from what could be considered a dérive, so we followed the route right and walked towards the World Financial Center. We tried to look into Ground Zero, though there were parts of the route which had been completely sealed from view. However, there were other parts of the route where it was possible to look downwards onto Ground Zero. The possibilities for the most wide-ranging views were from the windows of the World Financial Center (Figure 19.2). Being there reminded me of what Foucault (1975/1992) had written about panopticism and how the prison works as a system of power where inmates continually regulate their behaviour for fear of being watched by the wardens.

Then we decided that instead of using a map of New York we would use a map of Bangkok to disorientate ourselves. The Bangkok map also had a World Trade Center and so my brother and I would use this as the orientational marker for navigation around Ground Zero. We did not want to repeat the same route as before so we thought about how we could go underneath Ground Zero. We walked from Tha Ploenchit to Tha Phaya Thai to Expressway (2nd stage) and then onto Tha Ratchadammri. Walking in these places reminded me of how cities are shaped by 'political, economic and physical structures' such as freeways and other types of road networks (Joyce, 2003: 242). We got on the escalator which took us under Ground Zero. However it was difficult to dérive on the escalator precisely because its movement was fixed. We tried to find a river that was on our Bangkok map, but instead found the Subway PATH system.

The Subway PATH system was destroyed on September 11th 2001, but had now been fully renovated and was in public use. This was the closest that we

Figure 19.2 Photograph 2: The view from the World Financial Center.

would get to actually standing on Ground Zero, by being underneath it. It felt like a strange and awkward place to be. There was a high level of surveillance in this area, with many obviously placed security cameras on ceilings and walls. We knew that we were almost certainly being watched and this did make us feel awkward. We were not in the Subway to get anywhere but were there for a psychogeographical investigation. We were taking photographs and writing notes which could have been construed as unusual behaviour. This made us even more aware that the public, police and other security agencies could have been watching us. Patrick Joyce (2003: 148) has written about how people present themselves in everyday life in ways which are 'publicly acceptable' because we are continually being watched not only by others but also by cctv cameras and by the police. Joyce (2003) argues that this has the effect of changing the ways in which we construct our sense of self in contemporary society. I would argue that this all-pervasive technology of cctv cameras and increased surveillance of citizens is repressive and undemocratic in that as citizens we do not have choice as to whether we will be filmed, which we are told is necessary to prevent crime and terrorism.

Analysis of Map 1: Downtown Manhattan

This map (Figure 19.3) represents downtown New York with street names and locations from both Bangkok and New York maps. The grid-like patterns of the city are clearly represented along with rivers, the metro system and other buildings and bridges. The map is meant to create a disorientating 'reading' of the city. The

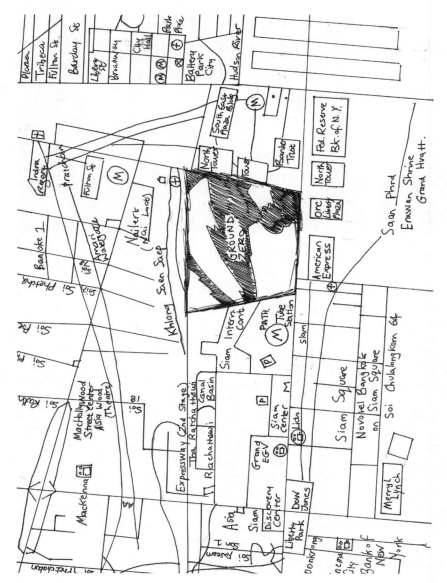

Figure 19.3 Map 1: A détourned map of Downtown Manhattan.

large blackened image in the centre of the map is where the World Trade Center once stood, now known as Ground Zero. This has been identified as a key site because I personally felt drawn towards it and this can therefore be compared to how particular areas of social environments are the 'constant currents, fixed points and vortexes' (Debord, 1958: n.p). In the original détourned map, I had glued a photograph of the World Trade Center into the centre of the map. Having done this, it seemed more appropriate to leave the centre of the map empty, to retain it as a memorial site, so I ripped off the photograph, which left behind a strange, blackened, destroyed scar-like pattern.

Conclusions

In this work I have demonstrated how psychogeographic methods can be used in psychology and have drawn importance to the practice of challenging the routinised ways in which we think and behave in environments. This practice serves as one way to challenge the dominant relations of power in places. This work has also raised questions about how to document social environments and our experiences both textually and visually. I have provided some examples from my research to demonstrate one way that walking could be used as a visual qualitative methodology with both the exposition of an autoethnographical narrative dérive account and with a detourned map. One of the key issues with documenting and writing about the visual world is that the exposition of the argument is written. The map, which was meant to stand as the visual document, was heavily loaded with words, words which referred to street names, buildings, bridges and so forth. This demonstrates one of the difficulties with visual qualitative methods in that it is very difficult to document the social world without using words. There are also limits as to what words can 'do' in terms of articulating experience (Frosh, 2002). When my brother and I arrived at Ground Zero we felt shocked and speechless. It was difficult to communicate in words what we felt because there are some types of experiences which cannot be stated in words, such as experiences of trauma, death of loved ones and feelings of love. This is why the early part of the narrative account in my PhD thesis is represented with space in the text and with dots, i.e. '.....................'. This practice is indebted to lettrist and situationist film-making technique with the aims being to disrupt, alter and negate dominant meanings and to engage audiences in alternative radical meaning construction.

My aims in this work were different to the situationists in that I wanted to conceptualise what a walking/map method would look like in psychology. I drew on situationism in relation to discursive theory and autoethnography. The dérive at Ground Zero was not strictly a dérive because my brother and I were constrained as to where we were permitted and not permitted to walk. It is clear that the act of walking does not in itself change the physical environment, but it can change the ways in which we think about and respond to environments. Psychogeographical walking can be used as a means to challenge the routine ways in which we move from 'A' to 'B' and is a deconstructive practice to challenge the taken for granted assumptions of how we should think and behave in places. *Dérives are always governed by the conditions of material circumstances. The aim of dérives should be to analyse these relations of material circumstances in order to intervene and change situations.* This method can be used to begin to consider what alternatives there can be to dominant modes of social organisation and space. The urban environment should be a contested space where alternatives to capitalist forms of organisation can begin to be formulated. The narrative account of dérives and détourned maps serves as a textual means of documenting the research process. Drawing on psychogeographic methodology is one way to further radicalise qualitative and critical psychological research (Hayes, 2003), with the wider aims being to transform the 'social organisation of place' (Pinder, 1996: 414) as well as the complete transformation of capitalist societies.

Note

[1] I would also like to clarify that I do not agree with any forms of violence and aggression.

References

Antony, R. and Henry, J. (2005) *The Lonely Planet guide to experimental travel.* London: Lonely Planet Publications.

Atkinson, P. (1997) Narrative turn or blind alley? *Qualitative Health Research*, 7(3): 325–344.

Barnes, T. J. and Duncan, J. S. (Eds) (1992) *Writing worlds: discourse, text and metaphor in the representation of landscape.* London: Routledge.

Bored in the City Collective (n.d.) *Psychogeography.* Retrieved 30 October 2008 from http://boredinthecitycollective.blogspot.com

Burnett, J., Cudworth, E. and Tamboukou, M. (2004) Women on dérive: autobiographical explorations of lived spaces. In Women and Geography Study Group, *Geography and Gender Reconsidered.* CD-ROM, August: 118–141.

Butler, J. (2004) *Precarious life: the powers of mourning and violence.* London: Verso.

Debord, G. (1958) Theory of the dérive. *Situationist International* [electronic version]. Retrieved 15 September 2004 from www.cddc.vt.edu/sionline/si/theory/html

Debord, G. (1967) The society of the spectacle. *Situationist International* [electronic version]. Retrieved 16 May 2004 from http://library.nothingness.org/articles/SI/en/pub_contents/4

Ellis, C. (2000) *The ethnographic I.* California: Alta Mira.

Ellis, C. and Bochner, A. P. (2000) Auto-ethnography, personal narrative, reflexivity: researcher as subject. In N. Denzin and Y. Lincoln (Eds) *The handbook of qualitative research.* Thousand Oaks, CA: Sage.

Foucault, M. (1992) *Discipline and punish: the birth of the prison.* London: Penguin.

Frosh, S. (2002) Things that can't be said: psychoanalysis and the limits of language. In *Afterwords: the personal in gender, culture and psychotherapy.* London: Macmillan.

Grup de Lesbianes Feministes (2005) Exploring new ways of insubmission in social representation. *Annual Review of Critical Psychology*, 1(4): 107–114.

Harley, J. B. (1988a) Deconstructing the map. *Cartographica*, 26: 1–20.

Harley, J. B. (1988b) Maps, knowledge and power. In D. Cosgrave and S. Daniels (Eds) *The iconography of landscape*. Cambridge: Cambridge University Press.

Harley, J. B. (1992) Deconstructing the map. In T. Barnes and J. Duncan (Eds) *Writing worlds: discourse, text and metaphor in the representation of landscape*. London: Routledge.

Hayes, G. (2003) Walking the streets: psychology and the flâneur. *Annual Review of Critical Psychology*, 1(3): 50–66.

Hollway, W. (1989) *Subjectivity and method in psychology. Gender, meaning and science*. London: Sage.

Holt, N. L. (2003) Representation, legitimation and autoethnography: an autoethnographic writing story. *International Journal of Qualitative Methods*, 2(1): 1–22.

International, S. (1959) Détournement as negation and prelude. *Situationist International* [electronic version] Retrieved 24 August 2004 from http://www.cddc.vt.edu/sionline/si/detournement.html

Joyce, P. (2003) *The rule of freedom: liberalism and the modern city*. London: Verso.

Khatib, A. (1958) Attempt at a psychogeographical description of Les Halles. *Situationist International* [electronic version]. Retrieved 22 September 2004 from http://www.cddc.vt.edu/sionline/si/leshalles.html

Kotanyi, A. and Vaneigem, R. (1961) Basic program of the Bureau of Unitary Urbanism. *Situationist International* [electronic version] Retrieved 28 September 2004 from http://www.cddc.vt.edu/sionline/si/bureau.html

Materialist Psychogeographic Affiliation (n.d.) *The materialist psychogeographic Affiliation*. Retrieved 30 October 2008 from http://www.materialistpsychogeography.co.uk

Pinder, D. (1996) Subverting cartography: the situationists and maps of the city. *Environment and Planning A*, 28: 405–427.

Pinder, D. (2000) Old Paris is no more: geographies of spectacle and anti-spectacle. *Antipode*, 32(4): 357–386.

Pinder, D. (2005) *Visions of the city: Utopianism, power and politics in twentieth century urbanism*. Edinburgh: Edinburgh University Press.

Precarias a la Deriva (2005) Housewives, maids, cleaning ladies and caregivers in general: care in the communication continuum. *Annual Review of Critical Psychology*, 1(4): 188–198.

Rose, N. (1999) *Powers of freedom: reframing political thought*. Cambridge: Cambridge University Press.

Sadler, S. (1998) *The situationist city*. London: MIT Press.

Sparkes, A. C. (2000) Autoethnography and narratives of self: reflections on criteria in action. *Sociology of Sport*, 17: 21–41.

Thrift, N. (2004) Intensities of feeling: towards a spatial politics of affect. *Geografiska Annaler B*, 86(1): 57–78.

Vaneigem, R. (1967) The revolution of everyday life. *Nothingness: the library*. [electronic version]. Retrieved 24 November 2004 from http://library.nothingness.org/articles/SI/en/pub_contents/5

Part IV

Ethical and methodological reflections on visual research

20 Reflections on the visual in community research and action

Darrin Hodgetts, Kerry Chamberlain and Shiloh Groot

Earlier chapters, and published work, have noted that the use of visual methods within psychology is informed by established traditions in visual ethnography, sociology and geography (Lykes *et al.*, 2003; Nowell *et al.*, 2006; Pink, 2007). Such research often combines insights from photographs and words to explore the textures of participant lifeworlds and how people negotiate what they see and know (Collier, 1957; Radley and Taylor, 2003a, 2003b). This chapter emerges out of our ongoing community research into homelessness using photo-production techniques (Hodgetts *et al.*, 2007b; Hodgetts *et al.*, 2008). The project is informed through broader social science traditions in order to investigate interrelated social psychological dimensions of homelessness, including identity, interpersonal relationships, the use of public space, and resilience. Visual methods provide a basis for understanding the hardship faced by homeless people in relation to situational, societal, material and relational contexts. Photography is proving useful for aiding our participants to show us what these hardships and associated circumstances look like and feel like. It also provides a useful basis for working with journalists, governmental officials and agencies trying to render assistance.

In this chapter, we discuss the use of photovoice and photo-elicitation techniques in community-based participatory research, where these techniques have commonly been used for showing deprivation to those in power and lobbying for change (Carlson *et al.*, 2006; Lykes *et al.*, 2003; Nowell *et al.*, 2006). This tradition is useful for bringing the perspectives of marginalised groups to the fore, and is a powerful means of initiating change through facilitating dialogue between various stakeholder groups. However, much of this research invokes potentially problematic assumptions about the concept of voice, largely in regard to assumptions about representation and transparency. In presenting this discussion, we are concerned not to simply offer a critique of community research involving the use of images but to develop a richer conceptual basis for such work. In light of this, there are two parts to the chapter. The first considers the origins of photovoice, the role of voice, and the importance of Freirian notions of dialogue in understanding what participants deliver through using the technique and its value for supporting social change. The second considers the process of picturing and how this can inform understandings of photo-production and associated efforts on the part of homeless people, psychologists, and community service providers to effect change.

Considering photovoice

Photovoice involves efforts to include the voices of people, often those who are marginalised from decision-making processes that shape their lives. It has emerged in applied and politically engaged areas of psychology, where a critical stance implies more than opposition to positivism and internal critiques of our discipline. Criticality also involves social action aimed at promoting inclusion and equity. The notion of giving voice comes from frustration on the part of psychologists engaged in challenging the exclusion of people from civic life and decision-making processes in society. Unfortunately it can lead to a romanticisation of marginalised people and to an anti-expert stance towards scholars, which promotes the idea that research participants are the only experts. This is an issue that can be addressed by keeping the theoretical roots of the method in frame and paying more attention to the act of making photographs or picturing.

Photovoice is informed by Freire's (1970/1993) work on critical consciousness-raising and community-based action research approaches to social transformation (Carlson *et al.*, 2006; Lykes *et al.*, 2003). Freire developed an approach to education that conceptualised teachers and learners as co-constructors of knowledge. He shifted power relations in education from a sermon-type approach to a conversational approach involving the mutual exploration of topics. This egalitarian orientation saw insight and knowledge as the product of joint introspection and exploration fostered through dialogue. Freire (1970/1993) outlined three levels of understanding and engagement with reality that members of marginalised groups can be guided through. At the *magical-conforming* level people are restrained by feelings of inferiority and helplessness. They see the status quo as natural and therefore do not question or challenge it. Their adaptation to adversity allows them to survive, but their passivity contributes to continued oppression. At the *naïve-reforming* level, people focus on the corrupt nature of the status quo. However, instead of challenging the status quo and injustice, they engage in in-fighting and blaming peers for the situations in which they find themselves. The *critical-action* level involves people reflecting on the ways in which values and assumptions shape their understandings of their situations and actions. People become aware of their own role in accepting or challenging the status quo. At this level, collective action is more likely and civic engagement can occur. In helping illiterate South American peasants move through these levels of consciousness, Freire attended to their daily practice as a site for the reproduction of social injustices. He used techniques such as drawing exercises to link such practices and emotional experiences to broader processes of oppression, and to encourage reflection and dialogue. Through these techniques, alternative understandings were cultivated as a basis for enhancing capacity to change and improve the world. Freire emphasised that such social change requires a combination of insights from actual experiences and daily life along with more abstract academic understandings of the social processes shaping such lives.

These ideas were taken up by Wang and Burris (1994) in developing photovoice methodology to assess the needs of rural Chinese women. This research drew upon auto-photography, where people take photographs of their daily activities and participate in follow-up photo-elicitation interviews and workshops to discuss their photographs. Photographs, drawings and stories were elicited from the women as a way of raising community concerns, identifying underlying influences, and working through possible courses of action to address these concerns. Photovoice enhanced participant reflexivity and contributed to participant knowledge of, and efforts to enhance, their own lives (cf., Klitzing, 2004). Photo-elicitation interviews based upon photographs allowed participants to show as well as to tell the researchers about their experiences (cf., Radley and Taylor, 2003a). The approach provides opportunities for participants to have more substantially engaged interactions with researchers that contribute to revealing deeper and richer information about daily existence than often comes from traditional one-off semi-structured interviews (Hodgetts *et al.*, 2007).

As a methodology, photovoice provides one means of documenting ways that participants make sense of how and where they live, and the opportunities and constraints on their existence. Photography projects are designed to engage in active dialogue and listening, provide opportunities for critical reflection to occur, and provide a basis for developing action strategies. They provide a means for engaging with, and building interventions out of, everyday experiences, a process that can enhance the usefulness of the resultant interventions.

Recently, Nowell and colleagues (2006) discussed neighbourhood renewal projects and their efforts to capture people's understandings of physical and social environments as a basis for fostering a sense of place, mutual support and health. They used photovoice to bring out the physical and social qualities of a neighbourhood, and to encourage reflection and group dialogue. The method was deemed appropriate for tapping into the lived realities of participants and allowing them to raise personally important issues, and for empowering them to improve the setting. The authors proposed that photovoice was useful because success with renewal initiatives is more likely if the strategies that psychologists employ are based on in-depth understandings of community settings and the everyday experiences and needs of the people living within those places. As is typical of photovoice projects, participants were trained over two evenings about the goals of the research and the ethics of photographing others. A professional photographer took them through basic photographic techniques. Participants carried cameras with them for five weeks and shot a roll of film each week. They were asked to select three images from each roll and communicate the meaning of these in response to framing questions concerning their lives and relationships with others, and what needed to change in the community. Participants attended weekly group reflection sessions where these themes were discussed in an effort to strengthen place-based affiliations and commitment to community renewal.

We have some reservations regarding the emphasis placed on giving voice to marginalised people in such projects. Although the perspectives of participants are essential, they should not displace academic interpretation, as is proposed by some community psychologists using the mantra that the participants are the experts. The emphasis on giving voice can lead to losing sight of the emphasis that Freire placed on the co-construction of knowledge. For Freire (1970/1993), the voices of marginalised people are problematic sources of knowledge, that should not be taken at face value and require interpretation. The voice of a participant is negotiated in dialogue with the practitioner/researcher. For Freire, dialogue is an essential epistemological process in learning about social power and exclusion and how to respond to it. Dialogue can facilitate the interweaving of everyday experience and theoretical insights into broader societal processes; it can enhance reflection, understanding and action through a process of walking forward together while questioning. Putting cameras into the hands of participants is a productive way of facilitating such collaboration between researchers and participants in the sense-making process (Felstead *et al.*, 2004; Hodgetts *et al.*, 2007a). However, participant training exemplifies how researchers are not simply giving voice to participants. Training is itself a dialogical process that influences the very nature of the photographs and accounts people produce, potentially limiting the raising of issues unanticipated by the researcher.

As a social process in research, making photographs does not provide direct access to everyday life; what is deemed worthy of photographing is subject to social conventions and norms around what is important and acceptable to show, and what a project is about (Bourdieu, 1990). The relationship between participants and pictures is mediated by the expectations of dominant social groups and the imaging practices of cultural institutions, including the news media (Hodgetts *et al.*, 2007a). For example, our homeless participants reflect upon efforts to convey their concerns in the context of media images already circulating in society (Hodgetts *et al.*, 2006). This raises questions about the transparency of 'giving voice', as participant attempts to show and articulate experience are mediated by these social conventions. Participants often refer to difficulties in displaying alternative images that depart from common media characterisations. It is through this tension, between needing to comply with social expectations to communicate effectively and the desire to represent oneself on terms that seem more relevant to one's everyday reality, that participants explore photographically what it means to be homeless (Hodgetts *et al.*, 2006). Their engagements with the ways homeless people are represented by the media opens a space within which they speculate about who gets to frame homelessness, its impact on their lives, and what can be done about it. This issue was important because our participants often picture the mundane, 'boring' and inherently 'pointless' aspects of street life as a strategy for deconstructing the overly dramatised images dominant in news reports (Hodgetts *et al.*, 2005). This constitutes a further dialogical level, emerging when participants discuss their photographs with researchers and deconstruct and challenge imaging conventions that can limit what they show.

As social products that reflect dialogue and different voices, photographs also provide materials for engaging officials and those in positions of power with a view to creating change (Wang *et al.*, 2000). In the process, links between lives, local contexts, society, history and culture are drawn into the research and community advocacy processes. If the dialogical construction of homelessness, and how communities might respond to it, extends out to a societal level through media deliberations, then surely we should involve homeless people's reconstructions in such dialogues. Below, we illustrate how photovoice can extend to such advocacy work via news media.

Hodgetts and colleagues (2008) investigated links between the representational space offered by newspaper portrayals of homeless men's use of a public library and their lived interactions in the library. This research was conducted in response to an item in a local newspaper raising concern about the appropriateness of homeless men being present in the city library. The item promoted the exclusion of homeless men by emphasising the deviancy of these men and the danger they supposedly posed for housed citizens. Our participants raised the issue of library access and the controversy in their talk and also through their photographs (see Figure 20.1). They responded to the news item by emphasising their 'appropriate' use of the library for reading and learning, and as a means of escaping disruptive practices, such as drinking in public, which were situated beyond the library.

Roger: It's where I spend my day. It's really cool. I learn a bit of history and read a few books there… There's a video and TV upstairs … right where the archive is and I watch a few documentaries up there … It's good to be off the street for a while to relax and do what everyone is doing. I can get to know people who go to the library without annoying them … It's not a big deal, but it's good to be able to go in there sometimes and just be somewhere.

Figure 20.1 Photograph of the public library entrance by Roger.

Participants presented the library as a place to engage in positive relationships with housed people. One participant made a photograph of a librarian outside the library showing 'the place and the person' and then discussed the photograph as depicting the importance of relationships occurring there:

Luke: That's a friend of mine at the library. We weren't allowed to take a photograph in the library unfortunately. And she's been like a backbone for me ... I see her in there and we sit down and chat for a while and she checks on how I am and we talk about all sorts of nothingness. It's just a lovely sense of someone who has their eye on me and who thinks positively about me. There's a really good caring streak to her and they're the type of things we underestimate a huge amount in life. And sometimes the most important people are those who speak kindly to us from time to time.

These comments raise the importance of interactions with library staff and patrons in supporting a sense of belonging, respite and refuge among homeless people. We used such photographs in a presentation to library and other city council staff to emphasise the importance of the library for homeless people. Discussion went on for two hours and functioned to reinforce support for the continued inclusion of all citizens in the library.

We also conducted further fieldwork in which we interviewed library staff and patrons, and worked with journalists on follow-up material to produce an alternative account of homelessness and library use. The result was a two-page feature article that foregrounded the positive function of spaces like libraries in homeless men's lives and challenged the previous account advocating the exclusion of 'the homeless' from prime public spaces. It introduced the opinions of homeless men, librarians and city staff on the issue, and documented how the library allowed homeless men to engage in academic pursuits and provided a space for them to move beyond the stigma of a homeless identity. It discussed the broader functions of libraries in homeless men's lives, as a space for safety, social participation and respite from a life predominantly lived alone in marginal spaces, and challenged the assumption that these men were dangerous. It included comments by housed library patrons who were more compassionate towards the homeless men, and raised the importance of interactions with library staff and patrons in caring for homeless men. Calls to exclude these men from the library were subsequently dropped, and the men's sense of place was restored.

The production of photographs can lead to the articulation of critical questions, here regarding relations between homeless and housed people, and who is included and excluded from public spaces. The library study illustrates how photovoice methodology can be extended through media advocacy to bring such political issues to the fore and as a basis for challenging exclusionary practices. The library example also emphasises how critical consciousness raising is important but needs to be linked with action, either on the part of marginalised people themselves or with those willing to get involved. What is clear for us is that we cannot simply locate responsibility for action with 'the homeless' because they are not necessarily in control of their homelessness. Many decisions shaping their situations are made beyond their lifeworlds and it is up to us, as critical scholars working with community groups, to help bridge this divide through advocacy and joint action. The use of photographs is important in this context because it renders the situation real and can be used to raise questions at different levels of the socio-political system that perpetuates homelessness.

Considering the picturing process

Now we extend our consideration of what people do when asked to picture and discuss their worlds during photo-production research projects. We examine this from three perspectives; picturing processes in the making of photographs, the co-construction of the meaning of images between participants and researchers, and the re-construction of photographs and their meanings in community practice and intervention.

Picturing, the making of photographs, involves an active engagement on the part of participants with the themes of the research as manifest in their lifeworlds. Looking at one's world with a view to making photographs orientates participants to the material aspects of their everyday lives, to artefacts important to them, and to the relationships that give meaning to these places and things (Hodgetts *et al.*, 2007a). The resulting pictures and associated accounts provide insights into the practices through which people construct themselves as social beings within specific locales, and enable us to link personal lifeworlds to wider societal contexts. If people make, rather than take, photographs (Barthes, 1981), these constructive processes of picturing are foundational to understanding photovoice.

Participants often produce photographs that attest to the existence of relationships and encounters, and the importance of events and locations, whether displayed in the frame or not (cf., Harrison, 2004a). Elsewhere (Hodgetts *et al.*, 2007a), we have proposed that to understand photographs provided by participants we must contemplate the scenes, events and relationships that lie beyond the frame, and even look to photographs that were never taken (see also Frith, this volume). This is particularly crucial because photographs have leaky or fuzzy frames that lead us onto considerations of things not fully evident, lying off to the side of the depiction. Rather than see photographs as bounded objects for interpretation, Radley and Taylor (2003a) propose that photographs are better understood as standing in a dialectical relationship with the persons who produce and discuss them. From this perspective, the meaning of a photograph does not lie in the material object, except insofar as this is part of the way that people talk about them. It is when we engage with and discuss photographs that we impute meanings into the image. In discussing the 'dialogical image', Benjamin (1982) proposes that processes of picturing allow people to surface and reflect upon taken-for-granted aspects of everyday life, and that the meaning-making processes are not necessarily restrained by the time and place of a particular photograph's creation. To reflect upon the photographs one has made is to explain and interpret the depictions (cf., Harrison, 2004b). From this perspective, picturing is not simply a technical process for producing material objects containing set meanings. Photographs can be seen as efforts at communication that are open to interpretation and various uses within ongoing social interactions (Bourdieu, 1990). In this way photographs comprise things that people can use to represent events, places, persons, and relationships; they can explain and show (cf., Brookfield *et al.*, 2008). The meaning of a photograph is thus more fluid and variable in response to the changing circumstances of the photographer, the viewers, and what is being done in the interaction between them. Reflecting this line of thought, Harrison (2004b) notes that 'Meanings of photographs will change, and the processes of memory, history making, narration and self-actualisation, are ongoing features of personal and social relations with photographs' (p. 25).

There is, however, a risk in focusing on the process of producing and exploring pictures. We might fall into the trap, evident in some variants of discourse analysis, of looking at how accounts are constructed rather than engaging with their meaning and sustaining a focus on their value for community action. We propose that a focus on the processes of construction, meaning making and community action should be inseparable. When participants produce photographs and discuss them with researchers, they critically reflect on their situations (Radley and Taylor, 2003a) and produce artefacts that can be used to plan change. Photo-based interviews can thus be thought of as conversations between respondents and interviewers about and around the specific scenes and how to respond to the concerns these raise. As interpretive practice, this is similar to Mitchell's description of representation as something assembled over time out of fragments and constituting an ongoing assemblage of insights woven together into an account (Mitchell, 1994). This perspective holds a key insight for avoiding simplistic notions of giving voice, and necessitates that researchers and change agents consider more than an understanding of photographs. It necessitates an understanding with the participants based on their efforts to picture their lifeworlds (Radley and Taylor, 2003b). Such an orientation involves tuning into conversations that extend beyond the photograph to an interpretative process involving 'looking at' and 'looking behind' the picture (Wright, 1999, echoing Barthes, 1981). This encompasses researchers and participants both looking at and behind from their different positions to determine the significance of the depiction for the research. In its most straightforward form, a participant might photograph an entrance to a library and then move, in discussion with the researcher, beyond this depiction to talk about why he goes there and the social relations shaping his access. These insights might then be used for lobbying, including through news media, to ensure continued library access for homeless people. It is common for photo-production participants to offer stories that take off from photographs, moving well beyond the depiction, and raising issues about the history of depicted events, relationships and places (cf., Harrison, 2004a). These accounts can take us somewhere very different from the location or relationships depicted in the photograph.

Further, participants can continue to picture an experience when reflecting again on a photograph made and discussed on a previous occasion. They can recount or reconstruct a possible past that is open to further negotiation and reconstruction as the person reflects on their contemporary life position (Harrison, 2004b). In the process, photographs can be re-described *as if* they were new photographs in the making. This is a crucial point because photographs are at once material artefacts and objects and memories to be recast through dialogue and further reflection. Hurdley (2006) found that people talk about objects displayed in their homes as if these represented their character and the relationships they hold dear. The meaning of these objects was not seen as fixed or static; the accounts people gave of objects depended on the aspects of self they wished to display and communicate in the context of the interaction and who they were engaging with. Personal things are invested with history and tradition, and often crystallise connections with other people and places. The retelling of the significance of an object invokes a nexus of meaning and relationships that exceeds the materiality of the object and invokes shared relations. Hurdley (2006: 721) notes that:

> Their materiality is not bound by temporal and spatial limits, since they are the material with which people build stories of absent presences, a horizon beyond which the past and future, the otherworld and ideal self dwell ...
>
> Objects were not only props to life histories but essential players; we were host and guest, yet also presenter and listener, judge and defender. The narrative was doing work, often in allowing the teller to display other worlds in an otherwise limited environment.

In discussing the ways in which a particular participant narrated an object, and, in the process, herself, Hurdley (2006: 726) states 'Her performance is an investment not only in the narrative, which in a sense is a memory of past action, but also in her present self. Past and present are thus literally materialized in the frame'. Discussions of photographs can also contain future intentions and actions not yet taken, such as leaving the street.

The idea of understanding homelessness *with* participants can also form the basis for working with service providers. Understanding the transitions occurring in homeless people's lives is crucial, and a focus on picturing can be used to foreground the agency of homeless people as they attempt to make their way in the world, and also to inform the practices of service agencies. For instance, we are using several case studies in workshops with agency social workers to encourage a broader understanding of why some interventions to assist homeless people to move off the streets are not working long-term. Below we discuss one such case to illustrate its potential for enhancing understanding and efforts for change. This case takes a longitudinal approach, allowing us to explore the complexities of a person's experiences of homelessness across both a range of settings and changed circumstances.

Joshua is a 45-year-old man who has had ongoing experiences of living on the street over the last four years. On our initial contact, Joshua had just come off the street and was entering a 'detox' programme, trying to address his alcohol and drug addiction problems. Over a period of 12 months, Joshua produced and

Figure 20.2 Homeless sleeping spot with poetry inspired by 'The Borg' (*Star Trek*).

discussed four sets of 27 photographs with us. These sets spanned his time in detox, a period when he was re-housed, and a later period back living on the street. They reflect key transitions in a homeless person's life that raise important issues about, and present insights into, the problems facing homeless people in resettlement.

In making the first set of photographs, a member of the research team accompanied Joshua on a tour of his street life, and he explained the significance of each photograph as it was made. In these photographs, Joshua took us into the hidden world of homeless people, producing several photographs of the private spaces in which they dwell (see Figure 20.2), drop-in centres in service agencies, and abandoned buildings. This is the underworld of homeless people, from which they step out to beg on the streets, rummage through bins, and squeegee car windows. Joshua wanted to portray what being homeless looked like. In the subsequent sets of photographs, we move out from this private domain into a more public arena.

The second set marked an important transition for Joshua, from the street to supported housing. When asked to image his life for a second time, Joshua had less idea of what to show us. He settled on presenting a perspective of domiciled life evidenced in public spaces. These are images of a city populated by housed people (see Figure 20.3), from whom Joshua is separated socially. This is the sanitised world of domiciled living in the city, beyond homelessness and, from his perspective, a somewhat *Disneyfied* world[1] (Amster, 2003). These images

Figure 20.3 Domiciled life on the streets of Auckland.

communicate the perspective of a man who is not participating in city life; Joshua is lost.

The third set was taken in a period when Joshua was transiting back onto the streets. In this set, the series of photographs depict interactions between homeless and housed persons. Here, lifeworlds overlap and collide in shared urban space. The set includes aspects of street life, such as an intoxicated 'streetie' asleep on a park bench and police regulating the activities of beggars. This set constitutes a visual diary of a typical day on the street for Joshua. It also conveys his use of creative signs when begging to gain resources (see Figure 20.4) that he shares with members of his street family, and out of which he builds relationships.

Joshua: My signs are a wee bit different. They're things like, 'Ninjas abducted family, need money for kung fu lessons,' and uh what else is it … I'm on e-bay for them apparently; quite a few people come past and recognise me … another one is, 'I'm starving and so is the idiot holding me', um 'Aliens abducted family, need money to build spaceship,' and things like this … it's all money-makers ....

Interviewer: Why do you put that spin on it?

Joshua: Because they're different and people actually come past and see them and it gives them a giggle. You know, instead of just the normal homeless bullshit that everyone's used to.

Figure 20.4 Joshua begging outside a McDonald's outlet in Auckland.

The fourth set depicts homeless people occupying prime public spaces and socialising together (see Figure 20.5). At this time, Joshua is re-embedded in street life.

While Joshua found it easy to articulate and picture street life, the same could not be said for his (brief period of) housed life. He found it difficult to identify with the housed setting, where he was like a fish out of water. From his acts of picturing and talking about his world, we are able to develop an understanding of what homelessness means for Joshua. Across the photographic sets we gain insights into how he is actually more at home when living on the streets with his street family. Joshua acknowledges that: '… 90 per cent of the boys who get places end up back on the street anyway. If I slip and get back on the piss it will happen'. In fact, Joshua never really left the street. Re-housing actually constituted a rupturing of his daily life and rendered him dislocated in an alien environment for which he was poorly equipped. We need to be aware that, when re-housed, homeless people may not have actually left street life, and the work of agencies remains incomplete. We can also recognise here the positive side of living on the street, with its advantages for the homeless person. Too often, professionals can lose sight of these positive benefits and focus too strongly on the negative effects of street life.

Here, the act of picturing – conceptualising and trying to make specific pictures and talk about them – is shown to be important for the agency of homeless people, and the articulation of their experiences and how we might respond to their

Figure 20.5 Joshua back with his street family.

concerns. Cases such as Joshua's illustrate the complexities of working to address homelessness. We do not resolve homelessness by using photo-production exercises, but we can develop better, more grounded, understandings of homelessness and insights into homeless people's lives from their use. These can facilitate change at a personal level through the engagement in critical reflection and dialogue, and at an institutional level through the use of the images to enlighten and engage people with the power to help. Our use of photography in this community-orientated research is informed by Freire's notion of praxis, informing theory with experience and practice with theory.

Discussion

The use of photovoice in applied community research enables us to explore everyday lives in ways that are often overlooked in research into topics like homelessness. The process of photo-production orientates participants to linkages between people and places, objects and relationships, and groups and society (Hodgetts *et al.*, 2007a, 2008). The method provides for insights into the ways in which people connect themselves to the significant and the mundane events and relations in their lives. In using this method we apprehend how the process of picturing enables participants to engage in critical reflection and dialogue with researchers, beyond that occurring through talk alone. By making photographs and talking to us, participants often do more than we have asked of them. Participants can extend the investigation in new and unanticipated directions.

They become makers of photographs and in the process interpreters of their lives, broader societal processes and the research, and ultimately generate material that can be used to lobby for social justice.

Most readers will recognise the value of giving voice to participants in qualitative research. In this chapter we have worked to strengthen such efforts by combining a conceptualisation of what people do when picturing adversity, or making sense with photographs, and generating workable strategies for social change. For too long, qualitative researchers in psychology have focussed on overly descriptive accounts of experience, and neglected the broader potential of research for making a difference in peoples' lives. Developing a richer conceptualisation of picturing allows us to demonstrate how, in using photovoice methodology, psychologists are doing more than simply acting as conduits for the experiences of others. We are developing theoretical interpretations of social processes that are central to the lives of homeless people, and which inform our efforts to address the needs of marginalised people. In closing, we should not lose sight of Freire's (1970/1993: 32) cogent point that: 'To affirm that men and women are persons and as persons should be free, and yet to do nothing tangible to make this affirmation a reality, is a farce'.

Note

1 Disneyfication refers to the process by which the public face of cities is increasingly transformed to reflect a Disney theme park, which appears clean and pristine on the outside, but which hides dirt and exploitation on the inside.

References

Amster, R. (2003). Patterns of exclusion: sanitizing space, criminalizing homelessness. *Social Justice, 30,* 195–221.
Barthes, R. (1981). *Camera Lucida: reflections on photography.* Trans. by R. Howard. New York: Hill and Wang.
Benjamin, W. (1982). *Illuminations.* Trans. by H. Zohn. London: Fontana.
Bourdieu, P. (1990). *Photography: a middle-brow art.* Cambridge: Polity Press.
Brookfield, H., Brown, S., and Reavey, P. (2008). Vicarious and post-memory practices in adopting families: the re-production of the past through photography and narrative. *Journal of Community and Applied Social Psychology, 18,* 474–491.
Carlson, E., Engebertson, J., and Chamberlain, R. (2006). Photovoice as a social process of critical consciousness. *Qualitative Health Research, 16,* 836–852.
Collier, J. (1957). *Photography in anthropology: photography as a research method.* Albuquerque: University of New Mexico Press.
Felstead, A., Jewson, N., and Walters, S. (2004). Images, interviews and interpretations: making connections in visual research. *Studies in Qualitative Methodology, 7,* 105–121.
Freire, P. (1970/1993). *Pedagogy of the oppressed.* Harmondsworth: Penguin.
Harrison, B. (2004a). Photographic visions and narrative inquiry. In M. Bamberg and M. Andrews (Eds), *Considering counter-narratives: narrating, resisting, making sense,* Philadelphia: John Benjamins, pp. 113–136.

Harrison, B. (2004b). Snap happy: toward a sociology of 'everyday' photography. *Studies in Qualitative Methodology*, *7*, 23–39.

Hodgetts, D., Chamberlain, K., and Radley, A. (2007a). Considering photographs never taken during photo-production project. *Qualitative Research in Psychology*, *4*(4), 263–280.

Hodgetts, D., Chamberlain, K., Radley, A., and Hodgetts, A. (2007b). Health Inequalities and homelessness: considering material, relational and spatial dimensions. *Journal of Health Psychology*, *12*, 709–725.

Hodgetts, D., Cullen, A., and Radley, A. (2005). Television characterizations of homeless people in the United Kingdom. *Analyses of Social Issues and Public Policy*, *5*, 29–48.

Hodgetts, D., Radley, A., and Cullen, A. (2006). Life in the shadow of the media: images of street homelessness in London. *European Journal of Cultural Studies*, *9*, 498–516.

Hodgetts, D., Stolte, O., Chamberlain, K., Radley, A., Nikora, L., Nabalarua, E., and Groot, S. (2008). A trip to the library: homelessness and social inclusion. *Social and Cultural Geography*, *9*(8), 933–953.

Hurdley, R. (2006). Dismantling mantelpieces: narrating identities and materializing culture in the home. *Sociology*, *40*, 717–733.

Klitzing, S. (2004) Women living in a homeless shelter: stress, coping and leisure. *Journal of Leisure Research*, *36*, 483–512.

Lykes, M. B., Blanche, M., and Hamber, B. (2003) Narrating survival and change in Guatemala and South Africa: the politics of representation and a liberatory community psychology. *American Journal of Community Psychology*, *13*, 79–90.

Mitchell, W. (1994). *Picture theory*. Chicago: University of Chicago Press.

Nowell, B., Berkowitz, S., Deacon, Z., and Foster-Fishman, P. (2006). Revealing the cues within community places: stories of identity, history and possibility. *American Journal of Community Psychology*, *37*, 29–46.

Pink, S. (2007). *Doing visual ethnography: images, media and representation in research* (2nd edition). London: Sage.

Radley, A., and Taylor, D. (2003a). Remembering one's stay in hospital: a study in recovery, photography and forgetting. *Health: An Interdisciplinary Journal for the Social Study of Health, Illness and Medicine*, *7*, 129–159.

Radley, A. and Taylor, D. (2003b). Images of recovery: A photo-elicitation study on the hospital ward. *Qualitative Health Research*, *13*, 77–99.

Wang, C., and Burris, M. (1994). Empowerment through photo novella: portraits of participation. *Health Education Quarterly*, *21*, 171–186.

Wang, C., Cash, J., and Powers, L. (2000). Who knows the streets as well as the homeless? Promoting personal and community action through photovoice. *Health Promotion Practice*, *20*, 81–89.

Wright, T. (1999). *The photography handbook* (2nd edition). London: Routledge.

21 Polytextual Thematic Analysis for visual data

Pinning down the analytic

Kate Gleeson

Despite an exhilarating recent upsurge in attention to visual research methods in psychology (Frith *et al.*, 2005), Psychologists have tended to focus on developing techniques that use visual methods to elicit data rather than attempt to analyse visual data itself. More recently, in some areas of psychology, it has become almost impossible to resist analysing visual data. Social psychology has become increasingly interested in the production of identity, dress, appearance and visuality generally (Kaiser, 1997). Health psychology has become concerned with appearance and visible difference (cf. Rumsey and Harcourt, 2005). While psychologists may feel they lack training in analysing visual images, the task is not beyond us. The processes involved in interpreting visual text may look a little different, but interpretation, whether of words or pictures, is basically the same process of bringing one set of texts to bear on another in order to make meaning.

Disciplines that have engaged more fully with analysing visual material, e.g. Media Studies, Visual Sociology, Anthropology, and Cultural Studies have been less inhibited by the enlightenment project than have psychologists. They are more relativist in terms of evidentiary claims and less apologetic and more creative in their analysis of images. Analytic process is rarely made explicit and assumptions about replication and generalisation are set aside in favour of truth claims based on sound argument and theoretical support. Those engaged in semiological analyses do provide a greater level of detail about analysis, but tend to incorporate substantial theoretical baggage (Rose, 2001) and offer no clear method for conducting analysis (Slater, 1998).

Cross-disciplinary raiding has encouraged social and health psychologists to shrug off the reductionist epistemology of the enlightenment and turn to qualitative methods. This has led to the development and appropriation of a wide range of techniques for analysing text. Many accept that discursive approaches need to make a further stretch to take in the visual but are still very committed to showcasing system and rigour. It is hard to shake off an 'upbringing' as a researcher in psychology. We have been steeped in a disciplinary culture which is underpinned by the assumption that all analytic procedures and sampling strategies must be visible and explicit. To us it seems reasonable to ask to see the 'working out' in an analysis so that we can evaluate any reading offered, approximate the steps other researchers have taken and align our own approach against those of others. It is perhaps for this reason that it is easier to focus on data elicitation than on analysis of the visual.

New analytic approaches may begin in a fuzzy way (e.g. Potter and Wetherell, 1987) but they are soon pinned down into explicit steps that provide an exemplary way through an analysis (cf. Smith, 2003; Willig, 2001). The battles for ownership of terms may frustrate us, the establishment of strict demarcation lines may be restrictive, but to their credit psychologists are trying to find a common methodological and analytical language. In other disciplines, it appears, at least to a psychologist outsider, that there is less impetus to do this. Rose (2001: 73) has argued that there is '... a tendency for each semiological study to invent its own analytical terms'.

In trying to find a method to enable a direct analysis of visual material, I have explored the methods used in those disciplines that do incorporate the visual, including Visual Ethnography (Pink, 2007), Visual Sociology (Kress and van Leeuwen, 1996; van Leeuwen, 2001), Visual Cultural Studies (Lister and Wells, 2001; Schirato and Webb, 2004), Media Studies (Bell *et al.*, 1982), and Visual Anthropology (Ball and Smith, 1992; Collier and Collier, 1986). All have something to offer, particularly in terms of providing an agenda of questions to address, but none offers a system for analysing visual data that works for me. I have nevertheless plunged into a visual analysis because I have research questions that make it necessary.

I am trying to find ways of understanding the personhood of people with learning disability. In this area, the usual techniques that go with explorations of the self and identity are simply not sufficient. To rely largely on interviews where many of your participants have less facility with language is to limit the possibilities of a study. This chapter describes my attempt to find a plausible means for analysing visual data for, in this case, a study of photographic portraits of people with learning disabilities that were presented in a calendar format. The calendars intrigued me because, in a cultural context where people with learning disabilities are almost invisible, here they are presented as a spectacle, specifically to be looked at. Both calendars were produced with the expressed purpose of presenting positive images of people with learning disabilities, but each was produced in very different circumstances and enabled different kinds of engagement and agency in the production of the images. I was interested in exploring the visuality of people with learning disability in terms of the cultural significances, social practices and power relations in which that visuality is enmeshed. I therefore needed an analytic that would allow me to compare sets of images thematically.

I have described this analytic as Polytextual Thematic Analysis. It is polytextual in that it assumes that all texts (including visual texts) are predicated on one another, and each can only be read by reference to others (Curt, 1994). It is 'thematic' in that it attempts to identify the repetitive features or themes in the data that enable patterns to come into view. My approach is very like a thematic analysis of the kind described by Hayes (2000). The analysis that I describe here is inductive, but the basic approach is also amenable to a Theory Led Thematic Analysis (Hayes, 1997).

Psychology needs to analyse the visual

Social scientists have long held that 'the visual representations of society are both methods of research, and resources, or topics to be studied in their own right' (Denzin, 2004: 237). And yet psychology struggles with the visual and lacks confidence in visual methods. If psychology does its job well and really captures human experience, its findings will appear as little more than common sense. My argument here has three elements. First, psychologists are embedded within cultures and construct knowledge from cultural resources and address questions that are culturally meaningful. Second, the things that they 'dis-cover', once extracted from culture, must be returned to it in order to be recognisable as knowledge. Once provided with insight into a cultural phenomenon by psychology, members of the culture must be able to recognise it from their own experience. It must be plausible to acquire the status of validity. Finally, although the 'common-sensicality' of our knowledge troubles psychology from time to time when our status as experts is affronted, it is nevertheless a bedrock assumption that underpins much qualitative research including those methods that incorporate participant validation. Our methods are essentially the basic human skills of watching carefully what people do and listening carefully to what they say. There is no magic in this. However, in the areas of psychology where the most basic methods apply, we find it hard to assert expertise if we do not claim some special technique to give credibility to our method.

Membership of the cultural group that we study, and knowledge of its language, gives us the sense that texts provide clear access to the thoughts ideas and experiences of others. We even have code books/dictionaries to help us check our interpretations. Psychologists would be reluctant to look at an image and offer an interpretation unless they have techniques to guide them (Beloff, 1997). We tend to assume that the meaning is embedded in the method (Tseelon, 1991). Other social scientists would have no such qualms because they feel the most important investment is in theory, and that it is the theory that gives weight to their claim to expertise, not analytical technique. Such claims are perfectly fair. Interpretations are based on theory, on a conceptualisation of what a particular behaviour might mean, rather than upon a method.

When we turn to the visual we have no rule books to support our interpretations and must fall back on a wider disparate range of texts and experiences to justify our interpretation of the image. Apparent consensus may occur. At particular times in particular cultural locations the meaning of a visual display is so frequently referred to and so widely discussed that a dominant interpretation may be accessible to the psychologist. However, when we look at an image and call it research, the reading of the data becomes more open to validity challenges, the status of the data becomes tenuous, and the author/researcher may feel pressured to engage with devices which add status to their analyses. These devices would include the development of complex systems of codes (the less accessible to the non-initiated the better) to create 'expertise' in visual analysis. The author/researcher would almost inevitably have to translate their understanding of the visual data back into language so that the analysis 'counts as an analysis'. Visual elements of the data can be used to illustrate, when they have been discursively 'worked over', but they cannot be used to convey or exemplify an interpretation. The interpretation rests in the language not in the image. I argue that we can resist our fear of being 'imposter' scholars.

An attempt to analyse photographic portraits

In 2006, two calendars were created, each of which contained 12 portraits of people with learning disabilities. I was intrigued by the fact that while people with learning disabilities are largely invisible in British culture, the calendars would define them as something to be looked at – a spectacle.

The calendars were both created by people with a stated interest in providing constructive and positive representations of people with learning disabilities. One was published by the Down's Syndrome Association and the other by an advocacy organisation – People First.[1] The additional text that supported the two calendars made it clear that the conditions of their production were quite different. The Down's Syndrome Association calendar was largely the work of Richard Bailey, a photographer and the father of Billie-Jo, a young woman with Down's syndrome. In the cover notes for the calendar he states that people with Down's syndrome

> …ARE expected to attempt the kinds of things that 'we' all take for granted. There is no reason why they shouldn't get married, there is no reason why they shouldn't attend mainstream school and go on to further education, there is no reason why they shouldn't go on to gain some kind of employment and make their own contribution to society. There is no reason why they shouldn't live happy and meaningful lives surrounded by the people who love them.

The second calendar is entitled 'Positive and Proud'. It was created to celebrate the year of disabled people in a joint project between Bridgend People First[2] and Valley and Vale Community Arts.[3] Each portrait is accompanied by a short poem written by the people portrayed. The statement that accompanies this calendar makes similar statements about aspirations for inclusion and fulfilment for people with learning disabilities. However, the message about its production is written in the voice of the people represented rather than on their behalf. It emphasises their own aspirations for their lives and states that the 'images and poetry represent the result of each individual's journey to self awareness and self discovery'.[4]

In light of the agentic differences in their production, I set out to analyse each calendar independently before comparing them. For the purposes of this analysis I was interested more in the content of the representations of learning disability offered rather than with more discursive questions about how these representations are constructed as real, truthful and natural.

There are only so many things that you can do with data

As a social constructionist informed by a critical polytextual approach (Curt, 1994), I was prepared to use any and all means for decoding and providing alternative readings of my data, but needed to settle on a single means for organising the data and finding pattern in them in order to construct a coherent analysis. I approached the analysis by first reading everything that I could find about visual data analysis. The material was limited and often less than explicit. Where it did exist, the approach tended not to be helpful in terms of how it conceived the sampling strategy, or in terms of the level of engagement with the data. The two most useful texts I read were those of Sarah Pink (2007) and Gillian Rose (2001). Pink doesn't offer techniques for conducting visual ethnography but does offer a very clear theory for a method. Rose provides a crystal clear account of a number of key approaches to visual methodology. Her clarity enabled my critique of the literature but did not offer any clear technique to guide the analysis.

I was offered many useful questions that could inform my analysis, but no one offered me any ideas about how to handle the data, how to order and organise them, how to find the pattern. I did however notice a pattern in the writing about visual analysis, and it was a familiar one. I had the same kind of feeling I sometimes have when teaching different approaches to analysing interview data. This is the feeling that there are only so many things you can do with data. Researchers explain and label what they do in different ways, depending on how they understand the processes of knowledge production through research. The same actions had different claims attached to them, but the actions taken to organise data and find pattern in them look pretty much the same, regardless of epistemology.

The interpretations we make are not contained within specific images, or interviews. Both interview transcript and photograph are polysemic and polytextual. We cannot interpret a text or image through that text or image alone, we draw on the meanings carried by other texts and images. As Derrida (1978: 25) so usefully pointed out, words only have 'meaning in relation to other words. Meanings are always in flux, relationships are arbitrary and ultimate meanings always deferred'.

For my study I needed an analytic approach that would allow for this intertextuality, but also allow me to deal with intervisuality. I consider the term 'intervisuality' as having a usefulness equivalent to intertextuality. Just as written texts cannot be interpreted without the use of other texts, not least a dictionary, images cannot simply be perceived. Every image is related to every other image available in culture and can only be interpreted by reference to those other images. In trying to draw out themes from the calendar photographs, I would have to rely on a visual language that is developed from looking at other images, basically all culturally available visual resources. I was less interested in drawing out any structural properties or rules underlying the construction of the images, than I was in recording, describing and organising the features of the images in a way that allowed me to focus on the content. I realised that there would be a number of useful reference points from which to explore the contingent and located intertextuality and intervisuality in these calendars. I needed an approach that would allow me to use anything and everything to make sense of my data.

Getting a broad understanding of patterns in data

One very useful technique for getting an overview of data and developing research ideas and research questions, is inductive thematic analysis. This approach puts the emphasis on finding common themes. It allows comparison between sets of data and it is descriptive before it becomes interpretative. This seemed an appropriate approach for comparing two sets of images of people with learning disabilities that were constructed with avowedly similar 'intentions' but within very different contexts of production. I needed a visual analytic that would allow an overview of quite a number of images. Thematic analysis was ideal as it provided a quick and easy method to give a view of the pattern in a sample of visual images. It is potentially rigorous, and makes the interpretative actions of the analysis as visible and as explicit as possible.

Illustrating Polytextual Thematic Analysis: The analytic process

I have therefore settled upon an approach that I have termed Polytextual Thematic Analysis. This refers to the analysis of visual data that looks across sets of images and tries to capture the recurring patterns in the analysis both in terms of form and content. The themes are recognised as the result of drawing on a range of other culturally available visual images and texts, and are interpreted in relation to these images and texts. This does not involve translation of visual symbols into written text, rather description of the elements of the visual texts that are recognisable and available in the visual and written knowledge of a culture.

The themes are written descriptions of visual elements, but could, and hopefully will be, illustrated visually in images that capture and represent the theme. Not that I have yet found an effective means for doing this.

The analysis

The analysis involves viewing the pictures repeatedly while reading and considering the various cultural images and texts that enable their interpretation. In the process we are looking for key themes, and key words that will capture recurring visual images.

Sampling strategy

The sample will always be determined by the research question. I have collected many different images of people with learning disability over the years as I have an interest in both visual identity and learning disability. The two sets that I focused on for the study were interesting in that they were both presented in the form of calendars, although one set was also presented in an art exhibition. As I have already said, there was something intriguing to me about the use of portraits of people with learning disability in calendars, as calendar portraits are explicitly defined as to be looked at.

In Polytextual Thematic Analysis sampling is, in keeping with other constructionist qualitative approaches, purposive and theory led. Criteria for inclusion should be stated clearly, but there is no need to address issues of representativeness. It is possible to use relatively large samples of images, and possible to compare different sets of data. I will set out the basic steps involved before illustrating the approach with an extract of the results from my analysis of the calendars.

The 'recipe'

1. Look at the images over and over again, singly, in groups, serially and in as many different orders as possible. Note any potential themes that emerge, taking care to describe the features of the image that evoke that theme. These initial things might be called proto-themes to signal the tentative and fluid nature of the themes as they are beginning to take shape.
2. Feel the effects that the images have on you and describe these as fully as you can in your notes. Go back to these notes and add additional comments as you continue to analyse other images to see if you are experiencing the pictures in different ways as you start to 'get your eye in'.
3. Where a proto-theme appears to occur more than once, collect together all the material relevant to that theme. Pull the relevant pictures together and look once again to see whether the proto-theme is distinct.
4. Write a brief description (or definition) of the proto-theme.
5. Once a proto-theme has been identified in a picture you will need to go back over all of the other images to see if it is recognisable anywhere else.
6. Once again pull together all the material relevant to that proto-theme. Revise the description of the proto-theme if necessary, and bring together descriptions of the elements from different images that best illustrate that theme. It is at this point that the proto-themes (i.e. first attempts at themes, or primitive themes) may be elevated to the status of theme. However, such a shift signals that the theme has been checked and considered many times. It does not mean that it is fixed in its final form.
7. Continue to work on identifying themes in the pictures until no further distinctive themes [that are relevant to the question(s) that you have brought to the analysis] emerge.
8. Look at the descriptions of all themes in relation to each other, and consider the extent to which they are distinct. If there is any lack of clarity, redefine the themes that you have identified. Write descriptions of themes that highlight the differences between themes. The object is to maximise differentiation in order to pull out distinctive features of the image.
9. Look at the themes to see if any cluster together in a way that suggests a higher order theme that connects them.
10. Define the higher order theme, and consider all themes in relation to it. As other higher order themes emerge consider each in relation to all other themes that have emerged.

11. It is at this stage that it is necessary to make a judgement about which of the themes that have emerged best address the research question so that a limited number may be selected for writing up. It will be helpful to incorporate any supporting materials that contextualise the images being analysed.

Presenting results

If themes are to be presented in the conventional way as written descriptions of the visual elements of the data, then each should be presented with a descriptive title, a definition and descriptions of the elements that make up that theme.

Because images are devoid of verbal language, although arguably always discursively produced (Foucault, 1972), the textual relocation of an image is easier and renders an image open to interpretation by an enormous range of people from different cultural locations. However, given the relatively inexpensive access to sophisticated technology for producing and reproducing images, it is not beyond the researcher's power to create composite images to illustrate themes. We could group and cluster images to juxtapose and show the relationships between particular features, perhaps in the form of a visual essay (Berger, 1972). I have not attempted this here.

An illustration – Learning disability in spectacular form

The analysis of the calendars resulted in a wealth of themes, sub-themes and, for want of a better term, super-ordinate themes. In the People First calendar there were 12 clusters of themes and two single themes that stood alone. In the Downs Syndrome Association calendar there were 8 clusters of themes. The theme map for the People First calendar was more complex and contained greater diversity than the Down's Syndrome Association calendar. Rather than try to present all the data here, I will illustrate a small number of themes in brief, but locate them in their cluster to show how this analytic technique has achieved its purpose of describing the features of the two calendars thematically to show some important differences and similarities between them. I have focused on differences here because they are easier to present briefly without full discussion of nuance.

One interesting difference between the calendars is the way in which gender is represented. In the Down's Syndrome Association calendar, no person is portrayed in a way that confronts gender norms, and the only gender-relevant theme to emerge was the theme of 'Gender Neutral'.

Gender Neutral

Although all people presented in the calendar are dressed in gender-normative ways, clothing is typically ambiguous, often a uniform. Where an infant is shown naked in multiple poses, only the top half of the body is shown making gender ambiguous. In most portraits the activities shown are gender neutral. None of the activities refers specifically to gender-related activities or positions.

In the People First calendar there was more emphasis on gender and a cluster of themes emerged – 'Powerful Women', 'Hyper-femininity' and 'Hyper-masculinity'. The themes of Hyper-masculinity and Hyper-femininity provide an informative contrast to the underplaying of gender in the Down's Syndrome Association calendar.

Hyper-masculinity

This theme refers to the way in which men in the portraits are presented in assertive, even aggressive postures, engaged in male stereotypical activities and associated with male defined artefacts. Be-suited Hywell leans against a sports car, Tom sits astride a motorbike in a leather jacket. Rhodri stands in outdoor gear, clutching binoculars, wearing a serious expression. His poem states 'I am an eagle, handsome, strong and free'.

Hyper-femininity

This theme is best illustrated in the portraits of Julie and Patricia. Julie is presented in a setting of high drama and glamour on a stage lit from below, surrounded by lush red curtains. Her full length dress swishes through the edges of a rich silk cape as she smiles up into the camera with the sexual confidence of a model or actress. Patricia wears the iconic ultra-feminine bridal outfit. She sits with lacy gloved hands neatly folded on her frilled, be-ribboned and layered satin dress, surrounded by her veil. While the theme captures the aspiration for a hyper-feminine identity, Patricia's accompanying poem asserts that this is a status denied her in her daily life. 'Look and see what can never be, my dream to have a family. Why can't I be a bride? Why has this been denied?'

Another contrast can be seen between clusters of themes about Relating. In the Down's Syndrome Association calendar there is a theme entitled 'In Love'.

In Love

This theme appears in only one portrait, but is explicitly identified by a caption 'love' (Figure 21.1 © Richard Bailey). It conveys a romantic image of couple-ness with no reference to sexuality. A young couple lean into each other's arms in an idyllic country setting. The man sits beside and slightly behind the woman, his arm around her shoulder reaching down to her hand on one side. The other arm reaches forward to her other hand. Their faces touch side on, their hands are clasped. There is no other intimacy between them.

In contrast, within the People First calendar there was a cluster of four themes about relating to others but also a cluster of six themes about sexuality. The theme of 'Sexual assertiveness' is an example of these.

Sexual Assertiveness

This theme is about expressing sexual intention explicitly. David lies on his side in a 'male-stud' pose, legs outstretched and crossed, leaning forward onto his arms,

Figure 21.1 The theme 'In Love'.

chin tipped downward so that he looks upward to the photographer (Figure 21.2 © Alison McGann). He is wearing jeans, a tight tee shirt and a medallion. The attached poem states that he is sexy and ambitious and that 'girls think I'm delicious'. Another young man in a suit, poses against a red sports car above a poem that describes him as 'handsome, smart and cute'. An older man in a leather jacket sits astride a motorbike with a younger woman leaning back into his arms. His poem describes him as 'sexy and bold'. These are assertive exuberant images of sexually confident people.

The final pair of themes to be contrasted relate to the contexts in which the people with learning disability are portrayed. There is more emphasis on individuals and identity in the People First calendar, sometimes very little of the location is visible in the portrait, or the location is neutral – perhaps with a single colour background. There is more emphasis on context in the Down's Syndrome Association calendar, and people are often presented in very beautiful settings. Indeed one of the themes, 'Idealised Setting', refers to idyllic settings where there

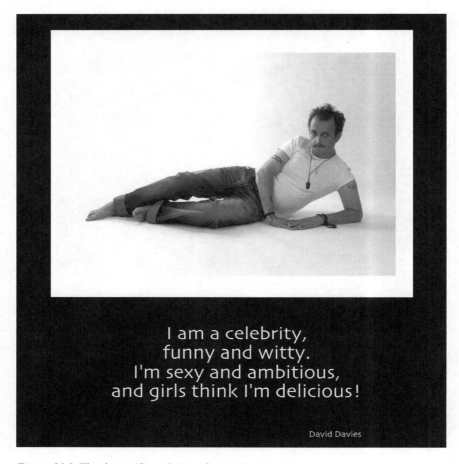

I am a celebrity,
funny and witty.
I'm sexy and ambitious,
and girls think I'm delicious!

David Davies

Figure 21.2 The theme 'Sexual Assertiveness'.

is nature in full flush, the sun shines and there is no clutter or litter to be seen. In fact the whole cluster of themes about setting was titled Mainstream Settings, because all of the contexts were apparently mainstream ones. The school settings in two of the portraits were mainstream schools. Other settings were valued locations such as theatre stages, sports tracks and workplace settings. The theme of Workplace is a very interesting example of a mainstream setting as it has a twist that casts doubt on the notion of inclusivity that is implied by the notion of mainstream.

Workplace

This theme explicitly conveys a recognisable workplace with work–related items and equipment clearly on view. It is drawn from two of the portraits that are taken

Figure 21.3 The theme 'Workplace'.

in workplace settings. The workers are in uniform, one a chef in a kitchen, the other shows two waiting staff taking a break (Figure 21. 3 © Richard Bailey). The settings are apparently mainstream, and therefore show people with learning disabilities actively engaged in valuable and productive work. However, in the picture showing the waiting staff on a break, there are two young women with Down's syndrome. It would be unusual to find two employees with a learning disability coincidentally employed in a small work setting. This may suggest that this is a supported work placement of some kind.

These themes confirm that achieving inclusion in mainstream settings is something that the Down's Syndrome Association calendar wants to convey. By contrast, there is a cluster of themes around power in the People First calendar that suggest that being permitted to enter mainstream settings is not as highly prized as being able to assert your own power. This is illustrated in an interesting way in the theme of 'Aggression'. There is nothing remotely approaching the notion of

Figure 21.4 The theme 'Aggression'.

aggression in the Down's Syndrome Association calendar where the photographer overtly sets up the portraits and directs their content.

Aggression

This theme captures aggressive postures, statements and gestures. In a vibrant red sweater, Brangwyn stares out of his portrait aggressively – his poem conveys an explicit challenge 'Step back! Why do you stare? Respect me, Respect you if you dare' (Figure 21.4 © Alison McGann). This is the only overtly aggressive and challenging image in either of the calendars, but it is clear and explicit in its assertive aggression.

Interpretation

There is not enough space to engage in a commentary on these themes or to relate them to the literature and to the debates with which they might engage. This chapter merely sets out to show the possibilities in such an analysis and to show that this analytic is effective in that it enables the powerful description of themes that illustrate important features in visual data. However, I would like to briefly share with the reader some of my reasons for believing that Polytextual Thematic Analysis of visual data enabled me to address my original research objectives in a productive way.

Even this brief description has shown that the analytic allowed me to identify identity-relevant themes. Having a systematic way of comparing the theme structures of the two calendars allowed me to make claims about the ways in which different groups attempt to assert positive visual identities for people with learning disabilities. The differences between the calendars showed that themes of 'inclusion' and 'mainstream' that are crucial elements of the Government's Valuing People agenda are treated differently by those who wish to promote valued visual identities for others, than by those who wish to lead their own identity projects. The themes from the People First calendar appeared to me to connect with an agentic foray into mainstream settings and engagement with mainstream identities that include a fuller range of grittier visualities including aggression, sexual intention and the individual's control over identity production. This finding alone shows that the cultural production of identities for people with learning disabilities in calendars can neutralise difference and normalise disability in ways that make people with learning disability more acceptable to mainstream society. It has also enabled me to discover that the calendar can also be a device that enables the identity projects and intentions of people with learning disabilities and allows them to assert visual identities that they value regardless of public opinion and government agendas.

In the first steps of analysis an attempt was made to stay at the surface level, to take the visual representations at face value and to describe them. However, there is, of course, another level of meaning below the surface that we can begin to see when we look across collections of images. These different levels of interpretation are often referred to in terms of creating higher order themes that are more abstract and capture something beyond an individual datum. A higher order of interpretation is possible with these data, in that themes about 'Agency' and 'Identity Project' allow us to consider the political implications of the two calendars. Unfortunately there isn't space to explore these here. It is my ambition to try to capture these themes visually so that people with learning disability might be able to engage with them and thereby help me further develop an understanding of what it means for someone with a learning disability to be portrayed in a calendar. I would also hope that by presenting the analysis in visual form there is a potential for handing over responsibility for interpretation to an 'audience' in the same way that ethnographers such as Trinh (1992) have tried to do with documentary film.

Last word

Shared meanings are relative to a group and are contingent on historic and cultural location. Our interpretation is always from within that group. We are users and experts of our historical and cultural location. The images, the words and our interpretations are not universal and value free. Neither need this be true for the visual images that we interpret. The fact that they are viewed and interpreted while wearing our 'cultural goggles' doesn't mean they are less useful within our world. If we can shrug off that old search for enlightenment, we can see that the fact that we use a specific lens to view the images is precisely the thing that makes our interpretation culturally useful. The lens is a language, just as the dictionary and other texts provide us with the language to analyse and interpret written text.

I will not feel that this approach to analysing visual data is complete until I have the means of presenting the analysis in visual form. But that means not only further developing my own creative skills, but also requires a shift in the culture of journals to enable visual data to be presented in a wider range of formats.

Now I have got to the point in the story where I am reminded of the emperor's new clothes. I am waiting for someone to ask 'Is that all?' Well, basically, yes it is. There is nothing magical in this approach, it is literally common sense, and involves attempting to draw upon cultural knowledge and shared perception. I have used anything and everything that I can recognise within the portraits, and I have tried to do it as explicitly and reflexively as possible. It is both simple and complex and a useful approach for analysing visual data. If someone had already written this chapter when I began my analysis, I would have happily used it.

Notes

1 The initial analysis of these data was presented at the Appearance Matters Conference in Bath 2007. A full account of the analysis and a more detailed description of the conditions of construction of these calendars will be made available in a paper under submission.
2 People First is a charity which enables advocacy and leisure activity for people with learning disabilities.
3 The photographer for the project was Alison McGann.
4 This quote is taken from the frontispiece of the calendar.

References

Ball, M. S. and Smith, G. W. H (1992) *Analysing visual data.* London: Sage.
Bell, P., Boehringer, K. and Crofts, S. (1982) *Programmed politics: A study of Australian television.* Sydney: Sable Publishing.
Beloff, H. (1997) Making and un-making identities: A psychologist looks at art-work. In N. Hayes (Ed.) *Doing qualitative analysis in psychology.* London: Sage.
Berger, J. (1972) *Ways of seeing.* London: Penguin.
Collier, J., Jr. and Collier, M. (1986) *Visual anthropology: Photography as a research method.* Albuquerque: University of New Mexico Press.

Curt, B., Eccleston, C., Gleeson, K., Lee, N., Stainton Rogers, R., Stainton Rogers, W., Stenner, P. and Worrell, M. (1994) *Textuality and tectonics*. Milton Keynes: Open University Press.

Denzin, N. K. (2004) Reading film: Using films and videos as empirical social science material. In U. Flick, E. Von Kardorff and I. Steinke (Eds.) *A companion to qualitative research*. London: Sage.

Derrida, J. (1978) *Writing on difference* (Trans. A. Bass). London: Routledge.

Foucault, M. (1972) *The archaeology of knowledge*. London: Tavistock.

Frith, H., Riley, S., Archer, L. and Gleeson, K. (2005) Editorial: Imag(in)ing visual methodologies. *Qualitative Methods in Psychology*, 2(3), 187–257.

Gleeson, K. (2006) When description becomes prescription: People with learning disabilities on display. *Appearance matters 2: Developing theory and practice*. Centre for Appearance Research and the South West Branch of the BPS, The Assembly Rooms and Guildhall, Bath, 6–7 June.

Hayes, N. (2000) *Doing psychological research*. London: Sage.

Hayes, N. (1997) *Doing qualitative analysis in psychology*. Hove: Psychology Press.

Kaiser, S. B. (1997) *The social psychology of clothing*. Oxford: Berg.

Kress, G. and van Leeuwen, T. (1996) *Reading images: The grammar of visual design*. London: Routledge.

van Leeuwen, T. (2001) Semiotics and Iconography. In T. van Leeuwen and C. Jewitt (Eds.) *Handbook of visual analysis*. London: Sage.

Lister, M. and Wells, L. (2001) Seeing beyond belief: Cultural studies as an approach to analysing the visual. In T. van Leeuwen and C. Jewitt (Eds.) *Handbook of visual analysis*. London: Sage.

Pink, S. (2007) *Doing visual ethnography*. London: Sage.

Potter, J. and Wetherell, M. (1987) *Discourse and social psychology*. London: Sage.

Rose, G. (2001) *Visual methodologies*. London: Sage.

Rumsey, N and Harcourt, D. (2005) *The psychology of appearance*. Maidenhead: Open University Press.

Shirato, T. and Webb, J. (2004) *Understanding the visual*. London: Sage.

Slater, D. (1998) Analysing cultural objects: content analysis and semiotics. In C. Seale (Ed.) *Researching society and culture*. London: Sage.

Smith, J. A. (2003) *Qualitative psychology: A practical guide to research methods*. London: Sage.

Trinh, T. M. (1992) *Framer framed*. New York: Routledge.

Tseelon, E. (1991) The method is in the message. *Theory and Psychology*, 1(3), 299–316.

Willig, C. (2001) *Introducing qualitative research in psychology: Adventures in theory and method*. Buckingham: Open University Press.

22 'So you think we've moved, changed, the representation got more what?'

Methodological and analytical reflections on visual (photo-elicitation) methods used in the Men-as-Fathers study

Karen Henwood, Fiona Shirani and Mark Finn

Why research the visual?

Within the social sciences generally (Kress and Van Leeuwen, 2001), and qualitative psychology specifically (Reavey and Johnson, 2008; Frith *et al.*, 2005), realisation is growing of the value of working with data in different media (audio, visual and textual), for giving researchers access to different modalities of meaning.[1] Since the 1990s (Henwood and Pidgeon, 1992; Henwood and Nicolson, 1995), speaking and writing have been key modalities for qualitative psychologists inquiring into the experiential, relational, embodied, socially situated, discursively constituted, and culturally meaningful ways in which people encounter others, live out their daily lives, and engage with their everyday worlds (see e.g. Camic *et al.*, 2003; Willig and Stainton Rogers, 2008). There is now a strong case for further expanding such research by recording and analysing *visual data* (e.g. photographs, paintings, films) where experiencing, representing and communicating meaning is accomplished in *visual mode*. Recording and analysing what is seen and how it is viewed, along with the ways of telling inspired by such viewings and sightings, gives access to different types of information not available by other means, enriching ways of representing experience and enhancing understanding of studied life (Reavey and Johnson, 2008).

General commentaries written about developing trends in social research methods attribute rising enthusiasm for visual research to such things as: visualisation becoming an integral part of everyday life and contemporary culture; easy availability of digital information technologies for making, collecting and showing static and moving visual images; and expanding skills and competences in using visual media, stimulating use of visual images within the research process (see e.g. Knoblauch *et al.*, 2008). Equally important is the coincidence of visual and technological literacy with the promotion of a more reflexive, perspectival understanding of the principles and practices of knowledge generation (Harrison, 2002). Multiple perspectives, or socially and culturally located viewpoints, are included as part of researchers' efforts at knowledge-making, and reflexive researchers are charged with bringing them together to produce a (more or less) theorised account of the qualities and textures of subjectivity and experience (Henwood, 2008; Henwood *et al.*, 1998). Increasingly, such perspectives are considered multilocal and centered on movement, involving wide-ranging sensorial engagements with the world. Being multimodal, these engagements include, but are not restricted to, sequential acts of listening and looking (Pink, 2008).

Writing in favour of a particular shift in perspective in visual research, Bohnsack (2008) proposes that visual researchers inquire into how people read visual images/what they do with the images, and do not simply use images to document studied life (see also Cardiff Hypermedia). Parallel developments in ethnographic study criticise the practice of reporting at a distance, and provide alternative ethnographic practices for studying visual culture as involving constructing points of view. Here, researcher and researched are brought into the cultural world, and questions asked about the authority, intelligibility, and cultural significance of their readings. Creation of knowledge out of what each viewer brings to photographic acts of viewing – portraying others and analysing patterns of representation – is a way of getting at what is more ambiguous, polysemic and difficult to interpret in visual images. It shifts interest to the audience's ways of viewing, and away from the producer's world of meaning. What people notice in an image, and make meaning out of, is part of the creative, knowledge-creating process involving the analysis of signification, usefully pointing to another key issue in visual study – the way it can involve shifts in mode of social interaction. For example, when looking at an image, people can experience a shared engagement with it, and a common knowledge of what is visible in the interview. Studying modes of communication and interaction (Jenkins *et al.*, 2008) reinforces the point that verbalising experience, and presenting oneself through the image, are not one and the same; the way we live and our feelings are not always readily available to verbal description (Reavey and Johnson, 2008).

Photo-elicitation is a multimodal technique for studying what people (come to) see in, and say about, pictures. It provides ways of combining the visual and verbal by using pre-existing, researcher- or participant-generated images, encouraging their careful and creative viewing by study participants, and eliciting extensive, verbalised responses to their symbolic qualities. As with open-ended interviews (Harper, 1994), researchers find ways to prompt, stimulate and give guidance to interviewees – listening and encouraging engagement with, commentary upon, and dialogue about the visual materials. Photographs are held to be uniquely informative about time and place because their particular properties (such as facial expressions, gestures, mannerisms, clothes of those photographed, photographic genres, and semiotic features) evoke an era, and link people to historical epochs of which they have no personal experience (Harper, 2002). Seeing themselves in, or experiencing (dis)identification with others in the image, can help people tell about their own personal lives, and engage with larger social realities (Harrison, 2002). Photo-elicitation techniques enable people to speak of thoughts, aspirations, hopes and fears in ways that are not strictly referential – speaking not of things that have actually happened, but that operate as part of the imaginary. As well as being singular and static, images can be viewed multiply – e.g. as part of narrative structures, and sequential analysis can promote accounting for continuity and change in time and place by respondents and/or researchers (Harper, 2005).

Working with visual methods in the Men-as-Fathers study

We address our own ways of working with a range of visual methods (specifically photo-elicitation methods) in a social psychological study of the dynamics of men's identities, relationships, and subjectivities as, and after, they become fathers for the first time (see Henwood *et al.*, 2008a; Finn and Henwood, 2009).[2] The study is inquiring into what it means to be a man and father in contemporary Britain, asking such questions as: How, and to what extent, are men's identities being refashioned within transforming gender relations, family relationships, and wider socio-cultural change? Are changing expectations for fatherhood producing new forms of masculinity?

Conceptually and methodologically, we are concerned to bring into focus how it is that men *come to be* men and fathers – how their identities and subjectivities become configured. We view the processes of masculine identity formation, and paternal subjectivity, as steeped in the men's everyday assumptions, experiences and perceptions about how things are, could and should be (now and in the future). Accordingly, we attend to the ways in which interviewees construct their points of view, drawing upon their own biographically/relationally conditioned psychological investments; finding different ways of negotiating with normative frameworks, expectations and beliefs; and invoking or activating culturally and socially situated discourses to account for, and interpret, the meanings that make up the fabric of daily life.

Like others (Frosh *et al.*, 2002; Wetherell and Edley, 1999), our way of studying identity and subjectivity foregrounds their emergence, production or constitution within ordinary acts of meaning making.[3] In view of critical methodological commentaries (outlined above), we have posed the additional questions: 'Does ordinary meaning making occur through the medium of talk or discourse alone'? Might it be necessary to augment purely talk-based (discursive) methods of inquiry by asking questions about sense making and the representation of experience, via other sensory modalities such as the visual? (Henwood *et al.*, 2008a).

Our study is qualitative longitudinal (QLL) in design, making it possible to investigate in biographical terms how identities and relationships change in and through time. One of the prime developers and advocates of QLL methodology, Saldaña (2003: 25) strongly advocates including visual methods as '*visual images, whether still or in motion, provide some of the richest and most tangible data for accessing change through time*'. Accordingly, we follow Saldaña's insight and consider how visual methods can help with using time as a vehicle of analysis, contributing to the development of a suite of micro-temporal methods for investigating the invisible temporal (Adam, 2008), complex temporalities (Henwood *et al.*, 2008b), and everyday, temporal and textual processes of change-in-the-making (Neale and Flowerdew, 2003; Neale *et al.*, 2007).

So how, then, can visual methods be used to elicit data and gain insights, potentially making accessible what would otherwise remain inaccessible using solely talk-based methods? We present, comment on, and compare three visual research methods (collage, visual sequence, personal photographs)[4] employed in our study involving two cohorts of variously skilled and socially positioned men from East Anglia (N = 30) and South Wales (N = 15). The East Anglia sample was interviewed intensively (three times) in 2000-1: subsequently 18 of the men were re-interviewed 8 years later in summer 2008. Interviews with the South Wales sample occurred during 2008–9, and followed the same pattern of three intensive interviews, one before and two in the first year after the child's birth.

Collage

The collage is a set of 18 photographs, presented simultaneously to participants on two A4 sheets: interviewees were asked to say what they thought about any images that stood out to them, and about the collage as a whole. Photographs depicted fathers in a variety of poses and activities in different settings, alone with children or with other people (wife/partner, other generations), and in a diversity of social circumstances (fathers were younger, older, apparently living in affluent or more impoverished surroundings, etc); covering a range of contrasting cultural ideas and ideals of fathers. The collage was used in 2000 when participants were first recruited to the study in East Anglia; we took the opportunity to ask about the same collage again with these men when they were revisited again 8 years later.

Practically speaking, presenting the collage fairly early on in interviews with the men (at first interview, during partner's pregnancy), was a way of stimulating interviewees to initially engage in thinking about fatherhood. Subsequently, more in-depth, conversational interviewing about the men's experiences as expectant fathers asked them about their perceptions of the pregnancy, and anticipated change in their lives and relationships with others. We envisaged that the collage would elicit nuanced data on how masculine and paternal identities signified for the interviewees personally and culturally, prompted by the images that had been selected to show diversity in fathering activities and identities, along with historical and contemporary fatherhood representations. The collage was a way of assisting the men to contextualise their own biographical experiences (viz. connect their own personal experiences with wider social realities), as they were being presented with others' lived social realities and different cultural possibilities. Following Harper (1994), we believed that the simultaneous presentation of a group of images on a page might have generative potential, for us as researchers, as specific images would gain more importance through being part of more elaborate visual statements.

Participants, overwhelmingly, selected 2 images that depicted father, partner and child in a happy and playful scenario, and said that the majority of the photographs were positive, with only 2 of the 18 images receiving no positive feedback from any of the participants. Perceiving positive father images was important as, without them, interviewees would have been less able to envisage their situations as expectant fathers, especially their imagined futures. However, the general perception of images in the collage as 'pretty positive' meant a lack of differentiation and limited discussion; some participants were unsure of what was expected of them, and how they should critically appraise the photographs; and, while all could indicate their favoured pictures, responses were generally quite limited as to the reasons behind this:

Malcolm: Here, number nine, that's really quite a nice picture certainly. Fourteen's quite nice, number one's nice, two's nice, he's playing with a child. Three, five's quite important because he's making him watch football!

Although, disappointingly, the men's responses were not extensive, the collage generated useful data. Through this technique it became apparent that images of modes of fathering which did not fit with the men's ideals and expectations were viewed as depicting bad fathers. For example, the men frequently distanced themselves from the image of Michael Jackson, describing him as 'the ultimate freak father' whose behaviour they had no desire to emulate. Whilst receiving a less critical reaction than the Michael Jackson picture, the image of a Victorian father and baby was also problematised for representing an outmoded form of fathering where the father was a distant breadwinner removed from a fun and emotionally close relationship with the child.

The collage proved a useful way of priming discussion of the ways of fathering men wanted to emulate, along with the difficulties they anticipated in doing this. Aside from the positive family images mentioned above, many men selected the picture of a man shaving whilst his small son looks on as a favourite because it represented teaching the child; an important father role. When it came to selecting images they thought would represent their own experiences of fatherhood, several of the men chose pictures they had earlier described in a fairly negative way. One of these images showed a smartly dressed father on a telephone whilst children were present but apparently receiving little of his attention, which participants saw as negative for suggesting the father had no time to spend with his children. Whilst wanting to emulate the playful family images they selected as being positive, these working father images raised concerns about how the men would reconcile work and family life.

Use of the collage enabled men to select the images they were most attracted to and subsequently highlighted several important issues: concerns about the integration of work and home life, the importance of being seen as a caring and involved father and a rejection of some non-normative types of fathering. However, many of these issues arose during the remainder of the interview and, by allowing the men to select images rather than talk about each one in turn, many of the pictures were overlooked, although it was not clear why. Was it because the men did not relate to them or because they were too normative to warrant comment? Did presenting such a large number of images perceived as 'generally positive' early on in the interview set up expectations around what good fathering involves, thus limiting the rest of the interview dialogue?

To develop our understanding of how the collage had worked as a method, and why it had been only partly successful, we presented it once again to the original East Anglia participants when revisiting them eight years later, at the end of that interview. Participants were asked not to select their favourite pictures, but what they thought of being shown the pictures as an expectant father then (if they could remember) and now. Many of the fathers had a strong recollection of the task, even remembering which images were chosen, although their reactions to being asked to do this were fairly mixed. Some of the men had enjoyed the task and repeated it again, picking out which ones they liked best and re-evaluating their original interpretations.

Simon: I can sort of remember, I remember a smiling dad with a pile of kids in a sitting room ... Hmmm. I found that quite useful, I mean if I remember the question was (2) yes, which ones do you relate to, how do you (1) what did I do? I think in my mind I interpreted it as which would you aspire to...which ones do you hope to be... Yeah I just absolutely fixed on that one... Yes and remember thinking 'yes, that's good' ... I still, that's a good one. You know ... because... I'm now informed that this is exactly what kids like more than anything; having a good old rumble about against dad, so I reckon I picked the right one at the time (laughs).

Like Simon, many of the men felt the pictures gained a new salience in light of becoming a father and having eight years experience of parenthood. This meant that second time around the men were more likely to comment on pictures that related to their own experiences, rather than picking up on aspirations or fears.

Unsurprisingly, the men were not really able to comment on the methodology, and were more likely to lapse back into the original task. However, none of the respondents had a particularly strong reaction against the collage, and their reflections illustrate the utility of presenting the images *before* the men became fathers in order to elicit responses about their concerns and aspirations. In hindsight, deploying further methodological strategies, and encouraging participants' more creative, and holistic, engagement with the collage (e.g. by stimulating discussion of cross referencing of images, sifting and sorting them into cultural categories, and agreeing on their meaning), might have produced more elaborated responses.

The temporal sequence (visual narrative)

The visual sequence is an assemblage of images presenting a temporal framing in visual mode of changing socio-cultural representations of fatherhood from Victorian to present day. It was used as an alternative photo-elicitation device, addressing more directly interviewees' perceptions of continuity and change, and questions about complex temporalities, with the second cohort of participants, from South Wales, who joined the study in 2008.

Figure 22.1 Victorian father as used in collage and sequence techniques; reproduced with permission from copyright holder for research purposes.

Concerns and drawbacks relating to the collage outlined above led us to significantly alter our photo-elicitation technique eight years later when another phase of the study was to be carried out with a new sample. We increased our use of historical photographs as, when using the collage, we had realised that an image of the Victorian father (Figure 22.1) provided an illustration of past ways of doing and displaying fatherhood and masculinity that may not be accessible through talk alone, better foregrounding issues of change and temporality. Harper (2002: 23) notes the evocative potentials of photographs in relation to (historical) time:

> Photographs appear to capture the impossible: a person gone; an event past. That extraordinary sense of seeming to retrieve something that has disappeared belongs alone to the photograph and it leads to deep and interesting talk.

Five images were used as a sequential narrative to represent fathering over different generations from Victorian to present day: (i) Victorian father, (ii) 1950s gender differentiated family image, (iii) 1980s father playing with child, (iv) 1980s Athena 'man and baby' image, (v) 2007 image of father and baby face-to-face in mutual gaze.[5]

The interviewer encouraged participants to interpret the visual images for their personally and culturally created, symbolic meanings, through offering them various conversational openings or question framings. This made it possible for interviewees to take up diverse interpretative stances, while reducing any discomfort at the task's open-endedness, making the task more intelligible, and allowing the images to elicit meanings relating to interviewees' own, personal lives.

I: We are just asking you to give some reactions to each of the images? Moving ahead in time...? I'm not going to give you much context, how do you read that? What's that representing? Can you see any of your own family in that?

By making visual features of the image foci of discussion (e.g. who is standing or seated; at the centre or margins of the photograph), the interviewer sought to bring out the interpretative significance of the visual to the interviewee, including specific socio-cultural meanings (such as dominance) afforded by representing aspects of parenting identities, practices and relationships in visual mode.

Joe: The dad's the focal point isn't he - in the first one you look at the dad and the kids there's no, you can't see any love there ...
I: No. I mean there's something ... about him being in the centre.
Joe: The central role in the family 'I'm the...' yeah that's what I'm saying, the disciplinarian 'I'm here, this is my family, I'm in charge' you know literally 'I'm the daddy' you know ... She's very much, she's kind of out in the corner 'I'm the wife but I'm over here' you know.

The sequential organisation of the set of images as a visual narrative was brought into play in the discussion, to facilitate reflections in and through time on movement, continuities, and changes in perspective.

Marcus: That's more where I see myself being.
I: So you think we've moved, changed, the representation's got more what?
Marcus: I think maybe it's got more tactile and more emotional and less functional.

The sequence picture of a Victorian father overwhelmingly elicited a negative response from participants, who saw it as an outdated mode of fathering, as with the collage image. The father was construed as unemotional, distant from the family, and the men failed to identify with it in terms of their own experiences or expectations; for them it remained a model of fatherhood rooted firmly in the past. Reactions to the 1950s image portraying a father kissing his housewife and children goodbye before leaving for work received somewhat more mixed reactions. Whilst most of the men recognised it as depicting a clear breadwinner/ housewife divide that would not be emulated in their own expectations, some of the men viewed the image positively by identifying with the man's role as provider, although still saying the father seemed too distant and roles were unequal.

William: Yeah that goes back to the working father, just come home from work and loves his family, is providing for them and food on the table. But it's very much stereotypical with her at home looking after the kids and him going out being the breadwinner … The fact that he is able to provide for his family, earn enough money, he's got the pride from doing that, that's appealing, um so there are elements of that that will be in my relationship. But I don't want the child to see two separate parents work and looking after, I want it to be quite equal really, if you know what I mean.

As the sequence progressed, participants felt better able to identify with the fathers who were depicted as involved with their children, as these images were closer to the men's experiences and expectations of what their own fathering would involve.

Engaging with visual representations of historical and modern themes enabled the participants to identify aspects of the past in the present and how they remained relevant for their understandings today (Henwood *et al.*, 2008a). The visual representation of socio-cultural shifts from a distant father to one playing with his child, to physical - and then emotional – bonding between them, facilitated talk of tensions in the men's identificatory imaginings (Finn and Henwood, 2009) of themselves as modern (involved, nurturing) fathers (see Figure 22.2).

Figure 22.2 2007 image of modern father; reproduced with permission from copyright holder.

Some of these tensions were ambiguous and difficult to detect, and may not otherwise have been accessed through talk alone. One example is the re-emergence of protection as a stubborn particular of paternal subjectivity: against the general perception that the modern father is better, visibly stronger masculinity and protectiveness remained tied together. Another is where images of the involved, interactive father come to be seen as objects of female desire.

Presenting images individually, with detailed probing of responses, led to much more detailed data from the sequence of images than had been obtained from the collage. This strategy led participants to comment on each picture, whilst the sequence also encouraged an element of comparison across time. The sequential narrative led participants to re-evaluate their responses as the sequence progressed, meaning each picture was framed by previous responses and influenced subsequent ones. This re-framing is particularly evident in Richard's case. Initially, after fairly negative responses to the first two images, Richard had a positive response to the 1980s image:

> That's nice 'cause I like the fact the father's playing with the child and supporting the child, and the fact they're all three engaged in the same activity so you've got two children and a father engaged in the same thing.

In his response he emphasises the engagement between father and child that was not evident in pictures of previous generations. However, when presented with a present-day image, Richard re-appraises his earlier view and depicts the 1980s picture in a less positive way:

> Um (2)[6] it's interesting 'cause that picture [2007 image] says to me something more about engagement than the previous picture [1980s image] did; I think the previous picture talked to me about support actually, it was possibly the positioning and the fact that the father's supporting the child in the buggy but it did say something to me about actually the father's role in supporting the children ... Whereas that [2007 image] says something more to me about engagement; the fact they're laughing at each other so they've got eye to eye contact.

Kevin also re-appraised his comments in light of subsequent pictures. Initially, Kevin was critical of the Victorian and 1950s images as showing an outdated mode of fathering from his own perspective, commenting on how unhappy he thought the individuals looked. However, after viewing some more contemporary images, there was an apparent shift as Kevin reconsiders his earlier comments:

> My take on it now (3) ... in some way the earlier photos are far better because there's structure, there's (3) more (3) there was more of a niceness about some of it, you know, more gentlemanly. But now there's no (2) day to day – and I've only started noticing it more definitely since I found out I'm going to be a father – is how people interact with their children, and I'm finding a lot of it appalling that (2) you know swearing in front of children and (4) screaming and arguing with their wives ... I'm not one to pass judgement but ... they're horrible – and they portray such a horrible image of what society, you think perhaps the 1950s was better.

It appears that these insights and reappraisals are particular to the sequential technique, which encourages participants to give a focussed answer on one image, yet each response is inevitably influenced by those images that have gone before. Presenting the images in a collage format is unlikely to elicit such responses as it does not set up temporal comparisons in the same way as the sequence. By using a sequential narrative and more focussed probing, participants gradually developed their responses, allowing us access to apparent contradictions and adjustments that are played out.

By displaying the sequence of images at the end of the interview, participants were able to refer back to and expand upon points they had mentioned earlier, but it also presented an opportunity to raise new issues that would otherwise have been overlooked. However, whilst there were several disadvantages inherent in the collage technique, by allowing participants to select images they were drawn to it gave the researcher an insight into aspects of fatherhood that were particularly important for the men (for example the father's role as teacher), which were not so apparent in the sequence.

From these studies we have identified photo-elicitation as a useful supplementary interview technique, particularly for complex discussions around temporality and personal experiences of cultural change. Whilst the technique itself requires careful contemplation, it is also important to consider the stage in the interview at which images will be presented and the depth of probing that will follow, given their impact on the data produced. Using images early on in the interview can set up expectations, whilst incorporating them towards the end allows for expansion of existing themes and facilitates the introduction of themes which may otherwise have been overlooked.

Using personal photographs

As a third strategy for expanding our use of visual methods, participants were asked to provide a few of their personal photographs for discussion in the interview. The aim was to generate images that could evoke more memories and emotions embedded in biographical experience, exploring their temporal extensions (Adam, 1995) in everyday life to reveal more about the temporal organisation of the lived experiences of men and fathers. We first introduced this strategy when participants in the East Anglia sample were re-interviewed eight years after their first child's birth, and so were familiar with the research and potentially had a range of pictures to select from. Our technique remains under development, as we are extending its use with our South Wales sample during their third interview, a year after their child's birth.

Well-known drawbacks to using personal photographs, documented elsewhere, are that they represent an ideal form of family life rather than a reality, a presentation of what families want outsiders to see, and are produced with particular purposes and viewing contexts in mind, a research interview not being one of them (Rose, 2007). Conversely, visual researchers advocating their use

(Kuhn, 2007) suggest that self-generated images make accessible biographical memories and emotions that are otherwise inaccessible using, for example, life-history interview methods. What is of interest to us in our project is exploring how, given their generation by participants rather than by us as researchers, such photographs potentially offer a quite different way to inquire into our participants' life and temporal experiences, and generate data on processes of personal and social change.

We did not ask men to analyse the pictures: this may have been difficult and uncomfortable for some of them. Rather, we asked them to tell us about especially liked images, and ones they felt were a good representation of their fathering. Interestingly, for several of the fathers, the fact that the pictures did *not* represent an accurate picture of daily family life was the reason they liked them.

Simon: this is by far currently my favourite picture ...
I: It's a very happy, smiley photo.
Simon: But reflecting on that in particular, you know it's, the key issue here is that all three of them are happy and that is *so* not normal, that's the thing
I: So not normal?
Simon: It's, you know because of everything that we talked about before, there's always, well not always, it's so common; one of the great drags has been one of them, one or the other, being grumpy at some stage all the time. And you know just 'cause of this sort of competition of being a three and there's not enough of us to go round to pay enough attention to three demanding individuals all at the same time and give them all what they want. So um, so these moments of all three being happy are wonderful moments and you know the more the merrier I would say. So that's what makes me smile about that one.

Like Simon, other interviewees tended to select pictures of their children only, rather than presenting pictures that represented their fathering.[7] In addition to talking about why the picture was selected, the men were asked how they felt about the pictures, and the general response from the men looking at photographs of their children was one of pride. Similarly when the men themselves were in the pictures and asked how they felt at that time, the most frequent response was 'proud'.

I: So who is he though, how does he feel? [pointing to picture of participant].
Malcolm: Proud ... Um 'cause they're close, they're showing they're happy (2) I think it shows (2) conceitedly how good looking they are. I don't know, it's just I'm proud, just a proud dad actually that's what it is, that's my kids (3) it's good.

Mothers were frequently absent from the selected pictures – usually explained by the fact that they were taking the picture – and their absence was commented on by several of the men.

We face a number of challenges in using such personal photographs. The utility of this technique is inevitably influenced by how participants use and collect them, which varies widely among participants. The majority of men kept family albums, most frequently in digital form, and were able to select favourites from this that they were happy to share with us. But, as with any data, the meanings are not transparent, and it is proving more difficult to generate the necessary kinds of interpretations, reflections, and reflexivity that work up the significance of such personal photographs with regard to the men's lives and their ways of living with others in contemporary times. Moreover, some men did not value photographs, and so felt using them in the interview would not be fruitful.

As we proceed with analysing our photo-elicitation data, using the collage and visual sequence techniques alongside our qualitative longitudinal interviews, we have begun to chart its significance, e.g. for the kinds of life-course disruptions and fateful moments that contribute to personal lives and change in the making (Shirani and Henwood, 2011a and b). The methodological challenge remains, however, to generate insights from our personal photograph data to contribute to our analytical work.

Concluding remarks

When employing photo-elicitation methods in research, there are many matters of method and technique to be considered. How will images be presented – simultaneously or sequentially? When in the interview/research relationship will the images be used? Will personal photographs be pre-requested or discussed spontaneously? These considerations have a substantial bearing on the data produced and their relevance for the research project.

Based on our comparisons, and reflections on methods inspired by them, we would be cautious about invoking prior methodological commitments regarding the particular value of ways of producing and presenting visual material in photo-elicitation studies. We have constructively critiqued our own use of photo collages. Our suggestion is that while they do, indeed, have limitations as we have used them - and so require further development, they can elicit responses to different expectations, norms and ideals, enable talk about hopes, fears and anticipated difficulties, and generally create conditions where speaking subjects can articulate researchable meanings.

Participant-generated images/personal photos are often seen as especially valuable when researchers wish to avoid imposing frames of reference on respondents' ways of seeing and telling, simply through their choice of pre-given visual materials. Our study has been especially successful in eliciting verbal data, reflexively linked to a researcher-generated sequence of changing socio-cultural representations of men as fathers, using pre-existing images. We conclude that engaging participants in the interpretation of visual narratives presented in visual mode can be methodologically appropriate, providing a reference point through which participants can represent aspects of their own reality to the researcher.

Has using visual methods strengthened our broader methodological project of developing QLL research, and our analytical work of studying the dynamics of men-as-fathers' identities in the making? Our contextualisation of modern fatherhood within the flow of a dominant socio-historical representation of fatherhood and masculinities has elicited data on men's identificatory imaginings, and how these ebb and flow in and through biographical and generational time (Finn and Henwood, 2009). QLL study is known for using time as a vehicle and topic of analysis (Neale, 2008); our visual narrative photo-elicitation technique adds to this repertoire and supports the development of the work. Nonetheless, there is far more to be done to develop the usefulness of a wide range of visual methods within QLL study, drawing attention to questions of movement, change and point of view, and focussing on sequential acts of meaning making in different modalities.

Acknowledgements

We thank the ESRC (award numbers RO22250167 and RES 347 25 0003) for funding the work; Joanne Kellett for collecting most of the collage data; our study participants for their time and permission to use their data; and Professors Barbara Adam, Amanda Coffey and Corinne Squire for their interest and advice at various stages of the work.

Notes

1 For discussions of the concepts of multimedia and multimodality, and the development of research strategies for bringing out the affordances of different kinds of data, see the work of Cardiff Hypermedia (e.g. MIQDAS Guide, see reference list).
2 The study is part of a cross disciplinary network (Timescapes) comprising a set of seven qualitative, empirical studies conducting research in a variety of locations throughout the UK, and collectively utilising qualitative longitudinal (QLL) methods to inquire into continuities and changes in relationships and identities at different stages across the lifecourse.
3 These theoretical approaches are variously called discursive, critical social psychological, psychodiscursive and psychosocial. For some discussion of what lies behind the variation in labelling see Finn and Henwood (2009).
4 Since the chapter was written we have been collecting responses to five contemporary images of fatherhood and masculinity in 2009; however, this aspect of the study is not considered here.
5 In addition to temporality, we took steps to intensify discussion of issues of masculinity in connection with fatherhood. The famous 1980s Athena 'man and baby' image was used to represent a cultural turning point in depictions of fatherhood and masculinity, along with a recent reproduction of this by rugby player Ben Cohen. Images of David Beckham and son, and the father from TV programme 'Shameless' were included as culturally recognisable fathers who participants may already hold an opinion about.
6 Numbers in brackets refer to length of pause in seconds.
7 Favourite pictures of the children were school photos, holiday snaps, or pictures from a momentous occasion such as weddings, when these photographs were representative of a particular moment or memory. For others, impromptu photographs were preferable as they captured the children naturally.

References

Adam, B. (2008). "The Timescapes Challenge: Engagement with the invisible temporal". In *Researching lives through time: Time, generation and life stories*, Timescapes Working Paper Series No. 1 ISSN: 1758-3349:7–12.

Adam. B. (1995). *Timewatch: The social analysis of time*. Cambridge: Polity Press.

Bohnsack, R. (2008). "The interpretation of pictures and the documentary method". *Forum: Qualitative Social Research*, 9: Art. 26, September.

Camic, P., Yardley, L. and Rhodes, J. E. (2003). (eds.) *Qualitative research in psychology: Expanding perspectives in methodology and design*. Washington, DC: APA Publications.

Cardiff Hypermedia. Available at http://www.cardiff.ac.uk/socsi/research/researchprojects/hypermedia/index.html

Finn, M. and Henwood, K. (2009). "Exploring masculinities within men's identificatory imaginings of first-time fatherhood". *British Journal of Social Psychology*, 48(3): 547–562.

Frith, H., Riley, S., Archer, L.M. and Gleeson, K. (2005). (eds.) "Visual methods". Special Issue of *Qualitative Research in Psychology* 2(3).

Frosh, S., Phoenix, A. and Pattman, R. (2002). *Young masculinities. Understanding boys in contemporary society*. London: Palgrave.

Harper, D. (2002). "Talking about pictures: A case for photo elicitation". *Visual Studies*, 17: 13–26.

Harper, D. (1994) "On the authority of the image: Visual methods at the crossroads". In N. K. Denzin and Y.S. Lincoln (eds.) *Handbook of qualitative research*. London: Sage, pp. 403–412.

Harper, D. (2005). "What's New Visually?" In N. K. Denzin and Y. S. Lincoln (eds.) *Handbook of qualitative research*. London: Sage, pp. 747–762.

Harrison, B. (2002). "Seeing health and illness worlds – using visual methodologies in a sociology of health and illness: A methodological review". *Sociology of Health and Illness*, 24: 856–872.

Henwood, K. L. (2008). "Qualitative research, reflexivity and living with risk: Valuing and practicing epistemic reflexivity and centring marginality". *Qualitative Research in Psychology*, 5: 45–55.

Henwood, K. L., Finn, M. and Shirani, F. (2008a). "Use of visual methods to explore paternal identities in historical time and social change: Reflections from the 'Men-as-Fathers' project". *Qualitative Researcher*, Issue 9, September: 2–5.

Henwood, K., Finn, M. and Shirani, F. (2008b). "Paternal subjectivities and temporalities: Emerging from the 'old' and creating the 'new'?" Paper presented at *Subjectivity: International Conference in Critical Psychology, Cultural studies and Social Theory*, 27–29 June 2008.

Henwood, K. L., Griffin, C. and Phoenix, A. (eds.) (1998). *Standpoints and differences: Essays in the practice of feminist psychology*. London: Sage.

Henwood, K. L. and Pidgeon, N. F. (1992). "Qualitative research and psychological theorising". *British Journal of Psychology*, 83: 97–111.

Henwood, K. L. and Nicolson, P. (1995). "Qualitative approaches in psychology". Special issue of the *Psychologist*, 8: 109–129.

Jenkins, K., Woodward, R. and Winter, T. (2008) "The emergent production of analysis in photoelicitation: Pictures of military identity." *Forum: Qualitative Social Research*, 9: Art. 30, September.

Knoblauch, H., Baer, A., Laurier, E., Petschke, S. and Schnettler, B. (2008) "Visual analysis. New developments in the interpretive analysis of video and photography", *Forum: Qualitative Social Research*, 9: Art. 14, September.

Kress, G. and van Leeuwen, T. (2001). *Multimodal discourse*. London: Arnold

Kuhn, A. (2007). Photography and cultural memory: A methodological exploration. *Visual Studies*, 22: 283–292.

Neale, B. (2008). Plenary talk at the *Understanding families and relationships over time – CRFR National Conference* 30 October 2008, University of Edinburgh, UK.

Neale, B. A. and Flowerdew, J. J. (2003). Time, texture and childhood: The contours of longitudinal qualitative research. *International Journal of Social Research Methodology: Theory and Practice*, 6: 189–199.

Neale *et al.* (2007) *Timescapes: Changing relationships and identities through the life course. A study funded under the ESRC Changing Lives and Times Qualitative Longitudinal Initiative* Feb 2007–Jan 2012, RES 347 25 0003.

Pink, S. (2008) "Mobilising visual ethnography: Making routes, making place and making images". *Forum: Qualitative Social Research*, Vol. 9, Art. 36, September.

Reavey, P. and Johnson, K. (2008) "Visual approaches: Using and interpreting images". In C. Willig and W. Stainton Rogers (eds.) *Handbook of qualitative research in psychology*. London: Sage, pp. 296–314.

Rose. G. (2007). *Visual methodologies* (2nd ed.). London: Sage.

Saldaña, J. (2003) *Longitudinal qualitative research: Analysing change through time*. Lanham, MD: Rowman & Littlefield.

Shirani, F. and Henwood, K. L. (2011a) "Continuity and change in a qualitative longitudinal study of fatherhood: relevance without responsibility". *International Journal of Social Research Methodology*, 14(1): 17–29.

Shirani, F. and Henwood, K. L. (2011b) "Taking one day at a time: Temporal experiences in the context of unexpected life course transitions". *Time and Society*.

Timescapes' website. Available at http://www.timescapes.leeds.ac.uk

Wetherell M. and Edley, N. (1999). "Negotiating hegemonic masculinity: Imaginary positions and psycho-discursive practices". *Feminism and Psychology*, 9(3): 335–356.

Willig, C. and Stainton Rogers, W. (eds.) (2008). *Handbook of qualitative research in psychology*. London: Sage.

23 On utilising a visual methodology

Shared reflections and tensions

*Ilana Mountian, Rebecca Lawthom, Anne Kellock,
Karen Duggan, Judith Sixsmith, Carolyn Kagan,
Jennifer Hawkins, John Haworth, Asiya Siddiquee,
Claire Worley, David Brown, John Griffiths, and
Christina Purcell*

Chapter summary

This chapter draws on the shared reflections and tensions from collaborative research in an experience sampling method (ESM) project exploring the use of the visual, particularly photography, in investigating everyday life experiences. The research was conducted among work colleagues at a Higher Education institution. In the current project, further developing the ESM method, participants photographed their activity at preprogrammed times, taped oral descriptions of activities and answered questionnaires concerning the activity and their subjective assessment of the activity. This enabled the building of a pictured account of everyday experience.

When the group reflected on the process of the research and potential interpretations of data, ethical issues became apparent. In this chapter, in line with the critical perspective of the book, we take the opportunity to reflect upon these ethical issues, privileging dissenting voices in the group reflections. The chapter documents the tensions inherent in the visual research focusing on power relations, with the intention of rethinking and reconceptualising well worn assumptions and structured formal ethical guidelines around informed consent, privacy in research contexts and reflexivity. In this sense, this chapter discusses the following key issues: power dynamics in the immediate audience of co-workers and academic members; the impact of the audience on the photographs; the inclusion of members' reflections on the process; questions around self-reflection in the use of photographs; and issues of confidentiality and anonymity in the visual. In conclusion, we highlight the importance of a critical debate around ethics in visual methodologies, and the claim that reflexivity has to be at the kernel of the research process.

Visual methods in social sciences

The visual is attracting increasing interest in social science research and, more recently, within psychology (Reavey and Johnson, 2008). Rose (2007) notes that photographic images, whether moving or still, are currently the most popular sort of image being created by social scientists because they can carry or evoke three dimensions of experience (information, affect and reflection) particularly well.

The polysemic (having multiple meanings) nature of the visual, as opposed to the mono-modal form of word-based text, has prompted Ruby (2005) to call for attention to social processes surrounding visual objects – a need to ask the same critical question of the eye as the voice, rather than assuming broad similarities. As such, the possibilities for visual information to offer different perspectives on the experience of everyday life have yet to be fully explored.

Reflexivity in visual methods

Research ethics are particularly important in visual methodologies (Rose, 2007). Given its visual content, issues such as anonymity are of particular importance. Ethical concerns related to visual methodology in researching everyday life and working relations should also be carefully considered. A central feature of the analytical interrogation of much qualitative data concerns reflexivity. In textual work, reflexivity tends to revolve around the position of the researcher and the impact the researcher characteristics might have on their subsequent interpretation of the data. The use of reflexivity in textual/verbal work tends to be a textual representation of the researcher in relation to a number of positional places and relationships (i.e. to participants, to data). However, image-based research requires the incorporation of other elements for reflexivity which are not dependent on verbal explication. For example, Pink (2001: 96) advocates a reflexive approach towards the collation and analysis of visual data which does not depend on translating 'visual evidence' into 'verbal knowledge' but exploring the relationship between the visual and the social and cultural contexts of knowledge production. Within this, issues such as construction and representation within the visual need careful exploration in terms of what and how knowledge is produced. In this respect, Wright (1999) makes the point that interpreting photographs involves a 'looking at' and 'looking behind' the picture. It is the careful interpretation of reflexivity and ethics around the visual that we explore in this chapter.

Rose (2007) highlights three contexts to be taken into account for the meaning production of visual work. These are: 'the site(s) of the production of an image, the site of the image itself, and the site(s) where it is seen by various audiences' (Rose, 2007: 13). Rose (2007) argues that for critical research, each of these sites should be seen in relation to three modalities: the technological (the apparatus), compositional (formal strategies to compose an image), and the social (economic, political, social relations surrounding an image). In this chapter we critically discuss the technological apparatus (e.g. meanings of the photographic camera), the compositional aspects (e.g. the impact of the immediate and broader audiences in choices of snapshots), and the social, political and social relation aspects in the production of images (i.e. picture taking within the institutional context).

The current project

The research described in this chapter draws on our shared reflections arising from a pilot project conducted within a participatory action research approach to explore experience sampling method (ESM) and the use of the visual in investigating everyday life experiences.

The ESM has been used for investigating everyday life experience, the relationship between the activity undertaken, skills, challenge and subjective experiences of well-being, focusing particularly around the role of enjoyment (Clarke and Haworth, 1994; Haworth *et al.*, 1997). Delle Fave (2007) notes that the ESM can be used to capture emotions, motivations and cognitive processes as they occur, an important tool for retrospective methods, though the ESM is seen as complementing and not replacing other research methods. Further consideration of the method and the data from this project can be found elsewhere (Hektner *et al.*, 2007; Kellock *et al.*, 2011).

The inclusion of photography as part of the ESM was initially used to study slices of time for the political-poetic statement on 'The Way We Are Now' project (Haworth, 2010),[1] developed from practice-led research into creativity and embodied mind in digital fine art.[2] Haworth (2010: 15) comments that there are a number of interpretive possibilities afforded by this visual method including an artistic object for contemplation; as individual visual profiles for comparative research; or as analysis of themes across a group of individuals, and between groups.

The research described in this chapter was conducted among a collective group of higher education staff (the social context). The co-researchers (n = 13) were work colleagues: supervisors, managers, students and support staff. Some have been previously engaged with the use of visual methods, participatory research and ethical issues in research (Mountian, 2009; Woolrych and Sixsmith, 2008). The key focus of the project was for the team to produce individual stories of their everyday life over the period of one week. The participatory approach included participants' involvement in the design of the project, set up of aims and objectives, and joint discussions over the data collected.

The ESM uses questionnaire diaries and electronic pagers which are preprogrammed to bleep at randomly selected times during the day to indicate response times. In the current project, a mobile phone was used to signal participants eight times a day, between 9:30 am and 9:30 pm during a week, in which the Monday was a bank holiday. At each signal, participants photographed their situation/activity, taped-recorded their assessments and impressions of the activity or any other comment, and answered six questions on the activity and subjective experience concerning enjoyment, interest, challenge, skills, visual interest and contentment. In addition, each participant completed a written individual reflection on their participation in the research process. A rich visual display was then created for each individual in the form of large posters. Individual images were also placed alongside the responses to questions in a data book that was compiled along with the individual reflections.

A focus group discussion was organised in which experiences of participation in the project were explored, taking the data book as discussion stimulus. Reflection is considered an important dimension of participatory action research (Reason, 1988) and as such, individual and group reflections have become an integral part of the current research project.

In this research, both visual and verbal data were, therefore, included in a three-part process: (1) picture taking and verbal description of the context of the picture, as photo-documentation, 'using photographs as documentary evidence' (Rose, 2007: 239); (2) individual reflections on the photos; and (3) focus group discussions of the research experience, using the snapshots to elicit the discussion, as photo-elicitation, the use of photographs 'as eliciting material for interviews' (Rose, 2007: 239). The extracts explored in this chapter derive from the visual data, focus group discussions, and individual reflections. The following analysis centres on a number of emerging issues concerning power relations in research, ethics in research and reflexivity.

Mapping power, reflexivity and ethics

A number of issues emerged from this pilot research concerning power and ethics in research, and particularly in relation to participatory action research (Burton and Kagan, 1996) and visual methodology (Jevic and Springgay, 2008). Beyond differences of power between 'participants' and 'researchers' (even though this was participatory research), issues of power related to the work place have had an impact on the research in various ways, particularly within the visual. For example, the interdependencies of power and work context were revealed in participants' choice of pictures taken and comments made in relation to the photographs.

Furthermore, in the context of participatory research where participants were both participants and 'researchers', reflexivity is a particularly intricate process. Reflexivity is a part of the research in which researchers reflect upon their analysis and the research process. Reflexivity and issues of power in research have been a key issue for qualitative research, and particularly for feminist research (Burman, 1998; Oakley, 1981; Batsleer and Humphries, 2000; Harding, 1996; Stanley and Wise, 1990). However, there is still a tendency in qualitative research to interpret subjective experiences as an individual characteristic or impression. Rather, as Parker (2005: 25) points out: 'reflexivity is [should be] a way of *attending to the institutional location of historical and personal aspects of the research relationship*'.

Foucault's (1998, 1991) work on power is crucial to articulate and deconstruct the various power positions taken in research, that of the institution, including academic institutions, of the research process (relationship between participants and researchers) and, in this case, of work relations. Power in this sense is not seen as an individual characteristic, but related to social structures, to structural power (hierarchical positions, differences in gender, race, class and so on), to techniques and rituals of power which are historically located. In this way the examples cited in this chapter are not read as individual characteristics, but rather as reflections on how power operates within academic settings, work relations and research dynamics.

Taking into account these power dynamics, reflexivity becomes fundamental to the analysis of the research, however, at the same time, these power relations may also appear in the reflexivity process itself, e.g. participants may not feel comfortable to comment openly about their ideas and motivations regarding the research process or to tell their motivations for choosing a specific snapshot. This requires us to rethink and reconsider reflexivity, particularly in relation to visual methods. Jevic and Springgay (2008) also comment on the tensions of joint work between researchers and students, and state that crucially, visual methods 'embrace proximity by understanding art making, researching, and teaching as living practices and as relational encounters that are provocative, hesitant, and complicated' (p. 67).

In this chapter we focus on some key aspects of power relations and ethics in research emerging from this pilot project. These include: (1) power dynamics between co-workers and co researchers, (2) the impact of audience on the composition of photographs, (3) the inclusion of participants in the reflections, (4) questions around self-reflection in the use of photographs, and (5) confidentiality and anonymity in visual methods. Particular issues concerning visual methods in relation to ethics and reflexivity will be further discussed through the examples cited in this paper. The analysis is based on the material generated in the first (individual reflections, photo documentation) and second (focus groups, photo elicitation) stages of the research. All the quotes in the paper are from group discussions unless otherwise stated (i.e. individual reflections).

Power dynamics in research

Academic practice and its constraints

The academic practice of research has its constraints and limitations. Clarity and transparency of research objectives and methods are of paramount importance to participants. Notwithstanding this, there are certain elements that are not or cannot be easily disclosed, thus the researcher is placed in a specific power position in relation to the participant. Some of these elements are, for example, how the material is going to be interpreted (e.g. the theoretical resources of analysis) and how it is going to be disseminated (e.g. the wide scope of dissemination). These elements, in the case of this research project, provoked some anxieties in some of the participants. Two participants in fact opted to withdraw from the research. Some participants commented:

> You don't know what it is that you're looking at, is it the activity or the environment or the object or (...) I can't see how these questions wouldn't be misinterpreted by different people.

This comment is seen here in relation to the interpretation of data. This theme reappears in the next example:

> This project felt more like work and felt invasive – to have my life exposed and discussed.

(individual reflection)

Here a number of issues appear intermingled: first, the participant did not feel comfortable in the position of the participant (life exposed and discussed), second, because the researchers are work colleagues, this might have put an extra weight on the idea of 'exposure'; and particularly in the context of a visual research project, photo-taking might represent another perspective within exposure, where participants may not feel comfortable to share snapshots of their private life with their colleagues and line managers.

Furthermore, although this research and pilot project was of a participatory action research perspective, questions around who is in charge of the research, and who has voice, still permeated the research process and outputs. There are some specificities of visual methods that we should also consider, as some participants expressed an unease around the sharing of the photographs (data) both to each other and to a wider audience, as seen in the next example:

> ... regarding the issue of showing the photographs ... if this issue is causing angst between us people who are active researchers – what of those we are working with? How can we make decisions about data and participants?

This example points to some aspects of visual methods wherein added pressures and anxieties regarding the exposure of the photographs and interpretation are described.

Regarding the research method and control over the data, some participants commented:

> I did not enjoy taking part in the project – for practical, personal and epistemological reasons. (...) I would have preferred to have been in control of when and where to record my states of well being (individual reflection).[3]

> ...she would say: quick take a picture of me [and] I said it doesn't work like that, you know I don't get a choice when to take it, it's just like when you are having a real good time, (...) well what's the point if it's wellbeing.

In these extracts participants pointed out specific aspects related to the research project, that is, of recording their activities according to pre-arranged times. These comments also highlight participants' anxieties regarding the control over the data generated by them, i.e. on the decision surrounding when to take snapshots.

Ongoing work relationships

Reflections on how the different professional positions of co-researchers in the academic institution impacted on the image production is further developed here, addressing the importance of the social, political and socio-relational context of the research.

First, there was the potential pressure to participate in the research, as participants who are in vulnerable positions may well feel that participation is important in being part of a wider research culture. Second, and crucially, in the analysis of the pictures taken and discussions in the focus groups, concerns and anxieties were expressed particularly by those in more vulnerable work positions, such as those in temporary or short-term contracts and/or not well established in their careers.

Some participants reflected their concern in showing pictures that portrayed them in working activities:

> ... the impact [of the research] on the participant has to be taken into account (...), so look at some of this week [pictures] and you see lots of computers screens

In this extract it is pointed out how a great number of the weekly pictures taken by the group are pictures of computer screens (Figure 23.1); in fact, most prominent in the snapshots of participants who were in less-established academic positions. This is one mode of academic work, while other researchers were more involved in other academic activities, such as meetings and discussions, which were also portrayed in their week snapshots. This made us reflect on the reasons why work-related pictures dominated this research. On the one hand, of course, these activities are part of the academic type of work, however, on the other hand, we highlight how some participants felt compelled to show more work-related pictures, as further discussed in this section. This is an outcome that can be related to the social and institutional context of the project, conducted among work colleagues.

Figure 23.1 is an example of a week portrait, where computer screens and work-related activities are predominant. The next extract also highlights this aspect:

> I'm often not doing the same activity in two pictures in a row (...), whereas other people I've seen you know kind of picture after picture almost that they are doing the same activity [computer screens].

Here, a participant comments on the perceived work effort being sustained over time. There is an explicit comparison with others who seem to be more fastidious in spending time on a particular task, such as sitting in front of a computer screen.

Issues concerning the private–public divide, and more precisely, private life and research in the work environment are pointed out next. Here key issues regarding suspicion and vigilance were highlighted by some participants:

> I think it is a very invasive technique and it makes the participant extremely vulnerable because we are exposing our life to a number of researchers and on top of everything to our work colleagues.

In this extract, exposure and invasion were raised as themes for this participant. The visual content of the research might have added an extra pressure in these ideas of exposure. Moreover, reflecting on the rites and instruments of power (Foucault, 1998), we consider how the mobile camera (the technological apparatus) was itself taken up as an instrument of surveillance and vigilance. This is further developed in the next section.

Impact of audience on the composition of photographs

The impact of the audience (the immediate group and the wider audience) in the research process is a key aspect to be taken into account in the use of visual methods, that is, how participants' awareness of the wider and immediate audience

Figure 23.1 Example of a week portrait, where computer screens and work-related activities are predominant.

impact on the choices of pictures to be taken (compositional aspects). Two main
issues are highlighted here in relation to the choices of pictures taken in this
project, first how participants negotiate the boundaries between the private and
the public; and second, the impact of the immediate audience of colleagues and
co-researchers and wider audiences (e.g. dissemination including conference
presentations and articles).

The boundaries between public and private are seen here in relation to power
position in discourse (Oakley, 1981). This dynamic related to the public–private

divide is seen in practice when awareness of audience inhibited participants in sharing pictures that could depict them in uncomfortable situations (in relation to wider audiences) and where these were portraying an image that did not match to that of the 'hard worker' (in relation to the immediate group: work colleagues and co-researchers). Some examples regarding the impact of the wider audiences are pointed out:

> If a participant decides to have a look at his life in an in-depth way and (...) [to] think about it, it can be enriching but once it [the picture] is exposed it [this exercise] stops being so much this opportunity for more analytic thinking, [when] it comes to the public- the space of the private is broken, so the pictures are taken being aware that there is a public ....

> The more public you make it the less accuracy [in terms of the research] you are going to get.

One participant went further to conclude that:

> The output others will see is a simple form of voyeuristic art that will act in only a limited way as a catalyst for environment and well-being but won't relate to the subject.

These extracts point to some deadlocks of research, i.e. the limits and difficulties of visual methods in research. Regarding the impact of the immediate audience (work colleagues) in the research, the next extract highlights the concern of the image of the hard worker:

> I did cheat, I am afraid, but by not doing something ... I did not play a computer game all week as I did not want the beep to go off whilst I was playing a game so I presume the phone 'watching' me made me do more work.
>
> (individual reflection)

In fact, in this particular example, it is possible to reflect on the technological apparatus (mobile phone) operating as a regulatory device, embodying a specific gaze (Foucault, 1991), in which the participant would respond accordingly, by curtailing desired activities in favour of those perceived as socially acceptable. Moreover, the confession style (Foucault, 1998) of the participant is clear when admitting she cheated. This brings forth the power relations of research and participant, and the embodiment of power in particular mechanisms and instruments, more precisely, in the mobile phone.

Inclusion of member's reflection on the process

Two aspects are emphasised here, first the limits of participation in the research, whereby not all participants felt comfortable discussing their reflections and concerns in showing photographs of their private lives to colleagues. Second, regarding the visual methodology, there was a sense that the visual needed support from the verbal, i.e. they wanted to add explanation to the visual.

As a group of social science researchers they wanted to talk about the pictures. Further, some participants highlighted that representation was an issue – this is not my real self, not a typical week or this is missing out key parts of my day. This authenticity argument seems not in tune with criteria to assess qualitative data where richness, transparency and multiple meanings are key. As Pinney (2004: 8) points out, photos can only be compressed performances. Accuracy and representation were further discussed in relation to the objective of the project and the textual/verbal comments about subjective appreciation of activities undertaken in the snapshots:

> I'm struggling that we are not considering how this [the snapshots and verbal accounts] doesn't represent wellbeing urm (...) we can go back and see what it has achieved but we are not being critical about what it hasn't achieved.

Regarding representation and participation in the research, participants commented:

> ... some people don't feel as if they have participated (...) You know well everybody feels they've participated but not in a participative framework.

> Some people feel that they have been almost you know the subjects of the research rather than participants.

Here participants expressed that the visual and textual data from the project seems to feature her/him as subject rather than co-participant. It is interesting to analyse these comments within the frame of participatory research, where participants are co-researchers, and yet there were still some preconceived ideas about research that permeated this pilot project, such as who is in control of the research and analysis. The participatory approach involved focus groups and individual reflections for consultation, shared interpretation and negotiation of data showing.

Furthermore, Piper and Frankham (2007) note that the mimetic (resemblance or representation) quality of photographs can serve as a trap where photos pose as singular truths whereas other forms of data (such as verbalisations) move subject positions around. In a piece of word-based text, individuals can shift subject positions whereas photos may locate people in a fixed position (e.g. as lonely, popular, motherly etc.). As a group of researchers particularly interested in qualitative work, photographs may well have positioned individuals more firmly than desired and in ways which contradict their usual social positioning within verbal or written text.

> This is quite an interesting process just in terms of those mechanisms because, because we've got that, that we are well that whole week essentially in that state of objective self-awareness we are objectifying ourselves (...) With the camera. Then even if we have forgotten that, when the alarm [mobile signal] goes we are thrown into that.

In this extract some characteristics of visual methods are highlighted, such as the fixity of the photographic image, and in this case, the self-awareness and objectification that the visual promotes.

Questions around self-reflection in the use of photographs

Participants reflected on the therapeutic use of photo-taking. As in any method in research, ethical concerns of those in vulnerable positions are chief (e.g. people who are distressed, traumatised etc.). Notwithstanding this, research is not a neutral device, since specific questions can trigger memories and thoughts that participants cannot always foresee. In the case of visual methodologies this is of particular importance. The visual can act as a reminder and as a trigger of memories and thoughts (Rose, 2007), which can be seen as a powerful device for reflecting upon everyday life.

In this pilot project, some participants felt that the snapshots of their everyday lives provided them an opportunity to reflect upon their situation, by raising awareness of the taking-for-grantedness of everyday life and re-signification of meaning, and the importance of recognising environments, contexts, events and people.

> I really enjoyed it and it made me question what I do with my life.
>
> (individual reflection)

> I should spend less time watching TV!
>
> (individual reflection)

However, some participants did not in fact feel prepared for this exercise:

> but you can imagine maybe if you did get something back that did make your life look dreadful and is too much work and not enough leisure or whatever, whatever you could form some kind of judgement and I suppose (...), that's where I got this feeling that X was talking about particularly the unintended outcomes of being shown that visual product to yourself and what other people are thinking of you.

> [If] somebody is not happy in their life whatever representation that that sort of how that manifests itself is going be emotionally quite challenging.

These extracts illustrate how the visual and particularly the visual in research about everyday life presents, on the one hand, a possibility for self-reflection and on the other hand, self-reflection triggered by the visual can appear as challenging for some participants, to look at a week in pictures and to reflect upon them. Within this, some participants commented on strategies to picture their daily routines in different ways, as seen below:

> ... if I was watching telly and it was something I took a picture because an alarm went off and then I was watching something I think I would think myself as an object (...) oh I'll still be watching telly and I'd take a picture of the dog (...) not exactly what's happening but gosh a few pictures in a row of *Coronation Street* (...) But what I was thinking about it there might have been a slight engineering of that because I've never been conscious of God I've taken another picture of watching telly you know looks like a couch potato.

In these extracts it is possible to see how snapshots provided participants with a space for self-reflection. Participants pointed out the exercise as a potential trigger for self-reflection and change. Nonetheless, the impact of the immediate and wider audiences on the exercise can also be seen in this outcome, as some felt wary and under surveillance, and used strategies to depict their everyday life in different ways. In fact, it is possible to note in the above extracts that self-awareness appears intertwined with a public gaze.

Confidentiality and anonymity

A key issue in visual methodologies is anonymity and confidentiality. As Parker (2005) points out, confidentiality cannot be ensured in qualitative research, as the details of participants' lives are examined and disseminated, however, anonymity can be insured. However, Parker highlights that anonymity has also to be reviewed in research, treated as an ethical question (Parker, 2005: 17), e.g. is the research being used as a way to further marginalise vulnerable people or to give voice to them, are ethics being used to protect the researcher or the participant?

In the case of visual methodologies, current ethical guidelines (British Psychological Society, 2006) for research highlight that participants must provide consent for the reproduction of their visual material. As well as protecting the participants, such consent can also serve as legal protection for the researcher. Beyond the legal framework of ethics, ethics in visual methods are particularly important and need to be further conceptualised. In the case of this pilot project, anxieties regarding anonymity and work relations were expressed by some participants:

> ... although we are all 'equal' and we all kind of know each other and we like the company of each other, it doesn't mean that we'd be happy to share everything and knowing that this information is [going to be] published in this way makes it a non-confidential non-anonymous work.

Regarding constraints of research in the work environment, the next extract highlights that:

> I know that we say this is confidential and all the rest of it but say for example if I took a picture of X, God love him, and put a comment this is my colleague I can't stand him, yeah, you know and here we are.

The discussion here relates to ongoing ethical and power dynamics that surround research – as researchers we are well versed in participative and engaged research strategies. However, the showing of data and subsequent analysis presented different challenges which surround the visual – which go beyond ethical guidelines around informed consent. These were related to visual methods and to the limits of this type of research in work environments, which could constrain the research and/or expose participants.

Conclusions

The aim of this chapter was to point out some of the tensions and difficulties involved in conducting visual research. A number of issues were raised via a critical examination of a pilot participatory action research approach using ESM and focus group discussions on the topic of subjective well-being and research in the work context. The analysis of pictures and comments from participants (co-researchers) were not read as individuals' characteristics, but rather as means to reflect on the power operations within academic settings, work relations and research dynamics. Although there are a range of critical issues in higher education (Duckett, 2002) to be considered, the analysis we provided focused on institutional power dynamics within the work place and how these dynamics emerge in research, and particularly in visual methods. Stronach, Garratt, Pearce, and Piper (2006) make the argument that in visual research what is not said has also to be considered, and this is what we have aimed to address in this chapter.

A range of complexities and tensions were reflected in the pictures (mostly work-related pictures) and in comments during focus groups and individual reflections. Some of these tensions could be seen in the wariness of participants, their feelings of suspicion and surveillance, the perceived pressure to participate in the project and concerns regarding the eventual interpretation of visual data. These were mostly expressed by participants who did not have well established careers or did not feel directly in charge of the research and/or methods, pointing out the need to consider the power dynamics in research, and to consider particular aspects of visual methods, such as anonymity, confidentiality and the fixity quality of image. Thus, by privileging dissenting voices, we aimed to address certain power dynamics in research in using visual methods, particularly around informed consent, ethics and reflexivity.

In this chapter we have focused on five main areas: power dynamics and the immediate audience of co-workers and academic members; the impact of the audience on the photographs; the inclusion of members' reflections on the process; questions around self-reflection in the use of photograph; and issues of confidentiality and anonymity in visual data. These aspects account for the technological apparatus, the compositional aspects and the political and social contexts of visual methods.

Within each of these areas, we have focused on the tensions and constraints of the research process. In terms of power and institutional dynamics, participants who were not in well established academic positions expressed their fears and concerns in diverse ways, including: pressure to participate; taking pictures showing them as hard workers and/or changing their activities during the project; awareness of the immediate public (working colleagues) and wider audiences; not feeling part of the research process and worry about interpretation of data; key aspects of anonymity and visual methods were also explored.

Our claim here is that visual methodologies and collaborative and participatory action research can function as a means of empowerment to research participants. However, we argue that reflexivity has to be central within the research process, addressed and reflected upon, taking particularly into account the specificities of visual methods. Power has to be crucially considered in relation to the position of the researcher, participants and institution, and these are paramount for research plans, reflections and outcomes.

Notes

1 www.creativity-embodiedmind.com
2 Funded by the Arts and Humanities Research Council in the UK; and research by Haworth (2007) into subjective well-being funded by the Economic and Social Research Council in the UK, www.wellbeing-esrc.com
3 This pilot study (ESM) required participants to take snapshots at pre-arranged times.

References

Batsleer, J. and Humphries, B. (ed.) (2000). *Welfare, exclusion and political agency.* London: Routledge.

British Psychological Society (BPS) (2006). *Code of ethics and conduct.* Retrieved 20 February 2009 from http://www.bps.org.uk/documentdownload-area/documentdownload$.cfm?file_uuid=5084A882-1143-DFD0-7E6F1938A65C242&ext =pdf

Burman, E. (1998). *Interviewing.* In P. Banister, E. Burman, I. Parker, M. Taylor and C. Tindall (eds.), *Qualitative methods in psychology – a research guide.* Buckingham: Open University Press.

Burton, M. and Kagan, C. (1996). Rethinking empowerment: shared action against power-lessness. In I. Parker and R. Spears (eds.), *Psychology and society: radical theory and practice.* London: Pluto Press, pp. 198–208.

Clarke, S. E., and Haworth, J. T. (1994). 'Flow' experiences in the daily life of sixth form college students. *British Journal of Psychology*, 85, 511–523.

Delle Fave, A. (2007). Theoretical Foundations of ESM. In J. M. Hektner, J. A. Schmidt, and M. Csikszentmihalyi (eds.), *Experience sampling method: measuring the quality of everyday life.* London: Sage.

Duckett, P. S. (2002). Community psychology, Millennium Volunteers and UK Higher Education: a disruptive triptych? *Journal of Community and Applied Social Psychology*, 12, 94–107.

Foucault, M. (1998). *The will to knowledge – the history of sexuality. I.* London: Penguin.

Foucault, M. (1991). *Discipline and Punishment – the birth of the prison.* London: Penguin.

Harding, S. (1996). Rethinking standpoint epistemology: what is 'strong objectivity'? In E. F. Keller and H. Longino (eds.), *Feminism and science – Oxford readings in feminism.* Oxford: Oxford University Press, pp. 235–248.

Haworth, J. T. (2010) Explorations in creativity, technology and embodied mind. In T. Freire (ed.), *Understanding positive life: research and practice on positive psychology.* Lisboa: Escolar Editoria, pp. 429–447.

Haworth, J. T., Jarman, M. and Lee, S. (1997). Positive subjective states in the daily life of a sample of working women. *Journal of Applied Social Psychology*, 27(4), 345–370.

Hektner, J. M., Schmidt, J. A. and Csikszentmihalyi, M. (2007). *Experience sampling method: measuring the quality of everyday life.* London: Sage.

Jevic, L., and Springgay, S. (2008). A/r/tography as an ethics of embodiment: visual jour-nals in preservice education. *Qualitative Inquiry*, 14, 67–89.

Kellock, A., Lawthom, R., Sixsmith, J., Duggan, K., Mountian, I., Haworth, J., Kagan, C., Brown, D. P., Griffiths, J. E., Hawkins, J., Worley, C., Purcell, C. and Siddiquee, A. (2011). Using technology and the experience sampling method to understand real life. In Nagy, S. and Hesse-Biber (eds.), *The handbook of emergent technologies in Social Research.* Oxford: Oxford University Press.

Mountian, I. (2009). Questions around social imaginary and discourse analysis for critical research. In Owens, C. (ed.), *Annual review of critical psychology*, vol. 6. Manchester: Discourse Unit. Avaiable at http//www.discourseunit.com/arcp/7.htm

Oakley, A. (1981). Interviewing women: a contradiction in terms. In H. Roberts (ed.), *Doing feminist research*. London: Routledge.

Parker, I. (2005). *Qualitative psychology – introducing radical research*. Buckingham: Open University Press.

Pink, S. (2001). *Doing visual ethnography: images, media and representation in research*. London: Sage.

Pinney, C. (2004). *Photos of the Gods: the printed image and political struggle in India*. London: Reaktion Books.

Piper, H. and Frankham, J. (2007). Seeing voices and hearing pictures: image as discourse and the framing of image-based research. *Discourse: Studies in the Cultural Politics of Education*, 28(3), 373–387.

Reason, P. (1988). *Human inquiry in action*. London: Sage.

Reavey, P. and Johnson, K. (2008). Visual approaches: using and interpreting images. In C. Willig and W. Stainton Rogers (eds.), *The Sage handbook of qualitative research in psychology*. London: Sage, pp. 369–314.

Rose, G. (2007). *Visual methods – an introduction to the interpretation of visual materials*. London: Sage.

Ruby, J. (2005). The last 20 years of visual anthropology – a critical review. *Visual Studies*, 20, 159–170.

Stanley, L. and Wise, S. (eds.) (1990). *Method, methodology and epistemology in feminist research processes in feminist praxis*. London: Routledge.

Stronach, I., Garratt, D., Pearce, C. and Piper, H. (2006). Reflexivity, the picturing of selves, the forging of method. *Qualitative Inquiry*, 12(6), 1–25.

Woolrych, R. and Sixsmith, J. (2008). *Understanding health and well-being in the context of urban regeneration: a participatory action research approach*. Final Report. Manchester: Research Institute for Health and Social Change.

Wright, T. (1999). *The photography handbook*. London: Routledge.

Index

MySpace xxvii, xxxiii, 87–102; data collection 92–3; methodology 91–2; profile pages 88–9; relations between profiles 95–6; relations between visual and textual 96–8, 99; uncommunicative relations 93–5

narcissism: female 35; Hollywood cinema 31; male 34; social networking sites xxxiii, 87, 98, 99
narrative picturing 60–1
narrative research 8, 71
narratives: Asian women's family and marital experiences 73–5, 77–80, 82; disabled students 271; electronic dance music culture 201; *Moving to the Beat* project 229; Ricoeur on 71; shared cultural 252; use of the term 66n2; visual images 71–2; visual sequences 335–40, 342; women's experiences of cancer 55–6
Neale, Stephen 35, 40
neighbourhood renewal projects 301
neo-tribalism xxxvi, 191, 193, 194, 195, 197–8
'new man' concept 32, 33
noise 92, 96, 97, 99
Noland, C. M. 71, 76
Nowell, B. 301

objectification 30, 31, 34, 36, 39, 40
objects, materiality of 307
observational methods 119, 135–6; autoethnography 286; video diaries project 140
observational style of documentary film 233–4
O'Neill, Rachel 39
'other-directed gaze' 158, 160
otherness 243, 245

Packard, J. 258
Parker, I. 104, 349, 357
participant-observation xxxiv, 136, 242, 244–5
participation 7–8; experience sampling method 355; risk communication 205–6, 208, 209
participatory research xxix, xxxv, 209; community-based 174, 299; experience sampling method 348, 351, 355; feminist 258, 272; group sessions 218; power and ethics 349, 358; reflection 349; transformative potential 185–6, 187; *see also* action research

'partnership' model 205–6
patriarchy 29, 34
PCP *see* Personal Construct Psychology
Pearce, C. 358
Pearce, Nick 175
Peirce, C. S. 4
People First 317, 321–7
perception, copy theory of 17
Perez, Gilberto 234
performance: autoethnography 146, 147; bisexual identity 255; to video camera 124–5, 127, 134
Peri, P. C. 227
Personal Construct Psychology (PCP) 272–4, 279–80
personal photographs 340–2
personality 2
Petford, B. 256
phallus 39, 230
Pharmacopoeia exhibition 192
phenomenology 4, 44–5, 51, 273
photo-elicitation 5, 6–7, 57, 252n1, 331–2; auto-driven 71; close relationships and marriage xxxii, 69, 72–5, 80–1; community-based participatory research 299; critical psychology 174–5; embodied experience 46–9, 51–2; experience sampling method 349; fatherhood 333–42; food risk knowledge 209; rural Chinese women 301; UNICEF 18, 19–23
photography xxix, xxx–xxxiii; bisexual identity 259, 263; close relationships and marriage 69–84; electronic dance music culture 193, 196–7; embodied experience xxxi–xxxii, 6, 43–54; experience sampling method 346, 348–9, 350–8; fatherhood xl, 333–42; gap between representation and responsibility 23; gaze of the other 252; homeless people 299, 302, 303–4, 306, 308–11; image/picture distinction 17–18; learning disabilities 315, 317, 319, 321–7; LGBT people 175–83; 'looking at' and 'looking behind' xxxi, 18–19, 27, 306, 347; picturing process 305–6; psychology's use of 1–3; social, cultural and community studies 174–5; social psychology of identity and representation xxxvii, 241, 243, 246–7, 249, 252; social sciences 346–7; UNICEF 19–23; women's experiences of cancer xxxii, 55–68; *see also* images